YANK AND REBEL RANGERS

RANGERS

Special Operations in the American Civil War

To my grandson Aiden Robert Croft

YANK AND REBEL RANGERS
Special Operations in the American Civil War

Robert W. Black

Pen & Sword
MILITARY

AN IMPRINT OF PEN & SWORD BOOKS LTD.
YORKSHIRE – PHILADELPHIA

First published in Great Britain in 2019 by
Pen & Sword Military
An imprint of
Pen & Sword Books Ltd
Yorkshire - Philadelphia

Typeset in Times New Roman 11/13.5 by
Aura Technology and Software Services, India

Printed and bound in the UK by TJ International, Padstow, Cornwall

Pen & Sword Books Limited incorporates the imprints of Atlas, Archaeology,
Aviation, Discovery, Family History, Fiction, History, Maritime, Military,
Military Classics, Politics, Select, Transport,
True Crime, Air World, Frontline Publishing, Leo Cooper,
Remember When, Seaforth Publishing, The Praetorian Press,
Wharncliffe Local History, Wharncliffe Transport,
Wharncliffe True Crime and White Owl.

For a complete list of Pen & Sword titles please contact
PEN & SWORD BOOKS LIMITED
47 Church Street, Barnsley, South Yorkshire, S70 2AS, England
E-mail: enquiries@pen-and-sword.co.uk
Website: www.pen-and-sword.co.uk

or

PEN AND SWORD BOOKS
1950 Lawrence Rd, Havertown, PA 19083, USA
E-mail: uspen-and-sword@casematepublishers.com
Website: www.penandswordbooks.com

Contents

PART TWO: YANK RANGERS

Acknowledgments

Foremost my thanks to my best friend, travel companion, advisor, publicity director, proofreader, critic, lover and wife, Carolyn Black, without whom I would be a ship without a rudder. To my pal and editor Chris Evans, to all my long-time friends at the US Army Military History Institute at Carlisle Barracks PA; Dr Richard Simmers, Richard Baker and staff. They have always been willing to show the path to that elusive document or volume.

Thanks to Martha Steiger and Julia Scott, Virginia tourism and Patty Rogers and the staff of the Leesburg Virginia Convention and Visitors' Bureau. Thanks are due to John and Bronwen Souders who shared their time and knowledge about the Loudoun Rangers in that beautiful village of Waterford, Virginia. Thanks to my daughter, April Black Croft, for her help at The National Archives and the Library of Congress. My appreciation to my brother Korean War Rangers, Nick Tisak of the 8th Airborne Ranger Company and Lew Villa of the 1st Airborne Rangers for their assistance in getting information about Sheridan Scouts, in particular the heroic Joe McCabe. They rescued his grave from obscurity. Thanks to the staff at the West Virginia Archives and the University of West Virginia Library as well as to the research staff of Dickinson College, Carlisle, Pennsylvania and the Pennsylvania State Library in Harrisburg. As one who knows joy when sitting in the stacks and uncovering some pearl of historical beauty, thanks to all archivists and librarians. They are the great guardians of our experience.

Prologue

Noon, April 3 1865. A long, grey and butternut-hued column of horsemen rode in dusty splendor along a Virginia lane near Sayler's Creek. Confederate infantry was on ahead, the sounds of gunfire far distant. The riders were in friendly territory. Men rode easy, some lulled to sleep by the cradle rock of their saddles. They were experienced cavalry. Revolvers were at their belts and carried in saddle holsters. Some tucked a spare fiream into a boot. Sabers, sharpened to a razor edge, were at their sides. They were four regiments of North Carolina cavalry, part of Fitzhugh Lee's Cavalry Corps, formed into a brigade under the command of Brigadier General Rufus Barringer. General Barringer had a good fighting reputation. Three times wounded, he had two horses killed under him. Those who did not know him tended to identify Barringer with faint praise by noting that 'Stonewall Jackson is his brother-in-law.'

Riding in the column with General Barringer were two of his staff officers and two orderlies. From time to time Barringer would turn in the saddle and look back to check the men. The movement was going well when Barringer noticed a small group of horsemen coming forward, chatting with men in the column as they came. It was nothing unusual; a regimental commander likely had a question or Fitz Lee had sent a party with new orders.

About fourteen men and an officer were in the group, laughing and joking, gathering around Barringer and his command group. General Barringer thought war a serious business and frowned at the easy familiarity of these men. 'Good afternoon, General,' said the officer, a wry grin creasing his dust-stained face. Barringer donned a frosty expression. 'You have the advantage of me, Sir!' The response was a hearty laugh. 'You're right, I have, General!'

Barringer's eyes widened as he stared into the muzzle of a brandished revolver. He quickly looked about, opened his mouth to shout, then decided it would be a rash and final action. He, his two staff officers and two orderlies were well covered by the strangers' guns. The weapons were held in such a way that the brigade riders to the front and rear could not see what was happening.

'Who are you, Sir?' queried General Barringer.

'Major Henry Young. I range this country for General Phil Sheridan,' said the officer. 'Now, General, let's ease out of the line of march. We'll take position on that little rise over there and let your men pass.'

With no other option, Barringer nodded and followed his captors out of the column and up onto the small hill. To his sorrow, General Barringer saw his command pass on without him. He was now a prisoner of war, captured by a Yankee Ranger.

Preface

Born in the early 1600s, the Rangers fought six wars in America before the United States was formed. They were men who blended European weaponry and discipline with the raid and ambush tactics of the American Indian. These men ranged outward from the settlements and from this practice they drew the name 'Ranger'. Primarily citizen soldiers who were skilled woodsmen, Rangers were the principal 'American' early warning and strike force of the Colonial period. By the time of the Revolutionary War they rejected the musket and adopted the 'long rifle' as their favored firearm. The Rangers became identified with the Pennsylvania rifle and ranger units and were often called 'riflemen'. They were the first units formed by the Continental Congress in the war for American independence. The deeds of Rangers Israel Putnam, Ethan Allen, John Stark, Nathan Hale, Francis Marion, 'Light Horse' Harry Lee and Dan Morgan are carved in American history. Unconventional in their methods and not regular soldiers, the Rangers were seldom looked upon with favor by the conventional generals of the regular armies of Britain or the United States. Useful in war, they were shunted aside in peace.

In the war of 1812, Kentucky Rangers played a major role in recapturing Detroit and were the key element in the American victory at the October 5, 1813 Battle of the Thames. The Texas Rangers were born as a military organization to take the war to the hated Comanche and Mexicans. They played a major role in the development of the south-western frontier. These Rangers proved the usefulness of the horse and the revolver. As with the Rangers of Colonial times, the Texas Rangers fought an enemy that gave no quarter and the Rangers responded in kind.

During the Civil War, 72 Union and some 270 Confederate units carried the name 'Ranger'.[1] Most had little or no relation to Ranger activities but used the name for its romance or in an attempt to glorify themselves. Such an example on the Union side was the 25th New York Volunteer Infantry also known as 'Union Rangers' or 'Kerrigan's Rangers'. They were briefly commanded by Colonel James E. Kerrigan, a 24-year-old budding politician who led by bad example. He was untrained, undisciplined, unworthy and unavailable for duty. Bored by an inspection of his unit, Kerrigan walked away, ignoring commands to return. One of the forty-two charges against him accused him of leaving his camp to 'visit and communicate with the enemy'. Not surprisingly, his men emulated their commander, even appearing on parade in their underwear, with parts normally considered private exposed. Kerrigan was tried by court martial and dismissed from the service on March 6 1862.[2] On the Confederate side were the notorious 'Florida Rangers', who spent their war stealing cattle from the farmers of Georgia. Young Samuel Langhorne Clemens, who would later make his reputation writing under the pen name 'Mark Twain', briefly served in a fifteen-man organization named the 'Marion Rangers'. He later wrote: 'I knew more about retreating than the man who invented retreating.'[3]

As they became identified with the rifle in the Revolutionary War, so the horse and revolver in large measure determined Ranger tactics in the Civil War. A soldier can be infantry or cavalry, indeed come from many branches and other services and be a Ranger. It is neither the weapon nor the type of transportation that determines if a military unit is 'Ranger'. It is not the name 'Ranger' being attached to a unit by some commander seeking to make his unit sound elite. Depending on which side was applying the name, Rangers in the Civil War were often referred to as bushwhackers, partisans, guerrillas and scouts.

What makes a Ranger is the power of will, extraordinary training, and the tactics they routinely practice. An American Ranger is a highly trained volunteer who has the courage, confidence and ability to spearhead attacks and invasions and operate behind enemy lines. Rangers are select troops who excel in intelligence gathering and are masters of the ambush and the raid. To develop knowledge, stamina and strength of will, the Ranger is tested and proven in the most trying circumstances. Rangers lead the way and they do so understanding that 'It is all in the heart and the mind.' Rangers are trained so that they can accomplish anything and are expected to. It is a tradition of the Ranger rooted in nearly four centuries of service to America that 'once a Ranger, always a Ranger.' We carry our traditions, the love of our brotherhood and the memory of our campfires and battles to the grave.

In the Civil War, most Rangers on either side were horsemen, though Rangers Turner Ashby, John Hunt Morgan and Nathan Bedford Forrest used the horse to deliver men to the point of action. They preferred to have their men fight dismounted. In addition to the Rangers, both North and South used regular cavalry units to stage deep penetrations and raids.

In a September 17 1863 letter to General Henry Wager Halleck, General William T. Sherman described the people of the South as being of four classes: the first was the large planters, the ruling class; the second was the small farmers and mechanics; the third was the Union men of the South; and the fourth was the 'Young Bloods'. Sherman wrote of this group: 'War suits them, and the rascals are brave, fine riders, bold to rashness and dangerous subjects in every sense.... This is a larger class than most men suppose, and they are the most dangerous set of men that this war has turned loose upon the world.'[4] It was this class of 'young bloods' that produced the Rangers of the Confederacy.

The fighting-at-home situation of the Confederate States of America provided a climate in which Rangers flourished. Some Southern officers began as Rangers and rose in rank and fame as leaders of large forces. Nathan Bedford Forrest was foremost among this number. Even when in command of sizable numbers of men, the roots of these men were Ranger. They fought in the manner used by Light Horse Harry Lee and Francis Marion in the Revolutionary War.

As with life, history is not fair. Some brave men have their stories told and fight in the glare of publicity; others battle on, their exploits little recognized, often forgotten. John Hunt Morgan, Nathan Bedford Forrest and John Singleton Mosby are among the best-known Confederate Rangers. Their actions are covered in my book *Ghost, Thunderbolt, and Wizard.*

John Imboden, Harry Gilmor, Elijah White, Hanson 'Hanse' McNeill, Turner Ashby and Phil and Bill Thurmond fought with valor for the Confederate cause. Along with the daring Union scout Henry Young, they are little remembered today. After the war, Elijah White would avoid all but local politics and end his life as a Baptist minister. Bill Thurmond was hounded by lawsuits stemming from his raids. Harry Gilmor was captured by Union Rangers. Turner Ashby, Hanse McNeill and Phil Thurmond would die in battle. War was in the blood of Henry Young. After the Civil War, he went west to fight in Mexico and was killed there.

This book is about Rangers in the American Civil War. Some were well known during the fighting, but many were not. Publicity is the life blood of remembrance and without that lasting attention many of their deeds, and the Rangers themselves, have faded to the background. It is my purpose here to shed light on these pioneering warriors whose names risked being lost to history. For that same reason, three well known Confederate masters of irregular warfare - John Mosby, John Morgan, and Bedford Forrest – are not featured here. Their legends are writ large and deserved a book of their own. For those wishing to learn more about Mosby, Morgan, and Forrest I encourage you to read Ghost, Thunderbolt, and Wizard.

INTRODUCTION

Opening Moves

In South Carolina, lawyer James L. Petigru observed that South Carolina was '...too small to be a Republic and too large for a lunatic asylum.' Nonetheless, South Carolina left the Union on December 20 1860 and other southern states quickly followed. At 4.20 am on April 12 1861, the fiery secessionist Edmund Ruffin pulled the lanyard on the first cannon to fire on United States soldiers at Fort Sumpter in Charleston Harbor. Five days later, Virginia seceded and its Governor John Letcher sent a message to Andrew Sweeney, the mayor of the city of Wheeling: '...seize the custom house, the post office, and all public buildings and documents in the name of the sovereign state of Virginia.' Mayor Sweeney responded: 'I have seized upon the custom house, the post office and all public buildings and documents in the name of Abraham Lincoln, President of the United States, whose property they are.' In Virginia the question was asked: 'Will brother fight brother?' The answer was 'Aye, when the mother is struck.'[1]

The war that followed would be primarily fought south of the Mason-Dixon line. Virginia would find its beautiful land ravaged and its people made destitute. It would lose twenty-five western counties that would remain loyal to the United States, breaking away to form West Virginia; all that lay in the future in the spring of 1861. As hot voices filled the air, women sewed uniforms and brightly-colored banners; men sharpened sabers and practiced musketry. A man said he felt patriotic. When asked what that meant, he replied: 'I feel as if I wanted to kill somebody or steal something.'[2]

With the two capitals of Washington and Richmond only 90 miles apart, the protection of each had a major impact on the employment of troops. The defense of Washington held vast numbers of Union soldiers in the ring of forts that protected the city. This action tied a rope to the maneuverability of the Union Army of the Potomac. The defense of Richmond resulted in much of the effort of the Confederate Army of Northern Virginia being put forth in the eastern portions of 'Old Dominion'. Still, armies fought in the western portions of the state. It was primarily in the outlying counties of Western Virginia – the Shenandoah Valley, Loudoun and Fauquier Counties – that the underlying current of Ranger warfare took root and flourished east of the Mississippi.

Terrain is the workplace of the Ranger. As it is the arena of conflict, knowledge of terrain played a major role in the success of Ranger operations. The chain of Appalachian Mountains of eastern North America reach from Quebec to Georgia. It was in the subordinate ranges of the Appalachians – the Blue Ridge Mountains in Virginia and North Carolina and Georgia, and the Great Smoky Mountains in Kentucky and Tennessee – that a true civil war of raid and ambush pitted brother against brother, neighbor against neighbor. For the larger 'Sectional' fight, the strategic importance of the Shenandoah Valley was evident to any worthy military planner with a Virginia map. For the Confederates, 'The Valley', as it was called, was a natural highway north-east to the city of Washington. For the Union armies going south-west, it led to very little of military significance and took them away from their primary objective of Richmond.

The Shenandoah Valley of Virginia is linked to the Cumberland Valley of Pennsylvania. The valley draws its name from the Shenandoah River and is bounded on the west by the Shenandoah Mountains and on the east by the Blue Ridge. For some 50 miles of its length, the valley is divided longitudinally by the Massanutten Mountain. The Massanutten often served as a curtain during the war, allowing troop movement to be concealed from the opposing force.

In 1861, the valley had numerous 'pikes' or macadam roads constructed by slave labor using crushed limestone. Such a pike of 100-mile length ran from Martinsburg south to Staunton and another from Winchester to Harpers Ferry. The rivers of the area, the Shenandoah and Potomac being the most prominent, are beautiful rivers wending through lush mountains and rolling countryside. They were also of military importance, serving as boundaries and hindering operations as barriers when in flood.

Located to the east of the Shenandoah Valley is Loudoun County, Virginia. Situated only 30 miles from Washington, Loudoun is a lovely land of rolling hills, bordered for some 30 miles on its north and east by the Potomac River. At the time of the Civil War there were thirteen Loudoun County ferries or fords across the Potomac.

While they went where ordered or opportunity offered, Rangers usually patrolled in the same area. John Singleton Mosby and Elijah White tended to operate east of the Shenandoah River. Turner Ashby and Harry Gilmor were in the Shenandoah Valley. Hanse McNeill and his son Jesse McNeill had an area of operations primarily to the west along the south branch of the Shenandoah River and along the upper Potomac River. In the mountains of present-day West Virginia were Bill and Phil Thurmond and a host of lesser-known Confederate Rangers, including 'Devil Anse Hatfield' of the post-war Hatfields and McCoys feud.

Agricultural wealth and generations of horse-breeding made the valley and nearby eastern counties prime areas of operation for Confederate Rangers. They were rarely supplied by their government so were greatly dependent upon local forage and food for their horses and themselves. The support of the populace and knowledge of the terrain allowed them to be sustained, move securely, and vanish when they desired.

As war began, the regular army of the United States numbered about 16,000 men. Many of these were scattered in western posts. North and South, mobs of civilians struggled with the new experience of learning to be a soldier. In the winter of 1861, Confederate rookie John McClinton, who would in time become a superb Ranger, found out the perils of war far from the battlefield. After a treacherous passage over an icy foot log above swirling water, he exclaimed to his captain that 'fighting war is mighty hard work and moreover is very dangerous, for I came near to being killed when I fell in the creek just then.'[3] Men who had never traveled more than 10 miles from home found themselves in strange places. In a letter home, a soldier described his location as '...Camp Misery, 15 miles from "the knowledge of God".'[4] Men had to learn where they fit in the army. South Carolina General Ebenezer Elzey was fond of whiskey. One night early in the war when Elzey and his staff were drinking, the general felt liberal and called the sentry into his tent to participate. Early the next morning while General Elzey was sleeping, the sentry came back on duty and shook Elzey awake, saying 'General! General, ain't it about time for us to take another drink?' General Elzey had the man placed under arrest and for months afterwards comrades would taunt the soldier with his words.[5]

Some men were clever and used the system against itself. A Union lieutenant approaching a volunteer on sentry was challenged with 'Halt! Who comes there?' Startled, the lieutenant, with contempt in every line of his face, expressed his ire with an indignant 'Ass!' The sentry's reply was quick and apt: 'Advance ass, and give the countersign.'[6]

During the confused opening of the war, numerous bands calling themselves 'Partisan Rangers' sprang up. They intimidated and preyed on any neighbor they suspected of supporting the Federal Government. Some of these men were motivated by patriotism, some by profit through robbery. Beatings and random murder were commonplace. A newspaper report described the terror that was created by these threats and attacks: '...many of the Union men did not sleep in their houses for weeks. Numbers fled the country for protection and to save their lives, caused by threats and every indignation that could be devised to intimidate them.'[7]

When President Lincoln called for 75,000 men to put down the rebellion in South Carolina, Virginia refused to contribute. On secession, it was obvious to Virginians that Union forces would be marching in their direction. The western axis of advance would likely be from Harrisburg, Pennsylvania through Chambersburg into the Shenandoah and Potomac valleys and from Ohio and Wheeling. The Ohio force could come down the Kanawha Valley in the direction of Saunton, Virginia, while that from Wheeling could follow the tracks of the Baltimore and Ohio (B&O) Railroad east toward Grafton. In late May 1861, the Union troops began to advance from Wheeling. On June 3 1861, Union forces, led by Colonel Benjamin Franklin Kelley of a Wheeling regiment and an Indiana regiment under Brigadier General Thomas A. Morris, launched an attack on the Confederates at Philippi. They drove the Confederates from the field in a rout that became known as 'The Philippi Races'. Union success continued with defeat of the Confederates at Rich Mountain. In September 1861, Union General William S. 'Rosy' Rosecrans hit the Confederate flank with a brigade and put the rebels to flight. The Confederate commander Robert S. Garnett was killed in the action. Garnett was the first general officer to die in a war that would see seventy-seven Confederate and forty-seven Union generals killed in action or die of wounds.[8]

Union General George McClellan was senior to Rosecrans and was supposed to follow him in the attack. Because he mistakenly thought Rosecrans was losing, McClellan did not attack and withheld the two brigades with him from the battle. Despite this, McClellan took credit for the victory and began to promote himself as a commander. Some newspapers called him 'The Young Napoleon'. It was a time when the public was hungry for heroes. With the old Napoleon being underground, the title 'Young Napoleon' was up for grabs.

George McClellan thought that Western Virginia was now firmly in the Union grasp. He claimed that 'The effect of our operations against the larger forces has been to cause the small guerrilla bands to disappear.'[9] By September 1861, a pattern of war had developed that proved McClellan wrong. Roving bands of raiders were terrorizing the countryside proclaiming themselves as Confederate Rangers. A *Cincinnati Times* report stated:

> There is not a county in all this part of old dominion that does not have a greater or less number of Secessionists, who have degenerated into assassins. They are committing murders daily, lying in ambush for that purpose. Not only the Union Volunteers, but their own neighbors, who peaceably and quietly sustain the cause of the Union, are the victims of their malice and blood-thirsty hate.[10]

Many on the Union side felt that the ambush was an unjust means of war. This was strange reasoning, as to lie in wait for an unsuspecting enemy and strike by surprise is as old as warfare itself. In America it was a tactic routinely employed by both Indians and whites from their early encounters.

Coming of Age

By early 1862, the Confederates knew the war was not going to end in their quick victory. Governor John Letcher of Virginia believed that with the Confederate army driven out of the western portion of the state, a way must be found to make Union occupation forces uncomfortable. A tactic was needed whereby the enemy could not move about without fear of attack. Letcher felt that guerrilla warfare seemed his best option. A small number of skilled raiders could force the enemy to draw off men intended for use at the battlefront. More Union troops would be required to guard vital supply routes and installations.

A guerrilla is defined as 'a member of a band of irregular troops taking part in a war independently of the principal combatants.' This definition clearly fit the situation in Western Virginia. There, local bands of mountain people were already in combat. If recognized by Virginia, their activities could be legitimized. Normally these units would operate independently under their own commanders. If operations brought them near to the Confederate army, they would take their orders from the regular army commander.

Governor Letcher appointed the officers of nine Virginia State Ranger companies on March 18 1862. The next day he provided leadership for the tenth company. Letcher did not have approval of the Virginia General Assembly. This was, in poker parlance, 'betting on the come'. Letcher knew that in the ardor of war his actions would meet with favor.

On March 27 1862 the Virginia General Assembly did as expected and authorized the raising of at least ten, but no more than twenty, Ranger companies. These were to consist of seventy-five enlisted men and three officers. Plans were made for organization of the companies into battalions and even a regiment, but events held activities to company level. The men were to be primarily enlisted from areas that had been occupied or were under direct threat by Union troops. Thus these Rangers would better know the area, have the support of the local populace, and higher motivation as they were fighting for their homes.

Recruiting went forth at a rapid pace. Soon untrained, undisciplined men began to roam the countryside. Within two weeks, passion, ignorance and greed combined to make some of these men hated by those they were organized to serve.

Conflict that pits neighbor against neighbor generates a special and personal ferocity. The Appalachian chain from Western Virginia south into Alabama and Georgia was home to mountain men who were seasoned hunters. They were free men who resented orders or intrusion from any outsider. They were often ignorant, violent, poor and clannish men who saw war as a license to take what they wanted. Sniping and volley-firing from heavy brush was a specialty that earned them the name 'Bushwhackers'. In the early part of the war, these tactics could be done with impunity as Union officers were ordered not to appear heavy-handed and the word of a suspect was accepted. If Union forces were in the area or they were captured, these men quickly learned to take the oath of allegiance to the United States. This was a way of remaining free to ambush their neighbors. Their oath had no value to them and therefore could be given freely. Some Confederates found it good sport to take and then disregard the oath of allegiance to the United States. They did it time and again.

Union Regular Army Indian fighter George Crook, promoted from captain to lieutenant colonel of Volunteers in a stroke of a pen, was assigned to command the 36th Ohio Infantry at Summersville, West Virginia. The 36th Ohio was a citizen soldier regiment described by its new commander as '...rare as a piece of beef'. The men were having a difficult time with their opponents. George Crook described the situation in his memoirs:

> The country was the home of counterfeiters and cut-throats before the war and the headquarters for the bushwhackers. It was well adapted for their operations, for, with the exception of a small clearing here and there for the cabins of the poor people who inhabited it, it was heavily timbered with thick underbrush, rocky and broken, with dense laurel thickets here and there. The thoroughfares and country roads that traversed this country were like traveling through a box canyon with the forest and underbrush for walls.
>
> It was here that the cowardly bushwhackers would waylay the unsuspecting traveler and shoot him down with impunity. Their suppression became a military necessity, as they caused us to detach much of our active force for escorts, and even then

no one was safe. It was an impossibility for them to be caught after shooting into a body of men, no difference as to its size. The question was how to get rid of them.

Being fresh from the Indian country where I had more or less experience with that kind of warfare, I set to work organizing for the task. I selected some of the most apt officers, and scattered them through the country to learn it and all the people in it, and particularly the bushwhackers, their haunts, etc.

Very soon they commenced catching them, and bringing them in as prisoners. I would forward them to Camp Chase [Columbus, Ohio] for confinement, by order of General Rosecrans. It was not long before they commenced coming back, fat, saucy, with good clothes, and returned to their old occupations with renewed vigor. As a matter of course, we were all disgusted at having our hard work set at naught, and having them come back in a defiant manner, as much as to say, 'Well, what are you going to do about it?'

In a short time no more of these prisoners were brought in. By this time every bushwhacker in the country was known, and when an officer returned from a scout he would report that they had caught so-and-so, but in bringing him in he had slipped off a log while crossing a stream and broke his neck, or that he was killed by an accidental discharge of one of the men's guns, and many like reports. But they never brought back any more prisoners.[1]

Throughout Appalachia, the war of small but bloody raid and ambush would create years of terror as neighbor fought neighbor without mercy. In the non-slaveholding mountain areas of Virginia, Tennessee, Georgia, North Carolina and Alabama, there were many opposed to secession. Alabama Cavalry rode for the Union and North Carolina furnished white Union regiments. There were no support programs for the families left behind. If the man was absent, women and children were left to fend for themselves and at the mercy of roving bands. There were thousands of southern men who did not want to be conscripted and leave their families to starvation or raiders. Draft evaders, called 'Scouters', and deserters often became bushwhackers to elude capture, and robbers to survive. Some 428 North Carolina officers and 23,694 men deserted the Confederate cause.[2]

It is likely that as many as 40,000 southern evaders or deserters took refuge in the forests of the Appalachian Mountains. They were forced to live like wild beasts and were ruthlessly hunted by Confederate authorities. Former neighbors robbed, tortured, shot and hanged each other. Hatred became so intense that no man, woman or child was safe. In the mountains of Central and Western counties of North Carolina, old women in their 70s and 80s, and pregnant women and children were beaten and tortured by Confederates to extract information about their men.

An example was Confederate Colonel Alfred Pike of the 50th North Carolina Regiment. The following report describes his torture of the wife of a Confederate army deserter:

> I went with my squad to Owens' spring where his wife was washing and inquired of her as to Owens' whereabouts, she said he was dead and buried, I told her she must show us the grave, she thereupon began to curse us and abuse us for everything that was bad, some of my men told me that if I would hand her over to them they would or could make her tell, I told her to go some twenty steps apart with them, she seized up in her arms her infant not twelve months old and swore she would not go. I slapped her jaws till she put down her baby and went with them, they tied her thumbs together behind her back and suspended her with a cord tied to her two thumbs thus fastened behind her to a limb so that her toes could just touch the ground, after remaining in this position a while, she said her husband was not dead and that if they would let her down she would tell all she knew, I went up just then and I think she told some truth, but after a while I thought she commenced lying again and I with another man (one of my squad) took her off some fifty yards to a fence and put her thumbs under a corner, she soon became quiet and behaved very respectfully, the rails were flat and not sharp between which I placed her thumbs, I don't think she was hurt bad. This is all I have done sir, and now, if I have not the right to treat Bill Owens, his wife and the like in this manner I want to know it, and I will go to the Yankees or any where else before I will live in a country in which I cannot treat such people in this manner.[3]

The 56th and 64th Confederate North Carolina Regiments CSA fought against the citizens of their own state. On January 18 1863 in the

Shelton-Laurel Valley in Madison County of Western North Carolina, Confederates of the 64th N.C. Regiment under Lieutenant Colonel James Keith shot down thirteen North Carolina men and boys execution-style. The killing was in retaliation for a raid to steal desperately needed salt by Madison County men.

The roots of the Confederate Partisan Rangers extend to militia units that existed prior to the war; these quickly became guerrilla organizations until March of 1862 when they were made Virginia State Rangers. James Carter Linger in his book *Confederate Military Units of West Virginia* credits the Confederate Rangers with a kill ratio of ten to one.[4]

On April 2 1862, Brigadier General Heth CSA wrote Governor John Letcher of Virginia expressing his displeasure with southern raiders who were calling themselves Rangers: 'The companies of this organization which have come under my observation are simply organized bands of robbers and plunderers, stealing the thunder of and basing their claims to organization upon the meritorious and daring acts of a few brave men.' Heth continued that many of the men were 'notorious thieves and murderers, more ready to plunder friends than foes…they do as they please – go as they please.' General Heth provided an apt warning, writing: 'A guerrilla force without being closely watched becomes an organized and licensed band of robbers. Properly managed in small parties they are very efficient.'[5]

Heth's concerns quickly came to reality. Two days later, a committee of citizens from Pocahontas, Virginia called upon him to complain of those who called themselves Rangers. Anxious to forward a written testament to the governor, Heth requested the complaint be in writing. Commonwealth Attorney William Skeen wrote Heth that

> the Rangers are a terror to the loyal and true everywhere, and cannot whilst in the murder of our citizens and the stealing of their property be of any service to Virginia or her cause…. Virginia has armed these men to murder, rob, steal and commit all other offenses of a less grade.[6]

Skeen denounced these men for three murders, three robberies and fifteen to twenty horses stolen in the community of Pocahontas. Men of Downs' and Spriggs' companies were calling anyone they wished to rob or murder 'Union men'. Burning with fury, Skeen and his committee demanded that the militia of Pocahontas be disbanded from service with the army and sent home to protect their families and property from their fellow Southerners.

General Heth took action. He informed the governor that under martial law he had the authority to disarm the men of Downs' and Spriggs' companies and that he intended doing that at once. He asked that no more similar organizations should be so recognized in his jurisdiction.

Heth was too late. In Richmond, the intent to form Partisan Ranger units was already well under way. Major John Scott, lawyer of Fauquier County, a former editor of the *Richmond Whig*, organizer of the Fauquier County Black Horse Cavalry and later with the 24th Battalion, Partisan Rangers, claimed authorship of one of the most important pieces of legislation in Ranger history. Scott wrote in 1867:

> I had conceived and drafted the Partisan Ranger Law, shown it to Secretary Randolph, and, with his approbation, had carried it before the Joint Military Committee of the two houses of Congress, whose Chairman was Mr. Miles, of South Carolina. I found the table of the committee covered with all kinds of projects relating to the irregular service. My plan was preferred, reported to the two houses, and without debate became a law. Colonel Mosby has often told me that upon that basis rested the superstructure which he afterwards reared.[7]

The words Scott claimed became the 'Partisan Ranger Act', established on April 25 1862 by the War Department of the Confederate States of America and published as General Orders No. 30. The orders spelled out the authorization by the Confederate congress for the army to 'form bands of partisan Rangers in companies, battalions or regiments, either as infantry or cavalry – the companies, battalions, or regiments to be composed, each of such numbers as the president may approve.'

These same orders gave those Partisan Rangers who were regularly received in the service the same pay, rations, quarters and status as members of the land forces of the Confederate States of America. This was important as it gave them legal protection under the rules of war. They were permitted to elect their officers, an old and unrealistic practice that some Confederate commanders would subvert.

Section 3 of the order would be controversial:

> Be it further enacted, that for any arms and munitions of war captured from the enemy by any body of Partisan Rangers, and delivered to any quartermaster at such place or places as may

14

be designated by a commanding general, the Rangers shall be
paid their full value, in such manner as the Secretary of War
may prescribe.

Thus Section 3 introduced a profit motive into membership in these
units. It set them apart from the line unit soldier who did not receive
such reimbursement. The prospect of monetary gain would attract some
undesirable men who were more interested in wealth than patriotism.
When uncontrolled, it was only a small step to robbery and murder not
just of the enemy, but of their own citizens. When controlled it was the
best recruiting tool the Rangers had. In most wars the manufacturers
make money while the soldier gets nothing but misery; under the Partisan
Ranger Act, a fighting man could become wealthy.

Virginia's effort to form local Ranger units failed due to lack of
supervision. The officers in some of these units could not or would not
control their men. Their criminal acts enraged both North and South and
cast a pall over future Ranger units and Ranger operations.

The Confederate Partisan Ranger Act would have a major impact on the
war. Many ruthless men sought to use it as a cover for their depredations.
Even William Clark Quantrill, the butcher of Lawrence Kansas, enrolled
his men under its protection of legitimacy. The actions of these murderers
detracted from the valuable service being done by authentic Rangers and
raiders. There was intense jealousy on the part of generals who often did
not have the knowledge to employ Rangers effectively, yet resented the idea
of independent commands.

North and South justified their use of the ambush and raid and condemned
its use by the opponent. Both sides complained this fighting of raids and
ambushes was outside the rules of war. Guerrilla, partisan and bushwhacker
were used derisively. John Mosby had no complaint about being called any
of these names. 'The word "guerrilla" is a diminutive of the Spanish word
guerra (war) and simply means one engaged in minor operations of war.
Although I have never adopted it, I have never resented as an insult the term
"guerrilla" when applied to me.'[8]

Regardless of the name, those who operated behind enemy lines seldom
remained together on completion of an operation. Most ambushes and raids
were a surprise strike followed by a quick withdrawal. Small unit raids might
last from one to six days. The assault frequently came at night when enemy
camps were asleep. The raids were performed without regard to the weather.
Rain, cold and snow were allies of the Rangers. J. Marshall Crawford of

B Company, Mosby's Rangers, wrote of a raid in which 'while riding we would put our reins in our mouths, and our hands under the saddle blankets, next to the horses' skins, to keep from being frozen.'[9]

When the raid was completed, the Rangers would return to their homes or to those of friendly families and await the next summons of their leaders. Dispersion in home area allowed the Rangers to support their families in better fashion than could be done by a soldier serving far from home with the army. Dispersion for security followed by concentration for the attack was the Confederate Ranger tactic. They frequently raided or ambushed Union troops, raised havoc with Union supply columns and earned the hatred of the blue-coated soldiers by their attacks on ambulance trains. In the eyes of Confederate Rangers, a wounded soldier was still a soldier and unless killed could get better and return to battle. They frequently wore captured blue Union overcoats, concealing their identity in order to get close. Confederate Ranger officers on occasion donned the garb of Union officers and bluffed their way into camps where they gathered information. Union Rangers frequently roamed behind Confederate lines dressed in Southern butternut or gray.

Horses were vital to mobility and raiding. Horses became such a passion that some men thought of themselves as horse thieves; an opinion of Confederate Rangers that held sway in the North. Crawford wrote that northern newspapers called Mosby 'Land Pirate', 'Horse Thief' and 'Murderer'. Officers on both sides referred to the Rangers as being under the 'Black Flag', meaning pirates. Mosby took a horse or horses as legitimate spoils of war, but he and his men insisted he personally never took loot. That was not the case with Mosby's men. In their writings, they tell of robbing passengers after train wrecks and lifting purses when the opportunity was there. The Rangers took considerable criticism for this. Personal profit was a prime reason why, when the Southern army was riddled with desertions, the Rangers had a goodly number of volunteers.

Southern Rangers prided themselves on their horsemanship and having the strongest and fleetest steeds. In the early years of the war the Southern horsemen had superior mobility. They disdained the saber and many did not carry rifles. The prime weapon of the Confederate Ranger was the revolver, and most men carried two or more.

Mobility over bulkier weapons reflected the belief that gaining advantage was critical, known at the time as 'bulge'. Forrest, Mosby and most other leaders with an attack philosophy talked of getting 'the bulge' on the enemy. Nathan Bedford Forrest said that 'Fifteen minutes of bulge is better than three days of tactics.'[10] A key advantage was to get in close and use the firepower of the revolver.

Some Southern officers of the regular establishment wrapped themselves in a cloak of chivalry. They had no hesitancy in killing or sending men to death, yet professed alarm at the Partisan Ranger actions. They resented independent Ranger commands not under their control. However, what the Rangers of the South did was worth many divisions to the Confederacy. Small numbers of Rangers sliced into the rear areas of the invading Union army and forced their opponents to guard everything.

Operating in their home areas with the support of the local population, who provided intelligence, early warning and sustenance, the Confederate Rangers used surprise, mobility, firepower and bulge as they destroyed lines of communication and supply. They had the best horses, weapons and equipment available as they made their selection from the vast supplies they captured. Sutlers – civilian contractors who followed the army selling from wagons loaded with provisions, supplies, liquor and delicacies not provided by the army – were a bonus target of the Rangers who excelled at taking them. A play in the North was even written about this practice, known as *The Guerrilla* or *Mosby in Five Hundred Sutler Wagons*.[11]

Union forces were operating on extended supply lines in unfriendly territory. In the beginning of the war, the Lincoln administration hoped that little force would be required to put down what they saw as a rebellion; they were quickly disabused of this. The song *Richmond is a Hard Road to Travel* would prove all too true. Rangers of the Confederacy were quick to see their opportunity and attack rear areas. The task of guarding vital railroad lines and protecting Pennsylvania and Maryland from attack drew off many divisions that were needed at the front. For the Union, fighting Confederate Rangers was akin to trying to kill a hornet with a sledge hammer.

Thousands of Union troops were required as rear area guards. Even great numbers of soldiers could not guard hundreds of miles of vital railroad tracks. The B&O Railroad was critical to the Union effort, but remained vulnerable to attack. The wagon trains that supplied the Union troops were soft targets that required hundreds of guards to arrive safely. The Union picket walking his lonely beat knew that at any moment a shot could come from the thicket that would end his life. The Rangers created fear in the enemy that captured the public imagination both South and North. In Union eyes, these Rangers did not operate under the rules of war and were not entitled to any protections of those rules. Initially, the intent was to hang captured Partisan Ranger officers, but the threat of retaliation of Union officers held captive prevented this course of action.

Backed by the potential of a mighty engine of war, Union Rangers had a different set of problems to the Confederates. Prior to conflict, President Buchanan's Secretary of War for the United States was avowed secessionist John Floyd. This traitor to his oath used his position to scatter the small 16,000-man regular army throughout the west. He sought to make it impossible for the army to put down an insurrection in the east. Floyd sent the best weapons south and provided the best assignments to Southern officers, thus giving them better training. At the onset of the war, 387 of the 1,108 officers in the army had gone south, but the Southern officers favored in assignment by Floyd were of high quality. Many Northern officers of potential had left the service. They often used their West Point training to find jobs as engineers or in business. Neither U.S. Grant nor William Tecumseh Sherman were on active duty. Among those that remained in uniform, there was initially a tendency to approach this war in the same manner in which previous ones were fought and to predict a quick victory. Sherman was among the few who predicted that the war would be long. As the army of the United States would learn, in a long war, the best source of officer development is the battlefield.

In the beginning, Union senior officers thought the terrain of the South and improvement in artillery would limit the effectiveness of the cavalry arm. Men who should have known better ignored mobility as a tool of war. Senior officers of the army of the United States intended to limit the number of Union cavalry to six regiments.[12] By the end of the war, 272 regiments of Union horsemen would be formed. Union generals also overlooked the advantage of firepower. Concerned about ammunition resupply, they bypassed the fifteen-shot Henry rifle in favor of the single-shot Springfield rifled musket.

Lacking the industrial might of the North, Confederate Rangers performed a vital service to their cause well out of proportion to their numbers. A total of less than 2,000 effective Confederate Rangers in Virginia tied down the equivalent of two Union corps. By forcing the army of the United States to guard everything, these Rangers kept some 30,000 to 35,000 Union soldiers from the battlefront.

As the war progressed, the army of the United States found the only effective tactic in combating Rangers was to destroy their support base. Initially, the Union approach was to leave the houses standing but destroy the barns and all food and fodder. The intent was to break the will of the civilian populace who were supplying the Rangers, to make these people dependent on the Union Army for sustenance. The burning tactic horrified those in the South who saw war as some kind of gentlemanly chivalric contest. Indeed, breaking the morale of the civilian populace is as old as ambush tactics in war. It has been employed by Americans time and again from the Indian Wars through the destruction of German and Japanese cities in the Second World War when incendiary bombs were dropped by the thousands and civilians burned out.

Union armies made the sky of Virginia hot with flame and black with smoke. In time, the winds of destruction grew even stronger and moved deeper south. Any southern man believed capable of carrying a weapon was rounded up and taken away. Anything that could burn was burned and the animals were taken or killed. There was nothing civil about the Civil War. With rare exceptions on both sides, it became mass murder and destruction. There was nothing left but hatred, misery, and a desire to see the war end.

'War is at best barbarism.... War is hell,' said General William T. Sherman.[13]

PART ONE

THE REBELS

Chapter 1

The Moccasin Rangers

In 1861, in the mountains of the Western counties of Virginia, a loose band of irregulars formed together under the generic name of Moccasin Rangers. The name likely stemmed from the deadly water moccasin snake.

The Moccasin Rangers were originally formed in early 1861 by two prosperous businessmen, Peregrin Hays and George Silcott of Arnoldsville in Western Virginia.[1] This unit appears to have had no formal organization but many leaders. Its primary area of operations included Wirt, Roane, Gilmer, Clay and Calhoun Counties, but the Rangers went where they chose and might operate as individuals, small groups or in bands. The Union newspaper, the *Wheeling Intelligencer*, found the Moccasin Rangers as a band or as individuals to be of particular interest to local readers. The newspaper published numerous articles about 'Bushwhackers'. The leaders of the Moccasin Rangers were as varied as their uniforms and equipment. At times they were led by Daniel Duskey, George Duskey, Perry Connolly, Jack Tuning and George Downs. The founding leaders, Hays and Silcott, were opposed to the depredations of these men and left the unit. Daniel Duskey saw this as desertion and sought to have Hays and Silcott arrested.[2]

Some of the men were originally members of the pre-war 186th Regiment of Virginia Militia. Dan Duskey had been a company commander in the organization. Duskey was a 52-year-old farmer from Calhoun County. He had an unmarried sister from whom Union General Benjamin F. Kelley tried to get information. Kelley promised the woman that if she would give the location of her brother he would help her find a husband among his staff officers. As she left, the woman asked a Union captain if Kelley had been serious. Assured that it was a genuine offer, she replied: 'Well I believe I'd as soon have the old man [meaning Kelley] as any of 'em.'[3]

In mid-December 1861, Dan Duskey and his son George led eleven other men in a raid on the town of Ripley in Jackson County. Guns were taken from the Court House. While in the process of looting, Dan Duskey kicked open the locked door to the United States Post Office and took 'About a peck or a half bushel of letters...'[4] Dan and George Duskey and thirty-two others of his men were rounded up a few weeks later, with George Duskey described as a '...devilish, defiant rebel...' by the *Wheeling Intelligencer* and Josiah Parsons escaped. Dan Duskey and Jacob Varner were initially indicted for robbing the mail but the Grand Jury, in a fit of exuberance, 'returned a large number of indictments for treason.'[5] The court fell into consideration as to whether robbing the US mail was treason. They decided they could only try the pair on robbery. Duskey's defense was that he was only trying to get information on troop movements. This defense raised the question about Duskey and Varner being legitimate soldiers acting under the authority of Virginia Confederate governor John Letcher. The court found no validity to that position. Dan Duskey was sentenced to four years in jail; Jacob Varner received a three-year term.[6]

In November of 1862, two Union officers of the 8th West Virginia Regiment were captured by the Confederates. The two men were held as hostages for Duskey and Varner, and in retaliation were imprisoned with hard labor in Richmond. Duskey and Varner were serving time in New York for their federal offense. It required a presidential pardon to free them and make the exchange.[7] The trial of Duskey and Varner demonstrated to the Confederacy that those operating in guerrilla warfare needed protection under the law. It likely contributed to the Confederate passage of the Partisan Ranger Act of April 25 1862.

Perry Connolly came from a family of mixed sentiment as his brother James fought for the Union. Perry stood 6ft 3in tall and, it was said, could cover 50 miles a day on foot. Connolly quickly gained the reputation of a merciless killer. He often rode to battle with his lover, Nancy 'Peggy' Hart. Nancy Hart would kill without compunction. On the several occasions when she was captured, she suddenly became a teary-eyed female, using her feminine wiles successfully on her captors.

Connolly specialized in raiding the B&O Railroad, a line critical to the Union effort. John W. Garrett, president of the railroad, was a close friend of Lincoln. Virginia had two governors, one from the south and one from the north. Pressure was brought on the northern governor of Virginia, Francis Pierpoint, to stop the depredations. This resulted in a 'wanted dead or alive' reward on Perry Connolly. Likely the most sought-after man in West Virginia, Connolly was operating out of Webster County, east of Charleston. In early January 1862, Connolly and some thirty of his Moccasin Rangers laid an ambush at Welch Glade for Union troops. They were unaware that another Union force had observed them and moved to take them in the rear. Eighteen of the Moccasin Rangers were killed at the first fire. Perry Connolly was wounded; he continued to fight, but as he gave no mercy, he received none in return. His position was overrun and Connolly was clubbed to death. He was buried south of the town of Cowen in Webster County.

Nancy Hart began to share blankets with another Ranger. She was later captured by Lieutenant Colonel William C. Starr leading a detachment of the 9th West Virginia Infantry. Miss Hart talked her guard into letting her have his musket so that she could show him that she knew military drill. She shot the guard dead, then took Colonel Starr's horse to make her escape. Soon back with the Moccasin Rangers, Nancy led 200 Confederate Rangers back to the site of her captivity. They captured Colonel Starr and his force.[8]

Captain George Downs of the 1st Virginia Rangers was a former miller, aged 40 in 1861. Downs and his approximately 100 Moccasin Rangers were located in Wirt County on the Little Kanawha River at Big Bend. They specialized in taking the property and often the lives of any who sympathized with the Union cause. Downs and his men and those of Captain Spriggs were criticized by Confederate General Henry Heth and Southern officials for robbery and murder. Downs was captured several times and, along with Captain Spriggs of the 2nd Virginia Rangers, was scheduled for hanging. The threat of retaliation against Union officers saved them. Later in the war, Downs served with the 19th Virginia Cavalry, was praised for his courage and promoted to major.[9] Most of the Moccasin Rangers who continued to fight were brought into line service, many as part of Company A, 19th Virginia Cavalry.

Chapter 2

The Hatfields and the McCoys

The fight between the Hatfields and the McCoys is the best-known feud in American history. In the Civil War both families had men who served as Confederate Partisan Rangers in the mountains of West Virginia. William Anderson Hatfield, also known as 'Devil Anse', would later lead his clan in the battle with his neighbors. In 1861, Hatfield was a brawling youth of 20 who was given his nickname by his mother. She believed he would fight the devil himself. Though only 5ft 6in tall, Anse Hatfield looked much bigger in a fight. That resulted in one of the McCoys later describing Devil Anse as '6 feet of devil and 180 pounds of hell'.[1]

When the Confederates decided to assign unit designations to the Partisan Rangers, Hatfield was first lieutenant of the 45th Battalion, Virginia Infantry. There were fifteen Hatfields serving in the 45th Battalion and eleven McCoys. Anse Hatfield claimed that his chief opponent in the post-war feud, Randall McCoy, had also served with the 45th Battalion. Anse Hatfield left the 45th without permission; one source says early 1863 or 1864. Asa Harmon McCoy supported the Union. He would be killed by Confederate guerrillas who some claim were led by Anse Hatfield.

The families lived in rugged country along that part of the Big Sandy River known as Tug Fork. Virginia was the mother state to both Kentucky and West Virginia, and the river is the boundary between the two present-day states. The feud did not begin until eight years or more after the Civil War. The beginnings of the animosity are uncertain; indeed, the cause of the feud is as foggy as a wet West Virginia ravine. Some claim it started in the Civil War, but it may have been a fight over a pig or a McCoy girl left pregnant and unwed by a Hatfield man. Blood-letting began when three McCoys killed Anse Hatfield's brother Ellison. Anse and his clan in turn executed these three McCoys. The feud would last for more than twelve years, with legal action taken by both sides and breaks in the conflict. When it ended in 1890, eight members of the McCoy family had been killed, two of them women. The McCoy girl who loved the Hatfield man died in grief at the age of 30. The Hatfield contingent lost four men, only one of whom was named Hatfield. A fifth member of this group died in prison as a result of the feud.

Chapter 3

The Thurmond Brothers

By 1862, the brothers of the mountain clan named Thurmond had decided to become actively involved in the war. Seven of the Thurmond sons served in the Confederate army; two would be killed.[1] Phillip James Thurmond and his brother William Dabney Thurmond both organized Partisan Ranger companies, drawing their men from the eastern West Virginia counties of Fayette, Greenbrier, Summers and Monroe. Phillip formed his company of some 120 men on May 2 1862 at the mouth of Wolf Creek in Monroe County. Within two weeks they were in action. William Thurmond completed his company during the summer months. The Thurmonds made life miserable for any neighbor who supported the Union. They also proved their commands were useful in doing reconnaissance work and conducting ambush and raid operations. Though later in the war some of the unit would secure horses, Thurmond's Rangers were primarily an infantry organization. In 1863, while on a raid with a larger Confederate force, Phillip Thurmond took his men behind Union cavalry positions and removed critical planks from a bridge that was on the Union route of withdrawal. He passed this information to his commander. When the Confederate charge came home, the Union cavalry sought to retreat by way of the bridge. Horses fell through the open planks and sixteen became wedged in openings of the bridge floor.

In the fall of 1862, Robert E. Lee moved his army into Maryland. His march would lead to a place called Antietam by the North and Sharpsburg by the South. Union units hurried to meet this invasion of the North. These units included many of those that had controlled West Virginia. The one-day battle at Antietam that Lee and McClellan fought on September 17 1862 resulted in 23,110 men being killed or wounded. McClellan began the fight with 90,000 men. Lee had 40,000 troops. McClellan thought himself outnumbered. He held out of battle some 30,000 troops as a reserve. These soldiers did not get to fire a shot. Only skilled generalship by Lee and incompetence by McClellan saved the Confederate army from destruction. Lee retreated. McClellan, who could have won the war at this point, proclaimed a victory and sat in place. His inaction confirmed the observation attributed to Lincoln that 'McClellan is a great engineer but he has a special talent for a *stationary* engine.'[2]

Confederate Major General William Wing Loring was appointed commander of the Department of South-Western Virginia on May 8 1862. A distinguished captain during the Mexican War in which he lost an arm, Loring had a habit of imploring his troops to give the enemy 'blizzards', hence his nickname 'Old Blizzards'. Loring was frequently at odds with his commanders, and variously commanded divisions; briefly corps and departments. He ended the war as a major general. Post-war, his friend Union General William T. Sherman assisted Loring to obtain the command of an Egyptian division; he then became known as 'Pasha Loring' in the United States.

The Thurmonds began a cooperative relationship with Brigadier General John Echols, a brigade commander under Loring. Echols appreciated the capabilities of Thurmond's Rangers and used them wisely as scouts and guides. Capably led by the brothers, the Thurmond Rangers began to build an excellent fighting reputation. In March of 1863, they ambushed two companies of Union cavalry, putting them in such a panic that the blue-coated soldiers abandoned their horses.[3]

In June of 1863, the Thurmonds learned that a Union Home Guard Cavalry Company at Fayetteville planned to link up with a Federal force at present-day Beckley, West Virginia. Acting on information supplied by a Confederate housewife, the Thurmonds planned to trap the column as it neared its destination. The ambush site was carefully selected. The upper side of the road was heavily wooded. Here the Thurmonds placed their Rangers in concealment. On the opposite side of the road the ground sloped away sharply. This area was not wooded, but covered with thick brush and briers. The length of the Union column had been well calculated. At each end of the ambush site a large tree had been cut by axes until they were a few strokes from being felled. This work was camouflaged. When the Union cavalrymen came riding by, the two trees were cut and felled, one sealing off the road to the front and the other preventing escape to the rear. The Rangers opened fire on the surprised men. The only avenue of escape was to jump the horses into the heavy brush below the road. Casualties are unknown, but those that managed to get away were torn and bloodied by the route of escape. Captain Ankrom who commanded the Union force lost his hat and a boot and was later seen limping about. Phil Thurmond got the hat.[4]

THE THURMOND BROTHERS

In December 1863, Union General William Averell was raiding southern railroads, and Confederate Brigadier General John Echols ordered Captain Phil Thurmond and 150 Rangers to make a night march to the Kanawha Valley. On December 11 at about 3.00 am Thurmond struck and dispersed an encamped Union force on Big Sewell Mountain, about 28 miles west of Lewisburg. Thurmond quickly realized this was the advance of a larger force. He sent a messenger to Echols, then fought a delaying action to buy time for the Confederates to react. The Rangers did excellent work to assist in trapping Averell's raiders, but Averell slid through to safety when another Confederate force failed to block a key bridge.[5]

In the early-morning darkness of October 26 1864, Thurmond's Rangers and Colonel Witcher's 34th Virginia Cavalry Battalion (reinforced) attacked an eighty-man Union detachment under Captain Reynolds at Winfield, east of Charleston on the Kanawha River. Though vastly outnumbered, the determined Union soldiers trounced the attackers. Phillip Thurmond was mortally wounded. His brother Elias was among the five Confederates captured. Elias Thurmond asked permission to remain with his dying brother and his request was granted. Phillip Thurmond died eight hours later and was buried at Winfield. Another brother, Lieutenant John Dudley Thurmond, assumed command of Phillip's company.

Thurmond's Rangers continued to serve the Confederacy well. They fought not only the Union forces but were assigned the mission of hunting the increasingly large bands of Southern deserters who by late 1864 had found refuge in the West Virginia mountains. There was also a belief that numbers of serving Confederate soldiers had recognized the war was lost and sought to cooperate with the United States forces through an organization called 'The Heroes of America'. Started in North Carolina, the secret organization spread northward along the Appalachian chain. To add to their woes, the Thurmonds found the Confederate army reorganizing their unit and putting them in a battalion under Lieutenant Colonel D.S. Hounshell, a man they despised for sitting on the sidelines during two years of bloody warfare.

On April 9 1865 Lee surrendered to Grant at Appomattox. Eight days later Colonel Hounshell performed the duty of surrendering his unit, most of whom had already gone home. Bill Thurmond became a surveyor, then built a town on the New River north-east of Beckley named 'Thurmond'. It became a booming coal town. Its other distinction prior to Bill Thurmond's death in 1910 was one of the largest red-light districts east of the Mississippi.

Chapter 4

The Iron Scouts

They came from Virginia, North and South Carolina, Georgia, Mississippi and Texas to serve with Robert E. Lee, J.E.B. Stuart and Wade Hampton. Their leaders were Bill Mickler in Prince William County and George D. Shadburne who became chief of scouts for Wade Hampton. Their mission was to go behind Union lines, often in civilian clothes or in blue uniforms, and gather information for their leaders. When they had the numbers and the opportunity, they would ambush or raid. From Stuart's 1862 ride to Chambersburg to the Trevilian Station fight against Sheridan and Wade Hampton's 1864 raid on Grant's cattle herd, the Iron Scouts were ranging to the front.

They were frequently assisted by southern civilians. Ranger Prioleau Henderson was visiting Miss Sophy Cooper at her home in Prince William County, Virginia when Union cavalry surrounded the house and began a search. Miss Cooper hid Henderson between the feather bed and the mattress in her room. When the soldiers searched her bedroom, the captain in charge of the search party sat on her bed while he questioned her. Henderson was suffocating, but stayed quiet as he heard Sophy tell the Union officer: 'You may look where you please, but you will find no "Iron Scout" here.'[1] Unable to find their man, the search party left.

Sophy Cooper's home was a favorite hiding place for Iron Scouts. When Bill Mikler was being chased by Union cavalry he went to Sophy's and hid in the same fashion between the feather bed and the mattress. There were a number of young women visiting. One of the women got into the bed on top of Mikler and pretended she was deathly ill. The search party found a room full of crying females weeping over their friend who was dying and begging them to let her depart this world in peace. The cavalry relented and rode away.[2]

General Robert E. Lee had a Ranger from Texas named Burke, who could dress in any disguise and go where he wished and be believed. Burke told Prioleau Henderson '...that he had three passes, one from

33

General Robert E. Lee, one from General Meade, chief in command of the Federal Army, and another from General Pleasonton, in command of Union cavalry.' On one occasion Mikler's Iron Scouts were watching Union movements between Bristow Station and Catletts when they saw a Union column riding along. Ranger Henegan said: 'Look Sergeant, at that officer on the right at the head of the column, don't you recognize him?' All of them looked in the direction indicated and readily recognized that it was Burke uniformed as a Union major.[3]

Coming from varied walks of life, the Iron Scouts brought many talents to the organization. They supported each other against anyone. Ranger Barney Henegan was 27 years old and 6ft 4in tall. He had studied law before the war and was skilled at debate. When General J.E.B. Stuart ordered an Iron Scout to be court-martialed and appeared as a witness for the prosecution, Henegan was defense counsel. He withered Stuart's argument and got his man off free.

The Iron Scouts were Rangers who lived a 'one for all and all for one' philosophy. When they deemed one man injured, all took action to repay hurt with hurt. On February 14 1862, Confederate Ranger Hugh H. Scott led a three-man ambush patrol near Brentsville, Virginia. They engaged a force of Union cavalry. One of Scott's patrol, a man named Bolick, was in love with a girl who lived near Arrington's Crossroads. The morning before they left, the girl jilted Bolick and he told her: 'I am going to be killed the first fight I get into.' Bolick was killed on the patrol. Scott and the other Rangers took his body back and buried him beside the house of the girl who spurned him.[4]

The Iron Scouts were men who had grown up with horses and guns. Many were skilled hunters. When most of these Rangers entered the Confederate army they had no understanding of military procedure. Such a man was Munce Buford who, after a rough beginning, would become one of the most successful of the Iron Scouts. Buford was from the Enoree River in Union County, South Carolina. He was just 15 when the war began and at 16 years of age became a member of Company K, 5th South Carolina Cavalry. Young Buford had likely never been more than 10 miles from home. In his first night in the army, his unit was on the coast of South Carolina. Without training, Buford was sent out on picket, his post being in some high weeds where it was hard to find him in the dark. When the corporal of the guard came to relieve him, failing to see Buford, the corporal called out, 'Sentinel, Sentinel, oh Sentinel.' This young green soldier, being tired of the misnomer, cried out in a loud voice to the corporal: 'I let you know, sir, that my name is not Sentinel, but Munce Buford of Enoree River, sir.'[5]

THE IRON SCOUTS

During Sherman's march to the sea, Ranger Hugh Scott was scouting for Wade Hampton near Snow Hill on the banks of the Neuse River. Scott was making a reconnaissance when he came upon a house and smelled food. As he entered, he found four of Sherman's foragers sitting at a table eating while they were served by the owner of the house. Scott posed as one of Union General Kilpatrick's scouts. While eliciting information from the men, he joined them in the meal and passing around a jug of whiskey. The four men were staying for the night and Scott was encouraged to remain. He said he had one more task to perform and then would come back. His remaining mission was to get some more of the Iron Scouts. They came back several hours later, awoke and captured the Union soldiers.[6]

While the troops were in camp, a Georgia woman came to visit her sick son. The young man died and was given a proper burial including a carved wooden headboard. One of the scouts noticed the name was B. Still.[7]

Sergeant George D. Shadburne was chief of the Iron Scouts. In March 1865, Shadburne, Sergeant G.D. Jones and Ranger James Taylor collided with a Union regiment at night and were captured while serving as couriers for Wade Hampton. They were hurriedly searched and taken before the regimental commander. The Union colonel saw a suspicious bulge in Taylor's coat and asked: 'What is that I see in your bosom?' Taylor replied: 'A pistol, Sir.' 'Why did you not surrender that?' enquired the colonel. Taylor responded: 'Because I wished to keep it, it is mine; and I thought maybe I might need it to shoot my guard sir.' 'The Hell you say!' responded the Union officer.[8] Taylor was relieved of his pistol.

Chapter 5

The Border Rangers

The Border Rangers were organized at Cuyandotte, Virginia on December 10 1860, reorganized on April 20 1861 and sworn into Confederate service on May 29 1861. They were citizen soldiers, willing enough but with much to learn. Angry at his horse, young DeKalb Hughes hit it over the head with the cumbersome weapon known as a horse pistol. The gun went off and knocked Hughes from the saddle, injuring him badly. A soldier named Blankenship was trying to get his shotgun unslung and capped; in the process he shot his brother in the chest, injuring him for life. In a later engagement a man named Thompson was trying to get away from some Union cavalry. While doing so, Thompson lost his hat and his false teeth. These incidents were all part of the learning process.

The Border Rangers fought at the Battle of Scary Creek and did well. They were proud of their battle flag, which by the end of the war had numerous bullet holes. One of the men of the company proudly preserved the Border Ranger flag. Twenty years later his wife needed some red material for a rug. She tore up the flag for that purpose. The Border Rangers became Company E of the 8th VA Cavalry and fought well throughout the war, ending at Five Forks. According to Ranger James D. Sedinger, when the war ended, 'The Cavalry all went to Lynchburg where we met on College Hill and talked the matter over and all concluded to go home and do the best we could.'[1]

Chapter 6

John D. Imboden

Born on February 16 1823 near Staunton, Virginia, John D. Imboden grew to be a part-time student at the Virginia Military Institute, a teacher, a lawyer and a member of the Virginia House of Delegates. At the onset of the war, Imboden lived at Staunton, Virginia. His VMI training led him to command the militia artillery in his home area. Imboden was a lawyer who looked for innovative solutions to the problems of the land. He wanted to see both secession and union, hoping that Virginia would sever its ties with the Union of the United States, but join a new one that would be formed, giving a wider latitude to the rights of a state.[1]

As the Confederacy came together, Imboden became an ardent supporter of the new nation. He spent his own funds to provide equipment to his artillery battery. On July 21 1861 at Manassas (Bull Run), Imboden and his gunners fought a spirited battle. Imboden came under the approving eye of the apostle of predestination, General Thomas Jonathan Jackson. When Jackson began his Valley campaign of 1862, Imboden was selected to raise and lead a Ranger regiment. This was done under the provisions of the Act of Congress approved on April 21 1862 and by Special Authority of the War Department. The unit was designated the 'First Regiment, Virginia Partisan Rangers'.

Imboden wrote a recruiting broadside stating:

> My purpose is to wage the most active warfare against our brutal invaders and their domestic allies; to hang about their camps and shoot down every sentinel, picket, courier and wagon driver we can find; to watch opportunities for attacking convoys and forage trains, and thus render the country so unsafe that they will not dare to move except in large bodies. Our own Virginia traitors...will receive our special regard.[2]

Imboden wanted to raise a regiment of ten companies and advertised for recruits in the *Richmond Dispatch*, making it clear that the service was intended for the mountains of Western Virginia.

On May 7 1862, Imboden activated a combined armed force of infantry, cavalry and artillery; a novel concept for the period and ideal for many raid situations. Imboden specialized in attacks on isolated United States garrisons. Though his First Regiment of Virginia Partisan Rangers was a major factor in setting the stage for other Ranger leaders, regimental-sized units were needed for conventional activities. Imboden's command was authorized to change his Partisan Rangers to a regular command on October 27 1862. It would become the 18th Virginia Cavalry. Many of the initial members of Imboden's Partisan Rangers made the change; Hanson McNeill and his followers did not and became a separate Ranger unit.

In 1863, Imboden's command would be enlarged to include the 62nd Virginia Mounted Infantry. It would be known as the 'Northwestern Brigade'. John Imboden became general officer and played a major role in actions in the Shenandoah Valley. In these battles he frequently had the Rangers of McNeill and Gilmor under his command. Imboden is buried at Hollywood Cemetery in Richmond, Virginia where Jefferson Davis and J.E.B Stuart are also interred.

Chapter 7

Turner Ashby

Turner Ashby was born on October 23, 1828 at his parents' estate named Rose Bank on the eastern base of the Blue Ridge Mountains in Fauquier County, Virginia. The plantation home was centerpiece in a scenic setting with mountains as a backdrop. From the mountain heights spewed the silver waters of Goose Creek. The creek tumbled downward to flow west to east through rolling country that was ideal for plantations and the hot-blooded young horsemen who galloped between them. These gallants sought to emulate the knights of bygone days. They rode pure-blood steeds on missions of romance, finance and sport. Turner, the third of six children, had two brothers and three sisters. The children were descended from four generations of military men. The Virginia ancestral root, Captain Thomas Ashby, had settled near Paris in Fauquier County, Virginia around 1705. He was an Indian fighter. Great-great-grandfather John Ashby had served as commander of the 2nd Virginia Rangers in the 1750s. Grandfather John Ashby was a captain in the 3rd Virginia Regiment in the Revolutionary War. Father Colonel Turner Ashby had served in the war of 1812.[1]

Grandfather Ashby had married Virginia Turner. Henceforth, both family names were honored. Turner Ashby's mother was Dorothea Green of Culpeper County. Dorothea was a woman of dark complexion and raven black hair. She passed her features to her son Turner. The boy was 6 years old when his father died. Dorothea did her best to manage the family holdings and raise the children. Tutors were provided for the youngsters. Friends and kinfolk taught the boys to skillfully ride and shoot.[2]

Growing up, Turner Ashby had responsibilities on the plantation, but they were those of a patrician. There was plenty of time to devote himself to stepping up into a saddle. Turner honed his skills as a rider, participating in fox-hunting, tournaments and steeplechase racing. By 1853, the family fortunes had declined. Dorothea Ashby sold Rose Bank. She moved to live with a married daughter at Stafford. Turner was now 25 years old and unmarried. He would be a lifelong bachelor. He stood about 5ft 8in

41

in height and normally weighed about 135lbs. Those who met him often commented on his luxurious black beard that hung to his horse's mane. Turner was close to his younger brother Richard who was 21. Richard had traveled, but came home to buy a farm close to their mother. Turner wanted to stay in sight of the old family estate. He purchased a farm close to Rose Bank and named the property 'Wolf's Crag'. As a gentleman farmer in his society, Turner Ashby owned slaves. He considered slavery the nature of man. He believed his society was born to the elite status of master. Ashby and his companions did not trouble themselves over the rights and wrongs of slavery. It had always been part of their society and was the norm of the time. The life of Turner Ashby and his friends revolved around testing themselves in a society that prized valor. Their joy was in death-defying feats of horsemanship, little dreaming that they would one day be called upon to be the lance of the South.

Each year a tournament would be held with a hurdle race. Ashby's biographer, later chaplain of his cavalry, the Reverend James B. Avirett, described a hurdle race at White Sulphur Springs as follows: 'The track was a mile long, and was crossed by two ditches, one twenty-one feet wide and the other eighteen feet, and by two fences each five feet high.'[3] Whoever was the young gallant to first successfully navigate the track would crown the Queen of Love and Beauty. The gallant and lady would lead off with the first dance at the Coronation Ball. Turner Ashby usually won. His closest competition was his beloved brother Richard.

Around 1855–56, a railroad that would be called the 'Manassas Gap Railroad' was built from Strasburg in the west to Manassas in the east. The workmen and the 'gandy dancer' section crews were a rough lot of men, inclined to violence. As the railroad ran close to his property, Turner Ashby recruited a company of young bloods to maintain order. Befitting their station, they formed a cavalry company, supplying their own mounts. Even when the railroad work gangs moved on, the men enjoyed doing cavalry drills together. What started as a few men grew rapidly into the unit that would be known as the 'Mountain Rangers'.

In the fall of 1859, on Sunday, October 16, the lush and peaceful valley of the Shenandoah was rocked by the appearance of abolitionist John Brown. The fiery prophet seized the United States armory and arsenal at Harpers Ferry. With thirteen white and five black followers he planned to raise an army that would sweep south to liberate the slaves. Brown had more fervor than planning ability. His raid was quickly crushed by ninety US Marines under the command of an army officer named Robert E. Lee.

Lee was on leave in his home state and therefore promptly available. The people of the South thought those in the North would rejoice in the capture of a scoundrel. They were surprised, mortified and angered to learn that to some northerners this revolutionary John Brown was a hero. Slavery was vital to the Southern economy. In Mississippi and Louisiana there were more slaves than free citizens and other states had large numbers of slaves. The end of slavery would mean a shattered economy and could result in loss of political control. A wealthy southerner was reluctant to travel in the North with his servants. There were those who would spirit them away. Of great concern to the South was that for every new free state added to the Union, a slave state would be added, thus maintaining a balance of power.

The feeling of national pride began to fade below the Mason-Dixon line. Strident voices of Northern abolitionists called for slavery to be abolished. Believing that those in the North intended to destroy their way of life, people in the South began to listen intently to the propagandists who had long recommended separation. The rationale was that Southern life tended to be insular, so why not look to the home state as the government that could be relied on? States were closer to the people and the power of the Federal Government was derived from the people through the states.

During the John Brown crisis, the men of the South had not been inactive. From near and far, militia units rallied in what they saw as defense of their homes and families. Foremost among the hotspurs who rode for battle was Turner Ashby leading his colorful Rangers. It had long been fashionable for young men to belong to a militia unit, preferably one with outlandish uniforms. The militia from Alexandria wore cerulean blue, those of the Valley Continentals buff and yellow, while men from South-West Virginia wore crimson.[4]

Turner Ashby had maintained his company of 'Mountain Rangers'. He had ridden the area of Point of Rocks and Harpers Ferry and knew it well. When John Brown made his raid, Ashby promptly led his men to Harpers Ferry. Then Governor Henry Wise of Virginia used the John Brown emergency to improve the training of militia companies. He would call them to active duty for several weeks as a unit, then would replace them with another group. Ashby and his Rangers stayed on. He made the acquaintance of, and no doubt got advice from, Robert E. Lee and J.E.B. Stuart. Another mentor, one to whom Ashby became close, was an eccentric instructor at the Virginia Military Institute named Thomas Jefferson Jackson.[5] A writer of the time described Jackson as a 'psychological event...and a querulous, tedious hypochondriac...for whom it was one splendid leap from bed to battery.'[6] Dick Ewell said he heard Jackson say that he never ate pepper because it weakened his left leg.[7]

Jackson was given to walking about holding his right arm in the air. He was very religious, so some people thought he was appealing to God. In truth, Jackson kept his arm aloft in order to improve blood circulation. He sat on the front edge of chairs to keep his intestines properly aligned. Jackson liked to suck lemons and was called both a *lemon squeezer* and *crazy* by associates in the Civil War.[8] Married to another prayerful soul, Jackson worshiped a God without mercy. He saw the Bible as a field manual for war. Believing he had no control over when his God would take him, Jackson was always prepared to meet his maker and therefore exhibited no fear. A proven, cold-eyed killer in the Mexican War, Jackson was different to Ashby who saw battle as an adventure. In the beginning they got along well.

Passion ran high as an invasion from the North was feared at any moment. As a skilled hunter with a natural flair for scouting, Ashby formed his men into teams that would patrol the border. During his time at Harpers Ferry, Turner Ashby spent many days in the saddle and came to have an understanding of the terrain. That knowledge would serve him well in the future. According to some reports, on several occasions he put his Rangers in civilian garb and entered the city of Washington to see what the now-despised 'Yankees' were doing.[9]

John Brown's passion earned him a hanging from a Virginia court. His body began moldering in the grave on Friday, December 2 1959, when he was hanged. A song became popular about his soul marching on. There was much truth to it. The tension did not dissipate. North and South were on a collision course over separation and slavery. In January 1860, Ashby went back to Wolf's Crag to resume farming. His men presented him with a sword as a token of appreciation for his leadership. In the summer of 1860, Turner Ashby was visited by an old friend, West Point graduate and United States Army officer Major Lewis Armistead. Ashby spoke of the likelihood of war. The gallant Armistead, who would die with his hand on a Union cannon at Gettysburg, was shocked. 'Turner, do not talk so,' he exclaimed. 'I know but one country and one flag. Let me sing you a song and drive away your gloom.' Armistead then sang *The Star-Spangled Banner*. Ashby joined in.[10]

On Wednesday, April 17 1861, Virginia seceded from the Union. Turner Ashby assembled his company, immediately leading them toward the United States arsenal at Harpers Ferry; the Rangers arriving on the 19th. Other Virginia units were converging on the arsenal as well, but they were too late to preserve it. Smoke and flames told them the garrison did not intend to let the arms fall into the hands of the rebels. John Imboden arrived with his six-gun artillery battery from Staunton. The two Ashbys and Imboden saved what they could of the war matériel, sending it on to Richmond. The Confederate force that assembled was commanded by Militia General Kenton Harper of the Virginia Military Institute. On Monday, April 21, Harper reported to Richmond that he had 2,000 men and had gained the cooperation of the Maryland officials. The Marylanders would provide early warning if Union forces approached. They had agreed that the Maryland Heights overlooking Harpers Ferry could be occupied when the Virginians deemed necessary. The active General Harper also sent outposts east and west and established telegraph communications.[11]

General Harper had Ashby's Mountain Rangers on outpost duty guarding the 12-mile stretch of Potomac riverbank from Harpers Ferry to the railroad way stop of Point of Rocks. Ashby was supported by Imboden's battery of artillery. There was a bridge at Point of Rocks to be guarded and the B&O Railroad and Chesapeake and Ohio Canal traffic to be monitored. Though he had no formal military school training, Ashby had the common sense to look out for the welfare of his men and supervise their activities. His was a genuine caring. He liked being out front to provide early warning of Union movements and he performed his mission with dedication and skill.

An order was published in Richmond on Tuesday, April 23 1862. It was a brief order, the body of which was just twenty-eight words. Major General Robert E. Lee was assuming command of the military and naval forces of Virginia.[12] On Monday, April 28, acting under instructions from Virginia Governor Letcher, Colonel Thomas J. Jackson, Virginia Volunteers, replaced General Harper in command of Harpers Ferry. Jackson began recruiting and training troops for regular service.[13]

Jackson had a dashing young West Point-trained lieutenant colonel of cavalry named James Ewell Brown Stuart. A devout believer in organization, Jackson sought to put Ashby under Stuart's command. This was the first of two clashes over organization that Ashby would have with Jackson. In conflict with senior officers the last weapon a subordinate has is to threaten to resign. This threat is a weapon best used sparingly. Both Ashby and Jackson used it on occasion and got away with it. In this instance, when Ashby threatened, Jackson rescinded his order.

The fervor of the South was reaching boiling pitch. It was an age of high-flying oratory with appeals to man, woman and God. Union Brigadier General Phillip St George Cooke, commander of the Potomac Department and father-in-law of Confederate J.E.B. Stuart, put forth a clarion call for men to come to the defense of their native state that included

> ...men of the Potomac border, men of the Potomac Military Department, to arms! Your country calls you to her defense. Already you have in spirit responded. You await but the orders to march, to rendezvous, to organize, to defend your State, your liberties, and your homes.
>
> Women of Virginia! Cast from your arms all cowards, and breathe the pure and holy, the high and glowing inspirations of your nature into the hearts and souls of lover, husband, brother, father, friend!
>
> Almighty God! Author and Governor of the world; thou source of all light, life, truth, justice and power, be thou our God! Be thou with us! Then we shall not fear a world against us![14]

With such rhetoric fueling the flames, recruiting went forward speedily.

Knowing he could not hold Harpers Ferry without occupying Maryland Heights, Jackson promptly took the high ground. It was not Virginia land. Jackson got his knuckles rapped by Robert E. Lee who, fearing it would anger the Marylanders and bring on Union attack, told Jackson his action was 'premature'.[15] Maryland was being wooed by both sides. On Monday, April 29, the Maryland state house of delegates voted overwhelmingly to stay in the Union. Up to this time Jackson had allowed the trains of the B&O Railroad to run without hindrance. Now he forbade coal trains to run at night, saying they disturbed the sleep of his troops. This forced the B&O to heavily increase traffic in the daytime. When he had them running the trains close together, Jackson shut down the line, seized 56 locomotives and 386 railroad cars and sent them south. These were moved to the east-west running Manassas Gap Railroad. They would later prove critical to the South in moving Johnston's army to the Battle of Manassas (Bull Run).

On Wednesday, May 15 1861, the newly-organized Confederate government started flexing its muscle. Orders came from the Confederate capitol at Montgomery, Alabama appointing Brigadier General Joseph E. Johnston in command of the Harpers Ferry troops. On the 24th, Johnston published an order assuming command and requesting Colonel Jackson to promulgate the order. Jackson had been given no instruction from Governor Letcher or General Lee to turn over his command; lacking that, he declined to step down. While done politely, he told Johnston 'No!'[16]

By the 26th, the confusion was resolved and Johnston was in command. While Jackson was in charge he had Ashby damaging the B&O Railroad at critical points and Johnston continued that policy. On Sunday, May 26, Ashby reported he was blasting rock overhang down on the tracks to prevent passage. One boulder taken down was estimated at over 100 tons. It was Johnston's opinion that the Confederates could not hold Harpers Ferry against attack. By Thursday, May 30 Johnston was pressing his case for withdrawal. In a message to Lee, he wrote: 'This place cannot be held against an enemy who would venture to attack it. Would it not be better for these troops to join one of our armies, which is too weak for its object, than be lost here?' Lee responded with a soothing letter asking that the ground be contested step by step.[17]

The Confederate States of America had put great stress on 'State Rights' as a reason for leaving the Union. It was a thesis that plagued the fledgling government, as soldiers tended to think of themselves in terms of their state. Jackson would not give way to Johnston until he had his position clarified by Virginia authorities. Johnston resurrected Jackson's reorganization. He now endeavored to put Ashby's Mountain Rangers under J.E.B. Stuart. Ashby would not comply and pointed out to General Johnston that he had orders to report his command to his Virginia Regiment and that Governor Letcher of Virginia had announced that Virginia troops mustered into the army of the Confederate states would preserve their regimental organization. Johnston gracefully backed down.[18]

Colonel Angus W. McDonald was a West Point classmate of Confederate President Jefferson Davis. On Tuesday, June 4 1861, McDonald was sent orders from Richmond to report to General Johnston at Harpers Ferry and raise a force of cavalry. After he had raised a command, McDonald was to destroy the over 300ft-long Cheat River Bridge and other bridges, roads and tunnels.[19] Johnston had no men to give McDonald, but patriotism was running high so recruiting went well. McDonald set about enlisting a regiment of cavalry consisting of ten companies. McDonald was 62 years old, a mentor and friend to Turner Ashby. McDonald invited Turner Ashby to join in the formation of the regiment. Ashby got permission to take his men from the regiment to which they had been assigned. He and his Mountain Rangers joined as Company A of McDonald's command.

General Johnston now had some 10,000 men under his command. The more Johnston planned the defense of Harpers Ferry, the less he thought it possible. Ringed by mountains and split by two rivers, Harpers Ferry gave a decided advantage to the attacker. A Union army of 12,000 under General Patterson was forming to the north of the Potomac. This force was in position to cut off Johnston and trap him in the bowl that was Harpers Ferry. The troops Johnston had were long on fervor and short on everything else. There were not enough weapons, ammunition, cannon, horses or uniforms and few of the men had military training. In truth Johnston had a 10,000-man mob. He wanted out of Harpers Ferry and his exchanges with Lee became more forceful. He wrote: 'You say that "the abandonment of Harpers Ferry would be depressing to the cause of the South." Would not the loss of five or six thousand men be more so?'[20]

Lee saw the possession of Harpers Ferry as critical to maintaining a tie with Maryland, a border state much wanted by the Confederacy. Under the present circumstance, if Harpers Ferry were abandoned it would open the valley of Virginia to Union occupation, thus depriving the South of great agricultural resources. Many in Maryland were realistic. While not spoken, it was obvious from looking at a map that if Maryland did go with the South, Maryland, not Virginia, would bear the brunt of the war. Lee took his disagreement with Johnston to President Davis who agreed with Lee.

Johnston's pleas to withdraw were only one of Jefferson Davis's troubles. From Greenbrier and Loudoun the cries were coming in from the civilian community: 'We need troops here to defend us!' There were not enough men or equipment to go around.

The threat of capture was real, and at length Johnston got his way. On Friday, June 14 1861, he began pulling out of Harpers Ferry. Every piece of machinery and matériel that could be salvaged from the arsenal had been shipped out to Richmond. Anything that could not be taken was burned. The bridge was destroyed and Johnston marched out his troops to set up a defense north of Martinsburg and Winchester.

In writing a Tuesday, June 25 1861 report to the Secretary of War, Colonel McDonald reported that on the 15th Captain Turner Ashby commanding a troop belonging to Colonel Hunton's Regiment (the 8th VA) had received permission to rejoin his regiment.[21]

On Monday, June 17 1861, the regiment that would later be known as the 7th Virginia Cavalry was officially formed; it contained a number of units that proudly carried the name 'Ranger'. Besides Ashby's Mountain Rangers, there were the Shenandoah Rangers, Bowen's Mounted Rangers and the Mason Rangers.[22] Colonel McDonald's age and health were not suited to long hours in the saddle. Turner Ashby, now 33 years old, was promoted to lieutenant colonel. Dr O.R. Funston would become major of the regiment. Funston would prove a warm friend and tireless supporter of Ashby. The Episcopal Minister James B. Avirett would become chaplain of the regiment and a devoted follower and biographer of Turner Ashby. Ashby's younger brother Richard assumed command of Company A. The two made a striking pair when riding side by side. Turner had a snow-white horse; Richard's was midnight black.[23]

Located at Romney in Western Virginia, the 7th Virginia Cavalry were central to their area of operations; they were 43 miles from Winchester and only 14 miles from Cumberland, Maryland where the B&O Railroad, the C&O Canal and the great National Road all converged.

The 7th Virginia served as border Rangers. Their first mission was to ride into the county of Preston and destroy the B&O Railroad bridge over the Cheat River. They did not succeed as Union infantry had the bridge well guarded. From a camp 6 miles south of Romney, Ashby's Rangers took up new missions, being employed in raids to destroy bridges, water towers and other supporting structures of the B&O. Union forces were well established on the border and Union sympathizers frequently crossed the lines to report on Confederate strength and dispositions. Ashby's men sought to ambush and kill or capture those crossing the border. Little mercy was shown by either side.

As previously mentioned, Ashby habitually wore a black beard described as being 'of unusual length'.[24] Astride his white horse, Ashby had the carriage and look of a mystical force. Union soldiers would see him on a ridge line, calmly observing them. When they tried to catch him he eluded them, only to appear again watching them in a silent taunting from above.[25] His passionate love of his cause and his men was known to both sides. His dark appearance made him seem like a Saracen knight of Saladin from centuries past. His boldness was infectious. To serve with Turner Ashby was an adventure. Men responded to this romanticism. They were eager to serve in his command. In turn, Ashby was totally devoted to Stonewall Jackson.[26]

Turner's younger brother Richard had left his wife and home to be the commander of one of the ten companies under Turner Ashby's command. Taller and with a more handsome appearance than his older brother, Richard 'Dick' Ashby was more worldly. The brothers were highly regarded; their deep devotion evident to all. On Tuesday, June 25 1861, while on a patrol with seven men, Richard Ashby was ambushed.

Attempting to withdraw, he was thrown from his horse. Richard refused to surrender. He went down fighting. Turner Ashby was leading another party. Hearing the gunshots, he rode to the scene. The Union force had withdrawn to Kelly's Island in the Potomac River. In a short, vicious fight Turner Ashby led a charge through the water and drove off the Union force. Ashby then went in search of his brother. Richard Ashby's horse and spurs were found in the camp and some distance away he was found badly wounded, his body torn by bullets and bleeding from saber slashes. Richard Ashby would live in pain for eight days before death claimed him. From the death of his brother, Turner Ashby had a very personal war against the North. A letter Ashby wrote to his sister Dora on Sunday, July 7 1861 included 'I had rather it had been myself. He was younger and had one more tie to break than I.' Turner Ashby buried his brother at Romney with the intent of taking him home to Fauquier County at the end of the war.

Since his withdrawal from Harpers Ferry, relations between Brigadier General Joseph Johnston and Richmond were at best uneasy. A June 26 letter from Johnston indicated a belief that Lee disapproved of Johnston calling up militia. This required a reassurance from Lee's headquarters. Johnston was soothed, but the relationship between Johnston and Richmond was cool. Johnston requested more cavalry as 'We cannot observe the river with one regiment.' On Thursday, July 4 1861, Johnston was sent something more valuable than a regiment of cavalry. Newly appointed Brigadier General Thomas J. Jackson of the Provisional Army, Confederate States was ordered to report to Johnston.[27]

Meanwhile, in Washington, hope flamed high that the war would be quickly over. To accomplish that aim, Union forces planned to enter Virginia on three avenues of approach: one leading through Manassas; the second through Harpers Ferry; and the third coming through Western Virginia.

On Wednesday, July 17 1861, McDonald, Ashby and their men were ordered to Winchester, Virginia, where they arrived on the 19th. Their mission was to provide early warning of, and if necessary delay, Union forces under General Patterson advancing from Charleston. In the meantime, a large battle was shaping up to the eastward at a place called Manassas near Bull Run. In need of reinforcements, General Beauregard ordered General Johnston to bring his troops east. The Manassas Gap Railroad that had once been a source of anger to Turner Ashby was now a blessing for the Confederacy. At Piedmont (now Delaplane), Virginia, Johnston's troops with lead elements commanded by Jackson began to move east by rail. In doing this Jackson gave the mobility of armies a great leap forward. Jackson arrived on the 19th and as a most welcome gift brought 2,500 troops to the surprised Beauregard. More of Johnston's men were following.

Ashby took his men ranging and found that Patterson did not show signs of moving. The regiment then returned, crossing the Shenandoah at Berry's Ferry, through the Blue Ridge at Ashby's Gap and spending the night at Upperville. They could hear the sound of artillery to the east, and rode to the sound of the guns. They arrived too late to take part in the Confederate victory the North called the Battle of Bull Run and the South called First Manassas.

On Sunday, July 21 1861, Confederate President Jefferson Davis wrote: 'We have won a glorious though dear bought victory. Night closed on the enemy in full flight and closely pursued.'[28] What Davis thought was a glorious victory for the South turned out to be something else. The Confederates did not press their victory. They had also been hurt in the fight and were still trying to turn mobs of men into an army. There was still this fervent belief that they could easily whip the cowardly Yankees. Their success at the Battle of Manassas (Bull Run) reinforced this delusion. Despite the pleas of Jackson and others, the Confederates did not march on Washington. The North learned from the battle and adopted a grim determination to triumph.

Colonel McDonald took the regiment back to Winchester where he led six of the companies into the South Branch Valley of the Shenandoah. Turner Ashby with four companies proceeded to Kearneysville to protect workers who were dismantling part of the B&O. When that mission was completed, Ashby moved his command about 4 miles south of Charleston and began patrolling. He clashed with a Union probe and forced them back across the Potomac.

In the mountains of West Virginia, a Union force was assembling under the command of General Rosecrans. Fearing an invasion that would cut behind his positions, Johnston sent the 7th Virginia on a 100-mile ride to Staunton. Rosecrans went in another direction and the 7th rode back to Winchester, the only benefit being that the men were becoming inured to the hard life in the saddle.

Johnston then split the 7th Virginia. McDonald and eight companies were sent to the south branch of the Potomac River. Ashby took the remaining two companies and returned to the vicinity of Kearneysville and the B&O Railroad line. The B&O was such a vital east-west link for the Union that the Confederates went to great lengths to control or destroy it. From Point of Rocks to Cumberland, Maryland, the gray-coated troopers occupied more than 100 miles of this vital railroad and they fought hard to keep it.

Soon more companies of the 7th were assigned to Ashby's command. From his camp at Shepherdstown, Ashby, with some 400 men, established outposts to provide early warning of Union movements. Behind these he utilized the remainder of his men in destruction of the railroad. Some 1,500 Union troops were within striking distance, and skirmishing between the two sides was frequent.

On Tuesday, October 8, a brigade-sized force of Union troops under General John Greary advanced on Harpers Ferry. They seized more than 20,000 bushels of wheat from the mill of a man named Herr. Union troops occupied Bolivar Heights overlooking the ferry. Turner Ashby took six of his own companies, 300 militia and two guns, then engaged and drove Greary's men from their position. Ashby was greatly aided in this by the fire of a 24-pounder. When the gun carriage broke an axle and was dismounted, Ashby was reduced to one light field piece. The Union troops now had time to reinforce and bring up artillery. Ashby withdrew.[29] He thought much about what the breakdown of a single gun had caused and thought about ways to combine artillery with fast-moving, hard-hitting Ranger tactics.

Eight days later Greary's command began moving from Harpers Ferry toward Charleston. On November 4 1861, General Jackson was given command of the forces in Shenandoah Valley and rode into Winchester, Virginia to make it his headquarters. Keenly aware of Ashby's knowledge of the area, Jackson sent for his Valley Rangers. The two men had mutual interests and the friendship flourished.

The elderly Colonel Angus McDonald was now wearied from active service. He had accomplished much in training men unaccustomed to military service, but from the onset most of the operations of the regiment were led by Turner Ashby. The men were fully aware of McDonald's age and looked to Ashby as their true leader. It was an uncomfortable situation for both men. Unable to continue, McDonald asked for reassignment and Turner Ashby took command of the regiment. He established his headquarters near Charleston, then led his men in patrolling the Potomac River.

An innovative leader, Turner Ashby developed two tactics that proved successful for him and became his trademark. Despite being a superb horseman, Turner Ashby recognized that aimed fire could best be accomplished from the ground. He used the horse as a means to transport his soldiers to the point of battle. When action was at hand he would most often dismount the men and send horses to the rear with designated horse-holders. His men would then fight on foot. Should they need to withdraw or pursue, their horses were close at hand.

Ashby's concern for artillery led to his development of mobile artillery that traveled with his troops. His guns and caissons were drawn by horses and his gunners were mounted. Thus his guns were immediately available and fought from positions often in the front line. Ashby's artillery could repeatedly move and shoot. While not new in military history,[30] the concept was unusual in the early days of the Civil War and proved highly effective.

To bring to reality his thoughts on artillery, Ashby rounded up three diverse guns and formed a battery led by the daring 18-year-old Roger Preston Chew. With James McCarty and James Thompson, two fellow students at the Virginia Military Institute, Chew had been part of a contingent that followed their instructor Thomas J. Jackson into service. These young gunners were joined by James Williams, an Iowa lawyer and politician.[31] Captain Chew and his three lieutenants recruited gunners and went to work. Chew's Horse Battery was organized on Wednesday, November 13 1861. Chew, who would be a 22-year-old colonel at the war's end, became one of the great artillerymen of the Civil War. What Ashby was to Jackson, Chew was to Ashby: a strong right arm.

Jackson had been promoted to major general on October 7. In mid-November, Jackson's former brigade was reassigned to his command. Having trained these men, he looked forward to committing them to offensive action. Though the Confederates had achieved great success in battles at Manassas and at Ball's Bluff near Leesburg, Virginia, they were having difficulties in the western part of the state. The Confederate defeat at the Cheat River on July 13 had resulted in the loss of General Garnett and some 700 men, while the Union casualties were less than a dozen. Now the Union forces controlled Virginia west of the Alleghenies. The mountains of Western Virginia are superb defensive terrain and no Confederate general was able to rout the Union troops from their works. Generals Floyd, Wise and Robert E. Lee each tried, but could not push out the stubborn Union forces. This was not good for careers. Lee was mocked in the Southern press and got the nickname of 'Spades' or the 'King of Spades' when he had his men dig in. When he withdrew to better positions, he was called 'Evacuating Lee'.

Union troops occupied Romney 40 miles west of Winchester and installed a garrison of 5,000 men. That move extended their control over the south branch of the Potomac. The North had the B&O Railroad operating from Baltimore to Harpers Ferry. Though the Confederate Rangers had destroyed some 40 miles of track to the west from Harpers Ferry to Hancock, the

Cheseapeake and Ohio Canal was open from Cumberland, Maryland to Georgetown at Washington. The Union line of communication and supply to West Virginia was open and functioning well.

Jackson chose not to turn west and fight the mountain battle. His plan was to attack north to the line of the B&O Railroad and then take a left turn westward following the line of railroad tracks. This would simultaneously sever Union communications and put Jackson on the left flank of his enemy. Jackson set about training his men for this mission. Most important for his effort was the consolidation of the various cavalry units and placing them under the command of Turner Ashby.[32]

In December 1861, Jackson ordered Ashby to Martinsburg, throwing out mounted pickets to the front to conceal his intention. Jackson then faked an attack toward Hagerstown, Maryland, followed by his planned turn toward the Potomac.

Jackson's intention was to attack and destroy the ability of Union forces to move troops and supplies on the Chesapeake and Ohio Canal. To achieve this aim meant destroying dams on the Potomac. He occupied his army in this mission from December 11 to 21. The most difficult objective was Dam #5 which was well protected by the rifles and artillery of Union troops. Destruction of the dam was accomplished by companies of the 27th and 33rd Virginia regiments. The troops did their work by going into the freezing water at night when the Union soldiers had difficulty seeing their targets.

Ashby led by example. He was constantly in the saddle, passing among his Rangers and encouraging them. He frequently traveled with only a small escort, allowing him to quickly pass from command to command. No single horse could sustain his long rides; he usually had three. He kept his men in position to serve as the eyes and ears of Jackson's army. As a result, his reports provided the information critical to Jackson's success. When the front was quiet, Ashby would take one gun of his mounted artillery over routes well scouted by his men. Putting the gun in position near an unsuspecting Union encampment, he would deliver a number of rounds of harassing fire and be gone before his opponents could react. When the enemy advanced he withdrew, frequently establishing an ambush that might be of dismounted horsemen or artillery covering a road. When the enemy withdrew, he advanced, harassing their movement.

There was a charisma about Ashby that few commanders achieve. His men loved him. When he went into the attack his cry was 'Follow me! Follow me!' The men would begin to shout 'Ashby! Ashby!' and charge after him.[33]

Logistics was the Achilles' heel of the Confederacy. So inadequate was the supply of clothing that many Confederate soldiers wore overcoats that had been captured. The 1st New York (Lincoln) Cavalry was operating against Ashby. John Casey, an Irishman in Company B, and some others were in hot pursuit of some Confederate horsemen. Casey got too far in front and two of the horsemen who were wearing blue overcoats suddenly turned and pointed their pistols at him. Casey was forced to dismount and surrender his horse and weapons. He was then turned loose as his captors took his possessions and rode off. Casey called to his sergeant, 'Sergeant Beach, those blamed rebels have got me horse.' Beach and some other New Yorkers galloped after the Confederates. Lieutenant Lewis, the commanding officer, was furious at the men for having ridden off and was yelling at them to come back. Beach closed on the Confederates who, in their effort to get away, let Casey's horse go free. As Beach and his troopers came trotting back with Casey's steed, the sergeant noticed a group of a dozen or so riders in Union blue overcoats watching them.

Thinking his men had broken the column, Lieutenant Lewis was furious. Seeing the riders beyond Sergeant Beach, the lieutenant yelled 'Come back!' Sergeant Beach said 'Those men are rebels!' Lieutenant Lewis paid no attention and spurred his horse past the sergeant, saying to Beach, 'I want to bring those men back.' Beach tried again. 'I tell you they are all rebels,' he shouted as he watched his officer ride up to the men in the blue overcoats. The officer in charge of the group of horsemen calmly watched Lewis approach and said: 'Do you wish to surrender?' Lewis was dumbstruck. The officer in the blue overcoat drew his saber and pointed it at Lieutenant Lewis. 'Do you wish to surrender?' he asked again. One of the men in the group said 'Lieutenant, if he doesn't surrender, shoot him.' Lewis jammed his spurs into the flanks of his horse and raced away, followed by a hail of bullets. As he reached safety, Sergeant Beach could not resist saying 'I told you those were rebels.' 'So I found,' was the dry response of Lieutenant Lewis. The men in blue overcoats were Turner Ashby's Rangers. Lewis was lucky to escape.[34]

Both sides felt God was on their side and prayed for more help. Stonewall Jackson went to church at every opportunity. He usually slept through the sermons, including one in which the minister prayed for President Lincoln.[35] Union General Nathaniel Banks also attended services. A staff officer noted:

> General Banks in his regimentals stood a little forward of the preacher. Immediately beside him stood a boy about twelve years old, ragged and snub-nosed, in the most independent

and critical attitude, devouring the General with his eyes, measuring him from top to toe, probably guessing how long it would take him to grow into a major general. The scene was American...[36]

It was not only the generals who looked forward to church. One Confederate soldier wrote: 'On Sundays the churches are generally full to overflowing with soldiers.... Many soldiers go to church just to get sight of a lady.'[37]

North and South were growing in strength and efficiency. At the end of December, Jackson was reinforced with troops from West Virginia under General Loring. Banks had his troops preparing to march south in the spring and take Winchester. Jackson intended to forestall this by being the first to take offensive action. Jackson planned to send troops along the B&O Railroad through Romney and to the Ohio River. He ordered Ashby to Dam #5 on the Chesapeake and Ohio Canal, then marched north on New Year's morning over frozen roads and through cold that caused great suffering in his army. Ashby was ordered to seize the town of Bath. This required hauling his guns over snow-and ice-covered mountains, but the mission was accomplished.

Winter campaigning in the savagery of the elements was hard on men and horses. The Confederates were long on spirit and short on supplies. There was no winter uniform or coats issued and men suffered terribly. Some horsemen were fortunate to have buffalo robes or elk hides. In these hard times Ashby demonstrated another quality key to being a good commander: he genuinely cared for his men, and did his best to look out for their welfare. Friendly contacts were established with regional farms. The men were supplied with food and given what warm clothing could be found.

Men delighted in talking about Ashby's skill as a horseman. A story made the rounds that Jackson and his staff were looking for a place to cross a stream. As they rode along looking for a ford, Ashby said to Jackson: 'General, I will cross here.' He pulled his horse back to get a running start and cleared the stream in one bound. No one else chose to try the jump or felt Ashby was showing off. He was clearly the best horseman in an army of good riders.[38]

On Monday, February 24 1862, Union General Nathaniel Banks pushed forward with an army of some 38,000 men including 2,000 cavalry and 80 guns and occupied Harpers Ferry. T.J. Jackson, called 'Stonewall' since Manassas, was now facing Banks with 5,000 men.[39]

Neither side had expected a long war. Political speeches described as 'horse-shit and gun-smoke' derided the opposition. Confederate General John B. Gordon would write:

There was at the outbreak of the war and just preceding it a class of men in both North and South who were 'most resolute in words and prudent in acts; who urged the sections to the conflict and then did little to help them out of it; who, like the impatient war-horse, snuffed the battle from afar – very far:' but who when the real war began...thought that it was better for the country and them to labor in other spheres. As an American humorist put it, to sacrifice not themselves but their wives' relations on patriotism's altar. One of these furious leaders of the South had declared that 'If we should secede from the Union there would be no war, and if there should be a war, we could whip the Yankees with children's pop-guns.'

When, after the war, this same gentleman was making a political speech, he was asked by a maimed soldier: 'Say, Judge, ain't you the same man that told us before the war that we could whip the Yankees with pop-guns?' 'Yes,' replied the witty speaker, 'and we could, but confound 'em, they wouldn't fight us that way.'[40]

Having expected a short war, much of the Southern army had enlisted for one year. The time of enlistment was growing short. By February 1862, men had found that it doesn't take much combat to satisfy one's curiosity. They were ready to go home. Part of Jackson's army had been taken from him to beef up the forces of General Johnston. Being outnumbered was a fact of life for Jackson; he sought more troops, but knew that in war there are many factors more important than numbers.

Richard Taylor, a learned and observant man who would become a lieutenant general, first met Stonewall Jackson when his Louisiana Brigade arrived to join Jackson for the Valley campaign. Jackson was pointed out as a man sitting on the top rail of a fence. Taylor looked and saw

a pair of cavalry boots covering feet of gigantic size, a mangy cap with visor drawn low. A heavy dark beard, and weary eyes – eyes I afterward saw with intense but never brilliant light. A low gentle voice inquired the road and distance marched that day. 'Keazletown Road, six and twenty miles.' 'You seem to have no stragglers.' 'Never allow straggling.' 'You must teach my people; they straggle badly.' A bow in reply. Just then my creoles started their band and a waltz. After a contemplative suck at a lemon, 'Thoughtless fellows for such serious work.'

57

Taylor wrote that Jackson sucked lemons, ate hard-tack and drank water, and praying and fighting seemed to be his idea of the 'whole duty of a man.'[41] During the Valley Campaign Jackson was much concerned about the preservation of his wagon train. Taylor noted 'The men said that his anxiety about the wagons was because of the lemons among the stores.'[42]

On March 11 1862, President Lincoln temporarily assumed command of the Union armies. He did this in an effort to allow General McClellan to concentrate on taking Richmond.[43] McClellan had 100,000 troops to the 60,000 Confederates under Johnston. President Lincoln was pushing for an advance and rapid conclusion of the war. Though his goal was worthy, Lincoln was greatly influenced in his war planning by Secretary of War Edwin Stanton. Stanton had the military ego of Napoleon with none of the great conqueror's military genius. Lincoln ordered all Union army commanders to assume offensive action. With glacial speed Banks began movement in the valley. The Confederates gave ground. Covered by Ashby's Rangers, Jackson withdrew through Winchester, clearing it on March 11. He then moved on to Cedar Creek. Ashby again covered the withdrawal. As Jackson fell back, Ashby ambushed Banks' lead elements at Fisher's Hill. He pounded the Union troops with Chew's artillery.

Ashby was promoted to colonel in mid-March. On Saturday, March 22 1862, he celebrated the promotion with combat, fighting at the edge of Winchester. While capturing several Union supply wagons, Ashby used his three guns to keep the Union forces under fire. One of the shells wounded Union General James Shields. Some women of Winchester incorrectly informed Ashby that many of the troops had gone to Berryville and only a rearguard remained. Ashby passed on the information and Jackson saw the opportunity to attack a weakened Federal force.

South of Winchester was a collection of houses named Kernstown. On Sunday the 23rd, Jackson came up while Ashby was skirmishing with Union troops. Ashby was employing his guns and horsemen skillfully, weakening a spot with artillery, then charging with his horsemen, himself in the lead on his white horse. The devout Jackson had reservations about fighting on a Sunday, but he had some 3,087 troops who weren't gainfully occupied so he prayed, then launched 2,742 of these soldiers and 27 pieces of artillery in a five-hour attack against General Shields. Jackson found that Shields had not sent off the bulk of his troops. Union forces were found to be nearly twice Jackson's number and Shields would not back down. After heavy fighting, the Confederates withdrew. Jackson reported that he had 80 killed, 375 wounded and 263 missing.[44]

Ashby's information had proven wrong, but his effort in the battle made the difference. Artillery Commander Roger Chew would write:

> I have always believed that his [Ashby's] audacity saved General Jackson's army from total destruction at the battle of Kernstown. Ashby moved boldly forward with his command, consisting of a few companies of cavalry and my three guns, and protecting his men from observation by woods and ravines, opened on them with artillery, and withstood from ten o'clock until dark the fire of the enemy's artillery, sometimes as many as three or four batteries. When the enemy moved forward he dashed upon and repulsed them with his cavalry. Had the enemy known our strength or not been deceived by the audacity of the movement, they could have swept forward upon the turnpike, turned Jackson's right flank and cut off retreat by way of the turnpike. They, however, made little effort to advance, and we remained in our position until Jackson had returned to Newtown.[45]

Jackson's command at the Battle of Manassas was now called the 'Stonewall Brigade'. At Kernstown the brigade was commanded by Colonel Richard B. Garnett. The brigade had fought hard and, not getting reinforced and in danger of being overrun, Garnett had ordered his men to withdraw. Jackson was furious, relieved Garnett and placed him under arrest with the intention of trying the officer by court martial.

Taylor wrote of Jackson and the incident:

> In that moment I saw an ambition boundless as Cromwell's, and as merciless...I have never met officer or soldier present at Kernstown who failed to condemn the harsh treatment of Garnett after that action.... I have written that he [Jackson] was ambitious; and his ambition was vast, all absorbing...he loathed it, perhaps feared it, but he could not escape it – it was himself – nor rend it – it was his own flesh. He fought it with prayer, constant and earnest.[46]

Thereafter, in anguish and shame, Colonel Garnett seemed to seek death. He found it while leading a brigade of Pickett's division in the attack on Cemetery Ridge, July 3 1863 at Gettysburg.

Jackson again headed south about 5 miles with Ashby's Rangers covering the withdrawal, then outposting the hilltops some 3 miles in advance of Jackson's army. Kernstown seemed like a modest Northern success, but the Battle of Kernstown turned the eyes of Lincoln's officers toward the Shenandoah Valley. Blinded by an 'on to Richmond' fervor, few had recognized that the valley was a Confederate bayonet pointed at the city of Washington. When the danger became clear, the Union leadership saw that troops intended for an assault on Richmond should be sidetracked to the west. This was of great concern to General George McClellan, who wanted McDowell's First Corps to be used in his long-delayed move against the Confederate capital. Instead, on April 4 1862, Lincoln and his advisors created two new headquarters: the Department of the Rappahannock commanded by General McDowell, and the Department of the Shenandoah under General Banks. A rapid-reaction 'Flying Brigade' was also organized, consisting of the 1st Pennsylvania and the 1st New Jersey Cavalry.

Four companies of the Pennsylvania 13th Reserve Corps assigned the name 42nd Pennsylvania Volunteers were added to the Flying Brigade. The 42nd was a unit whose reputation was growing. The Northern tier counties of Pennsylvania are mountainous and heavily wooded. The men of this area were primarily woodsmen or raftsmen engaged in logging. They floated their product down the Susquehanna River to markets. These men were accustomed to outdoor living and hunting. There were many skilled marksmen among them. Though their regiment was the 42nd of the line, the tail of a buck deer was their symbol so they were called 'The Bucktails'! One of the better regiments on either side, the Bucktails were commanded by Lieutenant Colonel Thomas L. Kane, a graduate of the US Military Academy at West Point.

While reorganization was proceeding in Union ranks, the Confederates saw that their recruiting was facilitated by battlefield success. In two and a half months Ashby's command swelled from ten to twenty-six companies and a battery of artillery. The companies were loose bands of untrained civilian volunteers who brought their own horses and arms. There was great need of manpower so the raw units were kept in almost constant contact with the enemy. Even if there had been a trained cadre, there was no time to conduct an organized training program. Though now a brigade in size, Ashby's command could not fight as one. The only officers coordinating the activities of the total command were Ashby and Major Funston. Ashby was not a West Point-trained officer; indeed, he had no formal military training and led by example. Jackson was a school-trained soldier and set about reorganizing Ashby's troops with the following order:

> The Commanding General hereby orders Companies A, B, C, D, E, F, G, H, I, K of Ashby's command to report to Brigadier General Talliaferro, and to be attached to his command; the other companies of the command will report to Brigadier General Winder to be attached to his command. Col. Turner Ashby will command the advance-guard of the Army of the valley when on the advance, and the rear-guard when in retreat, applying to Generals Talliaferro and Winder for troops whenever needed.[47]

The Puritan Jackson was only thinking of improvement. Mission-oriented and believing God had a hand in everything he did, Jackson had little regard for the sensibilities of his fellow men. Ashby had been totally dedicated to Jackson. Whatever the merits of reorganization, this act of Jackson's seemed like a betrayal. It hurt Ashby deeply. The Ranger leader stood up to his commander. He pointed out that his command had been given him by a former Secretary of War, not by Jackson. Then Ashby and Major Funston, the only other field-grade officer in Ashby's command, submitted their resignations. This was one of the few times in Stonewall Jackson's career that he backed down. He knew that Ashby's troops were devoted to their leader. If Jackson lost Ashby, a number of men would be leaving camp. Jackson's command would be gravely injured. The general rescinded his order.

His faith in Jackson restored, Ashby repaid the favor by effectively using his horsemen to screen the movements of Jackson's army. Behind this curtain, Jackson was able to rest his troops, then move with the secrecy, speed and surprise that became the hallmark of his campaigns. In mid-April 1862, Union General Nathaniel Banks moved south, placing the bulk of his army between New Market and Harrisonburg. He was now about 27 miles north of Staunton. Banks wanted to reach Staunton and was in search of Jackson's army. His scouts were unable to penetrate the screen that Ashby kept in front of him, thus Banks was uncertain as to where Jackson's army was located. The confusion was abetted by constant hit-and-run attacks Ashby was making on Banks' flanks and rear. Banks could never be certain when these were going to have the weight of Jackson's army behind them. General Banks had reason for concern. Brigadier

General James Shields' division had been taken from him and sent east. As McDowell was leaving Fredericksburg to help McClellan at Richmond, Shields' division would now move to Fredericksburg to replace McDowell. Had Banks been decisive and attacked south, he still had the strength to succeed, but constant harassment by Ashby's Rangers and his imagination held him in check. On April 17 1862, Jackson was at the base of the Blue Ridge Mountains in Elk Run Valley. He rested his army and planned his next move.

Events were going smoothly for the Union. McClellan was only a few miles from Richmond. General McDowell planned to march from Fredericksburg on May 24 to join McClellan. McDowell planned to use the new 'Flying Brigade' as skirmishers on that mission.

Northern plans were not limited to the Richmond area. General John C. Fremont had 8,000 men spread among the mountain posts west of the Shenandoah Valley. A Union reinforced brigade under Brigadier General Robert Milroy was coming out of the mountains of West Virginia to attack Staunton. They were opposed by some 2,500 Confederates under General Edward Johnson. Jackson could not afford to allow the troops of Milroy and Banks to link up at Staunton. He decided to attack Milroy while keeping Banks in confusion. When Milroy was defeated, Jackson would then attack Banks. Jackson kept a small force of cavalry with him, but the majority rode with Ashby to keep General Banks from interfering with the attack on Milroy. Ashby was up to the task and on Wednesday, April 30 1862 he attacked Banks' outposts. This created such a demonstration that Banks thought Jackson was at hand. He prepared for a defensive engagement. Ashby thus gave Jackson freedom of maneuver.

Jackson's plans were facilitated when Major General Richard Ewell arrived with 8,000 troops. Taking no unnecessary risks, Jackson held General Ewell's troops as a reserve and to cover him when Banks learned the truth about Ashby's strength. Jackson moved north, then crossed the Blue Ridge and reached Staunton.

From Jefferson Davis and Robert E. Lee to the rear rank private, the Confederates knew that Mr Lincoln's army had massed a huge force for an attack on Richmond. It was not large enough to suit Union General McClellan. Though only a few miles from the Confederate capitol, the Union commander was waiting for the 40,000-man corps of General Irvin McDowell to arrive from Fredericksburg. McClellan did not foresee a threat in the Shenandoah. He took Shields' division from General Banks to secure Fredericksburg after McDowell left. Robert E. Lee saw that the best chance of saving the Confederate capitol would be for Jackson to secure a victory that would pull off Union troops and send them to the west.

With troops drawn off in support of McClellan, Banks was now reduced to some 8,000 men. Not able to locate Jackson, his force remained in position, flailing at Ashby's Rangers who struck and quickly withdrew. Meanwhile, Jackson with about 4,200 men made a fast march of 18 miles to the west of Staunton. Milroy with some 3,700 Union troops was at the village of McDowell. It was at this small community on Thursday, May 8 1862 that Jackson made the first contact. Though taken by surprise, Milroy was in mountainous terrain that was suited to defense. Jackson did not choose to make a frontal attack. He began sliding around Milroy, who was forced to withdraw. At a second position Jackson found conditions favorable. He attacked, securing a significant victory. Jackson left his cavalry element to press after Milroy's retreating troops. Then he moved back to the valley, north of Staunton, to ready an attack on Banks.

Expecting a blow to fall, Banks began to withdraw. As he did, Ashby stayed close to him, constantly harassing the Union general and his men. Banks settled in at Strasburg. He prepared for a frontal attack, only to find he had a flank at Front Royal hanging in open air. Jackson planned to use this weakness to come in behind Banks and trap him.

Lee saw the opportunity for victory. He reinforced Jackson's force. Jackson soon had some 17,000 troops and 11 batteries of artillery. Ashby was given two more regiments of cavalry: the 2nd and 6th Virginia. Banks was now clearly outnumbered, with a two to one numerical advantage to the Confederates. Jackson wisely came at Banks from the latter's flank, approaching through Front Royal. Meanwhile, Ashby kept Banks blinded to the movement. Union Rangers could not get through to learn what Jackson was doing. Jackson was provided complete information on the Union force at Front Royal by Ashby and Belle Boyd, a young woman from Martinsburg in Western Virginia who was staying with a relative at Front Royal.

Jackson drove in the Union pickets at Front Royal, then fell on Colonel John Kenly and his 1st Maryland (Union). This action resulted in the 1st Maryland Regiment of the Confederates fighting the 1st Maryland Regiment of the Union. Colonel Kenly put up a spirited defense at Cedarville. Though they slowed Jackson's attack, Kenly's men were finally overwhelmed. Kenly was wounded by a saber slash. Some 700 Union soldiers were captured.

Kenly could not get word to General Banks of the attack because Ashby and his Rangers were at Buckton Station between the two Union forces.

Here Ashby had a stiff fight with Union infantry, but prevailed. He cut the telegraph line and tore up railroad tracks, preventing communications.

The reports that came to Banks seemed unreliable. He had been told that Jackson was attacking so often that now he believed this was just another raid by Ashby. Thinking defensively, Banks decided his best course of action would be to withdraw. Jackson was unsparing of himself or his men. He was a devoted student of the art of war, and as a result was doing many things right but not all. He knew the employment of artillery and infantry, but was not as sure-handed with cavalry. Seeking to cover all circumstances, Jackson made the same mistake as that made by some infantry commanders of cavalry and armor through previous years; he scattered his men about. Jackson gave George H. Steuart command of the 2nd and 6th Virginia Cavalry regiments, but made no provision to coordinate their activities with Ashby.[48] Jackson had eighteen of Ashby's twenty-six cavalry companies on detached duties with companies spread to the winds, watching passes and guarding roads, while others were used for pickets and couriers.[49] On May 24 1862, Jackson was marching fast, seeking to beat General Banks to Winchester and keep him pinned to the south. Banks was just as determined to get to Winchester and hole up. Jackson had ordered Ashby to cut the Valley Pike near Middletown, blocking Banks from marching east.

Near Middletown, Ashby, with 300 horsemen and his artillery, found a large body of Union cavalry withdrawing. Also to their front the Confederates could see an enemy wagon train guarded by Union cavalry. Now the mounted artillery again proved its worth. Though he was vastly outnumbered, Ashby charged.

As they closed to within 100 yards, the Ranger artillery halted and opened fire with cannister on the blue-coated soldiers. Like giant shotgun shells, the cannister rounds devastated the Union men, leaving a scene of horror. Several hundred survivors quickly surrendered. Ashby personally captured a number of Union soldiers. His second-in-command Major Funston attacked and captured wagons from a large supply column. It was Ashby's policy to attack the enemy at every opportunity. If the enemy broke, the pursuit was relentless. In the fight at Middletown the Union soldiers were routed and ran in all directions. Ashby's horsemen followed them in the same manner and became scattered. Jackson was critical; he accused Ashby's men of plundering the wagon train and not keeping together. However, trying to control horsemen who often operated in small groups in widespread areas was beyond Ashby's span of control.

Ashby's Mountain Rangers had been the foundation company of the 7th Virginia Cavalry Regiment; he personally knew and trained those men. They would quickly obey him. Increasingly his command gained strength. He could lead new men in battle, but could not oversee all they did. The men were not governed by the recently-passed Partisan Ranger Act of the Confederacy; they were expected to turn over what they captured to the government, but the men did not accept that ruling. Trapped in an inefficient supply system, they took what they needed. Jackson's infantry who followed on participated in the looting, but when looking for a scapegoat, Jackson found Ashby convenient. His men had let him down. Jackson reprimanded Ashby, who was greatly shamed. Always at the point of danger, Turner Ashby tried to supervise by pushing himself even harder, taking greater personal risks. He was in the saddle eighteen hours a day.

Now it was Jackson who experienced uncertainty. Would Banks continue north-east or go east? Several hours were spent in learning the truth, but they were critical hours as Banks cleared his supply column through Middletown. He continued heading toward Winchester. Banks made a few attempts to stem the rout of his troops. Reaching Winchester on the night of May 24, he thought himself safe. Jackson's troops had set a killing pace in pursuit. They were exhausted. Jackson, having overcome his religious strictures, intended to attack on Sunday, May 25. When a Confederate colonel told Jackson his men were 'falling by the road-side from fatigue and loss of sleep', Jackson said 'I am obliged to sweat them to-night that I may save their blood tomorrow.'[50] Banks learned that Jackson was hot on his trail. Banks was now heavily outnumbered. He determined to hold Winchester as long as he could and began driving his weary troops to prepare defensive positions.

As Jackson prepared to attack, Ashby was sent to block a retreat by Banks on the Berryville Road. Jackson had two regiments of cavalry, the 2nd and 6th Virginia, left with General Ewell to participate in Jackson's attack. These were under the command of West Point-trained Brigadier General George Steuart. Banks made his stand, but he was now weakened. By mid-morning on the 24th, the Union troops were again in retreat and Winchester was in the hands of the Confederates. Jackson might have bagged Banks and all that was left of his army, but having scattered his cavalry, he could not mount an effective pursuit. He sent an aide to order Steuart to lead the two cavalry regiments that were with Ewell in pursuit of Banks. However, George Steuart was the occasional West Pointer who is more concerned with form than substance. He refused the order as it did not come through his immediate senior, General Ewell. Hours passed before this inane reasoning could be overcome.

As darkness fell on May 25 1862, Ashby with Chew's battery, sought to continue the attack. They rode to Dranesville, 15 miles north of Winchester, then on the 26th, Ashby continued north to Martinsburg. He found that Banks' men had kept going north. The Union soldiers had left vast quantities of supplies behind them. The opportunity for plunder and an excellent rearguard action by the Union, combined with the scattering of Confederate cavalry, allowed Banks to safely cross the Potomac into Maryland.

Jackson had allowed no time for training of the cavalry recruits, had scattered Ashby's companies about and his own infantry had been involved in the looting. Steuart had ignored Jackson's orders to attack with the 2nd and 6th Virginia Cavalry. Despite all this, Jackson faulted Ashby for not having the cavalry together to pursue Banks.

A friend to both men, the politically powerful Colonel Alexander Boteler frequently pressed Jackson for Ashby's advancement. Though lukewarm to the idea, Jackson finally consented. On May 27, Ashby rode back to Winchester where he was promoted to brigadier general. Jackson did not personally present the promotion. Alexander Pendleton, a member of Jackson's staff, handed Ashby the promotion order and said: 'I do this with great pleasure, General Ashby, hoping that as you are soon to command a brigade, the country may expect less exposure of your life.' Obviously hurt by the rude treatment of Jackson, Ashby did not speak; he smiled and soon rode away.[51]

On May 28, Jackson's old brigade, now under the command of Brigadier General Charles Winder, had reached Bolivar Heights above the Union garrison at Harpers Ferry. Jackson intended to carry the war to the North, passing over the Potomac River and into Maryland. Ashby and Jackson had combined to forestall Union desires to seize Richmond, but a hornets' nest in blue had been disturbed. As Banks' soldiers recovered behind the Maryland line, President Lincoln called for an expansion of the army and ordered soldiers away from Richmond. General McDowell and his 40,000-man 1st Corps were sent through the Manassas Gap into the Shenandoah Valley to confront Jackson, General Fremont was ordered to come east from West Virginia, and Generals Banks and Sigel were ordered to attack.

The master plan of Robert E. Lee had worked. United States Secretary of War Edwin Stanton fell for Lee's trap and convinced Lincoln to send men after Jackson. The pulling away of McDowell's corps was sufficient to cause George McClellan to decide he could not take Richmond. The fall of the

Confederate and Virginia capitol would have gravely wounded the South. That it was forestalled likely prolonged the war for many months.

Three Union armies totaling some 65,000 men were converging on Strasburg with the intention to trap Jackson who had about 16,000 troops. Part of the Union force sent west was the newly organized 'Flying Brigade'. On May 27 1862, General McDowell's chief of staff issued the following order:

> Headquarters, May 27th, 1862
> General McCall,
> Falmouth.
>
> General McDowell wishes you to order to Catlett's, Bayard's Brigade as now constituted, viz, two regiments of cavalry, Kane's battalion of rifles, and the battery of mountain howitzers.
>
> Ed Schriver
> Chief of Staff.[52]

Now part of the capable Brigadier General George Dashiell Bayard's command (he would die of wounds in the Battle of Fredericksburg), the four companies of the Pennsylvania Bucktails boarded the cars at Catlett's Station and rode the rails westward with the 1st Pennsylvania and the 1st New Jersey Cavalry. They were part of Shields' division which was now coming back from Fredericksburg as the lead of McDowell's corps. Meanwhile, Banks was reinforced and prepared to move up the valley and Fremont was beginning to move from the west.

By the end of May, the knowledge that Union armies were on the march toward his rear forced Jackson to withdraw. He marched his army back to Winchester, his withdrawal covered by Ashby, whose skill again gave Jackson freedom of maneuver. Captain (later Colonel) Roger Chew would write of Ashby:

> When it was necessary to delay the enemy, who were pressing after Jackson in his retreat from Winchester...he [Ashby] displayed great skill and stubbornness in fighting from every hilltop. He would form a skirmish line and open on them with artillery, compel them to halt and form line of battle, and when their superior forces drew dangerously near to his men he would skillfully withdraw and form on the next hill.[53]

On the way south, Jackson learned that elements of Shields' division had already reached Front Royal. The Union forces were driving north-east to Winchester, pushing the 12th Georgia Regiment before them. Jackson was not pleased with the performance of this regiment. He had left it to watch the gaps of the Blue Ridge Mountains. Believing the 12th Georgia had failed, Jackson relieved the colonel commanding. Shields was now only 12 miles from the Union meeting-point of Strasburg. At Winchester, Jackson was 19 miles distant. Jackson also received a report that Fremont was approaching from the west. Union General Shields was dilatory; he delayed marching on Strasburg. On Saturday, May 31 1862, Jackson started a forced march to reach Strasburg before the Union armies. When asked what he would do if his line of retreat was severed, Jackson replied: 'I will fall back on Maryland for reinforcements.'[54] It was not an idle boast. Jackson believed that if forced to go north, he could clear Nathaniel Banks from his path. He believed that once over the Potomac, his threat against Washington would ensure him being sent reinforcements by Lee, enhance Southern recruiting and totally disrupt the Union effort against Richmond.

There proved to be no need for Jackson to go north. By rapid movement he could keep the armies in blue from cutting him off from the south. After a grueling march, Jackson won the race, beating Fremont to Strasburg by only a few miles. Though the Union forces were still separated, the forces of Shields and Fremont were within striking range. The opportunity existed for Shields to impede Jackson's path. Jackson was not disturbed by the close proximity of Shields and Fremont as Ashby and friendly civilians kept him well informed of the location of Union troops. He knew they had not joined forces. This information allowed him to pass his army between those of Shields and Fremont and march southward out of the trap. Shields moved back to Front Royal. The Union forces remained separate, open to attack and defeat in detail.

By the night of May 31 1862, Jackson had his prisoners, his captured matériel and all of his army gathered at Strasburg with the exception of General Winder and the Stonewall Brigade. They had the longest distance to travel and marched 28 miles on May 31.[55] Jackson now had the advantage of drawing the pursuing Union armies after him. This stretched out their supply lines and made these more vulnerable to Ranger organizations that were springing up since the passage of the April 1862 Partisan Ranger Act by the Confederate Congress.

To the east, Lee was watching McClellan. He saw a hesitant commander, one whose ranks were being hard hit by the swamp fever of the peninsula.[56]

In the Shenandoah Valley, Jackson was aided by the information on the enemy that Ashby presented to him. He equally benefited from the information Ashby denied the enemy. Northern scouts could not penetrate Ashby's screen. Unless Jackson was attacking them, they were never able to get a fix on Jackson's location or the number of troops he had. As a result, Union commanders safe-sided, crediting Jackson with far more men than he actually possessed.

As Jackson passed through the gap between Union forces, he took the 2nd and 6th Virginia Cavalry from the 'correct procedure-bound' Steuart (not J.E.B. Stuart), and put them under Ashby's command. Ashby held Fremont in position as he had previously done with Banks. For seventy-two hours he was in the saddle, using up one horse after another. On June 4, Ashby, at great personal risk, burned a bridge over the Shenandoah River. His beautiful white horse was mortally wounded under him in this action, but carried him to safety. To Ashby the death was that of a friend. He sat grieving beside this friend until the horse breathed his last. Men wondered how Ashby could survive. This general acted more like a point man. He was always out front, pressing the odds. He wrote to his friend Colonel Boteler of participating in more than 100 engagements and fights within less than 90 days.[57]

Captain Chew said of Ashby:

> Upon several occasions I suggested to him that we were lavish in the expenditure of our ammunition, but he said he believed in firing at the enemy whenever they showed their heads. He was reckless in the exposure of his person, and when he was cautioned about this replied that an officer should always go to the front and take risks in order to keep his men up to the mark.[58]

Brigadier General George D. Bayard's 'Flying Brigade' had been sent on in advance of McDowell's movement and linked up with Fremont's troops near Strasburg. Jackson's trains were too heavily guarded by positioned artillery to attack, so Bayard concentrated on protecting the Strasburg Railroad bridge for the future use of the Union forces.

As Jackson withdrew, Ashby again was his shield. Fighting the rearguard action put him in frequent view of Union officers. The Confederate Ranger was well known to, and admired by, his opponents. Colonel R.B. Macy, chief of staff of cavalry for General Fremont, would later write:

> I have been in advance with my regiment most of the time from Strasburg and the horse of General Ashby is a familiar object to us all, as he daily superintends the movements of Jackson's rear guard. As we see him on the outposts he affords an excellent mark for our flying artillery, as he is descried upon the hill in advance of us, seemingly never out of sight or absent from his post of duty. He is always the last man to move on, after satisfying himself as to the movement of our forces. Many and many a time on this advance I have seen the rifled piece brought to bear upon him, and the solid shot go shrieking after him, striking within a few feet of him, throwing up clouds of dust over him or else go singing over his head, dealing destruction to his men behind him.[59]

With Ashby as his primary rearguard, Jackson was fighting a delaying action and despite heavy rains was burning his bridges behind him. Bayard's brigade was committed to the pursuit. It was fighting in a wet hell; the ground was often so covered with rain that exhausted men and horses all stood in water ankle-deep. The soldiers were chilled and shivering, unable to light fires due to the closeness of the enemy. Some 5 miles below Strasburg the Confederates destroyed the Stony Creek bridge. It was a hard passage, but Bayard's 'Flying Brigade' found a ford the Union troops could use. Their advance continued. They put out fires, saving the mill bridge at Cedar Creek near Mount Jackson.

Soon Confederates destroyed the critical bridge over the north fork of the Shenandoah. Pontoons were rushed forward for Union engineers to throw a bridge of boats across the river. High water interfered and fresh floods came down, bringing logs and debris that tore the pontoons loose. As the bridge was replaced, Jackson gained eighteen hours on his pursuers. By 10.00 am on Thursday, June 5 1862, the bridge was functioning. Bayard resumed pursuit. The Pennsylvania Bucktails marched 18 miles before nightfall. The next morning their march resumed. By 2 o'clock on the 6th contact was regained, then lost at the outskirts of Harrisonburg. The Bucktails paused. About 3.00 pm the 1st New Jersey Cavalry, consisting of some 400 men reinforced with horsemen of the New York Mounted Rifles, trotted out on the Port Republic road. They pressed on south to determine the route Jackson had taken.

The 1st New Jersey Cavalry was commanded by a British soldier of fortune named Percy Wyndham. He had volunteered his services to the Union. It was said that Wyndham had been a colonel in the Sardinian army, had served under Garibaldi and was a Chevalier of the Military Order of Savoy.[60] Wyndham liked people to use 'Sir' Percy Wyndham when addressing him. This desire likely came from an ego as big as his gigantic mustache rather than an order by Queen Victoria. Wyndham had been appointed colonel by the governor of New Jersey. At the time Wyndham was appointed to command the 1st New Jersey Cavalry, the unit was in disarray with an inept commander and its only efficient officers under arrest. Wyndham trained his men well. They thought highly of him.[61]

Wyndham was given to bragging that he would 'bag Ashby'. He was about to have his chance. Wyndham's men rode in a column of fours with sabers drawn. The road was narrow and fenced on each side. A hollow gave way to a wooded hill, and beneath those trees a small group of Confederate horsemen could be seen. Wyndham ordered his men to form platoons. Though the horses were tired, he commanded: 'Gallop! Charge!' Attacking in three columns, the Union horsemen found their way blocked by fences that had to be dismantled. Wyndham's command became scattered. Only one column could see Confederates. Riding to the attack, these men were ambushed by a dismounted force of Southerners hidden in the woods. The New Jersey horsemen sheathed their sabers and tried to fight it out with revolvers.

So scattered was the 1st New Jersey Cavalry that Wyndham, who had entered the woods, could not be seen. His lieutenant colonel had been thrown from his horse, while the major of the regiment was occupied trying to escape Ashby's ambush. The regimental color-bearer had been thrown; the colors were lost. All was confusion. Ashby's Rangers were pouring fire into the milling mass of men.

Henry Pyne of the 1st New Jersey Cavalry would write:

> If a cavalry charge is glorious, a cavalry rout is dreadful. Pressing upon one another, strained to the utmost of their speed, the horses catch an infection of fear which rouses them to frenzy. The men, losing their places in the ranks, and all power of formation or hope of combined resistance, rush madly for some point of safety upon which it may be possible to rally. Each check in front makes the mass behind more dense and desperate, until horses and men are overthrown and

ridden over, trampled on by others as helpless as themselves to rescue or to spare. The speed grows momentarily greater. Splashing through the pools of mire, breaking down fences, darting under trees with the clang of sabers and din of hoofs, officers wild with shame and rage, shouting themselves hoarse with unavailing curses, and the bullets of the enemy whistling shrilly overhead, the mingled mass sweeps on, until utter exhaustion stops them, or their commanders, struggling to the front, can indicate a place to form. Thus the First New Jersey galloped from the field of their defeat, leaving their Colonel, three Captains, one-twelfth of their troopers, and the regimental colors in the hands of the enemy.[62]

Several hours after the capture of Wyndham, Ashby identified other blue uniforms moving toward him. General Fremont was under pressure from Brigadier General Bayard of the Flying Brigade and Lieutenant Colonel Thomas Kane of the Bucktails to allow them to go and rescue the captives and wounded of the 1st New Jerseys. Fremont did not want a major fight with the Confederates on this terrain. He agreed to what essentially was a combat patrol, but ordered Bayard not to bring on a general engagement. Bayard hurried on with a detachment comprising men of the Bucktails and the 1st Pennsylvania Cavalry. Ashby could not identify the troops coming his direction. As it might be the lead of the Union army, he requested infantry support from General Ewell. The 44th and 58th Virginia and the 1st Maryland Regiment which was commanded by Colonel Bradley T. Johnson responded.

Facing woods where the Confederate line was believed to be, Colonel Kane requested permission to lead his Bucktails forward. Knowing he had been ordered not to draw Fremont's army into a fight, Bayard gave Kane forty minutes to make a reconnaissance of the woods. If he encountered opposition, he was not to attack but to hold his position.

In the afternoon of Friday, June 6 1862, Kane led 104 men of the Bucktails into the woods. Bayard rode to high ground where he saw Confederate infantry coming up to the woods. Bayard tried, but could not get a message to Kane in time to call him off.

In the woods, the Bucktails encountered the lead of the 58th Virginians and delivered a hail of fire that drove the Confederates back. The success only served to pit them against a consolidated Confederate infantry. These men in butternut or gray were on the crest of a hill with a clearing in the woods before them. Backing up against increasing opposition, Kane paused at the clearing and the firing ceased. It was difficult to tell where the Confederate line was and how long it stretched. In an incredible display of self-sacrifice, Private Martin Kelly of Company G came to Kane and said 'Colonel, shall I draw their fire?' Kane acquiesced. Kelly stepped from behind the shelter of a tree and into the open field. Instinctively practically every Confederate infantryman who could see him opened fire. Kelly was ripped by leaden balls and instantly killed.[63]

The powder smoke from the gunshots outlined the Confederate position. Kane, who was hit in the leg during the Confederate fusillade, saw that the Bucktails were being flanked on the left. He ordered part of his force to attack that position. Now the Confederates on the same flank charged. The gunfire swelled to a roar. The Pennsylvanians could see several courageous Confederate officers mounted on horseback. Kane recognized the famed black beard of an officer and knew it was Turner Ashby. Such targets were a prime mission of the Bucktails. Kane saw the gun barrels of his men swinging toward the Confederate leader. Ashby's horse was shot from under him, but he jumped to his feet and came on. Kane's admiration for Ashby's courage was so great that he struck upwards two rifle barrels and called off another marksman who he could see was taking aim at the Confederate leader.

A horizontal rain of lead was ripping into the men of North and South. The 58th Virginians and the Bucktails clashed in a frenzy of fire and both were suffering greatly. There seemed to be a pause in the Confederate advance. Then Bradley Johnson's 1st Maryland (Confederate) came up beside the 58th Virginians and engaged the Bucktails. On foot, his long black beard clearly distinguishing him, Ashby sprang to the front, calling out to his men. Colonel Kane of the Bucktails was shot in the chest and went down. Ashby shouted: 'Forward, my brave men. Charge, for God's sake charge!' A Bucktail marksman took a steady aim. He caressed the trigger of his weapon and killed Turner Ashby.

Momentarily stunned at the loss of a Confederate icon, a roar of anger rose from the 58th Virginians and the 1st Marylands. Leaping to their feet, they bounded forward. The Bucktails were in desperate straits, their commander out of action and down to some sixty effectives. Captain Blanchard was shot through both legs. Captain Gifford was severely wounded, as was Lieutenant Swayne.[64]

Darkness was setting in as Lieutenant Wolfe approached the wounded Kane and said 'Colonel, shall I send two men to carry you back, we can't stay here any longer; if we don't get out right speedily we will all be captured.' Caught up in battle fervor, Kane responded: 'You are doing nobly

Lieutenant, give them hell.'[65] Just then, hell came from the other direction in the form of Bradley Johnson's 1st Marylands. Colonel Thomas Mumford of Ashby's command brought up two guns of Chew's battery and opened fire with cannister on the Bucktails' position.[66] Kane ordered the withdrawal. Under the darkening sky, Captain Charles F. Taylor (later colonel) of Company H gathered fifty-two of the Bucktails, broke contact and led them from the woods. Taylor then went back for Kane, not knowing if his colonel was dead or alive but determined to bring him back. When Taylor got to Kane's location he found the wounded officer a prisoner of the Confederates. Brave men have a unique bond in combat. Taken by Taylor's courage, the Confederates offered an immediate parole to Taylor. The Bucktail captain intended to be back in the war as soon as possible. He felt he could escape sooner than be exchanged. Taylor refused parole, as did Colonel Kane.

Men at war are often surprised at the amount of fury that can be compacted into a brief period of time. The fight lasted approximately thirty minutes. The Bucktails suffered 7 killed, 39 wounded and 5 missing (captured); a 50 per cent casualty rate. The Confederates held the field. The 1st Marylands attached a buck tail to their colors which they carried in remembrance of their victory.

Bradley T. Johnson of the 1st Marylands became a general. After the war he corresponded with his former foes. In 1898 he wrote the following to T.H. Ryan of the Bucktails:

> After 36 years I learn for the first time that you had only part of four companies – 104 men. I had 275 men present in ranks in the First Maryland and the Fifty-Eighth Virginia must have had 200 or more. So you fought five to one. Our loss was 17 killed, 50 wounded and 3 missing (70) in all. A game fight for you, and I heartily congratulate you on it. ...You put three balls into my horse and would have killed me, dead sure, if, when the second ball struck him he had not thrown up his head and caught the bullet intended for me.[67]

The death of Turner Ashby was like the death of a warrior prince. His friend and biographer Avirett wrote:

> To describe the lamentation of the troops when they heard the good and chivalrous Ashby had fallen would be impossible. Bronzed and scarred veterans, who perhaps for years had not

known what it was to shed a tear, wept like children; for truly, the decline of that bright June sun had ushered into eternity one of the best and noblest of them.[68]

Ashby's body was brought back from the site of his death on horseback. There are several versions of how this occurred. The most romantic is that four of his horsemen brought him back from the battlefield, riding stirrup to stirrup with his body across the front of their saddles. The body was taken to the small village of Port Republic where it lay in state wrapped in the flag of the Confederacy. A guard of honor stood silent watch. Throughout the night the soldiers who loved him came to pay their respects to their gallant leader.

The emotion of the men in the ranks was exemplified by Private Richard Black, a member of Company B from Romney (WVA), described by Avirett as '...perhaps the boldest and best scout in the army.' For long minutes Black stood before the body, his thoughts wrapped in silent grief, then the Ranger said: 'We shall miss you mightily, General – we shall miss you in the camp! – we shall miss you as we go out on the scout! But we shall miss you the most, General, when we go out to...' Unable to complete his words, Black broke down sobbing and hurried away.

The high regard in which Turner Ashby was held extended to the camp of his enemy. There would be some who would claim they fired the fatal shot or that Ashby was killed when he got in the line of fire from his own men. The Bucktails felt they knew which of their marksmen had killed Ashby. The man sought no glory from it and would not speak of the incident. A Union officer of General Fremont's command described Ashby as '...the brilliant leader of the enemy's cavalry, a man worth to them regiments, "a blast on whose bugle-horn was worth a thousand men." When we found the brave Ashby was slain, there was no rejoicing in our camps.'[69]

Ashby was devoted to Stonewall Jackson. When others including General Ewell thought Jackson was 'an old fool' and 'a crazy wagon hunter',[70] Ashby would not speak ill of his commander. In military matters, the devout Christian Jackson felt Ashby had insufficient control of the cavalry and Jackson was without forgiveness. Colonel Thomas Mumford wrote of Ashby's circumstance:

The companies composing his command were generally recruited from the border counties all along the northern and western lines. They had never been in a camp of instruction. Many of them could not perform the simplest evolutions in company drill. Provided with just such arms as they could pick up, with no organization, it was simply impossible for him to do anything with them but to *lead them.*

When informed of the loss of Ashby, Jackson had been interviewing the captured Colonel Wyndham. He immediately left the room. Ashby's descendant and biographer Thomas Ashby wrote that Jackson went to Ashby's quarters and shut himself up, presumably to mourn in prayer.[71] Jackson then went to view the body at Port Republic. In respect of the special relationship, the men left Jackson alone with Ashby's body till he had finished his grieving. Then Jackson turned back to the war.

The army rested on Saturday, June 7. The death of Ashby brought their own mortality before every man. An air of gloom had settled over the Confederate camp. Jackson recognized this and rode among the men praising Ashby and encouraging the men to continue his fight.

Successful military commanders are often admired, praised and respected by their men. Many are also disliked, even hated. Being a 'nice guy' is no substitute for victory. Few commanders can achieve both success in battle and the total love of the men they lead. Turner Ashby was an inspiration to his men; a seemingly mystical figure who rode into their hearts as a warrior prince engaged in a crusade. His great gunner Colonel Roger Preston Chew who was only 22 years old at the end of the war wrote that Ashby 'was the kind of man around whose character there was a halo of romance.'[72]

Few men experience combat without coming in contact with their God, but men worship in different ways. Jackson's was a visible and vocal faith. Ashby was not given to open prayer. Whatever Turner Ashby's line was to God, it was direct and private. In his faith, as in his leadership, example was his byword.

Jackson mourned Ashby as Lee would later mourn Jackson. Turner Ashby was the first of the great Confederate Rangers and none was more loved by their men than he. General Clement Evans who edited the *Confederate Military History* reported that Jackson wrote of Ashby: 'As a partisan officer, I never knew his superior. His daring was proverbial, his powers of endurance almost incredible, his tone of character heroic and his sagacity almost intuitive in divining the purposes and movements of the enemy.'[73]

Jackson now faced the two oncoming columns of Union troops under Fremont and Shields. On June 8 Jackson, though outnumbered, withstood Fremont's attack on the west side of the south fork of the Shenandoah at

Cross Keys. On Monday, June 9 1862, Jackson beat Shields at Port Republic. These blows ended the Union pursuit of Jackson. In some 48 days of marching, Jackson's army had moved nearly 700 miles and fought 5 battles. Except for his employment of cavalry, Jackson's aggressive tactics were superb; he prevented the attack on Richmond that would likely have been disastrous for the South.

Jackson's Valley campaign brought him just fame. There is an army tradition that a commander is responsible for all his unit does or fails to do. Certainly the responsibility for success is widely accepted. Failure frequently finds a subordinate scapegoat. Jackson deserved his honors for the Valley campaign. It should be remembered that his subordinate, Ranger Turner Ashby, contributed greatly to them. Some of the praise that Jackson so justly deserves is due to the fact that Jackson's enemy did not know where he was or what he was doing until they were suddenly attacked. This was due to the dedication of Turner Ashby who was more than Jackson's eyes and ears. Ashby was Jackson's blindfold, tied over the eyes of his opponent.

Turner Ashby was originally buried at the University of Virginia at Charlottesville. In 1866, the women of Winchester and the valley established the 'Stonewall' (the formal name is Mount Hebron) Cemetery at Winchester as a final resting place of the scattered Confederate dead. At that time the remains of Turner Ashby and his brother Richard Ashby were brought to the Winchester Mount Hebron Cemetery. They were buried with ceremony near the grave site that holds some 815 Confederate dead.

Chapter 8

Harry Gilmor

Maryland's contribution to the corps of Confederate Rangers included a young horseman from near Baltimore named Harry Gilmor. Born on January 24 1838, he was the son of a family whose sire came from Scotland, putting down American roots in 1767. The Gilmors built a successful shipping business and owned farms.[1]

Growing up with money, Harry Gilmor became a *beau sabreur*, a dashing, handsome young buck, arrogant, with a pronounced affinity and charm for the opposite sex. Gilmor was well-educated. His family was slave-owning and secessionists in their politics. He traveled to Wisconsin and Nebraska, spending some time in farming. As talk of war began, he returned to Maryland to prepare. Following the custom of his class, he became a member of the militia, serving as a corporal in a cavalry unit known as the Baltimore Horse Guards. Prior to the outbreak of war, Harry Gilmor was inclined to voice his opinions without regard to consequence. In May 1861, Union troops under Brigadier General Benjamin F. Butler occupied Baltimore. Butler had a way of dealing with dissent. In August 1861, Federal police ushered Harry Gilmor behind the walls of Fort McHenry for a two-week cooling off period of his rhetoric. After release, Gilmor made his way over the Potomac River to Charleston. He joined Turner Ashby, enlisting on Saturday, August 31 1861, in Company G, the Maryland Company, of the 7th Virginia Regiment. In time two brothers – Richard and Meredith Gilmor – and two cousins – Hoffman and William Gilmor – would also take up arms for the Confederacy. Gilmor was impressed with Turner Ashby. Admiring Ashby's leadership style, Gilmor said to himself: 'If I follow you, I go far enough.'[2]

The trouble with Harry was that he was a braggart, economical with the truth, a walking showboat. He was also bright, quick-witted, courageous, and a good shot. Ashby accepted him into his ranks. Gilmor was put on patrol with a Maryland-born man destined to carve his name in history as leader of the Ranger unit known as the 'Comanches'. Elijah V. White had settled near Leesburg, Virginia. Though only a private, Elijah White was leading patrols.

Gilmor began his war as a private and scout. Ashby's Rangers were guarding the south bank of the Potomac River. Contact was frequent as soldiers of the North and South crossed the river at its many fordable points on missions of reconnaissance or raid. There were short sharp skirmishes that were a good introduction to the advantages of firepower and mobility. Gilmor's first fight was in the town of Harpers Ferry. He did well. When volunteers were called for, Harry Gilmor was prompt to step forward. The Chesapeake and Ohio Canal adjoined the Potomac in Gilmor's area. Its barge traffic was critical to the Union. Gilmor became adept at sniping at barge crews. Harry's marksmanship brought high praise. Riding at a gallop, he could put a pistol ball into telegraph poles as he passed. He also shot a tin cup off his buddy Tom Gatch's head,[3] thus proving that Gilmor was a crack shot and Gatch was in need of psychiatric help.

In September 1861, Gilmor was leading a squad of eight men when he captured four soldiers of a Union patrol that had crossed the Potomac. In a fight at Harpers Ferry, Gilmor was beside a loaded cannon when Union forces charged up a street. Ashby gave orders to withdraw the gun. Gilmor wanted to fire one more shot, but the linstock was extinguished. He ran to a nearby fire, picked up a live coal in his hands and ran back to the gun. Despite being burned, Gilmor shoved the glowing coal in the touch hole. The gun recoil knocked him flat, but the shot killed or wounded eleven Union soldiers and gave time to draw off the gun.[4]

Raid and counter-raid occupied the month of November 1861. The Union forces were advancing slowly. In December, major activity quieted as opposing armies went into winter quarters. Patrolling continued along the Potomac. Gilmor became sergeant major of the 7th Virginia Cavalry Regiment.

Harry Gilmor had a lust for life and a love of pranks. When he learned that Regimental Chaplain Mr Averitt had a bottle of whiskey, Gilmor professed alarm that men of God should be drinking alcohol. He stole the parson's whiskey and shared it with his friends. The chaplain was not amused.[5]

The winter cold, snow and ice increased the difficulty of patrolling. On missions, the men cut pine boughs that they used to sweep away the snow and as a mattress beneath them while they took what sleep they could. Ashby frequently used Gilmor as his messenger to General Jackson. The rides were harrowing and often made under fire. Success required expert horsemanship and the best of horses; Gilmor had both. General Jackson wanted telegraph wires cut above and below the town of Hancock and the water tank burned to trap a Union garrison. It was a dangerous mission. Ashby told Jackson he thought Gilmor could do it. Harry was sent off with a guide. He spent a night climbing telegraph poles while Union pickets tried to shoot him with their rifles. He succeeded in cutting the lines, but could not burn the water tank as it was made of stone. Jackson was laying down when Gilmor reported in after his harrowing mission. All that Jackson said was 'Good' and 'Good night'.[6]

The next day Gilmor was out again leading a two-squad patrol on a raid to the Alpine Depot on the B&O Railroad. They found a huge quantity of Union supplies beside the tracks; supplies that were unguarded. Sugar, coffee, whiskey, rifles and clothing were stacked in a quantity Gilmor valued at half a million dollars. The men took all they could carry and Gilmor brought Captain Clark's entire Maryland company back to carry off all they could. They made another trip so they could cache supplies for the future. On Ashby's orders, they burned the rest.

Gilmor's career was interrupted when two of Ashby's men got into a fight, intending to kill each other. Trying to separate the men, Gilmor was shot in the hip. He would be out of action until March of 1862. As he healed, Gilmor, with Ashby's support, began recruiting men to serve in his mounted infantry company. The men served as Rangers, but like most other Ranger units had a formal alphabetical and numerical designation. Gilmor's unit would be Company F of the 12th Virginia Cavalry. It was natural that most of the men Gilmor recruited would be from his home state of Maryland. There were many who hoped the daring deeds of Harry Gilmor would inspire the state of Maryland to heed the words of the secessionist song *Maryland, My Maryland*, leave the Union and come to the aid of the Confederacy.

Harry Gilmor would be wounded four times during the Civil War. He had a remarkable ability to find women to look after him before, during and after recuperation. Histories published after the Civil War made it appear that sexual activity paused during the conflict. On the contrary, sex was as always practiced with alacrity. 'Horizontal refreshment', as fornication was called, was the eagerly sought alternate form of campaign for those in situations where gunfire was frequent. On several occasions Gilmor came close to capture or death because his lust and bravado made a dangerous combination. To properly impress the female of the species, Gilmor and his brother would take their time about leaving their women when Union troops came to call. The Gilmors would bid adieu to the girls while pausing to squeeze off a round or two at the advancing blue coats. Gallantry required that they make their escape in a last-minute ride-for-life. Family wealth had provided Harry with horses that were among the best in Maryland. He could outrun Union cavalry, clearing fences and walls that stymied his opponents. The dashing Harry Gilmor had the hearts of Confederate belles aflutter.

As March 1862, closed, Gilmor had completed his combination of recovery from wounds, love-making and recruiting. He was elected captain of his company. Gilmor was next ordered to Harrisonburg where Lieutenant Colonel J.R. Jones was provost marshal. Jones had a problem and turned to Harry for a solution. There were men who supported the Union; others who did not want to be drafted into the Southern army. Several hundred of these were hiding in the gorges of the Blue Ridge Mountains in the vicinity of Swift Run Gap. It was beyond the capability of Gilmor's small force to round up these people, but with some companies of sharpshooters and artillery supplied by Jackson he brought them to bay. Gilmor took forty-eight prisoners, dispersing the rest of the sulkers and Unionists.[7]

Near Lacey Spring, Gilmor with a few of his men were leading the way for some 240 men of Ashby's cavalry under Captain Samuel Myers. Suddenly they were charged by a large force of Union cavalry. The Confederates launched a counter-charge, resulting in an earth-shaking collision as horses piled into each other and a close-quarter fight began. Gilmor was fired at by a Union officer; Gilmor repeatedly returned fire. Much to his surprise, the bullets had no effect. Both officers emptied their revolvers and engaged with the saber. Men of Harry Gilmor's class were often trained in foil fencing as the foundation of fighting with the blade. Such men did not waste time or energy in wild, swinging slashes as though the saber were a club. Gilmor knew how to guard himself properly, to control his parries and to use small feints and cuts that had a downward action, slicing like the blade of a razor.

The Union officer he was opposed to was trained in the use of the blade, but not as skilled as Gilmor. After his attack was parried, Gilmor executed a movement called a *moulinet*, which sent the saber spinning from his opponent's hand. As Harry raised his saber to cut the man down, the officer, a man named Hasbrouck, surrendered. Gilmor was surprised to learn that Hasbrouck was wearing body armor, a steel breastplate that Gilmor's shots would not penetrate. Hasbrouck was hurried to the rear. He would be the only prisoner taken. Union horsemen charged again, putting the Confederates to flight. Seven of Gilmor's men were lost.[8]

In May of 1862, it was reported that Stonewall Jackson was in retreat with Turner Ashby's Rangers, including Harry Gilmor serving as the covering force. The wily Jackson had stolen a march on his opponents; he was not retreating but attacking in another direction. Collecting all the railroad cars and engines he could find, he moved his troops westward by rail to Staunton. The Confederates fought a successful battle at McDowell and Jackson pressed his advantage. He marched his troops at great speed, covering as much as 30 miles a day, the men earning the title of 'foot cavalry'.

In the pursuit of the Union troops, Harry Gilmor earned praise when he led his men in a charge into a narrow gap in the mountains, capturing a position others had failed to take. With Ashby's troops watching and cheering, Gilmor cleared the way for Jackson to continue. Gilmor then began alternating duty, leading the advance guard of the army and serving as Jackson's courier. While Gilmor and Jackson were riding together, Union artillery felled a large tree that landed at Jackson's side. Gilmor was astounded that Jackson paid no heed to the incident, and said of Jackson: 'Fear had no lodgement in that man's breast.'[9]

Sent as escort officer to take captives to the prisons of Richmond, on return Gilmor met with Jackson. The Confederate general had just beaten Union Generals Fremont and Shields at Cross Keys and Port Republic. Turner Ashby had been killed. Gilmor was put under the command of Brigadier General Beverly H. Robertson whose instructions were 'Captain, I leave it all in your hands, to act as you think best. Keep me well advised of the enemy's movements and keep them well stirred up.' Gilmor thought that was 'a very acceptable commission for a Partisan Ranger.'[10]

Four companies were added to Gilmor's command, giving him control of a total of six. In the next action Gilmor's troops were surprised by the 1st Vermont and the 6th Ohio Cavalry. In a running battle, Gilmor and another Ranger killed a Union captain while the Confederates broke free. The base of the Union cavalry was in Big Spring, 2.5 miles from Luray, but several squadrons of blue-coated horsemen were kept in advance, patrolling on the riverside near Luray. Two or three times a day, Gilmor's men skirmished with these troopers. During these brushes with the enemy Gilmor's skill with pistol and saber stood him in good stead. As with most Partisan Rangers, Gilmor was more comfortable when performing independent action. On several occasions he received peremptory orders from General Robertson to report without delay. These orders seemed to indicate a desire to bring Gilmor to heel. When Robertson moved to Orange Court House to oppose John Pope's advance, Robertson left Colonel Ayrshire Harmon in command of Gilmor. Harmon and Gilmor were close friends.

Harmon sent Gilmor to Winchester under a flag of truce to release some Union doctors that had been captured at Winchester. With obvious glee, Gilmor reported 'hundreds of ladies came over to see us'.[11]

In August of 1862, Union Corps commander Nathaniel Banks attacked Jackson at Cedar Mountain (Confederates called it 'Slaughter Mountain'.) As the Confederates withdrew, Gilmor was assigned rearguard duty. A lieutenant named Featherstone was killed at Gilmor's side when a shell took off most of his head. The shell then passed through one horse into another where it exploded, blowing the second animal to bits. Four men were killed, three of them being decapitated by the same shell. Confederate General A.P. Hill came to Jackson's assistance. In fierce, close-in fighting that often featured the bayonet, Banks' troops were driven back. After the battle, Gilmor began to suffer from a high fever. He was out of action until the end of the month when he participated in the Second Battle of Manassas (or Bull Run). There, Lee ended Pope's hope of fulfilling the Union battle cry of 'On to Richmond!'

At Fairfax Court House, Gilmor led his men in an attack that drove the Union cavalry he opposed back to Falls Church. As Pope retreated into the Washington forts, Lee determined to advance. He moved via Leesburg to cross the Potomac River into Maryland. This move would be the prelude to the Battle of Antietam. Passing through Leesburg, Gilmor led his men to Frederick, Maryland. Always eager to have a social life, Gilmor left his command on the night of Saturday, September 12 1862 to visit a relative, and from there he and a companion rode within 7 miles of Baltimore to make another visit. This rash action brought him into the arms of a Union ambush and he was taken prisoner. After being taunted, he was taken to the Western Police Station House where he was remanded to prison at Fort McHenry and listed on the roster as 'A Spy'. No one seriously thought Gilmor was a spy, but the written word has power. What normally would have been a quick exchange of captured officers dragged on for five months. Harry Gilmor was such a pleasant companion that he became friends with the officers of the 6th New York Heavy Artillery and the 18th Connecticut who garrisoned the fort. He was well-treated, had care packages from home, visits from family and female friends. He was even allowed to walk the ramparts.

On December 21, Gilmor was sent to Fort Monroe where he stayed living on what he described as 'sea-biscuit and bad bacon' until January 2 1863. Much to Harry's disgust, he was pulled from the exchange process just as freedom appeared a step away. Jefferson Davis had put out a proclamation that he wanted Union officers tried for inciting Negroes to revolt. That was bad news for captured Confederate officers. In retaliation, Harry Gilmor was detained and sent to prison at Fort Norfolk. Ever the *bon vivant*, Harry saw no reason why jail should deprive him of the joys of life. It was not long before he talked his jailor into allowing visits from women who Harry said brought 'luxuries of every kind'.[12]

Unable to sit out a war, Harry planned an escape but before he could flee, the exchange process began. He was well supplied, ready to go back to the war wearing new cavalry boots and a new hat. At Fort Monroe he was stripped of his luxuries by one he described as 'a miserable little assistant of the provost marshal.' From there his route of exchange took him by City Point and on to Richmond. En route he caught a cold and could not speak for several days; a disaster for a man of Harry Gilmor's loquacious charm.

When his voice returned, Gilmor went to visit Stonewall Jackson who, referring to Gilmor's capture, said: 'Want you to keep a sharp lookout hereafter.' Gilmor had dinner with Jackson and the general's staff, then requested he be returned to his command. In early March, he left Richmond and returned to the Shenandoah Valley where his former command was stationed. The men cheered his return, but Harry Gilmor was not given command. He got his sorrel horse 'Old Bill' back. To reaccustom the animal to his master, he rode the horse from Newmarket to Luray. It is important that a horse gets rest so he stopped at Luray, his remembrance being 'Here I found all my lady friends as kind and charming as ever, and three days were spent most pleasantly.' Never lacking for money, Gilmor next purchased a powerful half-mustang horse to provide him with additional mobility. The horse went where it wanted to and in several skirmishes with Union cavalry almost took Gilmor back to prison. He got rid of the animal, calling it 'the most unmanageable horse I ever saw this side of the Missouri River.'

Looking for action, Harry rode over to Culpeper and joined the merry band that was J.E.B. Stuart's staff. He felt at ease with Major John Pelham and the rest of this jovial crowd and partied with men, few of whom would live to see the end of the war. Tuesday, March 17 1863 came up bright and clear; it was St Patrick's Day. Major Puller, a staff officer, hurried into the room and told Harry that Union cavalry had crossed the Rappahannock River at Kelly's Ford and Stuart and his men would ride to meet them. Gilmor ran to the stable to have his horse saddled, then went to Stuart who accepted Harry as a volunteer staff officer. Booted, spurred, mounted and armed with pistols and saber, Harry Gilmor was almost ready for battle. Only one duty remained, a duty Harry remembered as 'Raising my hat to the pretty little Miss Bessie_____, I dashed down the main street after Stuart, who had already started at a rapid gallop. On turning the corner, I saw Miss Bessie on the balcony waving her handkerchief to me as I passed out of sight.'[13] Harry Gilmor knew how to make an exit.

The Union cavalry had suffered much from mismanagement. Scattered about on picket duties, through no fault of their own, they were often used as mounted guards for the Washington forts. The times were changing; a new awareness of the importance of this mobile arm had come to Union commanders. Joe Hooker had brought his horsemen together into fighting units and now some of these came to fight under the command of William Woods Averell.

Harry Gilmor was riding beside John Pelham. Knowing that Harry would have some tasty morsels in his kit, Major Puller called out with the macabre humor of war: 'Harry, leave me your haversack if you get killed.'[14] Stuart was looking through field glasses with Fitz Lee at his side. They were studying some Union cavalry in Jamison's Woods. Fitz Lee thought it a small force and said to Stuart: 'Hadn't we better "take the bulge" on them at once?' Stuart concurred. Captain James R. Bayley rode forward with dismounted marksmen while the horsemen were assembled for a charge. Harry Gilmor went into action with Bayley in an attack that failed. Bayley's horse was killed. Averell had concealed four pieces of artillery on the flank. The guns fired cannister, oversized shotgun shells that ripped the Confederate lines. There were many more Union horsemen than Fitz Lee expected. When the 3rd Virginia Cavalry charge got to within 150 yards of the Union lines they were met with a hail of fire that emptied saddles, driving them back. Stuart went to the front, rallying his withdrawing horsemen. Union and Confederate regiments began to mix in hand-to-hand fighting with sabers. Stuart told Gilmor to take an attack order to Colonel Thomas Rosser. Gilmor joined this young Confederate leader in a charge, both of them believing they were not engaging a large force. They rode toward the ford into a heavy fire from dismounted sharpshooters. As their advance took them past a heavy wood they found two brigades of Union cavalry drawn up in columns of squadrons and a rain of fire descended upon them.

Gilmor was trying to assist Rosser when he heard Rosser call out: 'Major Puller, why in the name of God don't you assist me in rallying the men?' Gilmor turned and saw Puller bent forward in the saddle. The young officer said: 'Colonel, I'm killed.' Rosser replied: 'My God, old fellow, I hope not, bear up, bear up!'[15] but Puller was dying, shot through the chest, and he soon pitched from his horse.

Half an hour later Gilmor and Pelham were on the right of the 2nd Virginia Cavalry as it moved to a new position. The place the regiment had occupied was under fire. A shell exploded nearby, its jagged metal tearing into the back of Pelham's skull, mortally wounding him. At that moment a force of Union cavalry appeared nearby. Gilmor hurried to carry Pelham's body to the rear, calling upon some soldiers to take him to an ambulance. With his uniform coated with the 21-year-old Pelham's blood, Gilmor took the news to Stuart who bowed his head and wept at the loss of his friend and gallant commander of artillery. The battle was going against the Confederates. Stuart ordered Gilmor to Culpeper to send a telegram for assistance. On the way he found the men who carried Pelham's body. They had not sought an ambulance and were carrying the wounded officer draped across a horse. Gilmor was furious. He succeeded in getting the message sent to Lee and an ambulance for Pelham. It was too late; whatever chance for life Pelham had was gone. The Confederates stabilized the battlefield. Much to the anger of his seniors, Averell withdrew. He went secure in the knowledge that the Union cavalry had come of age. An exhausted Harry Gilmor lay down beside Pelham's body and slept soundly. It was, as he would write, 'The fortune of war.'[16]

Gilmor woke up feeling sick. He would be bedridden for ten days, perhaps suffering from the mental and physical shock brought on by participation in a fiercely-fought battle. He had performed well at Kelly's Ford and was visited and praised by Stuart, Fitz Lee and staff officers.

Both Stuart and Fitz Lee in their March 17 1863 after-action reports praised Harry Gilmor but misspelled his name. Stuart wrote that he was 'especially indebted' to Pelham and 'Captain Harry Gillmer, 12th Virginia Cavalry who accompanied me as volunteer staff.' Fitz Lee wrote: 'Captain Gilmer, Twelfth Virginia Cavalry, a volunteer for the occasion on the Major General's staff, I also commend for his marked bravery and cool courage.'[17]

Gilmor also received 'many kind messages and beautiful bouquets', the latter not likely coming from J.E.B. Stuart and his officers. With this inspiration and a visit from his brother Meredith, Harry came back to health. Meredith had been run out of Baltimore by the Union Provost Marshal Colonel Fish for being a rebel. He was now free to fight for the cause.

On Wednesday, April 1 1863, the two brothers arrived at Luray. Harry Gilmor assumed command of a squadron of the 12th Virginia Cavalry including his former company of primarily Maryland men. On April 20, Gilmor's dreams came true when he was given authority by the Secretary of War to raise an independent battalion of Partisan Rangers. On May 7 he received his commission as a major and began recruiting. While subordinates were finding volunteers, Gilmor took ten trusted men and went scouting behind Union lines. His mission was to gain information that would be useful to General Early when Early moved against Union General Milroy.

At Woodstock Gilmor met Belle Boyd who, not surprisingly, he had known before. Belle had a lust for adventure and promptly asked Harry to take her with him. Thinking to get rid of her, Gilmor said she would have to have permission from General Jenkins to go on the mission. The next morning Harry rose early, thinking he could be on his way before Belle woke, but she had taken his pistols and saber. The result was that Belle Boyd got her way and rode off with Gilmor carrying two small pistols in patent leather holsters snugged around her waist. They went to the headquarters of General Jenkins where Belle made an impassioned plea to the general to be allowed to go on the mission. Gilmor stood behind her making signs to the general that he did not want her along. When General Jenkins refused her request, Belle ceased to be ladylike and vented her anger. It was to no avail. Harry went unaccompanied by Miss Boyd on a three-day trip into Union areas where he plotted the location and numbers of enemy troops.[18]

Harry Gilmor now came under the orders of Confederate General Richard 'Dick' Ewell who was moving north by way of Front Royal. Belle Boyd tried to get Ewell to let her fight, but Ewell took a dim view of women being on the battlefield. At the First Battle of Manassas (Bull Run), Dick Ewell and John B. Gordon were sitting on their horses when a young Virginia girl of some 16 years of age rode up in great excitement to tell them what she felt was important military information.

Ewell saw some Union artillery unlimbering and said to the girl:

> Look there, look there, miss! Don't you see those men with blue clothes on, in the edge of the woods? Look at those men loading those big guns. They are going to fire, and fire quick and fire right here. You'll get killed. You'll be a dead *damsel*, in less than a minute. Get away from here! Get away!

The girl looked at the Union guns and gunners, disregarded them and continued talking. Ewell turned to Gordon and said: 'Women – I tell you, sir, women would make a grand brigade – if it were not for snakes and spiders!' He then added more thoughtfully: 'They don't mind bullets – women are not afraid of bullets; but one big black snake would put a whole army to flight.'[19]

Dick Ewell was one of the colorful characters of the Civil War. General John B. Gordon, who came to know Ewell well, wrote: 'He was a compound of anomalies, the oddest, most eccentric genius in the Confederate army.'[20] In an army that included Stonewall Jackson, that took some doing. Gordon related that Ewell had deeply loved a woman when he was young. The lady married another man, but Ewell never forgot her and during the war he put her son on his staff. The woman, whose name was Mrs Brown, became a widow. When Ewell was wounded, she nursed him back to health, fell in love and married him. Ewell could never believe in his good fortune at finally marrying the woman he adored. He would introduce her as 'My wife, Mrs Brown, sir.'

Harry Gilmor was in Middletown with the mission of preventing Union patrols from penetrating Ewell's position to gain information. When some forty Union cavalry attacked his pickets, Gilmor went after them with ten men. Five of the cavalry were captured, the remainder riding toward Winchester with Gilmor's troops in hot pursuit. The chase did not feel right to Harry Gilmor; he began to suspect they were being drawn into an ambush, so the pursuit was broken off. Captain Raisin of the 1st Maryland Cavalry (Confederate) came up with some seventy riders eager to take part in the fight. Still suspecting an ambush, Gilmor offered to scout to the front. The pursuit was resumed. About 1.25 miles short of Newtown the Union cavalry wheeled about, drew sabers and challenged the Confederates to charge. Gilmor signaled Raisin to halt his men; the signal was misunderstood and the Confederates charged into a waiting ambush. Union infantry rose from concealment on the side of the road and opened fire; two hidden guns were unmasked that plied the gray-clad horsemen with cannister. The Confederates were routed.

In June of 1863, the recruiting of Gilmor's new command was still under way. Gilmor kept himself occupied by riding with various units that were skirmishing with the enemy or ranging the countryside for General Richard Ewell. The Confederates had defeated the Union troops at Berryville. Gilmor was sent to scout in the vicinity. On return he met a man dressed in Confederate uniform, riding a fine gray horse. Gilmor identified the man as a Union 'Jessie Scout'. For reasons unknown, Gilmor was expecting to meet an enemy Ranger. He had prepared himself by tying a white handkerchief around his neck, leaving a long end hanging down over his shoulder. According to Gilmor, this was the sign of identification by which the Union scouts knew each other. Why the small band of Union Rangers would not know each other and why men whose lives depended on blending into their surroundings would tie conspicuous white scarves around their necks, Gilmor did not explain in recounting the story. The Union scout was suspicious, but Gilmor convinced the man that they both belonged to the same command. Seeing the Union Ranger was carrying handcuffs, Gilmor distracted him by asking to see them. When the man reached for the handcuffs, Gilmor ran him through with his saber and took his horse.[21]

In June of 1863, the commander of the 1st Maryland Cavalry having been wounded, Harry Gilmor was assigned to lead the unit. On orders, Gilmor with 200 men moved toward Frederick with a view to destroying the Monocacy Bridge, but found the bridge too well guarded to attack. Ranging north, Gilmor moved on to Hagerstown, Maryland, then on to Chambersburg and Shippensburg, Pennsylvania. He set out for Carlisle, learning en route that Ewell's corps had moved from Carlisle toward Gettysburg. Gilmor led his men through Papertown (now Mount Holly Springs) and Petersburg (now York Springs) to Cashtown. It was July 1 1863 when Gilmor reached Gettysburg. Ewell's lead elements were striking the flank of the Union position, forcing the Union troops to give up the high ground on Seminary Ridge. They were falling back through Gettysburg to form a new line on Cemetery Ridge. Gilmor wrote that 'the face of the earth seemed covered with *blue-coats* all running toward the town of Gettysburg in the wildest confusion.'[22] During the confusion, Gilmor rode among the running Union troops. Using his saber, he captured the colors of the 149th New York Infantry.

With the blue-coated soldiers hurrying through Gettysburg, Gilmor with one of his men entered the town to find it littered with loaded muskets discarded by the fleeing Union troops. Gilmor, who would claim he and his companion were the first Confederates in the town, was fired upon by a Union soldier, who missed. Gilmor used one of the dropped muskets to shoot the man.

The new Union line on Cemetery Ridge was hinged on the right flank by a wooded, rocky height named Culp's Hill. This was critical terrain, recognized as such by General Lee who ordered General Ewell to 'press those people'. Lee's order included the words 'if practicable'.

Lee saw that possession of Culp's Hill would allow him to roll up the Union line on Cemetery Ridge. Union General Hancock also recognized the importance of Culp's Hill and was hurrying troops to defend it. Gilmor wrote that he was present when division commander General Early said to Ewell, his corps commander, 'I can take my division and drive the enemy beyond those heights; and if this is not done, you will find a line of works that will cost us dear.' It is 33 miles from Carlisle to Gettysburg; Ewell thought his men were exhausted from the long march and the fight that followed. Ewell felt that Lee's orders had been discretionary. He did not move on Culp's Hill. Thus the first great mistake by the Confederates at Gettysburg occurred.

On the second day of the Battle of Gettysburg, Major Ridgely Brown returned to duty and took command of the 1st Maryland Cavalry (Confederate). In his memoirs Gilmor claimed he was ordered by Ewell to serve as provost marshal of Gettysburg and to search for prisoners, ammunition and arms. Actually another Maryland officer, Captain Frank Bond, had the temporary title and Harry Gilmor was along for the ride. More than 2,500 muskets were found and stacked in the town square. Before they could be removed the battle went against the Confederates and the Union troops recovered the collected weaponry.

On July 3 1863, Gilmor accompanied Brigadier General Harry Hays of Early's division and his Louisiana troops in an assault on the Union lines. After heavy fighting they were repulsed. The shock of the Confederate defeat weighed heavily on Gilmor. He joined the general retreat, taking the route used by Brigadier General John D. Imboden, who had the mission of protecting the Confederate army trains and wounded.

On July 4 a horrendous storm descended on the area, with rain so thick that men could not see and canvas could not provide protection to the wounded. The sheets of rain were accompanied by a wind that made hearing orders almost impossible. It was 4.00 pm when the long train started from near Cashtown in the direction of Chambersburg.

The Confederate wagon train from Gettysburg would be 17 miles long. It was a 17-mile-long cry of agony. The wagons loaded with torn and bleeding bodies were further brutalized by the bouncing and jarring over rain-soaked and heavily rutted roads. Imboden wrote that from nearly every wagon as the teams trotted on came cries and shrieks:

> 'O God! Why can't I die?'
> 'My God! Will no one have mercy and kill me?'
> 'Stop! Oh! For God's sake, stop just for one minute; take me out and leave me to die on the roadside.'
> 'I am dying! I am dying! My poor wife, my dear children, what will become of you?'

The cries, the moans, the prayers, the oaths, the agony and despair set into the unrelenting storm burned itself on Imboden's memory. He would write:

'During this one night I realized more of the horrors of war than I had in all the preceding two years.'[23]

As Imboden and Gilmor sought to protect the column, they had to keep moving, had to break clear before the dawn and the sun brought Union cavalry in pursuit. Imboden changed his route. He left the main road near Fairfield traveling cross-country to Greencastle which the head of the column achieved on the morning of July 5. They were now within 15 miles of a Potomac River crossing at Williamsport. At Greencastle, the local townspeople turned out with axes, cutting the spokes from wagon wheels and dropping wagons in the street. Imboden sent his horsemen against them. Union cavalry was on the scene and stiff fighting was going on. They made it to Williamsport on the afternoon of the 5th. The entire town became a hospital for the thousands of Confederate soldiers wounded at Gettysburg. Imboden told the townspeople that they would either cook for the wounded or their kitchens would be occupied for that purpose. The surgeons went to work. The Potomac was running at flood stage and the wounded had to be ferried across in small flat boats. Men had their wounds dressed on the south side of the river. Many wounded, being proud infantry, would not go back into wagons but walked on.

Imboden had his back to the wall with all the wounded, the wagons and some 10,000 animals of the army. He was short of supplies. Fortunately the sheep and cattle that Ranger Hanse McNeill's men had taken from Pennsylvania and the foraging done by Imboden's men were providing some relief.

Imboden learned that Union cavalry was closing on him and prepared a battle line with his artillery set up in the hills near Williamsport. Major Harry Gilmor was left with organizing the teamsters, quartermasters and commissary along with the wounded who could fight. The normally rear echelon troops were issued the weapons of the seriously wounded and put into the line. To be defeated meant the loss of men and matériel that were critical to the South.

The Union cavalry launched a dismounted attack that came home on McNeill's Rangers and Imboden's troopers. The Confederates held firm. Imboden counter-attacked with McNeill's Rangers, the 18th Virginia Cavalry, the 62nd Virginia Mounted Infantry and Gilmor's ad hoc command. With some 180 men, Gilmor made a dismounted attack on Union positions at the White Hall estate. The battle was fought building-to-building. Gilmor lost thirty-four men in the effort, but managed to stall the Union troops until the 62nd Virginia Mounted Infantry under Colonel

George H. Smith came to his assistance. Though the Confederates suffered fifty-nine casualties in the process in heavy fighting, the Union cavalry was forced to withdraw. The sound of guns on the enemy flank proclaimed that J.E.B. Stuart and his cavalry had arrived. The Confederate wounded and trains were saved.

Imboden was impressed with Harry Gilmor's impromptu command. He wrote: 'The wagoners fought so well that this came to be known as "the wagoners' fight".'[24]

Exhausted by his endeavors, Gilmor fainted. When he came to, he was a prisoner of the 5th US Cavalry Regiment of Brigadier General Wesley Merritt's brigade. The cavalry had its attention on the battle at hand. Gilmor was left to be guarded by two men. He slept, and when he awoke he found it was raining. His guards had spread a blanket over him. They were laying on the outer edges, but both were asleep. Gilmor wriggled out from beneath the blanket, found his horse and arms and rode off. When he reached his men at Williamsport, he sent a detail back to capture his guards.

Recruiting for his command was slow, while demands for Gilmor's scouting were large. As new companies were in various stages of growth, Gilmor took the single company that was organized to range in front of J.E.B. Stuart, performing reconnaissance missions. Contact with the Union troops was frequent, including opportunities to converse with each other. There was often a desire to read what the other side's newspapers were saying. At the invitation of Captain Charles W. Fenner of the 12th Pennsylvania Cavalry, Gilmor rode to the Union side of the Potomac to swap newspapers. A Union Ranger wanted to kill Gilmor, but Captain Fenner prevented it.

Stuart sent Gilmor into Maryland to determine the direction that Meade's army was taking. Taking ten men, Gilmor got as far as Frederick when he learned that Union commanders were aware of his presence. Troops were moving to block his routes of escape. Gilmor moved from between Williamsport and Hagerstown on a detour that took him to Harpers Ferry, Virginia. Returning south, they attacked a Union outpost from the rear, capturing a lieutenant, two non-commissioned officers and twelve men. The information Gilmor provided was valuable to Stuart who soon moved off to Eastern Virginia. Gilmor went to the Shenandoah Valley to finish raising his command.

Gilmor next moved to a camp near Mount Jackson. From that base he ranged outward, scouting in the area of Winchester, Martinsburg and

Charleston to discover Union intentions. On September 26 1863, Gilmor reported from Newtown:

> General S. Cooper
> Generals Slocum's and Howard's Corps are going to reinforce Rosecrans, and will be under Joe Hooker. They move 5,000 every night over the Baltimore and Ohio Railroad, and commenced last night, 25th. I have sent a courier to General Ewell with full particulars, and will try to damage the railroad tonight.[25]

Near Charleston, Union forces comprised the 9th Maryland Infantry commanded by Colonel Benjamin Simpson and two companies of cavalry. Near the end of September, Gilmor led fifty men of his command on a raid to seize government horses and mules reported to be pastured near Hagerstown. The raid did not develop. On the return, Gilmor's scouts came in from the Charleston road and told him that twenty-five Union cavalry had been seen moving toward Smithfield. Gilmor and his men were soon in pursuit. En route they met a man who Gilmor knew to be for the Union, but they did not stop to take him prisoner. By the time they reached where they expected to find the enemy, the Union troops were gone and the horses of Gilmor's men were exhausted.

Gilmor pushed on to head off the enemy column. When he reached a house owned by a Mr Morrow, 2 miles from Summit Point, he allowed his men to stop and get a drink from the spring. While the men were dismounted, Union cavalry who had been informed by the man Gilmor met on the road opened fire from a nearby hill. Despite the urging of their commander, Captain George D. Summers of Company F, 2nd Maryland Cavalry, the Union horsemen did not assault. Gilmor's men took up position behind a stone wall and began shooting. Summers rode at Gilmor, firing his revolver as he came. Gilmor took his time in aiming and at twenty paces killed Summers with a head shot. The Confederates then charged the Union troops. In the course of the fight that followed, Gilmor and a Union officer fought with sabers. The struggle ended when Gilmor parried a cut at his neck and delivered a deep wound to his opponent's face. Gilmor reported 4 Union troops killed, 3 wounded and 23 men and 29 horses captured. One Confederate was killed, three wounded and one taken prisoner.

The Union report differs. Colonel George D. Wells, Brigade Commander, wrote that on October 7, Colonel Simpson had sent a patrol of twenty horsemen on the Berryville road. It was soon learned they were cut off. Captain Summers with the forty-three men available went to the relief of the patrol. In the meantime, the guerrillas made the safety of the town, though closely pursued. Colonel Simpson sent infantry in support, who reported capturing three horses and four men of Companies A and F, 12th Virginia Cavalry. Captain Summers was returning when he encountered Gilmor's party. Summers charged and was killed by a volley from behind a stone wall. The Union force reported the Confederates as Baylor's and Morrow's companies of the 12th Virginians and Gilmor's battalion. Summer's cavalry broke off the action when he was killed. The men reported Summers and one enlisted man killed and four wounded.[26]

In war the accounts of a battle usually differ depending on which side is making the report. Within the battle men who are fighting on the same side, often within a few feet of each other, will give conflicting reports. An example is an action involving Harry Gilmor's command as seen by both sides that occurred in mid-October 1863 when Gilmor's bivouac was in the vicinity of Strasburg, Virginia.

Gilmor wrote that he started with forty men to move toward the Paw Paw Tunnel on the B&O Railroad. They left Newtown at 2.00 pm on October 14 and headed for the North Mountain. As they passed a residence called 'Carter Hall', Gilmor and a companion stopped, in Gilmor's words, 'for a few moments to see the ladies there. We stayed rather longer than we intended, and the sun was nearly down when we set out to join the command which I had directed to take a certain route.'[27] Captain John C. Blackford was the senior officer who remained with the troops.

Gilmor could not find his command on the route he said he directed them to take. Gilmor and his companion roamed the hills looking for his troops without success. Gilmor wrote:

> The route they had to go was the most dangerous on the whole border; and, although Blackford was a brave man and a good scout, I knew him to be rather incautious and totally reckless of danger, and could not rid myself of a strong presentiment of something disastrous befalling them. The result showed how well-founded were my fears. As they passed Back Creek Valley, the men were allowed to straggle into houses tenanted by their worst enemies. The consequence was, they went into camp for the day with no scouts or pickets out; they all laid down and, while asleep, a force of infantry and cavalry

surrounded and fired into them, capturing all but five or six, who managed to conceal themselves in the bush. Not an officer escaped. They were the best men and horses of the command, and were selected for the occasion.[28]

A Union report of the action gives a different account. As the war progressed, many Union commanders began to develop Rangers who roamed behind Confederate lines. They were daring men. Working alone or in small groups, they posed as Confederate soldiers or Southern civilians. When they took prisoners or had important information, the Ranger would return to the advance party of his regiment, turn over his captives or findings and go back into Confederate territory. Union Rangers were effective and much hated by the Confederates. Edwin F. Savacool was detached from Company K, 1st New York (Lincoln) Cavalry to Ranger service. When patrols captured Southern mail carriers, Savacool often took the mail sack and played the role of mail carrier as he roamed behind Confederate lines.

On October 14 1863, Savacool was in his chosen role when he encountered Gilmor and his men who were setting out on their raid. When questioned, Savacool responded that he was going about his mail duties. The Confederates were suspicious, but Savacool knew that in his mail bag he was carrying a letter to Gilmor from a woman. All questioning stopped at this time, Gilmor liked what he read and Gilmor's men relaxed. Savacool learned they were on the way to Back Creek to burn the railroad bridge. Eager to see the woman who wrote the letter, Harry Gilmor left his command to go calling on her.

Captain Blackford and the men were ordered on, with Gilmor intending to join them later to accomplish the mission. Blackford took the men to an assembly area near a small hamlet called 'Tomahawk'; this was about 5 miles from the bridge they were ordered to destroy. The Confederate Rangers would wait in thick woods and brush till nightfall, when they would attack.

Meanwhile Savacool circled back, riding rapidly to inform his command. He notified the infantry who guarded the bridge. He then informed his commanders. Detachments of the 1st New York and 12th Pennsylvania Cavalry regiments were sent in pursuit of Gilmor's troops. Captain Richard G. Prendergast of the 1st New Yorkers was senior officer, with Captain Henry of the 12th Pennsylvanias second-in-command. With Ranger Savacool as guide, Captain Prendergast scouted Captain Blackford's position. The Confederate Rangers were concealed in a wooded ravine. Prendergast posted his two detachments of cavalry in ambush positions.

He then sent infantry from the bridge guard to come at the Confederate Rangers from the rear, flushing them into the ambush. The Union plan worked smoothly. Some of the Confederates ran for their horses, others ran for the woods. A Northern reporter styled 'Grapeshot' penned that the Confederates 'took to their heels, and ran in a style exceedingly creditable to chivalrous pedestrianism. We routed them, foot, horse and dragoon, capturing nearly the entire party.' In all, two captains, one lieutenant, twenty-five men and thirty horses were reported taken captive. The writer Grapeshot called Gilmor 'an eminent and worthy bushwhacker' and chided him as 'a thorough lady's man'.[29]

The common factor in both reports is that Harry Gilmor deserted his command when they were in the midst of a raid to be with a woman or women. Gilmor blamed Blackford for being incautious and reckless, while his own actions were downright foolhardy. Men were shot for less serious offenses during the Civil War.

John D. Imboden took command of the Valley District, establishing his headquarters at White Post. There, Gilmor reported to Imboden for instructions. The Union garrison at Charleston looked vulnerable to a raid, so Imboden sent Harry Gilmor on a scouting mission. Taking sixty men, Gilmor made a reconnaissance. He determined the attack was feasible, but only if executed by Imboden's full command. On October 18 1863, Imboden's column moved from Berryville toward Charleston with Harry Gilmor, sixty-five mounted men and thirty new recruits without horses leading the way. It was a 12-mile march to Charleston over rough terrain, but there were no stragglers in the foot troops. Gilmor's men would take up positions separate from the main body, performing a blocking mission to cut off any Union retreat or reinforcements moving between Charleston and Harpers Ferry. Gilmor's command moved first, departing at 1.00 am. Imboden followed with the main body at 2.00 am.

Union Colonel B.L. Simpson had failed to establish sufficient security. Imboden was able to encircle his adversary. With the town surrounded, the aroused Union garrison took up defensive positions in buildings including the jail and the court house. These buildings had firing loopholes cut in them for opposition to infantry. Buildings were not protection from Imboden's artillery. When Imboden called for surrender, Simpson tried to stall, then replied: 'Take us if you can.' Imboden could. He lined up his artillery firing at 200 yards range, shelling Simpson's troops into the streets. Simpson tried to withdraw from town by the Harpers Ferry road. The retreating Union troops ran into the blocking position of Gilmor and the 18th Virginia Cavalry.

Few Union troops escaped. When the soldiers of Gilmor and Simpson clashed, it was Maryland versus Maryland with men on each side calling out to each other by name. Imboden reported to General Lee that he had captured between 400 and 500 officers and men and many horses, mules, wagons and equipment. Colonel Simpson managed to escape, but without his command. He thought his troops suffered 250 casualties.[30]

A Union reaction force promptly came down from Harpers Ferry. Imboden withdrew after a very tidy raid. Gilmor's and McNeill's Rangers covered the withdrawal, fighting hard to hang on to what they had captured. Gilmor had three horses wounded under him in the fighting. There were too many bluecoats and not enough forage, so Imboden hurried off his prisoners and captured equipment and informed General Lee he was retiring up the valley to Shenandoah County.

When he returned to Berryville, Harry Gilmor put his mind to other priorities. He wrote: 'I rode into town to see some of my old acquaintances among the ladies, and found all very enthusiastic in their reception of us.... I received a kiss from more than one pair of ruby lips, and gave many a hearty hug and kiss in return.'[31]

The winter of 1863/64 was particularly fierce; still the attack philosophy kept men in the saddle. Raiding a Union camp in a night attack over ice and snow, Gilmor found himself with an empty revolver. He became engaged in a hand-to-hand fight trying to wrest away the revolver of a Union captain. Gilmor slipped and fell. In the darkness, pierced only by the flickering light of the camp fires, Gilmor looked up to see his opponent taking aim. Thinking he was a dead man, Gilmor closed his eyes. The Union officer fired, the ball sending a shower of ice and snow over Harry Gilmor but going into the earth beside him. The Union officer did not wait to see the effect of his bullet, but moved away.[32]

In the harsh winter, Gilmor's men kept well fed and clothed with captured supplies from the North. In early December Gilmor and his men were scouting Union activity, reporting the blue-coated troops in force at Front Royal on the night of the 11th[33] and on the 12th reporting to Lee that a scout to Millwood had discovered Union forces amounting to 2,000 infantry, 700 cavalry, 8 pieces of artillery and 80 wagons.[34]

On December 19 1863, Gilmor's men attacked a railroad bridge guarded by Companies H and E of the 1st New York Cavalry. The opposing forces clashed in close-range fights that were often hand-to-hand. The Union troops saved the bridge, but seven of the cavalrymen were captured along with their horses.[35]

Gilmor's Rangers along with those of Mosby, White and McNeill made guarding the miles of railroad tracks a mission impossible. Water towers so critical to steam engines were destroyed, as were bridges and engine repair facilities. Trains were wrecked as rails were removed at critical points. Battlefield success helped with recruiting. Gilmor's command grew to six companies. Gilmor was of great assistance in the Confederate defeat of Union General Franz Sigel in the Shenandoah Valley.

Whenever women and wine were available, Harry Gilmor made them part of his battle plan. When following Rosser's command, Gilmor found a distillery and looked forward to a drink. His plans were frustrated when he learned that Rosser had ordered that no spirits be sold to the troops. Gilmor pretended to be General Lee and wormed his way into the heart of the elderly lady of the establishment. Thinking he was the great general, the woman gave Harry her prize bottle of vintage peach brandy; one she had saved for thirty-three years. Harry was ashamed of himself, but he and his staff drank the brandy.[36]

Meanwhile, Captain John Blackford, who had been captured while Harry was wooing the ladies, had quickly escaped from prison at Fort McHenry and managed to get home. On January 6 1864, Union Ranger Ed Savacool was leading a party in search of Blackford. Trying to get close without being detected, Savacool with one other man approached Blackford's house as darkness fell. The snow lay thick upon the ground with fresh tracks visible. The fenced garden was thick with bushes that concealed anyone within. Suddenly two men were seen climbing the fence. As one of the men dropped to earth, Savacool and his partner opened fire with their revolvers. The man on the ground surrendered; the other, who was on the fence, yelled 'Don't fire, I'm shot, I'll surrender', but then quickly dropped to the other side of the fence and ran. While his partner guarded the prisoner, Savacool scaled the fence and began a running gunfight with the fleeing man. As they each carried two revolvers the gunshots came fast, one upon the other. Firing while running was not effective. As though by silent agreement, both men stopped and faced each other, firing simultaneously. Savacool fell with a bullet in his thigh; Blackford was also down, one pistol empty, the second near his hand. The Confederate Ranger asked for a drink of water and died.

On seeing John Blackford's body, the women of his family raged at the Union soldiers, crying 'He was worth the whole Yankee army.' The men of the 1st New York Cavalry were glad that Blackford was no longer a threat. A soldier praised him, remarking 'He would have been a worse plague to us than Mosby.'[37]

In January 1864, Gilmor and McNeill led their Rangers in the Virginia hills, scouting for Tom Rosser. Not wanting to bother to take some rails down, Gilmor tried to have his horse jump a fence. The jump failed, he fell heavily and was rendered unconscious. Gilmor awoke in a cabin where one of his men was making love to a mountain girl. Gilmor wrote that there were five or six more girls sitting around. The next morning Gilmor had to be helped on his horse. He was not specific as to the cause.

Still recovering, Gilmor sent most of his men with Hanse McNeill on a cattle raid. Unable to rest, he went with Rosser in an attack on Burlington. Rosser wanted a railroad depot destroyed at Frankfort and Gilmor knew the area. Borrowing a squadron of Elijah White's Comanches, Harry Gilmor went raiding. The depot was guarded by two companies of Union infantry and was shielded by a board fence to its front. When the charge went home, the fence stymied the horsemen. An expert rider, Gilmor threw the weight of his horse against the boards and knocked down a section. He wrote of what followed:

> Turning half round in my saddle to call on the men, I received a sudden shock, and felt deathly sick, and at the same instant, saw a man trail his gun and run off. I killed him before he had gone three steps. His ball had passed through two coats, and stuck in a pack of cards in my left side pocket; they were quite new, the wrapper not having been broken open. The suits were each distinct; the bullet passed through all, stopping at the last, which was the ace of spades![38]

From then on, whenever Rosser saw Gilmor he would ask 'If spades are trumps'. The depot and supporting buildings were taken and burned.

All Confederate Rangers enjoyed the excitement of wrecking trains. The problem with running an iron horse off the rails was that the opportunity for looting was difficult to resist. Despite the orders of their commanders, the Confederate Partisan Ranger Act offered men the chance to act in the manner of buccaneers. What they took from the Railroad Express agents and Union paymasters was legitimate spoils of war. To rob passengers cast these men in the role of highwaymen and to many in the North put them outside the laws of war.

Raiding by night, hiding by day in barns and wooded groves, Gilmor with twenty-four of his men approached Kearneysville, Virginia. On Thursday, February 11 1864, they blocked the tracks, derailing a Baltimore and Ohio express train. Gilmor went after the Express Agent and the mail but could not find him. The clever agent, Mr. Tshude, had hidden under mail bags and preserved the $4,000 he was protecting in the in the safe.[39]

A hasty Confederate withdrawal was necessary when another train arrived carrying Union troops. When Gilmor got back to the cars he found some of his men robbing passengers. His orders had been to leave women alone and not to take personal possessions on pain of execution, but the temptation was too great for the men.

Northern newspapers fanned the flame of outrage. This disturbed Robert E. Lee who wrote the Confederate Secretary of War James A. Seddon: 'Such conduct is unauthorized and discreditable. Should any of that battalion be captured the enemy might treat them as highway robbers.'[40]

Some of Gilmor's men next robbed a caravan of Jewish merchants on their way from Richmond to Baltimore to replace their stocks. These people had political connections in Richmond. Lee ordered Gilmor to be tried by court martial. Gilmor was ordered to Staunton, Virginia where his trial convened in early April 1864. The trial lasted a week, ending with Gilmor honorably acquitted of all charges and specifications. The findings required Lee's approval. Fortunately for Gilmor, Lee was engaged in battle with Grant. Gilmor fretted until he was rescued by General John C. Breckenridge who had assumed command of the Valley District. Breckenridge ordered Gilmor to re-muster his command of Partisan Rangers, but stripped Gilmor of much of his independence. By direction of the Secretary of War on May 5 1864, they were made part of the Maryland line and called the '2nd Maryland Battalion of Cavalry'.[41]

General Sherman was preparing to march on Atlanta. Robert E. Lee had found Grant a general who just kept coming on. Gloom was settling on the Confederacy. As the Battle of the Wilderness heated up, there was a lot of praying going on among the troops on both sides. General John B. Gordon noted that a young soldier who was asked to lead a prayer began: 'Oh Lord, we are having a mighty big fight down here. Now if you will take the proper view of the subject...' Many of the worshipers were unable to maintain their composure.[42] Jefferson Davis was finding leadership of a losing cause brought attacks from allies as well as the enemy. The governors of Georgia and North Carolina keenly believed in their State rights and Davis was hard pressed to achieve unity by mere persuasion.

Anxious to get back into action, Harry Gilmor left Staunton for New Market, arriving around May 6. He found Imboden's command about 3 miles south of town. A member of Imboden's staff told Gilmor that his men were on the picket line covering from Mount Jackson to Edinburg. Again in the saddle, Harry anxiously went out to find his battalion. What he found was not encouraging. Some troops were still at Staunton. Losses had taken his strength down to eighty-five men. As the men were relieved from picket duty, Gilmor began to assemble them. While this was in progress and the men were feeding their horses, firing was heard nearby. A column of the 21st New York Cavalry under Major Charles Otis was moving south. Despite the warnings of a subordinate who had seen the size of the Union force, Gilmor ordered his men into the saddle and charged the Union column. The Confederates were in turn charged and had to gallop away. Both sides were using the Hawkinstown road for rapid movement. To keep their troops under control, both leaders kept their commands in column formation. As the Union column became strung out in pursuit, the Confederates turned to fight; again they were forced to turn and ride for safety.

Gilmor stayed in the rear of the column, counting on the accuracy of his fire to delay the Union troopers. He saw his first shot send a man reeling in the saddle; the second shot brought down a horse. Alternately firing and retreating, he slowed the Union pursuit. Three of his men returned to help. Two of these men were shot. As Gilmor turned again to fire, he saw a Union officer dismount, take a carbine from a soldier, then resting the weapon on a fence post, take deliberate aim. In a desperate attempt to avoid the bullet, Gilmor wheeled his horse to gallop away. Gilmor felt the blow as he was struck in the back. The bullet had hit within 2in of the spine on the upper part of the right hip bone. Fighting pain but with surprisingly little bleeding, Gilmor rejoined his troops. The pursuit broke off when they neared Mount Jackson. Now Gilmor was able to look to his wound. He had been fortunate: the bullet had struck the crupper of the saddle and glanced off and upward. In so doing, the force of the shot had been reduced. The bullet was deflected, striking in a glancing fashion. Harry's principal concern was that he had been shot in the rear end. With the macabre humor of war, such a wound made a man subject to ridicule.

Soon back in the saddle, Gilmor led his men, ranging outward to locate Union cavalry couriers and patrols. His mission was to work in support of General Breckenridge who was preparing to engage General Shields at New Market. Using all the troops he could rally, including more than 200 young cadets of the Virginia Military Institute, Breckenridge drove General Shields' troops in retreat to Strasburg. For a time the Union pressure on the Shenandoah Valley was eased.

During a truce, Gilmor met Major Charles Otis of the 21st New York Cavalry. He learned that Otis was the officer who fired the shot that caused Gilmor's wound. In this war where opponents spoke the same language, there was frequent vocal exchange. The two officers got along well. With macabre humor, they gleefully promised to kill each other at the earliest opportunity. Otis had a strong sense of humor. When the Union troops captured Staunton, Virginia, he signed the registry book at the American Hotel 'Major Charles G. Otis, 21st New York Cavalry, first Yank in town.'[43]

As patrolling resumed, Gilmor sent back the information he gathered to General Breckenridge. To his surprise the answer came back from General Imboden that Breckenridge and the Confederate infantry had been ordered east to help General Lee. Only Confederate horsemen remained in the valley. The defeated Union General Shields was relieved of command, to be replaced on Saturday, May 21 1864 by General David Hunter. This officer fought total war. He believed in laying waste to his opponent's territory. It was soon evident that Hunter was being reinforced and gathering troops for a raid southward to Staunton and Lynchburg.

Harry Gilmor had the mission to delay Hunter's movement to give time for larger Confederate forces to return to the defense of the valley. Finding Union patrols thick in front, Gilmor took his small band into the rear of Hunter's force, seeking to disrupt communication and supply. John Singleton Mosby would at times come over from Loudoun and Fauquier Counties to lend a hand.

On May 24 1864, Gilmor learned that a Union wagon train was en route from Martinsburg to Winchester. It is rare in war that both sides report the same numbers engaged, casualties and results. This action was no exception. Gilmor felt he was up against 175 cavalry and 80 infantry. Union reports say it was a 125-man detachment from the 15th and 21st New York Cavalry regiments escorting twelve to fifteen wagons. Both sides agreed that medical supplies were the cargo. Gilmor concealed his men in thick woods near Bartonsville. His scouts had shadowed the train as it passed Winchester. As the train neared Gilmor's position he could not see any infantry so he assumed they must be hiding in the wagons. This led him to allow the train to pass and attack it from the rear.

Lieutenant Colonel Augustus Root of the 15th New Yorkers was the officer commanding the Union detachment. Riding with Colonel Root was Captain Robert H. Brett of Company K of the 1st New York Veteran Cavalry who was returning to his own regiment. Lieutenant Burritt N. Hurd of the 15th New York Cavalry headed the advance guard. The Union column passed Winchester and on to Newtown without any sign of the enemy.

Gilmor and his fifty-three men hit the column in the rear as it entered the town. The Confederates rode in a column of fours divided in two sections. Gilmor led the first section and Captain John R. Burke the second. The Union rearguard faced about and fired their carbines, but the impetus of Gilmor's charge brushed them aside. Excited by the action, Gilmor's horse ran away with him, carrying him into Union ranks. Lieutenant Hurd and the cavalry in advance doubled back and charged Gilmor's column. Captain Brett was killed and Lieutenant John M. Rulifson of the 15th New York Cavalry severely cut with a saber slash. The Confederates beat back the Union cavalry and forced them to retreat. The reports of both sides say that Gilmor's men seized the wagons. Gilmor claimed he burned the wagons, taking forty prisoners including six officers plus seventy horses.

Gilmor claimed he talked with Captain Brett before the officer died, consigning Brett's body to civilians with instructions that it be sent to Union lines at Martinsburg. Union reports differ greatly. Union claims are that the cavalry had not retreated far when they encountered a Union infantry regiment marching to Winchester. Gilmor and his men were occupied with going through the wagons when the combined force of infantry and cavalry came charging in on them. The Union troops got back the wagon train and Captain Brett's body, but the fight was a swirling brawl. Lieutenant Hurd captured Harry Gilmor, but Gilmor's men freed him. The fight cost the 15th New Yorkers sixteen men wounded and/or captured. Several later died at Andersonville prison.[44]

David Hunter was well aware that Confederate attacks in his rear area often came as a result of information and logistical support supplied to the Confederates by the local populace. Hunter issued an order that if his pickets were bushwhacked or trains attacked he would burn houses in the area. Gilmor wrote a message that he would execute the prisoners he held if Newtown were burned. Gilmor felt his threat of retaliation spared Newtown. The Union reports do not credit Harry Gilmor.

Major Joseph K. Stearns of the 1st New York Cavalry was given command of the detachment to burn Newtown. He discussed the order with his officers and men, then met with the citizens of the town. Stearns made the decision to disobey Hunter's order, though he felt it would be the end of his career. On return Stearns reported to his commander, saluted and said 'General Hunter, I am the officer that was ordered to burn Newtown and didn't do it.' Hunter grunted and went back to his work. No action was taken against Major Stearns.[45]

On May 26 1864, Hunter moved south, leading the right wing of a two-part raid ordered by Grant. To the east, Sheridan would also be attacking. Both generals had the mission of breaking Lee's line of supply by cutting the railroad, depriving Confederates of their support base and forcing Lee to defend at several points.

William E. 'Grumble' Jones, the cussing, singing warrior who loved the sound of a banjo, led a Confederate force back into the valley to oppose Hunter. The two forces clashed at Piedmont on Sunday, June 5 1864. After hard fighting that claimed the life of General Jones, the Confederates were routed. The Union march south continued. The flag of the United States flew in Staunton, Virginia for the first time since 1861. Hunter pressed on, heading for Lexington and Lynchburg, his path marked by smoke and flames.

On June 17 1864, a worried Colonel E.G. Lee, Confederate commander in the Staunton area, was writing to Richmond:

> I would respectfully call attention to the fact that there is now only McNeill's sixty men between me and the Potomac, and he will under Major Gilmor's order be removed...would it not be well to permit Gilmor and McNeill to remain below...I ask that they be instructed to keep me advised of the enemy's movements, and especially of all that threatens this point.[46]

Gilmor was having his own adventures. He withdrew to a wooded assembly area in Clark County where he concealed his men. Taking five other men, he went to a house some distance off to have breakfast and get food for his men. As the Confederates were beginning to eat, the host, who had been keeping a dilatory watch, sauntered in and told them there were horsemen nearby. The riders proved to be the efficient and deadly Union scouts. Gilmor persisted in calling these men 'Jessics', though that organization had long since been disbanded and most Union commanders had their own bodies of Rangers. Gilmor and his men broke for their horses, seeing that behind some ten to fifteen scouts was a large body of Union cavalry.

One of Gilmor's men was surrounded and refused to surrender, firing until he was riddled with bullets. The Union Rangers chased Gilmor and the rest of his men about the countryside in a pursuit Gilmor compared to a 'fox hunt'. The fox escaped. Still hungry, Gilmor went to another house for dinner, the women of the house providing him with strawberries and cream. While Gilmor was eating, cavalry caught up with him again. One of Gilmor's men came into the house yelling that the Union troops had captured five and killed one of Gilmor's troops at a nearby blacksmith's shop. While the women screamed with excitement and were jumping up and down, holding out his hat, saber, pistol and haversack, Gilmor gulped down his strawberries and hurried away.

Riding to Mount Airy, Gilmor found that David Hunter had been there. The livestock had been slaughtered, the houses ransacked. There was much weeping and wailing among the womenfolk. This was not the Southern predictions of 1861 when the hot rhetoric claimed that one Southerner could whip three Yankees and in a short war of a few weeks, the battlefield would be tidy except for the Union dead. Now the South was seeing the face of war and feeling its fist.

Horses are fright animals, many becoming unmanageable in battle. Gilmor was annoyed with horses that ran away, taking him into enemy columns. He took time to purchase a trustworthy mount. To his disgust he found that he had to pay $3,500 in Confederate money for the animal he wanted. It was not encouraging to know that he could have bought the horse for $400 in United States currency. His command was beaten up. The best he could muster was forty men; still, his commanders needed to know what Hunter was up to so Harry Gilmor went ranging.

On June 12 1864, General Lee ordered Jubal Early, who was at Gaines Mill, to take the 2nd Corps of some 8,000 infantry and two battalions of artillery over to the Shenandoah Valley, strike Hunter from the rear and defeat him. If possible, Lee then wanted Early to move north in the valley to threaten Washington. It was hoped that this would relieve Grant's pressure on Lee's army. As a result of Lee's counter-moves, Grant's two-pronged raid was only partially successful. Sheridan had been blocked at Trevalian Station in the east and Early foiled Hunter's plans in the west. The two Union columns could not unite, but they left their mark upon the southern rail lines and countryside. Hunter was now withdrawing with a strong rearguard.

When joined with Confederate forces already in the valley, Early had 10,000 infantry and 2,000 cavalry. He sent his infantry marching after Hunter, telling Gilmor to push ahead, that Hunter's troops were demoralized and Gilmor could capture hundreds. Gilmor and his men were exhausted; they had been in contact with Hunter's rearguard and knew better. Gilmor wrote: 'I told Early very plainly I was overworked, and could not hold out long, but like all infantry officers, he thought cavalry ought to know no flagging.'[47]

Gilmor's 40 Marylanders were joined by 250 Virginians. With this mixed lot he pitched into the rear of Hunter's rearguard. He was soon reinforced by General Ramseur and some 200 sharpshooters. Thus pressure was kept on the Union rear. On June 19 1864, the two sides skirmished near the quaint town of Liberty, Virginia. Harry Gilmor never let battle interfere with the more fundamental aspects of life. A lovely home and a bevy of beautiful girls caused him to pause in the fight. One of the girls gave him a glass of water. When finished drinking, Gilmor placed the glass on a fence post. A stray bullet struck the post and the empty glass fell to earth. Frightened, the girls screamed and ran inside the house, one of them losing her slipper in the process. Gilmor and Henry Kyd Douglas leaped from their horses and raced for the slipper with Gilmor claiming the prize. Remounting, he teased the owner of the shoe, saying she must come outside to claim it. Two girls came out, but another whizzing bullet sent one running for cover. The owner of the shoe stayed outside. Gilmor wrote:

> I sprang to the ground – down on my knees to replace the slipper. The beautiful foot was soiled with grass. What diligent efforts I made to remove every stain; it is astonishing how long I was about it; and then how awkward I was in getting on the shoe! No doubt it was very tedious to her, but the time was *very short* to me. Such are some of the few happy scenes that brighten a soldier's life.[48]

Having Harry Gilmor feeling her ankle must have made a lively entry in the diary of the young maid from Liberty. As Gilmor would write: 'A soldier *will* make love wherever he goes, for all the girls expect it. They say "Poor fellow! He'll be killed, wounded or captured soon, and we shall never see him again; let us give him all the pleasure we can."'[49] Henry Kyd Douglas, loser in the race for the slipper, noted with satisfaction in his memoirs that he went back to the girl's house that night while Gilmor was sent elsewhere.[50]

The mobility that was a strength of Gilmor's command depended on their horses. Broken down from continuous service, the horses needed rest and care. Early had no one else who could do the out-front ranging that was required, so twenty-one tired men on twenty-one tired horses set out to determine what Hunter was about. They soon had their answer. From the crest of a mountain they saw the smoke and flames arising from houses, mills and barns. Gilmor scouted Hunter's army plus finding roads and byways that Early could use. He ambushed a small Union signal party killing two men, then watched Hunter's army continue to march north. Early was not closing fast so Gilmor rode on to Salem where Hunter had just passed. Near Salem they encountered a detachment of the Union rearguard and captured two men. One of these, a sergeant, had a superb white horse that Gilmor took for himself. Contact was established with General John Imboden who was in the lead of Early's army. Gilmor had located an element of William Averell's cavalry division feeding their horses. A running battle was opened that lasted over 4 miles of road.

The Confederates could only wistfully envy the Union soldiers who were armed with seven-shot Spencer carbines. It was fortunate for Harry Gilmor that he had captured the white horse as the one he was riding was killed under him in the next action. Soon thereafter Early ceased to follow Hunter, choosing to go into camp in Roanoke County. Gilmor joined him there. He was one of the few with whom Early shared his plans of going north to cross the Potomac and threaten Washington.

Strict secrecy was observed. The troops were not informed; indeed, Gilmor's men thought that Early had returned to Richmond. Gilmor was once again ordered to get out front and patrol to keep messengers from passing back and forth. Early did not want any indication of his plans reaching northern lines. Gilmor made certain none did. As July opened, Jubal Early began moving his army north through Winchester. On July 4 1864, Early tried to cross the Potomac while seizing Harpers Ferry. Union resistance was too strong, so Early bypassed the opposition and the next day crossed the river at Shepherdstown, moving into Maryland. Much effort had gone into getting Maryland into the Confederacy. By mid-1864 it was clear to the Confederates that their wooing had been in vain; Maryland was not coming to their aid. About seventy-five Maryland men did come into Confederate ranks. Their arrival almost doubled Gilmor's strength. General Early made his feelings about Maryland clear when he ransomed the town of Frederick for $200,000 under the threat of burning.

The army of the United States had put together a stopgap force of short-term men under General Lew Wallace.[51] On July 9, Early hit this outnumbered force at the Monocacy River to the south-east of Frederick and routed them. Wallace lost the fight, but gained time for the Union. Defenses were hurriedly strengthened at Baltimore and Washington with two experienced divisions of Major General Wright's Union 6th Corps rushed north from City Point, Virginia. Early still hoped to get to Washington, but he was running out of opportunity.

While a colonel, Bradley T. Johnson of Maryland had developed a plan to kidnap President Lincoln. There was great interest in the plan, but Union troop movement put Confederate priority elsewhere. At Staunton, Johnson had been promoted to brigadier general and given command of what had been the cavalry brigade of the deceased 'Grumble' Jones. Johnson's mission was now to capture the Union prison at Point Lookout and free the Confederate prisoners. Early had an idea of arming these men with captured weapons and using them to help take Washington.

Gilmor was ordered to join Bradley Johnson. Johnson detached Gilmor's command to serve as the advance guard of an infantry division reinforced, commanded by General John Breckenridge. Gilmor reported to his new commander at Boonsboro, not far from the 1862 battlefield called Antietam by the North and Sharpsburg by the South. On arrival Gilmor found he was also being given command of the 1st Battalion, Maryland Cavalry. As Early pushed northward through Maryland, Gilmor and his two-battalion-sized force did out-front scouting. Despite the skirmishes, there was time to stop at 'Glen Ellen', his parents' estate in Baltimore County, for a visit with his father, mother and siblings.

At the house of a man named Ishmael Day, Sergeant Eugene W. Field, Gilmor's ordnance sergeant, ordered Day to take down a United States flag Day was flying. When the order was refused, Field dismounted to take down the flag. Day seized a shotgun, mortally wounded Field, then fled to safety. Gilmor's men burned Day's house and outbuildings in retaliation.

Riding north, Gilmor's men neared the bridge where the Philadelphia, Wilmington and Baltimore Railroad crossed the Gunpowder River. When a passenger train was seen coming down the tracks, Gilmor dispatched Captain James R. Bayley and twenty men to capture it. A correspondent of the *New York Herald* was on board and in a July 13 1864 article described the attack on the express train from Baltimore to New York:

> We reached the Gunpowder River all safe, and immediately after passing the long trestle bridge speed was increased. The train was in charge of Asher Pancost, engineer and T. Brison conductor. About two miles from the bridge at Magnolia station, two or three pistol shots were heard when the train suddenly stopped, and a cry was raised, 'The rebels are on us.' But a few seconds elapsed before they entered the cars

carrying pistols in their hands. The first question asked was 'Are there any ladies in this car'...they ordered every lady to sit down. This was immediately followed by another order to 'Clear Out'. It was while leaving the cars that purses and watches were taken from the passengers. The request to hand them over was enforced by a cocked pistol held at the head of the victimized passengers...after the baggage and express cars were emptied, steam was then got up, the engine reversed and the train of blazing cars run down to Gunpowder bridge. A column of dense black smoke was soon seen rising in the direction of the bridge. When rebels who had been in charge of the train returned, they said the bridge was burning finely and would be totally consumed.[52]

Gilmor was disappointed as he had planned to run the train to Havre de Grace and burn bridges and a steamboat there. That plan was frustrated when the engineer Mr Pancost escaped. Among the passengers was Union Major General William B. Franklin, a corps commander going home for rest and recuperation. The general was in civilian clothes when a Confederate asked who he was and Franklin replied: 'Nobody of any account.' A woman passenger from Baltimore who was a Confederate sympathizer recognized the general and soon identified him to Gilmor's men. Franklin was taken prisoner, given his luggage and a captured buggy to ride in. To bring home an enemy general officer was worthy of praise. Gilmor was careful about who he selected to guard Franklin.

The women were all aflutter about being captured; among them were Maryland women who knew their captors. As Confederates rode up to the car windows, the *Herald* reporter heard women crying out 'Why Tom, is that you?' and 'How are you Harry?' When the raiders were inside the cars, some of the women kissed Gilmor's men. The captured men were treated well but were robbed of money, watches and jewelry, the secessionist women joining in the looting. One doctor had to give up his boots. For four hours the captives remained with the raiders and there was much conversation. Gilmor's men said the war was 'Old Abe's doing, and if they ever caught him they intended to tie him to a tree and make him kiss a nigger.' They did not think much of Union generals, but considered McClellan was the best of a bad lot.

Gilmor kept five Union officers including General Franklin as prisoners. Some of the Union officers escaped as they were in civilian clothes. Lieutenant Colonel Smith of the 8th Connecticut walked away while the guards were busy elsewhere. Several officers were turned loose by Harry Gilmor because they were Masons and wore an identifying breastpin. The brotherhood of Free Masonry was a cherished thing in the Civil War. Men frequently helped others of the fraternity when they were in difficulty.

A second train of twelve passenger cars had come up so the act repeated itself, even to the point of the engineer escaping. Gilmor was the soul of courtesy. He had the baggage of both trains unloaded at the nearby station, making certain that claim checks were available and sorted out. Then the cars were set afire and the flaming mass of the train backed out on the bridge. A burning engine and cars fell into the river as the bridge collapsed. A Union gunboat that could only watch had to raise anchor and move on. Harry continued his display of courtesy by signaling the gunboat that it could land and take passengers aboard. This was done.

Though some ungrateful passengers later reviled him, Harry Gilmor added new luster to the art of raiding. His gallantry was pure romance. Unfortunately the dashing cavalier had to put up with the 'stand and deliver' attitude of some of his troops. The *New York Herald* correspondent concluded his article by writing

> ...I am but performing an act of simple justice by stating that Major Harry Gilmor was not cognizant of the conduct of his men. He strictly prohibited all stealing from prisoners, but the event proved that the lawless troopers under his command could not be restrained from filching a purse or a watch when a fair opportunity presented itself.

Writing in the Saturday, July 16 1864 *New York Times* under the heading 'The Magnolia Raid', Surgeon N.P. Rice of the US Volunteers reported that he and his baggage were so thoroughly looted that when he arrived in New York City he had nothing left but a toothbrush and five paper collars picked up from the ground. Reid was outraged at the conduct of the women on the train who supported the Southern cause. He wrote:

> It is almost impossible to describe their conduct that day; their exuberant enthusiasm over the rebel flag; their familiar intercourse with the various rebel officers and soldiers. It is simply necessary to say that before he left, Major Gilmor had not a button left on his coat – all having been cut off to present to these friends.

Gilmor was on home ground and had many friends in the area. He determined to push on in the direction of Towsontown, 7 miles north of Baltimore. Locals told him the militia had been called out and the streets of Baltimore were being barricaded against him. At Towsontown, Gilmor was informed that a large force of cavalry was coming out of Baltimore to engage him. There was considerable concern in the ranks that this would be their last mission, but he kept the troops firm. In the dark of night, fifteen men were sent forward to meet the opposing horsemen and develop the situation. Gilmor followed close behind with the main body. When his advance was driven back, he ordered that every man yell at the top of his lungs and charge. The Union cavalry fled back to Baltimore. Gilmor was delighted to learn that his only casualty was a wounded horse.

As his men were exhausted, even sleeping and snoring in the saddle, Gilmor rode at the rear to collect stragglers. He was also tired and dozed off. When he awoke it was at the challenge of a Union picket. In the darkness, Gilmor posed as a Union scout while making his way clear. When he found his men they were sound asleep, including the hand-picked guard over General Franklin. The high-ranking prisoner had escaped. Gilmor wrote: 'I swore with unusual energy.'[53] Men were rousted out and began to search for Franklin, but were unsuccessful. All that was left was his valise of personal effects. Gilmor would make certain these were returned to Union lines.

Rest is critical to leadership. The need for sleep is the constant enemy of those who operate behind enemy lines. The exhaustion and tension of combat builds until the mind will not function. Duty requires men to press on. Sleep is a time of vulnerability, but in time the need for sleep overcomes all other considerations. Gilmor had gone beyond his limit and his eyes were closing while men talked with him. After sending out patrols, he gave in to nature and slept the night away. At sunrise, Gilmor was refreshed and led his command toward Rockville. En route, Gilmor learned that Early had withdrawn to Poolesville, then was going back south over the Potomac. Early had found the defenses of Washington more than he could handle. One of the forts his men had fired on was Fort Stevens. A Ranger from the Black Hawk War, President Abraham Lincoln stood under fire on a parapet of the fort, thus becoming the only serving United States president to participate in a battle while in office. General Jubal Early wrote in his report to Lee: 'Washington can never be taken by our troops unless surprised when without a force to defend it.'[54]

After riding through the day and the night that followed, Gilmor brought his men back to Early's command, rejoining the cavalry under General

Breckenridge. While Gilmor had been engaged, Maryland-born General Bradley Johnson had ordered the burning of the home of Maryland's governor Augustus W. Bradford. A detail of Maryland Confederates under the command of Lieutenant Blackstone of Maryland accomplished the mission. Johnson said it was 'in retaliation' for the burning of Virginia Governor John Letcher's home by General David Hunter.

Experiencing infrequent skirmishing, Gilmor's men moved from near Leesburg to the Shenandoah Valley at Rippon. Gilmor was still in charge of some 200 troops that comprised the 1st and 2nd Maryland Cavalry (Confederate). His small force was kept busy ranging to the front of Early's army. On July 26 he went via Martinsburg to Hedgesville, then on the 29th was ordered to make a reconnaissance of Potomac River fords. It was obvious to Gilmor that Early was planning another move north into Maryland. When General John McCausland's brigade came up, Gilmor came under McCausland's command. With Gilmor's men leading the way the Confederates crossed the Potomac at McCoy's Ford and were once again in Maryland.

Gilmor's mission was to clear the road for the Confederate main force. It was not long before the Maryland Confederates were engaged in stiff fighting with the 12th and 14th Pennsylvania Cavalry. Three of Gilmor's men were shot down. McCausland wanted to march via the village of Clear Spring to reach the road to Mercersburg. He ordered Gilmor to clear the Union troops from Clear Spring without delay. With skirmishers out front, Gilmor moved forward to find he was facing a strong position. To his left front the road was lined with a post-and-rail fence. There was open terrain in that area and Gilmor could see dismounted Union troops in linear fashion along the fence and beyond those some mounted cavalry. To Gilmor's right front at a greater range, a stone fence lined the road and behind that was a thick wood. Pressed for time, he reasoned that he could charge down the road firing into the flank of the dismounted troops and ride down the cavalry behind them.

Gilmor took the lead, with his men whooping and hollering as they galloped down the road with pistols blazing. As they passed the dismounted Union men, both sides exchanged heavy fire. Gilmor did not stop; he intended to get behind these blue-coated soldiers, rout their supporting troops and collapse the Union position. What he found, to his dismay, was that two squadrons of Union cavalry were waiting in ambush. As the Confederates galloped past the woods, a devastating fire struck them from the right flank. The command was immediately thrown into confusion with men falling wounded, crying out in pain, horses rearing and plunging as riders attempted to turn them. Gilmor's men turned and rode for their lives with the Union cavalry in hot pursuit. A unit may fight in large and famous battles and suffer few casualties, then suddenly get hit hard in some place none of the men have heard of. Seventeen Confederates were killed or wounded. With good reason, Gilmor wrote: 'I do not like to think of that fight.'[55]

That night Harry Gilmor overtook the main body of Early's army. All his men were exhausted. He had been without sleep for forty-six hours, yet the mission continued. After a brief stint of rearguard duty and brief rest, Gilmor was ordered to take his men into Chambersburg, Pennsylvania in advance of the army. Armies are armies. There was nothing more noble about the Confederate army than that of the Union. In their campaigns into the North, the Confederate army burned houses, stole property, took livestock and ransomed towns, all the while taking the self-serving position that it was only done in retaliation. In their holier-than-thou view, the men from the South were not to blame. It was all Union General David Hunter's fault. In Maryland, Gilmor's home state and that of his men, the Confederates went in singing *Maryland, My Maryland*, then ransomed Hagerstown for $20,000 and Frederick for $200,000. They wanted payment in gold or US greenbacks. General Jubal Early called the Maryland ransom money '...a contribution...'[56]

On July 30 1864, General Early's army moved into Pennsylvania. The town of Chambersburg was captured by the troops of General John McCausland. Early demanded the town hand over a ransom of $100,000 in gold or $500,000 in greenback currency or be burned. Gilmor wrote that people laughed and would not pay because they thought Union cavalry was near. The principal citizens arrested by Gilmor said they told him that 'there was not probably $50,000 currency at hand.'[57] Probably both stories are correct. Will Kochersperger, a sergeant of the 20th Pennsylvania Cavalry, was in Chambersburg. He talked to a member of the town council who said they would not pay 5 cents. Harry Gilmor was ordered to have his men apply the torch, while Confederate soldiers were permitted to ransack the town. McCausland had been beaten by Hunter at Lexington and was eager for revenge. He said that Hunter had burned property in Virginia (Hunter said that was in retaliation for bushwhacking of his outposts and wagon trains); McCausland's burning of Chambersburg was in retaliation. If there was a moral high ground between the two commanders it will be for others to distinguish.

Gilmor wrote: 'Deeply regretting that such a task should fall upon me, I had only to obey.'[58] His decision highlights the courage of Major Stearns, 1st New York Cavalry, who disobeyed Hunter's order to burn Newtown, Virginia. In the military, it is not easy to go against an order from one's commander. Harry Gilmor did not and his troops began to burn the houses. Gilmor wrote that he ordered his men to be kind to the women and children, to assist them and to see that no excesses were committed. According to eyewitness reports, some Confederates were outraged by the destruction and helped people, while others ran rampant.

What occurred at Chambersburg, Pennsylvania was described by Confederate General Bradley T. Johnson of Maryland in a report to the Confederate adjutant general:

> It is due to myself and the cause which I serve to remark on the outrageous conduct of the troops on this expedition. I informed General McCausland during the expedition that I should perform this duty. Every crime in the catalogue of infamy has been committed, I believe, except murder and rape. Highway robbery of watches and pocketbooks was of ordinary occurrence; the taking of breastpins, finger-rings and earrings frequently happened. Pillage and sack of private dwellings took place hourly. At Chambersburg, while the town was in flames, a quartermaster, aided and directed by a field officer, extracted ransom of individuals for their houses, holding the torch in terror over the house until it was paid. These ransoms were from $750.00 to $150.00, according to the size of the habitation. Thus the grand spectacle of a national retaliation was reduced to a miserable huckstering for greenbacks... drunken soldiers paraded the streets in every possible disguise and paraphernalia, pillaging and plundering and drunk. A soldier packed up a woman and child's clothing, which he had stolen, in the presence of the highest officials unrebuked.[59]

Under McCausland's orders, Harry Gilmor supervised the burning of Chambersburg. He spared one fine home. The lady who met him at the door was the wife of the colonel of the 1st New York Cavalry, William Boyd. Gilmor had been fighting against Boyd for several years and had a high respect for him. Gilmor wrote: 'I left a guard; and well I did, for an officer who had been drinking too much came up soon after, and tried to force the guard and burn down the house.'[60] Sergeant Will Kochersperger noted: 'When they left, nearly two-thirds of their party were in a state of intoxication, hardly capable of sitting on their horses.'[61]

McCausland headed off with a string of burned-out buildings behind him. When he reached Hancock, Maryland, McCausland attempted to ransom the town for $30,000. Gilmor and other Maryland officers and men were outraged. Gilmor noted that McCausland's Confederates were inclined to plunder. After talking with General Bradley Johnson, the Maryland men were determined to resist the offense to their state. The strange circumstance developed of Confederates protecting property from other Confederates; Gilmor stationed two men at each house and store for their protection. A confrontation did not occur as General William Averell's Union horsemen were in pursuit. They hurried McCausland south.

Gilmor commanded the rearguard action in Hancock. For the benefit of the onlooking ladies he played Horatio at the Bridge. There was no military reason for Harry Gilmor to sit on his horse in the open while bullets rained about him. In the process, his horse was wounded. The women of the town were pleading with him to move out of danger. Gilmor wrote: 'It is astonishing what perfect fools men will make of themselves when with these beauties.'[62]

From Hancock, McCausland moved to Cumberland where he was checked by Union General Benjamin F. Kelley. McCausland was in trouble. Gilmor described the situation as

> I cared not how soon we returned to Virginia. We had Kelley,
> with twice our force, in front in trenches; Averell coming up on
> our rear; the Potomac, seven or eight miles, off to the left; the
> mountains of Pennsylvania on our right, with our commanders
> not on the best terms with each other.[63]

Gilmor was assigned the mission of leading the Confederates out of the looming trap. To succeed, he needed a local guide to show the way. The only guide Gilmor could find supported the United States. A cocked pistol held at the man's ear was sufficient encouragement to help the Confederates. Gilmor's men moved toward the Potomac by night, leading the way for McCausland's troops. During the darkness they skirmished with Union pickets. At dawn Gilmor's advance was ambushed, suffering one man killed. Bradley Johnson came up with more troops. Near the bridge at Oldtown, the two Marylanders discussed the situation.

116

Union troops had possession of the Virginia side of the Potomac; there was no ford near that would bypass them. Union soldiers brought up a train with cars reinforced inside with railroad ties to form breastworks. The train included flat cars built up with railroad iron to protect emplaced artillery. The locomotive was in the center of this configuration. The guns of the armored train covered the ford and bridge approach to Oldtown. The weapons of the train were complemented by a large blockhouse with 100 men under the command of Colonel Stowe of Ohio. Supported by Bradley, Gilmor tried to ford the river, losing a dozen men before the south bank could be reached. Gilmor met with Bradley and McCausland. He told them it was critical that artillery be brought up to deal with the Union train.

Lieutenant McNulty's Baltimore Light Artillery put a shell through the boiler of the locomotive. Another shot went through a porthole, dismounting a gun on the train. That was enough for the troops on the train; they left their positions and ran.

Bradley Johnson sent a Virginia regiment against the blockhouse. The attackers suffered heavily as they were beaten back. It was decided to threaten to massacre the garrison if they did not surrender. Hearing this threat and believing it, the Union commander Colonel Stowe noted that the term of enlistment for most of his men was almost expired. Stowe sent a message to the Confederates that if the Union defenders would be immediately paroled, they would surrender. One man can make a difference. Had it not been for Colonel Stowe's lack of courage, Union generals Averell and Kelley would have been able to trap McCausland's force.

With Gilmor still ranging ahead, the Confederates crossed the river and headed in the direction of New Creek. After two days of skirmishing Gilmor described as useless, they moved to the Moorefield Valley of West Virginia. Gilmor was disgusted. He wrote that 'Most of the regiments were demoralized, principally because of the amount of plunder they were allowed to carry.'[64]

Averell caught up with McCausland at Moorefield, attacked and routed the Confederates early on the morning of August 7 1864. Gilmor was sleeping when awakened by a pistol shot. He found himself confronted by two men in Confederate uniform. One fired at Gilmor and called upon him to surrender. Gilmor shot him. The other soldier yelled that Gilmor was firing on his own men. Confused, Gilmor asked what command the man was from. The response was 'Captain Harry Gilmor's command.' Major Gilmor immediately knew he was facing a Union Ranger. He shot and killed the man. Averell's horsemen were right behind their Rangers. They rode down the Maryland men.

The rout was on with McCausland's men under the Union saber and pistol. The roads were strewn with loot taken from Pennsylvania and discarded in flight. Averell captured 3 battle flags, 4 pieces of artillery and took 420 prisoners including 38 officers. More than 400 horses and various equipment were part of the spoils. Union losses were seven killed and twenty-one wounded.[65] Gilmor alone lost six officers and forty-five men of his 2nd Maryland Cavalry and their battle flag. Harry's brother Richard and a cousin, William Gilmor, were taken prisoner.

Around August 12, what was left of Gilmor's command moved to Fisher's Hill to join Early's army. As is frequent with Ranger units, Gilmor was put close to Early's headquarters. This provides additional security to the headquarters, plus the men are immediately available to go out on reconnaissance or other missions as the commander desires. General Lunsford L. Lomax was now commander of Confederate cavalry in the valley, with Gilmor serving under his direction.

General Phil Sheridan was now in command of the Union forces in the Shenandoah Valley. Observing the movements of Confederate units to his front and east, Sheridan decided to withdraw from Strasburg to Winchester. Confederate Jubal Early promptly moved to follow Sheridan. For a change, Gilmor was assigned the rearguard duty of rounding up stragglers. That would not do for Harry Gilmor. Putting his men in charge of a junior officer, he rode to the front of the column where he was accepted as a volunteer on General Ramseur's staff. While carrying a message during a battle, Gilmor drew not-so-friendly friendly fire from Georgia troops and his horse was killed. He confiscated the horse of a captured New Jersey officer. During this fight Gilmor captured some twenty-five Union soldiers by riding among them shouting out commands to imaginary units. Success emboldened him to call for the surrender of a company from the 1st New Jersey Cavalry. The lieutenant in command of the unit was bluffed and surrendered some forty-eight men to Gilmor and one of his riders.

About August 24 1864, Gilmor took part in an attack near Charleston. In this action he was given command of the 19th and 20th Virginians plus his Marylanders. Taking a good defensive stance, he held the position in an attack by the 12th Pennsylvania Cavalry. Colonel William Bell, commander of the 12th Pennsylvania Cavalry, was mortally wounded in the attack. The adjutant of the 12th was the son of Pennsylvania's Governor Curtin. When young Curtin's horse was killed, he mounted Colonel Bell's splendid charger. Gilmor wounded the horse and took Curtin prisoner. After recovery from its wound, the horse was given to General Lomax. The Confederates withdrew to Charleston. They spent three days in reorganization while Gilmor's command continued patrolling through August 27. The many fights had taken a toll of their strength. Only 175 men were fit for duty in the 1st and 2nd Maryland battalions.

Trying to regain the initiative, Generals Lomax and Fitz Lee sought to again cross the Potomac into Maryland. Gilmor was sent to Falling Waters. His orders were to attack any Union pickets on the south side of the river and if possible to cross, take possession of the town of Williamsport, then hold it until Fitz Lee could make the river crossing. The Union pickets were driven off after a stiff fight that cost the Confederates one dead and three wounded. The arrival of a large force of Union cavalry ended this plan to cross to the north bank of the Potomac.

Gilmor was next ordered into an assembly area with the cavalry divisions of Lomax and Fitz Lee. While the troops and horses were eating, Harry Gilmor was called to a meeting with General Lomax. At Lomax's headquarters he learned that a force of 200 Union cavalry was attacking Confederate lines near Leetown. The Union riders were making a considerable nuisance of themselves, disrupting the Confederate picket line. Gilmor was ordered to relieve the Confederates on picket duty and drive off the blue-coated horsemen. Once more, Gilmor's bugler sounded the call to mount and ride. Gilmor led out on the Smithfield to Leetown road. He had not proceeded more than a mile and a half when he encountered the Confederate regiment of Colonel Evans that was on picket duty. Gilmor and Evans agreed that after being relieved, Evans force would form to the left while Gilmor sent skirmishers forward on the right to cover the withdrawal back to the main line. Holding the 1st Maryland in reserve, Gilmor sent the 2nd Maryland forward. However, before the relief could be effected Union horsemen of the 6th US Cavalry attacked Evans' men.

Gilmor counter-attacked with the 2nd Maryland. As it seemed the battle was swinging in his favor, a swarm of Union cavalry appeared. They were riders of George Custer's and Thomas Devin's brigades seeking a way to raid the Confederate rear.

The routed Confederates ran for some 3 miles, mixed with their pursuers in what Gilmor called 'this scene of horror.'[66] Riding at a gallop, men were cursing and shouting amid the clash of steel on steel as sabers met and the sharp crack of pistol-fire rent the air. Men emptied the chambers of their revolvers at each other, then used them as clubs. Gilmor's revolver was empty when a Union officer charged him, put a pistol against his side and pulled the trigger. The hammer fell on an empty chamber. Gilmor delivered a blow with the saber that knocked his opponent from the saddle. The officer jumped to his feet, only to have another Confederate shoot him through the head. Waiting in reserve, the 1st Maryland Cavalry was swept up in the flight that continued to within a mile of Smithfield. The Union cavalry then broke off the attack, contenting themselves with firing artillery after the Confederates. Gilmor mourned the loss of twenty-six more of his men. The scouts Lomax had sent to the front had not gone far enough. They had missed the critical information that Sheridan's cavalry was moving forward. Lomax and Fitz Lee were forced to withdraw. In the fight, Gilmor's cousin Hoffman Gilmor was shot in the arm at the junction with the shoulder. Sent to Winchester, it would be months before the young man could recover.

Skirmishing continued, with the tide of war rising against the Confederates. The Union cavalry arm was ever improving in arms, power and confidence. As their numbers declined, the Confederates tried to maintain the offensive, using attack to maintain a viable defense. On September 3 1864, Lomax, with three brigades of Virginia cavalry, struck William Averell's division near Bunker Hill. These Confederates were armed with single-shot Enfield rifles. In Gilmor's opinion these were useless to mounted men. Harry Gilmor said he would 'rather command a regiment armed with good oaken clubs.'[67]

The attack was slow in gathering momentum, with Union pickets preventing the location of Averell's lines. Gilmor was ordered to take his men forward on reconnaissance to find the enemy. When he made contact, Gilmor used fire and maneuver, with one element pinning the enemy with fire while the other flanked a position. Gilmor's men forced the picket line back to its reserve camp on the edge of a wood. There was food here: pickled pork and biscuit. The withdrawing Union pickets tried to burn this, but the effort only gave the hungry Confederates a hot breakfast. With ammunition almost exhausted, Gilmor came up against Averell's forward positions about half a mile from Darkesville. The point of Confederate advance found itself facing what Gilmor estimated at two regiments armed with seven-shot Spencer carbines. The Union troops were on a ridge line behind a fence-rail barricade. Their line covered the road and was well established, with the flanks securely anchored. To the front were three open fields separated by beaten-up fences.

Gilmor called for reinforcement. He was sent the 18th Virginia Cavalry from Imboden's brigade. This regiment, the pride of John Imboden, did not rate highly with Harry Gilmor. In Gilmor's opinion, the 18th Virginia Cavalry 'had probably the worst reputation of any in the valley.'[68] Gilmor thought it was the fault of the officers of the 18th (several of whom outranked him), that the regiment had problems. General Lomax felt that Gilmor had experienced the terrain and knew the situation best. Lomax held the two Maryland battalions in position and put Gilmor in temporary command of the 18th Virginians.

Leaving the senior officers of the 18th behind with a squadron to serve as a reserve, Gilmor formed the men in a single mounted line and advanced under fire. The first field was crossed at a walk and the fence taken down. They passed over the second field at a trot, halted and took down the fence. By this time some six men and a dozen horses had been shot. They re-formed and moved forward, passing from walk to trot to gallop. As they closed on the Union position they had to leap the barricade. Many men were hurt by their horses falling on them. The Union cavalry withdrew to their horse-holders and rode off. Gilmor claimed that while no Union soldiers were killed, he pursued them to Darkesville and captured some forty men.

Beyond Darkesville was Averell's main line. Union horsemen were soon on the attack. They forced the Confederates back, first to the barricade, then into a general withdrawal to Bunker Hill. Gilmor now had the 1st and 2nd Maryland and 18th Virginia Cavalry under his command. A furious fight occurred at a stream crossing with the Confederates having to cross under heavy fire. They then turned on the Union horsemen who were closest behind. Gilmor claimed thirty-six Union casualties were suffered here. The 18th Virginians were withdrawn to rejoin Lomax as Gilmor sought to hold the crossing. Artillery support was needed but, when Confederate artillery opened fire, the shells fell among the 1st and 2nd Marylands, killing two and wounding five men. Gilmor asked for an adjustment of fire and got it. Now the shells exploded directly over their heads. Routed by friendly fire, Gilmor withdrew his men.

The battle was a swirl of men, now charging, then retreating, re-forming and charging again. Gilmor led a charge. When he looked over his shoulder it was to find that fewer than a dozen men were following. Gilmor was furious that he was not receiving support from the Virginia troops. He claimed he later heard that Lomax told the Virginians, 'Are you not ashamed, to see a handful of Marylanders cut to pieces fighting for your state, while like a pack of cowards, you stand off and refuse to assist them?'[69]

Gilmor was waving his saber over his head, encouraging his men, when he felt the impact of a bullet. The shot had come from the side, hitting him in the left shoulder. The bullet broke the shoulder blade near the joint, then continued on to break the collarbone and pass into the neck. Then the bullet came out under the jaw, narrowly missing severing the carotid artery. Gilmor tried to hold his seat in the saddle and encourage his men to attack, but his wound was too severe. With the aid of General Lomax, he was placed in an ambulance to suffer the jolting and jarring of the ride to the York Hospital in Winchester. His wound proved not to be life-threatening. As the groans of those whose limbs had been amputated prevented his rest, Gilmor made his way to the home of a widow he knew. There he was solicitously nursed back to health by the lady and her two attractive nieces. The sight of a woman always lifted Harry Gilmor's sprits. Recuperation in these surroundings was good duty. Gilmor gushed: 'The three weeks of physical suffering spent in that house were among the happiest of my life.'

Visitors came to Gilmor's side, among them General Lomax who told Harry that he had consolidated the two under-strength Maryland battalions. They would be under Harry Gilmor's command. Not all the 1st Marylands liked this arrangement and some officers resigned. Gilmor gave orders from his bed. He said that his Marylanders did most of the scouting for the army. Riders visited frequently, keeping him well-informed of events. The news they brought was not good.

For an attacking force, a ratio of three to one odds in strength is desirable. Sheridan had achieved that number and more. On Monday, September 19 1864, Sheridan's horsemen under General Torbert crossed the Opequon Creek north of Winchester to take the Confederates in the flank. Meanwhile, Sheridan's infantry struck Early's soldiers, driving back the Southern troops along the Berryville pike and killing Confederate General Robert Rodes. In Winchester, all was confusion. Early's Confederates were in flight. Barefoot and dressed in a loose calico shirt slit up the back by his nurses, Gilmor made his way downstairs. He saw 'a scene of flight and confusion.... Troops of all kinds were dashing through the streets in the wildest manner, and though many ambulances passed, not one could be induced to stop.'[70] One of the young women ran from the house and, seizing the bridle of a passing officer's horse, asked the rider if he would help a fellow Confederate officer. To the good fortune of Harry Gilmor, the rider was Lieutenant Mason McNew of Company B, 1st Maryland Cavalry. McNew generously gave up his horse to Gilmor. Without time to adjust stirrup length, Gilmor hauled himself upon the horse, then rode to Sheep Hill where the Confederates were trying to rally.

At Sheep Hill, Gilmor found an ambulance to ride as a patient to Kernstown. He ordered that McNew's horse be taken back to him, then spent the night laying on the floor of a house among many wounded and weary soldiers. The angels of mercy that were the women of the South moved among the groaning men, tending as best they could the wounds of battle and spirit.

In the Civil War many men would experience the efforts of women to be of assistance. General John Gordon told the story of a beautiful Southern girl who was helping in the hospitals and asked a badly wounded soldier if she could do anything for him. The young man told her it was too late; that he had not long to live. The girl said: 'Will you let me pray for you? I hope that I am one of the Lord's daughters, and I would like to ask him to help you.' The soldier looked at her lovely face and replied: 'Yes, pray at once and ask the Lord to let me be his son-in-law.'[71]

Early's army was running. Gilmor saw a Confederate wagon train galloping by with wagons three abreast. An officer said that the enemy was only fifteen minutes behind. Again, Gilmor could not get an ambulance to stop. Again, a passing man of the Maryland cavalry gave up his horse to the well-known Ranger. Gilmor rode the 8 miles from Kernstown to Newtown, arriving at about 10.00 pm. Sick and feverish, he went to the house of a friend he called 'Aunt Mary'; there several of the young women helped him dismount and put him to bed. Generals Early and Lomax took time to stop by. They made certain that Gilmor received an ambulance. Once more he rode as a patient, this time to Woodstock, then Mount Airy. Again, ladies took him in, Gilmor was put to bed and cared for.

On Thursday, September 22 1864, Sheridan routed Early at Fisher's Hill. Gilmor once again was forced to flee. Accompanied by his nurses, he attempted to clear the Union line of march, seeking to get over the Blue Ridge Mountains into Nelson County. Jubal Early counter-attacked and Sheridan withdrew. Gilmor came back across the mountain, riding to Staunton. He was appalled by the destruction he saw. General U.S. Grant was determined to break the will of the South; to deprive the Southern armies of their support base by placing such hardship on the populace that they must devote their energy to survival, not support of the Confederate army. Gilmor wrote: 'I found all the barns, stack-yards and, in some places, the dwellings burned, and the people destitute of everything.'[72] Grant's policy was working. Harry Gilmor was hungry, but the only thing he could find to eat was a cake made of chopped horse feed.

The Confederate retaliation was to kill any Union soldier they caught burning. Gilmor said that of one group of twenty-eight Northern soldiers, none escaped with their lives. Harry made a triumphal entry into Staunton and set hearts to fluttering. He wrote: 'All were delighted to see me back again and, being wounded, I got many a kiss from pretty girls, and without much pressing; they did not fight hard, for fear of hurting my wound.'

He rode on to Newmarket where ladies told them a Union Ranger in Confederate uniform had gleefully told the women that he had dinner with Harry at the American Hotel in Staunton. Gilmor had not suspected the man. The Union Ranger, while an efficient scout, had the common failing of a man talking freely with women. Gilmor knew from what the women told him that the Confederate dispositions had been thoroughly scouted.

Confederate counter-attacks met with success until October 9. George Armstrong Custer, who was now a division commander, joined with Wesley Merritt's division in routing Rosser and Lomax. Confederate morale was cracking. Gilmor saw Generals Lomax and Johnson begging men to stand and fight in a futile effort to rally their troops, then the two generals charged forward with only a few men in support. The running fights were chaos.

Lieutenant McNew of the Baltimore Light Artillery could not get cavalry to stay with him long enough to give security to his guns. Seeing that capture would occur, Gilmor suggested one gun give covering fire to allow three to escape. A fleeing Confederate horseman rode over a loader. Before the gun could be fired, the Union cavalry were on them, swinging their sabers. The gun and gunners were captured. Gilmor was forced to surrender to a Michigan trooper who wanted to follow the practice of 'going through' a captured opponent, taking his belongings. Fortunately for Gilmor, the Union cavalry commander ordered the prisoners left behind for follow-on units and directed another charge.

Gilmor took a stray horse and rode for safety. He was riding hard with a Union soldier mounted on a beautiful but runaway horse beside him. Neither man could fight. Gilmor had surrendered his weapons. The Union soldier was trying to control his frantic animal. A Confederate courier rode close behind the Union soldier and put a revolver bullet in his brain. The Confederate and Union horsemen were so scattered and intermixed that Gilmor heard Union cavalry commander General Alfred Torbert give the command to cease the pursuit and re-form.

Harry Gilmor had tried hard to encourage Maryland men to support the Confederacy. Many including Phil Sheridan thought that Gilmor was the likely man to lure this border state to the Stars and Bars. By October 1864 that Confederate flame of hope was but a flicker. Now came the news that in a close vote, Maryland had voted to abolish slavery. Rumors were rampant. One that persisted was that many of Sheridan's troops had been pulled from the valley and sent to assist Grant against Lee. Early's scouts were unable to refute this. Though his left arm was still in a sling, Harry Gilmor decided to make a reconnaissance into Sheridan's army from the east. To get into Union lines, Gilmor needed to ride into what he called 'Mosby's Settlements'.[73] This was a reference to those portions of Loudoun and Fauquier Counties in Virginia that were increasingly being known as 'Mosby's Confederacy'. On October 13 Mosby had derailed a B&O train. He captured two US army paymasters with more than $170,000 in what would be known as the 'Greenback Raid'.

Going east, Gilmor found a handful of his Maryland men who were enjoying themselves by skirmishing in more even-handed battles with Union pickets. Gilmor's mission was to get information. He instructed his men not to engage any Union force larger than fifteen men. Despite a wound that was oozing pus, Gilmor led his men, circling westward across the Shenandoah River and into the rear of Sheridan's army. The weather was inclement so Gilmor made best use of the rain. The Union army had issued thousands of oilcloth ponchos to their men. When taken from Union soldiers, the ponchos were also worn by Confederate troops and fully covered their uniform. As dark hats were often worn, it was impossible to tell which side a man belonged to.

According to Gilmor, they rode up behind a company of Union cavalry led by an officer. Gilmor sent one of the men forward who had applejack in his canteen. Posing as one of Union Captain Richard Blazer's Rangers, the Confederate offered the officer a drink. The officer was then given the opportunity to fill his canteen at the rear of the column. When he rode back among Gilmor's men, he was taken prisoner. Gilmor related that his other troops went forward one or two at a time to offer the Union horsemen drinks of applejack and by this means took thirteen prisoners. According to Gilmor, they called this 'taking 'em in out of the wet'.[74]

Likely as a result of the captures, Gilmor's men now had blue overcoats. It was not unusual for Confederate Rangers to wear them as they were issued none by their own government. It was a chilly fall, so Gilmor's men frequently wore the overcoats. While so dressed they encountered four Union soldiers who, thinking they were talking to other Union troops, said they were some of Blazer's men on their way to vote for Abraham Lincoln in the presidential election. Union troops voted strongly to support President Lincoln. Gilmor told the four men his command was part of the Union cavalry and his story was believed. When they relaxed, these unsuspecting men were also taken prisoner. According to Gilmor, he was able to use their papers and ballots to go into Sheridan's camp, where he and others voted. They considered McClellan a good general so they voted for Abraham Lincoln.[75]

Gilmor brought back the information to Early that Sheridan was not leaving the valley; a report Sheridan would soon verify by action. Gilmor was sent out again after Sheridan's Rangers and unknown people who were committing murders and robberies. There were deserters from both armies who used war as an opportunity for private gain. Gilmor came close, but did not succeed on either count. The weather turned so cold that he could not remain in the mountains. The thought of women in Shepherdstown was sufficient to warm Harry Gilmor's blood. He rode into the town and visited with some ladies he knew. They were afraid for his safety in a Union town so Gilmor decided to show off. He related that he stood in the doorway (obviously with his uniform covered by a blue overcoat or poncho), and gave orders to a passing Union squad. He told the senior man to go to the guard-house and tell the officer there to 'send a squad immediately to a certain low drinking-house, and arrest some men who were creating a disturbance.'[76]

On November 10 1864, Gilmor and his men left from near Shepherdstown at midnight to continue their scouting mission. By morning they had covered some 30 miles and were riding off road, but on trails and through a thick forest. It was in the woods that they came upon Union Captain Richard Blazer's men lying concealed. Gilmor reported some sixty Union soldiers which was about the total of Blazer's unit. In this war of Ranger against Ranger, Blazer and his men were an all-volunteer organization who ranged outward, hunting in particular for John Singleton Mosby, Bill Thurmond and other Confederate Rangers.

Had sixty Union Rangers been in an ambush position, the Gilmor story would likely have ended. More likely Blazer's men were in a bivouac area, resting after a night of searching. Gilmor and his men squeezed off six rounds, hitting two of Blazer's men, then broke contact and rode for safety. They were hotly pursued for some 5 to 6 miles with Gilmor leading the cross-country flight. Mounted on his reliable horse 'Old Bill', Gilmor chose horsemanship as the means of escape. He led his men on a difficult cross-country route, jumping the stone walls that girdled farm fields and ditches. At a staked fence Gilmor made the leap, but the horses of his men could not follow. He turned back to re-jump the fence, but this time Old Bill lost his footing and horse and rider fell heavily. Gilmor was knocked unconscious. His men brought him off to the house of a friend. Gilmor was severely bruised. His wound reopened and he would be in pain for several days.

On the morning of November 12 Gilmor could hear firing. He learned that his commander General Early was at Strasburg trying to counter-attack. Though he and his horse were stiff from their fall, Gilmor mounted and made his way through Union patrols. He rejoined Early near Newtown and briefed the general on what he had seen while ranging the countryside.

In weakened physical condition, Gilmor went to Mount Airy for several days to rest. It was predictable that he would find a woman or women. In this case General Sherman had allowed two young females to pass through his lines to go to Columbia, South Carolina. The gallant Gilmor became their escort and experienced what Harry Gilmor called 'a most delightful trip'. They traveled to Lexington, Lynchburg, Richmond and Columbia, South Carolina, arriving in South Carolina's capital city around December 12 1864. Here Harry Gilmor indulged himself in a week of pleasure.[77] While in Columbia, Gilmor had the opportunity to meet South Carolina governor and part-time general, Milledge L. Bonham. It is deadly to a general and advantageous to a politician to be forgetful; Bonham excelled at the latter. When home on leave from the army in 1861 he saw a boy and said 'Hello Bill, how's your pa?' 'He is dead sir,' replied the boy. Later that day Bonham saw the boy again and said 'Hello Bill, how's your pa?' 'Still dead sir,' was the reply.[78]

Leaving his female companions in Columbia, Gilmor went via Richmond to Staunton. Reporting to General Early, Gilmor was ordered to take his command to Western Virginia. Early was issuing Gilmor orders that would be controversial. They were put in writing by Special Order No. 137 which read:

> Major H. Gilmor will take his battalion to Hardy County, for the purpose of operating in that and adjoining counties. The companies of McNeill and Woodson, already there, will report to Major Gilmor, and will be permanently under his command.
>
> J.A. Early
> Lieut. Gen. Commanding Army of Valley District.[79]

The problem with this order was that it was not well-received in Western Virginia. Hardy County was the home turf of McNeill's Rangers. They were accustomed to deciding who their leaders would be. On arrival at his new command, Gilmor found he was not welcome. Confederate Ranger John Hanson McNeill had been killed, but his hot-blooded son Jesse and the capable Lieutenant Isaac Welton were rivals to replace the deceased leader. McNeill's Rangers had been fighting well, knew their home territory far better than any outsider, and felt they had earned and been promised by the Confederate government that they would be an independent command.

Unable to get cooperation, Harry Gilmor complained to his commander. General Jubal Early was furious that McNeill's Rangers would dare to question his orders and took the opportunity to lash out at all Ranger activities. On January 31 1865, Early wrote Robert E. Lee from Staunton:

> General R.E. Lee
> Commanding Army of Northern Virginia
> GENERAL: I wish you would get the Secretary of War to revoke the exemption granted McNeill's company from the operation of the act abolishing partisan Rangers. This command has refused to acknowledge Major Gilmor's authority, whom I have found it necessary to send to Hardy to take charge of McNeill's and Woodson's companies and the remnant of his own battalion. One of my principal objects in this was that he might cut the railroad and impede the passage of troops over it, and this has been thwarted by the refusal of these companies to acknowledge his authority. The fact is that all those independent organizations, not excepting Mosby's, are injurious to us, and the occasional dashes they make do not compensate for the disorganization and dissatisfaction produced among the other troops.
>
> Very Respectfully
> J.A. Early
> Lieutenant-General[80]

On February 3 1865, Lee forwarded the recommendation to the Secretary of War and added his request that McNeill's Rangers be removed from the provisions of the Partisan Ranger Act.

Gilmor had some 100 men of his own command. He was counting on adding 200 Rangers from Western Virginia. He maintained ties with Confederate sympathizers in Maryland, actively seeking more recruits from his home state. The feeling of local community was strong in Hardy County. Gilmor was an outsider. It would take time and success to build a feeling of unity between the Marylanders and the men of Western Virginia. In 1865, the Confederacy had little time or success.

Harry Gilmor did what he could to recruit and equip the men while he waited for a break in a winter of terrible cold. Numerous Confederate deserters roamed the countryside, creating an additional danger. Gilmor ordered out pickets and patrols. These were not properly supervised. Unless leaders are willing to go where they send men, patrols and outposts soon make themselves as comfortable as possible. There were cabins in the mountains where warm fires crackled in the hearths. It was more comfortable there than freezing by the side of a snow-covered trail.

In the small hours of Sunday, February 4 1865, Harry Gilmor and his cousin Hoffman were tucked up in a warm bed and fast asleep. Whatever dreams Gilmor was having were interrupted when he woke to find himself looking into the muzzle of a revolver. Ranger met Ranger as the man on the trigger end of the weapon was Major Henry K. Young, commander of the select band of Phil Sheridan's scouts.

Hustled into captivity, Harry Gilmor was provided a special escort commanded by Major Young who, though friendly, was watchful. General Phil Sheridan gave his opponent praise when he wrote of Gilmor: 'He is an energetic, shrewd, and unscrupulous scoundrel and a dangerous man. He must be closely watched, or he will escape.'[81]

Gilmor was taken to Fort Warren in Boston and sat out the remainder of the war in prison. Having a taste for adventure, fine food and wine and doting on a social life, Harry found prison life irksome. He maintained a rather forlorn hope that he would be exchanged, but there was little chance he would be allowed back in action. As the South collapsed, Gilmor found '...thanks to our fair guardians in Boston, the time...was made to pass more pleasantly by frequent presents of strawberries, currants, and other delicacies to us.'[82] Were these unusual presents coming from hard-bitten prison guards or does 'fair guardians' represent contact with the women of Boston? With Harry Gilmor, nothing was impossible.

Released on July 24 1865, Harry Gilmor took the oath of allegiance. For a time he lived in New Orleans and in 1866 published his memoirs entitled *Four Years in the Saddle*; these have been criticized as being too self-centered, but they are 'his' story. If the times had permitted free literary expression regarding sexual activity, Harry Gilmor might have added a whole new dimension to the record of the Civil War years.

As his heart was in Maryland, Harry Gilmor returned home. He married Mentoria Nixon Strong. He was police commissioner of Baltimore from 1874 to 1879 and a colonel in the Maryland National Guard. He died on March 4, 1883.[83] Gilmor was aged only 45 when he died, likely from the lingering effects of his wounds. He is buried in Loudon Park Cemetery in Baltimore.

Chapter 9

Elijah V. White and the Comanches

Elijah Viers White was born near Poolesville, Montgomery County, Maryland on August 29 1832. As a youth he spent four years in the North, two attending Lima Seminary in Livingston County, New York and two at Greenville College in Licking County, Ohio.[1] White grew to be a strong-featured man, 5ft 11in tall, fair-complexioned with blue eyes and light hair. His nickname was 'Lige'. Despite his time in abolition country, Lige White was a dedicated adherent to the practice of slavery. He cared sufficiently that in 1855/56 he went to Kansas where he joined a group of Missourians who were abolitionists. Leaving this contentious and murderous strife, he returned to Maryland and in 1857 he settled on a farm by the Potomac River in Loudoun County, Virginia. On December 9 1857 he married Sarah E. Gott. White secured a few slaves and farmed while the tensions of war were building.

Like most young men of his area and station, White belonged to a militia unit, serving as a corporal in Captain Shreve's Loudoun Cavalry. He was one of those who responded to the 1859 John Brown raid at nearby Harpers Ferry. When war began, White left the Loudoun Cavalry to begin service in Mason's Rangers, a unit organized in June 1861 and comprising Maryland men under the command of Captain (Dr) Frank Mason.[2]

This organization became part of Angus McDonald's and Turner Ashby's 7th Virginia Cavalry. White proved to be a superb scout. On a patrol in Maryland he may have captured the first northern prisoner of the war, a lieutenant named Costine who was an officer on Union General McCall's staff.[3]

While on these scouting activities he was occasionally joined by another young Maryland adventurer, Harry Gilmor. White's home was very close to Leesburg and the Potomac River. There were militarily important ferries over the river near Leesburg. Union commander General McClellan had suggested a 'slight demonstration', so on Monday, October 31 1861, his subordinate, Brigadier General Charles Stone, sent troops across to Virginia in the vicinity of Ball's Bluff. The Union troops were under the command of Colonel Edward D. Baker, a senator from Oregon. Baker was one of President Lincoln's closest friends, and an ardent supporter of the president. Initially the attack was successful, but in the afternoon Baker was killed and the Union troops routed. Their retreat over the steep bluff found many of them stranded without boats. The Union suffered almost 1,000 casualties. Though not an officer, Lige White played a significant role in the Confederate success. This was his local area, he knew the terrain, he was an experienced scout and had courage. White guided the 18th Mississippi to successful action, won a shoot-out with a Union soldier, then in darkness scouted the Union situation. He found Union soldiers trapped below Ball's Bluff trying to get back to the Maryland shore. White gathered a group of volunteers, primarily from the 8th Virginians, and led the Confederates back to the edge of the bluff where they fired into the men below until surrender was obtained. Some 320 Union soldiers surrendered.[4]

For this service, White was recommended for a commission in the Confederate army. He was told there were no vacancies, but that his name would go on the waiting list. White declined this. On the advice of Colonel Eppa Hunton, the Confederate commander at Ball's Bluff, White applied for a captain's commission in the provisional army. The commission was granted. White was authorized to raise a company to perform ranging service on the Maryland/Virginia border.

White started his career as a Ranger leader in December 1861 with fifteen men. His first duty was courier service providing a link of riders between Leesburg and Winchester. One of the men who joined him was a young firebrand, a fellow Marylander named Frank M. Myers. Carrying a deep hatred of anything Northern, Myers became White's principal lieutenant. In later years he would be the unit historian. Born as an independent unit, White's command consisted of about twenty-five men. On January 11 1862, they were enlisted for the war.[5]

Much to their disgust, White and his men were mustered into regular service on October 28 1863 as the 35th Battalion, Virginia Cavalry. Later General Thomas Rosser gave them the nickname 'The Comanches' for the manner in which they charged, yelling war cries. Raised in the Loudoun County border area with Maryland, the unit included men from both states on their rolls. They were often required to serve as an integral unit of the army. When given freedom of action they operated in much the same area and manner as Mosby's Rangers. Union reports frequently refer to both Mosby's and White's men and the Northern soldiers were under the erroneous belief that both these Ranger commanders coordinated their actions.[6] Confederate reports do not show any significant coordination between the organizations of Mosby and White.

In January 1862, White's small command moved to Waterford in northern Loudoun County. Waterford was a Virginia community (primarily German and Quaker), and few Waterford men believed in slavery or secession. White's Rangers had the disagreeable duty of rounding up militia men who did not report for duty. The duty required those who would not serve because of their religious belief to pay exemption fines. White was also ordered to range Loudoun and Fauquier Counties to impress wagons and slaves for use by the army. Loyalty was put to the test as farmers were required to surrender what they held as their rightful property.

White executed these contentious duties, but sought to get into the fight. On his own, he scouted the Potomac River crossings looking for line crossers and preventing slaves from escaping. On occasion he crossed over the river and scouted the Union camps. These efforts did not provide a rich haul of captures, but were of great benefit in training White and those who would later be his key men.

Disgusted with the inertia of his commander, President Lincoln ordered General McClellan to get his army moving south with Saturday, 22 February 1862 as the effective date. Confederate lines began withdrawing before McClellan's elephantine movement. White's Rangers left Waterford for Leesburg on Tuesday, March 4 1862. The route took them through the Catoctin Mountains. From these heights they could see the Confederate army pulling back, leaving a wasteland behind them. Mills, woodyards and crops that would benefit the Union army were being burned. The sight of the destruction was sobering. War was no longer a game. The rich lands of Loudoun County were suffering at the hands of their own men, the first of many trampled by armies engaged in the waste of war.

The Confederate army evacuated Leesburg, but White got permission to remain behind for a few days. The Union advance was glacial. Seeing no activity, White left Leesburg. Soon thereafter, the arrival of Union troops brought into the open those who supported the United States. The arrest of key Confederate sympathizers occupied the attention of Union cavalry.

White took his small command southward to link up with Colonel Thomas Munford, who was operating with four companies of cavalry along the Loudoun-Fauquier Counties' border. At Rector's Crossroads, White attacked a Union picket of about half a dozen men who withdrew toward Middleburg. At this town White's men killed one Union soldier and wounded another. Thanks to a timely warning by a townsman, they narrowly escaped being ambushed by the 28th Pennsylvania Infantry. White followed this action with a raid at Salem where his men captured the baggage train of that Pennsylvania regiment.

In late April 1862, White was ordered to report to General Richard Ewell for scout and courier duty. White and his men arrived at Liberty Mills on May 1 1862. They were assigned as part of Ewell's force, joining General Thomas Jackson in the valley. Ewell, who was older and always referred to by Jackson as 'Old Ewell', told Richard Taylor that he admired Jackson's genius, but was certain of his lunacy and that he never saw one of Jackson's couriers approach without expecting an order to assault the North Pole.[7] A gruff old soldier who had an acid wit, Dick Ewell exercised a firm discipline that had his men in terror. Any who used the expression 'Don't know' to Ewell would feel that their hide was being flayed from them. Ewell had seen long service in Indian country. He had brought east an Apache Indian boy in a semi-adopted state. Ewell doted on the boy. Taking a character from *Robinson Crusoe*, Ewell called the youth 'Friday'. Myers called him 'the ugliest, dirtiest and most aggravating and thievish little wretch.[8] Richard 'Dick' Ewell would rise to be a lieutenant general in the Confederate army. He had graduated from West Point in 1840 and, except for the Mexican War, spent his years in small frontier posts where Ewell said he had 'learned all about commanding fifty United States dragoons, and forgotten everything else.'[9]

Jackson set out to make a probe on Union General Milroy's force, leaving Ewell's 8,000 to hold the line against the Union forces of Banks and Shields. They did not attack, but Ewell was naturally anxious and snappish. Anxious for a kindly face, White's men were glad to see their old friend Colonel Munford who commanded Ewell's horsemen of the 2nd and 6th Virginia Cavalry.

Subordinate commanders were finding service under Richard Ewell required the utmost of tact. The general was quick to show his temper. Ewell ordered Munford on a mission. Just before departure at midnight, Munford went to see Ewell to check for last-minute instructions. Ewell was upstairs in bed in a nightshirt but leaped from under the covers. The general threw a map on the floor, got down on his knees and by the light of a lard lamp read it. Munford thought Ewell's bald head and long beard made him look more like a witch than a major general. Ewell was talking excitedly, describing Jackson as 'a great wagon hunter'. While the two officers were talking, a courier came looking for Munford. The soldier's saber was improperly fastened and banged on each of the steps as he came to Ewell's quarters. When the courier knocked at the door and said he was looking for Colonel Munford, Ewell let him in and told the man to light another lamp:

> 'Look under the bed,' snarled the major general to the startled courier. 'Do you see him there? Do you know how many steps you came up?' 'No Sir,' replied the courier. 'Well I do,' growled Ewell, 'by every lick you gave them with that *thing* you have hanging about your feet, which should be hooked up when you come *to my quarters*. Do you know how many *ears you have*? You will go out of here less *one and maybe both* if you ever wake me up this time anight looking for your *Colonel*.'[10]

Later the terrified courier begged Munford never to send him to General Ewell again.

In mid-May 1862 White led a scout consisting of some of his own men and a detachment of the 16th Mississippi Infantry. After a time most of this party was sent back to camp. White and a few other men continued on. They passed into Union lines, where one more man was sent back with information. White, Myers and Captain Brown of the 16th Mississippis reached the house of a Mr Rhodes and convinced the family they were Confederates. At the Rhodes' house, they were fed and given information about two Union cavalrymen at a nearby house, collecting horses. Moving quietly on foot, the three Confederates captured the two Union soldiers and their horses.

White sent Myers and Brown back to get the Ranger horses while he took the two prisoners to another location. Union Rangers wearing Confederate uniform were operating in the area. The locals were suspicious of everyone. At this point in the war, there were still men in the area who were not in the Confederate military but anxious to participate. These civilians would shoot from ambush and thus were considered 'bushwhackers'. Seeing White with the two prisoners, five of these civilians thought he was a Union Ranger coming to free the prisoners. The leader of the group, a man named Sheetz, was carrying a double-barrelled shotgun. White and Sheetz fired at each other, but both weapons missed. White got off the first shot, breaking Sheetz's right arm. Sheetz tried to switch to the other arm, but White put a bullet through that. The civilians retreated, firing. One put a ball from a hunting rifle into White's head, narrowly missing his right eye. The two Union prisoners were naturally confused by all this fighting between Confederates.

When Myers and Brown got back they found a confused scene with Sheetz and White down, White so covered with blood that his death seemed certain. Captain Brown rode for White's camp to bring back an ambulance, a doctor and most of White's men. The doctor decided White could be saved, loaded him into the ambulance and took him away. Myers had a difficult time keeping the Rangers from killing the civilian bushwhackers.

With Myers commanding the Rangers, the unit moved as part of Jackson's army to Winchester in the pursuit of General Banks. The Rangers were scattered, assigned a variety of duties including scouting, escort and courier. North of Winchester they were reunited as a unit, issued twenty new carbines and captive equipment including sabers and revolvers. Myers was ordered to take twenty men to Charleston to search through and inventory captured Union supplies. When this was accomplished, the Rangers joined the 6th Virginians in skirmishing with the enemy until Jackson and Ewell came up with the army.

Myers asked Ewell for permission to use the new carbines to snipe at the Union troops. Ewell thought it a dangerous idea, but gave permission. Myers and two others crept forward to fire. They had brief success but two companies of infantry soon opened fire on them, the balls coming like rain. Myers was wearing a new red shirt that was torn by three bullets. Rightfully terrified, he thought his end was at hand. Ewell fired his artillery at the Union infantry, saving his three scouts.

On Sunday, June 1 1862, Jackson's army had withdrawn to Strasburg. Union General Shields was at Front Royal and Union General Fremont was only a few miles from Strasburg. The two Union armies were poised to trap Jackson, but he slipped his army between them. The troops learned that over in the east on May 31 the Battle of Seven Pines had been fought. Confederate commander General Joseph Johnston had been severely wounded. Ewell thought General Lee might replace Johnston. This worried the troops, who thought Lee had not done much in his West Virginia campaign except earn the nickname 'Evacuating Lee'.

General Turner Ashby's name was on everyone's lips with praise for his close-combat encounter at New Market where Ashby and a companion took on seven Union cavalrymen in a fight with sabers. The next day, June 5 1862, Ashby was killed by a shot from a marksman of the Pennsylvania Bucktails. On Sunday, June 8, Ewell fought Fremont at Cross Keys and stopped him. On June 9, Jackson beat Shields at Port Republic. Jackson's Valley campaign was a Confederate triumph. During these last fights, the Rangers had been scouting enemy positions. They, like the rest of the army, were developing a great respect for Thomas 'Stonewall' Jackson. During the Battle of Port Republic, Jackson had ridden ahead of his men. He found himself in Union lines. To return for his troops, Jackson had to use a bridge covered by several pieces of Union artillery. Though his uniform was usually shoddy, Jackson had an air of command. He rode up to the Union major who commanded the guns. Assuming his best air of authority, Jackson pointed down river and shouted: 'Turn your guns, sir, turn your guns; the enemy is coming from that direction.' The officer complied and Jackson galloped across the bridge. The artilleryman got his guns turned back in time to give Jackson a whiff of grapeshot, but missed him.

Around June 20 1862, Lige White was sufficiently recovered from his wound to rejoin the company. Jackson left the valley, taking his army to the support of Robert E. Lee. At Charlottesville, Virginia, Lige White's command was joined by a Maryland company under Captain George Chiswell. The men knew that in April the Confederate Congress had passed the Partisan Ranger Act. This was the duty White's organization had been raised to perform. The men were anxious that their unit be reorganized under the new law. They found, however, that they were linked to General Ewell and ordered to march with his division as it went with Jackson to serve in Eastern Virginia. In the east, they combined with the 13th Virginians in the destruction of an ammunition train on the York River Railroad. The locomotive ran into the Chickahominy Creek. Cars blew up with such force that some of White's men bled from the nose and ears.

What is known in history as the Seven Days' campaign was drawing to a close. On Monday, June 30 Lee, seeking to split McClellan's army, attacked United States forces at White Oak Swamp (Frayser's Farm). Jackson took his army across the Chickahominy at Grapevine Bridge to begin blasting Union forces with seventy cannon. The Confederates thwarted McClellan's goal to reach Richmond, but could not trap and destroy his army. White's Rangers captured German-made instruments for a Union band and a curious set of protective armor that would withstand a pistol ball. They also skirmished with the Pennsylvania Bucktails.

The Seven Days' campaign bloodied both armies; the Confederates taking 20,000 casualties and the Union forces more than 15,000. Ewell ordered the Rangers to keep contact with the enemy, thus early July had White's men scouting Madison County. White now had about 100 men in his company. He led reconnaissance and combat patrols, often engaging Union cavalry who were performing the same mission. The combat operations usually consisted of departure in the hours of darkness and cross-country movement in blackness, with an attack at first light. They fought a successful fight with a detachment of Union cavalry and infantry near Madison Court House, capturing six men. At the end of July, White, Myers and twenty men captured a seven-man Union picket post. They followed that by setting up an ambush for a Union cavalry patrol that made a daily trek along the road from Robertson River to Madison Court House. The blue-coated soldiers were often kept informed of Confederate positions by slaves who had an effective communications system. Possibly forewarned, the patrol did not show. Disappointed, the Rangers rode back to camp. Coming back into friendly lines has through history been a particularly dangerous experience. In this case the Confederate pickets made no attempt to halt them but opened fire.

With bullets flying, White's men galloped away. Lige White rode directly at the pickets, cursing them with vigor. When the shooting stopped, the Rangers rode back. They found their captain eloquently describing the ancestry and intellect of the men who formed the picket. The pickets were upset at being spoken to in this manner. One man grumbled 'If you wasn't a captain you shouldn't [wouldn't] talk that way.' That remark tore what little restraint White had left. 'No I ain't,' he bellowed. 'I'm no captain; I'm Lige White and can whip you any way! Come on! I dare you!' None of the pickets chose to fight. White rode off, cursing cowards.[11]

Patrolling lasted into August of 1862. On Saturday the 9th, General Jackson arrived to confer with General Ewell. General John Pope was commanding the Union army which was located around Culpeper. Jackson had his army south of Culpeper. Both generals were thinking of offensive action. Myers saw Jackson walking around with his arm in the air. He assumed that the general must be asking for God's help. Union Corps Commander General Nathaniel Banks made the first punch, attacking Jackson. White and Myers rode out to the battlefront. They were thrilled at the sight of a well-drilled Union cavalry regiment executing all maneuvers by the sound of a bugle. General Ewell rode up, calling on White to have his men drag a battery of artillery to the top of Cedar Mountain (also called Slaughter Mountain). Putting the guns in position, the Rangers soon found themselves called upon to help service them. The Confederate guns were delivering accurate fire, while the counter-fire of the Union artillery had shot and shell bursting around the Confederates.

Myers noted that some of the Confederates would run to a spot where a Union shell had just exploded. This was done based on the unscientific theory that lightning never strikes in the same spot twice. Some of the soldiers learned the hard way that this is not true of artillery. The battle raged after dark while Myers thrilled to the streaks of fire and glow of flames. He noted, as many a man found in war, that a night battle can be a beautiful thing provided one is an onlooker and not a participant.

On the 10th, White's men prowled the battlefield, taking stragglers prisoner while looking for plunder and Northern newspapers that would provide information. White was in conversation with a man from Loudoun who had brought White's wife over for a visit. The man was telling where White's wife was located. The Confederate officer who had command of the outposts rode by. He told White that the outposts were withdrawn, there was only enemy to White's front. White acknowledged this, but caught up in the news of his wife he took no action.

A Union cavalry detachment on patrol had captured Major Christie, Ewell's ordnance officer, while he was trying to get ammunition from a broken wagon. Now that detachment in a size Myers probably overestimated as a squadron swept in on White and his men. Taken by surprise, the Rangers leaped to their horses. White's horse did not have a bit in its mouth, but he was a skilled rider. As so often happened in early Civil War fights between cavalry and the Rangers, the cavalry tried to use sabers while the Rangers used revolvers. As usual, the revolvers won. The cavalry were repulsed and galloped away. Major Christie, the ordnance chief, had been rapped about the head and shoulders with Union Cavalry sabers, but was not much the worse for the experience. Christie was a grateful man for being freed; thereafter the Rangers were well supplied with ammunition. General Ewell had seen the fight from the top of the mountain. Ewell called it 'A beautiful thing'.

The stormy Richard Ewell continued to be the terror of his subordinates. Lige White had a one-night pass to visit his wife. While White was absent, several Rangers built a large fire out of some hay. Ewell yelled down the hill that the Rangers had better extinguish it or he would 'throw a pistol ball among them if they did so any more.' Feeling they could not be identified in the dark, the Rangers shouted back that they would return all the pistols balls he threw at them. Nonetheless, they put out the fire.

An unfortunate lieutenant did not perform a courier mission properly. While attempting to justify his failure to Ewell, the officer used the expression 'I supposed'. Ewell flew into a towering rage. 'You supposed; you supposed, you say; what right had you to suppose anything about it, sir; do as *I tell you* sir; do as *I tell you*.'[12]

While White's men were camped at Somerset they began to talk about home in Northeast, Loudoun County, Virginia. Many of the men were from the vicinity of Leesburg or over the Potomac in Maryland. A Unionist miller named Sam Means from nearby Waterford had raised a company of Rangers. This was home turf to White's men. There was a great desire to ride against the former neighbors who were now called Yankee renegades.

Jackson was moving his army westward toward Manassas. Lige White asked for and received permission for his men to continue on for a strike at Means' Union Rangers. On Monday, August 25 1862, White's men, now numbering approximately 100, rode west. They passed Manassas, then moved to the Bull Run Mountains that lie on the eastern edge of the Loudoun and Fauquier mountains. They rested here, getting information and food from friendly local people. On the night of August 26, they moved on guided by two men: Captain Randolph of the Black Horse Cavalry and Captain Gallaher who had served under Ashby. These men had knowledge of area trails. As they approached Waterford they were guided into concealment. Patrols were sent out while the main body rested. While the men lay hidden in the darkness, an eight-man Union patrol came down the road from Leesburg. They were moving with the careless noise and conversation of those who believe the enemy is not near.

White had learned that Means' men were located at a Baptist church about 100 yards from the farm buildings of a Mr Hollingsworth. At the Hollingsworth barn, White dismounted twenty men, putting them under the command of Captain Randolph. The dismounted men were to move forward to capture or drive the Union Rangers from their quarters. At that point, White with his mounted men would sweep down from a nearby hill to kill or capture the lot. Randolph's element moved at first light, crossing and concealed by a field of growing corn. As they approached the church they found Means' Union Rangers outside the church. White's men believed the Union Rangers were listening to the report of the patrol that had just returned.[13]

About twenty Union Rangers were present, the rest being on picket or another patrol. Captain Means was at his home in Waterford. Lieutenant L.W. Slater was the senior Union officer on site. The Union record is that there were unconfirmed rumors of Confederates in the area, that a guard mount was in process and some of the men were inside the church when they heard the sound of men coming in their direction.[14]

Confederate Ranger Myers claimed Captain Randolph disobeyed his orders and fired too soon. Union Ranger Goodhart wrote that Slater called out 'Halt! Who comes there?' and was fired upon. How the battle started is lost in the fog of war. Firing of shotguns and revolvers by the Confederates did commence. Lieutenant Slater was seriously wounded and command fell to the efficient Union drill master Charles Webster.

White led his mounted contingent in a charge down the road from the nearby hill. The effort was ineffective. Most of Webster's men had withdrawn inside the church and were now firing. Four Union men climbed through a basement window to escape; two of these were captured. Waterford was a Union hamlet with hiding-places quickly offered to the other two men. White led his men to Means' house, but the Union commander had heard the firing and had left. White and his riders galloped back to the church. The Confederates surrounded the church and poured a heavy fire into it. Webster was not lacking in courage and maintained a counter-fire. He prevailed upon a Mrs Virts to carry in an offer of surrender to Webster. As Mrs Virts lived directly across the road from the church and in the line of fire, she had a vested interest in stopping the shooting. When Mrs Virts took White's surrender terms to Webster, she was rebuffed by expletives not considered fitting for a church or the ears of a lady of the period.

The firing went on for about an hour and a half until the ammunition of the Union Rangers began to run low. Horses were a prize and men took risks to get them. Confederate Ranger Peter Kabrich tried to untie a horse that was tied close to the church. He was shot by Webster. The gallant Mrs Virts carried in a second offer of surrender and again was rebuffed, hopefully in more gentle terms. There was no water in the church and the list of wounded was growing. White and Webster agreed to meet in the street outside the church under a flag of truce. White's losses were Rangers Brook Hayes killed in action and Corporal Kabrich mortally wounded. Several others had slight wounds. Webster had Ranger Charles Dixon killed in action and Ranger Henry Dixon would die of his wounds. Lieutenant Slater was wounded in five places and eight other men, including Webster, had been hit.[15]

The two sides disagree on the results of the action. The Confederates claim 30 prisoners taken along with 56 horses plus equipment along with 100 revolvers and 100 carbines. The Union report lists the names of 19 men and 30 horses. Both agree that those captured were paroled.

This fight was one of those rare occasions in the Civil War when many of the enlisted men engaged had been neighbors and possibly friends. The even rarer circumstance occurred of brother fighting brother. Confederate Ranger William Snoots wanted to shoot his unarmed brother Union Ranger Charles Snoots. Brother Charles was demanding that they fight it out hand-to-hand. White's officers put a stop to the squabble.

Leaving the dying Ranger Kabrich to the care of Union hands, White's men took two hostages and rode off in triumph. White left Lieutenant

Myers with the main body and made a personal excursion to Leesburg to show the flag and his pistols. He was welcomed in this Confederate bastion. Leesburg, which was later described by Union soldier Henry Morhous as 'a perfect sneering nest of rebels',[16] greatly welcomed White. After promising liberation and enjoying the home folks, White rode back to his command, joining them at Aldie. His wife was waiting for him there.

While White's men were occupied at Waterford, the opening guns of the Second Battle of Bull Run (Manassas) were being fired. Union commander General Pope had been confused by Robert E. Lee. Jackson had outflanked Pope's Rappahannock River position and wreaked havoc on his supplies. There was hard fighting at Groveton on Thursday, August 28 1862. On that day General Richard Ewell received a severe wound that would result in the amputation of a leg. White's command had once again been assigned as Ewell's couriers; they carried him from the field of battle.

Ewell was the man who gave White's Rangers orders and Ewell was down. Forgotten about by new leadership, White's command took up station around Ewell's house. Myers was sent back to Loudoun County to recruit. General Pope lost the Second Battle Of Manassas and withdrew. At Chantilly, another fight took place in which Jackson forced the blue-coated soldiers to withdraw. The brave Union Major General Philip Kearny who had lost an arm in the Mexican War was killed here when he was shot in the buttocks and dragged through the mud behind his horse. A sad way for a warrior admired by both sides to end his life.

General Pope had lost influence in Washington and would be relieved of command. General McClellan was gathering the Union army in a protective ring around Washington and Baltimore. Lee's plans to take the war to the North were shaping up. As Elijah White led his men over the Maryland border they had high hopes that the people of the 'Free State' would rise to their cause. They were doomed to disappointment. Maryland had seen enough of the war to prefer that it be fought out elsewhere. To total Confederate Ranger Frank Myers, the Maryland position was unconscionable. He wrote:

> ... she was now a subjugated thing, too much afraid of the power that had bound the slavish chain upon her very soul, to lift the folded hands from which the tyrant's fetters had just been so bravely torn, even though upon her own soil the conquering battle-flag of Dixie waved high above the bloody Northern standard.[17]

Myers compared Maryland to a lamb when the Confederate army expected her to be a lion.

Understandably caught up in the passion of his fight, Myers could not see that to many Marylanders, the United States flag was not a 'bloody Northern standard', but the flag of their country. Though some of its sons went south, Maryland was not going to cast its fate with the Confederate states of America.

Most generals prefer to be the center of attraction at military affairs. The talented and flamboyant J.E.B. Stuart exemplified this. As he liked women, Stuart had every reason to expect that he would be the star of the show as the Confederate army moved into Maryland at Poolesville, so he was miffed when the eyes of the home folks were on one of their own. As Henry Kyd Douglas of Jackson's staff observed of White and his men:

> The Marylanders were especially wild in their enthusiasm and one of them, Captain E.V. 'Lige' White whose home was near there, threw himself from his horse among a group of mothers and daughters, and kissed such a lot of them in five minutes, that I venture to say the record was never broken.[18]

Happy to be on home turf among people he knew, White set about recruiting for his unit.

It is an unfortunate thing when a good soldier comes under the ire of his commander. Whether it was for showboating, jealousy or some other reason, Captain Elijah White soon had the misfortune of getting into a dispute with Major General J.E.B. Stuart. The cavalry commander decided to shed himself of White. He ordered the captain to take his command back to Loudoun County. White felt he was in his birth state of Maryland and had earned in combat the right to fight there. He protested till the argument fell into senseless repetition, with Stuart believing that White was bragging that he had done as much as any Southern soldier and White protesting that he had not said that, but that he had fought as hard as any man to get the opportunity to fight on the soil of his birth state of Maryland.

The two men went together to General Lee, who was not about to be witness to an argument between a major general and a captain. White waited outside while Lee and Stuart talked. White was consoled by Stonewall Jackson, who encouraged him to just follow orders. With the wisdom of Solomon, Lee solved the problem by sending White back to patrol Loudoun

County, thereby backing up Stuart's orders but taking White from Stuart's command and having him report directly to Lee.

The animosity between White and Stuart died hard. This prevented White from having the support and latitude of operation granted to Mosby. White and his men had been recruited as and clearly preferred operating independently as Rangers. As horsemen, they were in time brought back under the control of cavalry commander Stuart. To the disgust of White and his men, Stuart tended to treat them as a regular cavalry unit and hold White's battalion under close control.

On the night of Saturday, September 12 1862 White, now joined with Maryland men under Captain Chiswell, made his way back across the Potomac. They stopped at Waterford and bivouacked at the Baptist church where they had fought the Loudoun Rangers. There was no opposition from the Union Rangers as they were absent. While White was in Maryland, Myers had remained in Loudoun County recruiting. White and Myers linked up at Waterford where White now prepared to carry out his orders from General Lee.

Where the Confederate army went, the Union army followed to keep itself in position to prevent an attack on Washington. Union troops in large numbers were at Harpers Ferry. It was not good defensible terrain. Union General Miles had, in effect, placed himself in a bottleneck. Jackson was taking advantage of this with his artillery voicing itself. The Catoctin Mountains were an excellent vantage point for White's men. They did not know the Union Rangers under Sam Means were in Harpers Ferry and destined to play an important role in guiding Union cavalry to safety.

Elijah White was now operating on very familiar territory including his own farm. It was there he engaged a detachment of Union infantry and cavalry. The horsemen got away, but White's men captured thirty-five foot soldiers which Myers and a guard took to Winchester. White moved back to Unionist Waterford, but on Wednesday, September 17 1862 he learned that a Union detachment of some 400 men was moving on Leesburg. White had thirty men in the saddle; without waiting for more he rode to the defense of his beloved Virginia town. He found Company A of the 6th Virginia Cavalry commanded by Captain Gibson along with some forty Mississippi infantry. The Confederates were preparing to evacuate. Union troops that were coming were under the command of Judson Kilpatrick who had 400 horsemen and 4 guns. The Confederates tried to stage their defense on the outskirts of town. Kilpatrick, thinking the Southern soldiers were also in Leesburg, opened fire on it. The Union commander then sent cavalry through the town. At the outskirts they encountered White's men and other Confederates.

White ordered a charge. As he led his men forward, the Confederate infantry fired. Riding in advance, White was struck by a ball meant for the enemy. The ball took him under the shoulder blade, coming to rest under the skin at the base of his neck.[19] White tumbled from his horse and the Confederate attack dissolved. White's men picked up their wounded captain and the Confederates withdrew.

The small action was scarcely noted by the armies, who at the same time were locked in a day that surpassed all others of the Civil War in bloodletting. North of Leesburg, near Hagerstown, Maryland on a battlefield called Antietam by the North and Sharpsburg by the South, the two great armies engaged in slaughter. More than 26,000 soldiers were killed, wounded or went missing in that battle, with the North coming out slightly to the better. It was a great opportunity for the army of the United States to end the war, but as President Lincoln observed about Union commander McClellan, 'he has a case of the slows'. Though he had the force to end the war, McClellan watched as Lee withdrew. For Lee it was the end of his first thrust into the North.

While Lige White was hidden from Union search parties, Frank Myers took command, setting up his headquarters at Snicker's Gap. The command patrolled Loudoun and Fauquier Counties, reaching as far east as Fairfax Court House. There were intermittent brushes with Union troops, but no major activity except in the eyes of the men being shot at. Lieutenant Myers was exercising command over several captains. He felt more comfortable when on October 19 1862, Captain Trayhern arrived and took command of what was now about 130 men organized into 4 companies of about 33 men each. Myers kept command of Company A. On the 20th Trayhern moved his companies to near Berlin, where they sat on hilltops and watched Union troops at drill on the Maryland side of the Potomac. Early on the morning of the 21st, Myers found one of his picket posts gone and recognized that they had been captured.

Trayhern led the Rangers in pursuit, only to find that Lovettsville was now occupied by Union troops. Attempting to attack a detachment of infantry, Trayhern nearly ended up in a trap. Soon the 6th New York Cavalry, under Colonel Thomas Devin, was in hot pursuit of the Confederates. They caught up with the Southern riders in a fenced area and some of the Rangers were unable to get away. Union infantry blocked their flank. Ranger Bussard, one of the originals of White's men, was killed and Jacob Robertson badly wounded; twenty-three of the men were captured. The survivors of the fight were vocal in their criticism of Captain Trayhern's tactics. Considering this unjust, he promptly resigned and left. Frank Myers once again was in command.

On Tuesday, October 28, as the main Union army inched its way into Virginia, Confederate Maryland's main man Colonel Bradley T. Johnson came from Stuart's staff. After assisting in reorganizing the unit, Bradley mustered it into the regular service as the 35th Battalion, Virginia Cavalry. The hope of being under the Partisan Ranger Act ended. Elections were held and Lige White became major. Frank Myers won the votes to be captain of Company A and would be second-in-command. Companies A to E were formed. White was still recuperating. He contented himself with leaving instructions with Myers before he departed for home and the care of his devoted wife.

The army of the North kept pressing south, driving through Loudoun County and into Fauquier. Myers led the men to share Snicker's Gap with a gun from Chew's battery and a company of the 2nd Virginia Cavalry. Union horse soldier General Alfred Pleasonton was on the prowl, leading a Union column toward the gap. On Thursday, November 6 1862, there was a lively little fight near Snickersville (Bluemont) that Chew's gun crew brought to a close. On the 9th the Union troops were back, pushing steadily forward.

White was now back in command. He withdrew by Castleman's Ferry to Confederate lines on the west side of the Shenandoah River. White was the last man to cross. Bullets kicked up the water about him, while his men feared for his life. It was a good fighting withdrawal. Stuart showed some pleasure at the performance of the command. He had a congratulatory note sent down to White. Though not personally signed, it showed some easing of the anger between the two men.

Toward the middle of November 1862, White's men were in camp near Castleman's Ferry in position to observe Union activity in Snicker's Gap. The sight of large fires on the slopes of the mountain indicated a possible Union withdrawal. A probe into the gap revealed that the enemy had withdrawn. White and his men followed General Burnside's soldiers, capturing sutler wagons that were following the column. A withdrawing enemy army offered excellent opportunities for raiding. White sent out patrols that captured more than 200 prisoners and some 20 wagons with supplies. This was followed the next day by the capture of additional wagons. A four-man charge on the wagon train of the 98th Pennsylvania Infantry resulted in the capture of its colonel's headquarters wagon with that officer barely escaping. Near Mount Gilead, sixty Union infantrymen who were guarding stores were captured.

The various detachments were all meeting with success. During the Union army withdrawal White's men estimated that they took more than 1,000 prisoners and 200 wagons, while the Union troops were forced to destroy additional supplies to prevent capture. With the help of General Jackson, the men of White's command who had been captured were exchanged and rejoined the unit.

At 7.00 pm on Monday, November 24 1862, Captain Chiswell of White's command led out forty-six riders to Conrad's Ferry about 4 miles below Leesburg. Here Chiswell's men concealed themselves while scouts crossed the river and searched the opposite side. Finding no opposition, Chiswell led his men across and rode for Poolesville, Maryland. About 2.5 miles short of that town they captured four Union soldiers guarding medical supplies. The prisoners told them there were another sixteen men guarding supplies in the town. About 6.00 am Chiswell and his men charged into Poolesville, capturing the remaining men. They found a wealth of supplies including weapons, tents, clothing and medicines. Taking what they could carry on their horses, they destroyed the rest. Chiswell's men were primarily Marylanders who had friends and family in the area. They knew the terrain well. Sending out scouts as far as Frederick, Maryland, Chiswell learned that 200 Union cavalry and some 200 convalescent infantry were there. Chiswell then led his men back across the Potomac at White's Ferry. They rode back into camp around 8.00 pm on November 25. White reported they had traveled 70 miles in about twenty-six hours and had not lost a man.[20]

On November 28 1862, White's men were on outpost duty at the Shenandoah River fords from Front Royal to Key's Ferry. Headquarters and the main body was near Berryville, beside the turnpike, about 3 miles from the river. On Saturday, November 29, a large force of blue-coated horsemen rode up on the opposite shore of Castleman's Ferry. To Lieutenant Barrett and his men of Company A who were guarding the crossing, it had become routine to see detachments of General Julius Stahel's Union cavalry on patrol on the opposite side of the river. This force kept growing while Barrett prepared for an attack and sent a messenger to Captain Frank Myers at the main camp. The messenger did not think his mission important. He simply told Myers that there were 'Yankees' on the other side of the river. He did not know if they looked like they would attack. Fortunately the Confederates were preparing for a move. Their wagons were loaded and the drivers preparing to march.

At Castleman's Ford, the Union cavalry suddenly charged across the ford, driving Lieutenant Barrett and Company A before them in a mad race for the Ranger camp. Barrett and some twenty of his men were overtaken and captured. White was informed of the action and came riding up. While trying to stem the flight he was shot in the thigh. With his wagon and mules flying down the road and most of his command on the run, White gathered a dozen men and fought a rearguard action to Berryville.

At Berryville, Lieutenant Colonel Burke and his 12th Virginia Cavalry were in camp. Hearing the firing, they quickly saddled up. Burke started his wagons on the road to safety and sent men to White's assistance. These were beaten back with the 12th Virginians losing one man mortally wounded, two others wounded and seven captured.[21] The relentless pursuit of White's command continued for 7 miles past Berryville. It was a whipped-down bunch of Confederate riders that headed up to Winchester. General W.E. 'Grumble' Jones cussed them out. He made them turn about and head back to Berryville.

Having achieved what they wanted from their raid, the Union cavalry was crossing the river en route back to their camp. The difficulties experienced by White's troops illustrates the importance of communication. Lieutenant Barrett had chosen the wrong man to be his messenger, sending one who was more interested in getting to the comforts of base camp than relaying his commander's concern. Myers felt the courier should have been court-martialed and shot. White reported Captain R.B. Grubb, Lieutenant W.F. Barrett and twelve privates captured, one man wounded and two wagons lost. The 9th New York Cavalry was positively identified as taking part in the raid. Burke believed the 2nd Pennsylvania, 1st (West) Virginia, 1st New York and 8th Illinois Cavalry regiments were also involved.

In December 1862, White's men captured Charles Webster, the drill master of the Loudoun Rangers. The story of Charles Webster is related with that of his unit later in this work. Webster was a dangerous man; one hated by Elijah White.

In the east, General Burnside's Union army occupied Fredericksburg. The soldiers in blue looked across the Rappahannock River at heights they would soon be ordered to scale. Slocum's Union corps was passing through Loudoun County en route to join Burnside. White led his men from camp on the morning of December 12, marched to Hillsborough and camped for the night. On the 13th he captured twelve Union infantrymen who, when questioned, told him that the Union column was moving toward Leesburg and had about a three-hour start. White sent these prisoners off under guard, then pushed on after the Union column, keeping an advance guard well to the front. These men captured six more Union soldiers.

ELIJAH V. WHITE AND THE COMANCHES

At about 3.00 pm White took his men into Leesburg and saw the Union cavalry who were the rearguard of the train in the process of leaving the town on the Centreville Road. Riding hard, they caught up with the cavalry about 3 miles below Leesburg, captured two men and wounded three others. The Union horsemen fell back on their infantry support. White felt it prudent not to attempt to attack; he withdrew and put his men into camp near Waterford for the night.

On the morning of Sunday, December 14 1862, White led his men on to Waterford where they clashed with Captain Sam Means' Loudoun Rangers. White claimed Means had about sixty men and that he killed one of Means' lieutenants, captured a sergeant and a private, putting the rest of Means' men to flight. White then split his command, sending a squad to Harpers Ferry while he led ninety-three men across the Potomac River at Conrad's Ferry and on to Poolesville, Maryland, arriving at about 8.00 pm. The men who went to Harpers Ferry surprised a Union outpost and captured twenty-six soldiers, later released on parole.

White was among friends and relatives at Poolesville. He learned that a company of about sixty men of the 10th New York Cavalry occupied the town. About half of these troopers were away on a scout; the remainder were billeted in the town hall. White divided his force in half and charged into the town from two directions, catching the New Yorkers by surprise. A shoot-out occurred at the town hall with a Union lieutenant and a sergeant killed and eight cavalrymen including the commanding officer wounded. In total the Confederates took twenty-one prisoners, all of whom were paroled. They captured forty-three horses with equipment to take home and destroyed the equipment and supplies they found in the town. Major White then led his men back across the Potomac River at White's Ford and into camp.[22]

The remainder of December was spent in scouting northern Loudoun. Eight more prisoners were taken near Leesburg on the 20th. The command was successful in and enjoyed the Ranger experience. There was discontent when orders were received to join General Jones at New Market. They rode into camp there on Christmas Day 1862.

Rumors were afoot that were disturbing to the men. In January, rumor became fact. White's Rangers were now to be absorbed into the regular establishment and be assigned as a cavalry unit in the brigade of Brigadier General William E. Jones, the colorful, cussing, banjo-picker whose disposition had earned him the nickname 'Grumble'. The men had experienced regular army service in 1862 when they were placed under Lieutenant Colonel Tom Munford and they were even less keen about going under Jones. By 1863, every Confederate horseman knew the monetary benefits of the Partisan Ranger Act. That was what White's men wanted.

It was more than dissent: the reaction to being made regulars bordered on mutiny, with Maryland men threatening to pull out of the war and old-timers claiming they knew what they volunteered for and what they had been promised. White was greatly disappointed by these orders, but could do nothing to change them. Soldiers in the Civil War could be shot for disobeying orders. The threat of execution buried anger under obedience. The original members of White's battalion never ceased to feel that they had been betrayed by their government.

On Wednesday, February 4 1863, Elijah White was promoted to lieutenant colonel and Frank Myers was made major. An administrative lieutenant named Watts was brought in to develop the paper trail so vital to regular units. Through February and March the men endured ceaseless drill to perform as cavalry. In early February, General Jackson sent White on a strange mission to arrest men who would then be brought to Richmond to testify against Charles Webster. Putting witnesses under coercion was not a hindrance to wartime law.

Morale in the unit was low; many of the men and officers objected to the restraints and discipline they now had to endure. For the first time the court martial system was in effect, but the battalion officers who sat on the court handed out such light sentences that White was embarrassed. Numerous command requests for reports were coming down the line. In this, as in all wars, some required reports and got worthless answers.

General Rosser was disgusted that he did not have an ordnance report from White. Rosser wrote General Lee questioning if Lee had the power to get answers. One of Lee's staff arrived at White's battalion, looked at the scanty records and questioned what he perceived as the loss of 260 guns. White seemed trapped by a piece of paper. A quick-witted Ranger nearby said 'Why Colonel, ain't them the guns that busted in West Virginia?' 'I golly, yaas,' exclaimed White, grasping at a life-line, 'they did bust; you sent us a lot of them drotted Richmond carbines, and they like to have killed all the men.' It was an answer that could not be disproved. That was all the staff officer needed. He wrote down '260 guns busted in West Virginia' and left.[23]

A critical mission of Confederate forces in the valley was to draw off Union troops facing General Lee. This was accomplished by periodic moves northward that were a threat to Washington, Maryland and Pennsylvania.

Union offensive thinking quickly changed to defense when this occurred. On Tuesday, April 21 1863, Colonel 'Grumble' Jones headed his brigade through Brock's Gap in the North Mountain into West Virginia. The purpose of the raid was to disrupt the B&O Railroad. Moving through a rugged and wondrous land, the raiders rode to Moorefield, then on to Petersburg where, aided by local guides, they crossed the South Fork at spring freshet, a dangerous time to challenge the roaring waters.

If water disrupted their passage, it was not long before Union troops did as well. At Greenland Gap on the east of the front ridge of the Allegheny Mountains they encountered a Union log fortification manned by West Virginians who were skilled with their rifles and full of fight. They had to be burned out before they would surrender. The Confederates tried a double envelopment which ended in them not only firing on the Union troops but each other. Jones's men suffered 100 casualties. They killed seven of the Virginia Unionists and captured eighty. Now the Confederates were in mountain country. They soon found themselves shadowed by bands of armed mountain men who did not attack but were always there.

Some plundering had taken place, but they were under regular army rules now. Grumble Jones made a man who had liberated a hoop skirt wear it around his neck. A man who had stolen an umbrella was required to carry it open before him for an afternoon in front of the brigade. Jones would lay his hands on every horse and cow he could find, but other property he would not allow to be taken, even if paid for.

The brigade passed through Morgantown and on to Fairmount, arriving on about May 1 1863. Here they met about 700 Union home guard trying to protect the railroad. These were poorly-armed civilians who soon surrendered. Railroad bridges, track and rolling stock were damaged or destroyed by the Confederates. They marched on, bypassing some tough Union infantry at Clarksburg, then on to Philippi and Bridgeport where the Confederate 1st Maryland Cavalry was thrashed by well-positioned Union infantry. The 6th Virginia Regiment attempted to attack the vital railroad works at the Cheat River but was repulsed. Jones took the command to Philippi where he put guards on the prisoners and livestock and sent them off to the Shenandoah Valley. The command then moved from Buckhannon in Upshur County, through Weston in Lewis County and on to West Union in Doddridge County. Jones was dividing his command, sending strong and wide-ranging search-and-destroy parties. West Union was another railroad facility ineffectually guarded by mostly rear-area shirkers who quickly surrendered. Not a man on either side was lost. Jones's men destroyed railroad buildings and track. One of White's companies was involved in lighting coal oil and burning out the wood supports of tunnels, thus causing them to collapse. On through Cairo went the raiders, riding through the counties of Pleasants, Ritchie and Wirt to the Little Kanawha River.

They were constantly sniped at by Union bushwhackers, but the light hunting rifles of the mountain men did not have the range of the soldiers' weapons. The bushwhackers did keep men from straggling. Myers found West Virginia an 'apparently interminable sea of mountains'.[24] Now the raiders were after oil production. Around May 10, they called on Oiltown where they found production in high gear. Wells driven by steam engines were pumping black gold. There were barrels of oil and river barges, specifically constructed to serve as oil tankers. Explosions rocked the works, while the air was filled with flame and smoke. An estimated 150,000 barrels of oil were destroyed.

Back in the saddle they rode through Calhoun, Gilmer, Braxton, Nicholas and Fayette Counties, through Lewisburg in Greenbrier County and on to the famed Greenbrier resort at White Sulphur Springs. There, Jones paused to give the men Sunday, May 17 1863 as a day of rest. The springs were a popular rest spot from 1778 with their natural hot water reputed to have healing qualities. The raiders enjoyed the great hotel. Built in 1858, it was called 'The Old White' and represented the latest and best in accommodation. Leaving one comfort, they marched to another famed resort area at Hot Springs, a resting-spot for both Washington and Jefferson. Then they rode on to Warm and Alum Springs in Bath County and through Augusta, going into camp near Mount Crawford in Rockingham on the evening of Thursday, May 21 1863.

The thirty-two-day 700-mile raid was a great success. Major Frank Myers estimated about 20 railroad bridges and tunnels destroyed, some 950 Union troops killed, wounded or captured, over 1,000 small arms and a cannon taken or destroyed and 1,000 cattle brought back.[25]

Enjoying their success, the men rested, repaired equipment and tended to horses and weapons. New orders were on the way. On Monday, June 1 1863, Colonel Jones put the brigade in motion to join General J.E.B. Stuart to the east near Culpeper Court House. Major Frank Myers had taken sick on the raid and he was angry. While Myers was on the long raid, Captain George N. Ferneyhough, senior captain in the battalion, succeeded in having the previous election set aside and himself elected major. By virtue of this action, Myers was once again a captain. The undeserving demotion was not the only bad news. Wounded in error by his own troops on May 2 during the Battle of Chancellorsville, General Thomas Jackson died on Sunday, May 10 at Guiney's Station, Virginia.

It was good to be 30 years old, a major general commanding 10,000 cavalry and the darling of many ladies. Such a combination impelled General James Ewell Brown Stuart to hold a great review of his force. Make that two reviews. On Saturday, June 6 1863, Stuart held a first review at Brandy Station. Many women in carriages and railroad cars were witness. Female delight and compliments were sweet as honey to Stuart's ears. Therefore another grand review would be held on Monday the 8th. For this parade it was hoped to have General Lee in attendance. Stuart had his riders tall in the saddle. For men in the ranks, a dress parade represents considerable work. Much scrubbing and polishing is required to make everything neat. There are the long minutes or hours waiting to pass in review; usually it is dusty and hotter than Hades. The eternal grumbling in ranks since Pharaoh's army can be heard of 'Let's get the troops out of the hot sun.' This incipient sign of rebellion has never fazed the general officer corps of any army. Everyone likes praise; Stuart adored it. He would have his shows.

Stuart did have a mission. The Confederate army was at Culpeper; Lee was contemplating a move north. Stuart's cavalry were responsible for watching the fords over the Rappahannock River, but few officers were concerned. To many Southerners, the much-maligned 'Yankee' cavalry existed as a source of supply for the Confederates. Thus the parade went off well. There was pride and even humor. The Texan John Bell Hood had brought an entire infantry division over to watch the fun. Infantry and cavalry delight in mocking each other.

On Tuesday, June 9 1863, some 10,000 blue-coated horsemen crossed the Rappahannock River going south in two columns, one at Beverly Ford and the other at Kelly's Ford. There was not the exuberance in these ranks that was found in the Confederate cavalry at Stuart's review. There was more of a grim determination, a sense that they had suffered greatly in the learning of this hard trade. Now these men were ready to prove their worth. Their commander was Alfred Pleasonton moving to carry out orders from General Hooker to find out what the gray-coats were up to. Pleasonton had some up-and-coming cavalry leaders under him, John Buford and George Armstrong Custer among them.

The now well-spitted-and-polished Confederate cavalry were in their blankets, as Frank Myers put it, 'wearied out by the military foppery and display of the previous day's review.'[26] Reveille was the crack of Union carbines. 'Boots and Saddles' had the 6th Virginia Cavalry of Jones's brigade beaten back, with Stuart close to losing his artillery. The gunners' horses were in pasture and the 8th Illinois Cavalry were burning out their gun barrels from rapid firing at the gunners. Jones had trained his men well; they were quickly in action, the entire brigade trying to save the guns. Jones's 12th Virginians were being beaten back when Lige White committed his men in a headlong charge into Union ranks. The ferocity of the attack slowed the Union momentum, allowing Confederate artillerymen to draw off their guns. Union cavalry cut off and captured forty-six of White's men.

Jones tried to warn Stuart of an impending attack on Stuart's flank. He received the answer: 'Tell General Jones to attend to the Yankees in his front, and I'll watch the flanks.' Jones predicted accurately that Stuart would 'soon see for himself.'[27] Gregg's Union division had crossed the Rappahannock and was fast approaching Stuart as Jones predicted. Save for three pieces of artillery, the nearest Confederate force was Harman's 12th Virginia Cavalry and White's men. They were about 1.5 miles away from Stuart's headquarters at Fleetwood. Both of these units galloped to meet Gregg's men. They came up on the high ground to see Colonel Percy Wyndham and the 1st New Jerseys not 50 yards away, advancing in a column of squadrons with colors and guidons displayed.[28] The 12th Virginians were in the lead. As they clashed with the 1st New Jerseys, the Virginians were forced back around the house Stuart was using as a headquarters. The action divided the formation of the New Jersey riders. Lige White ordered Major Ferneyhough to charge Union cavalry in front of the house, while White took the rest of the command to attack another Union force at the rear. White succeeded but Ferneyhough was having a difficult time. Colonel Harman had used White's attack to re-form the 12th Virginians and now they joined Major Ferneyhough. The Union cavalry was forced to execute a fighting withdrawal.

The blue-coated horsemen had been ably supported by a battery of the 5th New York Artillery that was positioned to the east at the foot of the hill. White was ordered to take these guns. Re-forming his command, he put them into a gallop into the fire of the artillery and its cavalry support. The Union gunners fired their cannon until White's men were among them, then fought with rammers, pistols and knives. White would later report: 'There was no demand for a surrender or offer to do so until nearly all the men, with many of their horses, were either killed or wounded.' White tried to turn the Union guns against their former owners. He was looking to Stuart for support, but it did not come. Union Cavalry came sweeping in and White's men were in turn driven from the guns they had captured. They took four enemy standards, but lost two of them. With attack and counter-attack, each time losing men, White's command was hard hit. Ninety men were killed, wounded or missing, three of them company commanders. Many of the best horses were killed or wounded.

Brandy Station was an easy march for Confederate infantry. On being informed that the foot soldiers were near, Union General Pleasonton decided his mission had been accomplished. He began to withdraw. The Confederates had the field, so Stuart proclaimed it in General Order No. 24 as 'the victory of Fleetwood'. It wasn't much of a victory. Stuart had been surprised. The Union cavalry had given the Confederates all the fight they wanted. Brandy Station was the Confederate victory that made the Union cavalry. Increasingly the end of a fight would show the Stars and Stripes waving in triumph. It would culminate in 1865 when 28,000 Union horsemen proved themselves the terrible swift sword of the United States.

General Richard Ewell, now equipped with an artificial leg to replace the one lost near Manassas, was back in action, Old Baldy being assigned to take command of the corps that had been Jackson's. Lee planned to invade the North. Ewell, needing Rangers out front to perform his part, asked for Lige White's command. Though they were now Confederate line troops, White knew he would once again have a latitude he did not have while part of Jones's brigade or Stuart's cavalry. White asked Ewell for permission to take the men home to the northern Loudoun and Maryland border. Ewell granted his request.

Lee was moving, but neither the Union command in Washington or under General Hooker in the field knew where the main Confederate body was located. In the valley, General Ewell was thrashing General Milroy near Winchester and beginning to send advance units north across the Potomac. White left his camp at Snickersville and moved north, crossing the Potomac near Berlin. He believed he would find the Union Loudoun Rangers near Point of Rocks, Maryland. He split his force, taking 100 men with him to ride along the Potomac River using the Chesapeake and Ohio Canal towpath. White sent Lieutenant Crown and Company B to take another route via the Frederick Road and come down on Point of Rocks from the rear (north).

Crown soon met a detachment of Cole's Union Maryland Cavalry under the command of the experienced Captains Vernon and Summers. This day belonged to the Confederates. A hard charge by Lieutenant Crown put the Union cavalry to flight. Crown reported thirty-seven men and horses captured. Meanwhile, Lige White had tangled with the Loudoun Rangers. These men had been on the move, participating in the Battle of Winchester, then scattered on scouting missions east of the Blue Ridge seeking to learn what Lee's army was doing. Three of the best Union Rangers captured one of White's men near Waterford, taking him to Harpers Ferry for questioning. Most of the Union Rangers had gone back to the Maryland side of the river to an encampment at the base of the mountain near Point of Rocks. The men were exhausted from hard riding and Captain Means did not properly supervise security. Some men were spotted coming into camp; a guard later said they were in Union uniform so he did not suspect them.

Dressed in blue or not, these were Lige White and his 100 riders. He hit the Loudoun Ranger camp hard, capturing thirteen men and horses. The B&O tracks that ran directly by the Potomac and C&O Canal included a railroad station with telegraph and sidings. White's men cut the telegraph line, burned storehouses and a train on the siding. They set another train ablaze and ran it back toward Baltimore. It was a good day's work. Lige White took his men back to Loudoun County, distributed the booty, then camped near Hillsborough. The men had the chance to visit families and friends, but the visits were short. Lee's army was moving north.

On Tuesday, June 23 1863, General Ewell had his corps in Maryland moving north. Generals Longstreet and A.P. Hill were following, beginning to cross the Potomac. Lige White took his men across the Potomac River at Shepherdstown, then rode north past the mournful Antietam/ Sharpsburg battlefield. The riders passed through Hagerstown and crossed into Pennsylvania. They joined Ewell at Greencastle near Chambersburg. The Confederates were enjoying the fruits of a northern invasion. At Chambersburg, Carlisle and Shippensburg shops were searched and matériel taken. Ewell sent 3,000 head of cattle south and 5,000 barrels of flour were identified for shipment. Carlisle Barracks dated from 1758. It was the home of the Cavalry School of Practice. General Ewell had been stationed at Carlisle Barracks and had fond memories of it. He asked General Lee if he should burn the old post. Lee told him not to do it.[29]

White's battalion was greatly welcomed by Ewell's corps. At this time they were the only cavalry with the advance corps of Lee's army. Two brigades of Stuart's cavalry had been left with Lee under Robertson. These cavalry brigades were trailing the Confederate army. Their mission was to keep General Hooker's Union scouts from penetrating through Ashby and Snicker's Gaps while Lee used the Blue Ridge Mountains as a screen for his movements. Stuart moved on June 25 to join Ewell but found his path blocked by Hooker's army. He would have to bypass this force to join Ewell. That would take time.

ELIJAH V. WHITE AND THE COMANCHES

The capture of a northern state capitol would be a major psychological blow to the Union. Harrisburg, the capitol of Pennsylvania, was before the Confederates and readily available. Ewell sent White's men to join General Early's division on the road to York. General John B. Gordon's brigade was Early's lead. Gordon's orders were to move on an axis of Cashtown and Gettysburg to Wrightsville where there was a railroad bridge over the Susquehanna River. Securing this bridge would allow the Confederates to strike Harrisburg from the flank. White's battalion was the point of Gordon's effort.

In the afternoon of June 26, with Company E in the lead, they brushed aside home guard defenses at Gettysburg consisting of the 26th Pennsylvania Emergency Regiment (militia) and the Adams County Cavalry. White's entire command was less than 200 men, but they knew what they were doing. The opposition was terrified by the Ranger charge, fleeing in panic through the streets of Gettysburg. Myers wrote that the Union infantry who could not flee 'threw down their bright new muskets, and begged frantically for quarter. Of course, "nobody was hurt", if we except one fat militia captain, who in his exertion to be first to surrender managed to get himself run over by one of Company E's horses and bruised somewhat.'[30] One Union soldier was killed. Private George W. Sandoc of the Adams County Cavalry would be the first Union soldier to die at Gettysburg. White's men took 175 men of the militia unit prisoner and paroled them. There was plenty of liquor available in Gettysburg which White's men quickly put to use. Many troops were soon roaring drunk. This small action was the first combat White's men had experienced in the North. Carried away with the success, men felt that total victory was close at hand. They could not know that these few shots were but a prelude to the vast action that was to come at Gettysburg. After about two hours of lubricated pleasure in Gettysburg, going through captured soldiers liberating watches and greenbacks, the party ended. General Early came into town and ordered White's men off in pursuit of the Union troops. They did not find any and occupied themselves in rounding up Pennsylvania horses before enjoying the enforced hospitality of civilian homes about a mile from town.

Early sent Gordon to take York, Pennsylvania. Gordon had White's battalion and Tanner's battery of artillery as his lead units. On Saturday, June 27 1863, White's command confiscated horses and had a skirmish with some Union troops near Hanover. Union General Hooker had his army at Frederick, Maryland. He was about to be relieved and replaced by General George Meade.

On Sunday, June 28 1863, White's men led the way into York, which surrendered to Early. The general put a heavy ransom of $100,000 on the town. He did not get all the money he wanted, but settled for $28,600 in US currency, and clothing including 1,000 hats.[31] White's men rode into Hanover and went shopping, taking whatever they wanted from merchants, then paying with Confederate money. The flourish of a revolver brought prompt service. Gordon's men reached Wrightsville on the banks of the Susquehanna River. If they could capture the railroad bridge, Harrisburg seemed within their grasp. The Wrightsville Railroad bridge was described as being 1.25 miles long. There were 1,200 Pennsylvania militia protecting the crossing. They were well dug in and prepared to fight, but they did not have any supporting artillery. When Gordon's guns began to roar, the Pennsylvanians retreated across the bridge, burning it behind them as they ran.

However, the Susquehanna River was not deep. There were many places where the river could be forded. At the moment when success seemed certain, Lee learned that the Union army was now across the Potomac and coming north. He ordered his scattered army to begin consolidation in the vicinity of Gettysburg. Ewell was starting for Harrisburg on June 29 when he received orders from Lee to join the main army at Cashtown.[32] Knowing they would not be going to Harrisburg, Early had White's men destroying Union rail communication. The Rangers burned twenty-two railroad bridges throughout the countryside. With Early now marching to Gettysburg, White's men were in the lead. There were occasional brushes with the enemy. The Union forces begin to show considerable skill; they were no longer local home guards.

Meanwhile, J.E.B. Stuart, with three brigades commanded by Fitz Lee, Hampton and Chamblis, had crossed the Potomac above Washington and ridden through Rockville and Westminster, Maryland and Hanover, Pennsylvania. Fitz Lee's brigade had the advance. About 12 miles from Carlisle, Stuart learned of Lee's presence at Gettysburg and went in that direction with the brigades of Hampton and Chamblis. Fitz Lee was ordered to continue on to Carlisle. When he arrived, he found it occupied by Union troops under General Smith. Carlisle had been his first assignment after graduating from West Point. Fitz Lee had been welcomed in homes and made many friends there. Now it was war and his call for surrender was refused. He sent in word to put the women and children in the basements, then opened fire with his artillery.

As the first shell screamed into the center of town, the New York troops who were in the town dove for the ground. A woman who was standing near the square saw the men laying flat and thought she was the only survivor.

ELIJAH V. WHITE AND THE COMANCHES

Darkness fell on the night of July 1. While Fitz Lee made plans to attack Carlisle in the morning, Stuart sent word for him to bring his brigade on to Gettysburg. Fitz Lee sent men to burn Carlisle Barracks, the gas works and a lumber yard. He was popular in Carlisle after that. School children would chant:

> In eighteen hundred and sixty-three
> Carlisle was shelled by Fitzhugh Lee.

Lige White's command arrived back at Gettysburg on Wednesday, July 1 1863, marching to the sound of the guns. Heth's division of A.P. Hill's corps was engaging Buford's cavalry and the oncoming men of Reynold's Union corps. Marching from Carlisle, the Confederate general struck the Union forces in their right flank. Significant forces of both armies were now engaged. Lige White and his men screened the left flank of Ewell's corps, had some skirmishing and were fired at by Union artillery. They took a few prisoners, but much of the time the men were onlookers to the battle. The same was true of the second day, their only involvement being two patrols consisting of one officer and six men searching out the right flank of the Union army. One of these ran into elements of the 2nd Cavalry Division of the Union army. They reported that experienced Union horsemen were on the scene.

General Lee unsuccessfully sought to turn the Union right flank at Culp's Hill, having unsuccessfully sought to turn the Union left flank at Little Round Top. Lee reasoned that if his enemy was strong on both flanks they must be weak in the center. Union commander General Meade had reasoned Lee would believe this. The center of his line was strong. Despite objections from General Longstreet, Lee determined to attack the center of the Union line on Cemetery Ridge. He would send cavalry leader J.E.B. Stuart, who had finally linked up with Lee's force around the Union army, to strike at the rear. This would exploit the success of the attack on the Union center. Meade also foresaw that possibility. He left Union cavalry behind his infantry.

Lige White's men spent the night of July 2 1863 bivouacked near a deserted farmhouse at Rocky Creek. On the morning of July 3, the battlefield was quiet save for an occasional shell, one of which set fire to the nearby house. The hours ground by in nervous anticipation. Artillerymen were pulling batteries into position so White's men knew a battle was about to open. At about one o'clock one of the Confederates' two breech-loading

English-made Whitworth cannon fired a signal shot. Immediately 150 guns of the Confederate artillery opened a furious cannonade. This was answered by Union guns. The roar of the guns was deafening.

It was now time for White's men to move out in a support role. They cantered out on the York road and soon came into contact with Union pickets. The Union outposts were driven in but backed up by a considerable force of Union cavalry. White reported this and an infantry brigade under General 'Extra Billy' Smith was committed to the action. Smith had no intention of hanging his brigade out in space. He stopped short, leaving White's men exposed. As Lige White's men had already committed, they had a hot action filled with charge and counter-charge. It was with considerable pleasure that White saw a body of cavalrymen materialize into Stuart and the Confederate cavalry. Four brigades of Confederate cavalry totaling some 6,000 men were now on the scene. More Union horsemen engaged. The action swelled as a great cavalry battle raged. Men fought together with revolvers and in hand-to-hand combat, hacking each other with sabers. After the fight, bodies were found locked together, rent with bloody wounds.

At Cemetery Ridge, Lee was unsuccessful in an attack that, to the ire of North Carolinians, has long been dubbed 'Pickett's Charge'. General Pickett was a division commander of Virginia troops. Men of Generals Pettigrew and Trimble's divisions participated and outnumbered the men of Pickett's division. Though reluctant, General Longstreet was the officer commanding the attack. The monument at the scene of the battle correctly identifies it as 'Longstreet's Assault'.

The cavalry battle was in conflict inconclusive, but in the context of the overall battle, a Union success. Stuart was unable to attack Meade's infantry from the rear, Stuart withdrew and the Union held the field. Lige White's men participated in one successful charge on Stuart's right flank, earning a compliment from Stuart.[33]

In Washington and on the battlefield, there was great anger at General Meade for not pursuing Lee's army after Longstreet's Assault was smashed on the third day at Gettysburg. Union cavalry commander Alfred Pleasonton risked the termination of his career when he said to Meade: 'General, I will give you half an hour to show yourself a great general. Order the army to advance, while I will take the cavalry, get in Lee's rear, and we will finish the campaign in a week.' Meade's assessment was that Lee had plenty of fight left in him and would welcome the opportunity to use good defensive terrain to smash a Union attack.[34]

ELIJAH V. WHITE AND THE COMANCHES

On July 4 1863, the weather suited the mood of the Confederate army, the heat of the previous day being replaced by dense gray clouds and a heavy rain. Lee held his army on the field, covering the withdrawal of his wounded, ready to meet Meade's forces should they attack. The day was given over to the task of collecting the dead and loading shattered bodies into wagons for a ride of agony to the south. A wagon train 17 miles long packed with the wounded bounced along the rutted roads. Behind them, soldiers were stacking amputated arms and legs, and gazing with horror at a battlefield where entire units of Union and Confederate dead lay in rows and piles.

Wrapped in his own grief, Lee did not know that the Confederacy had been dealt a double blow. On this July 4, the Confederate bastion of Vicksburg surrendered to General U.S. Grant. Seeing that Meade would not attack, Lee issued orders to withdraw on the evening of Sunday, July 5.

Both White's and McNeill's Rangers played a fighting role in the retreat from Gettysburg. Companies A, D and F of White's command under Major Ferneyhough were detached to remain with A.P. Hill's corps who led the Confederate withdrawal. General Ewell's corps was at the rear of the Confederate army. Lige White with Companies B, C and E served as rearguard. There was frequent fighting. Brigadier General John B. Gordon's brigade would pitch in at times when White found the Union pressure too strong. When the Potomac was crossed, Lige White again came under the command of General Stuart. White asked for permission to take his troops back to Loudoun County to operate in the Partisan Ranger role they preferred.

Stuart granted the request. The Rangers moved rapidly down the west side of the Blue Ridge with White heading his men toward Snicker's Gap in northern Loudoun County. He hoped to be able to launch raids as Union troops and supplies passed through this gap in the Blue Ridge Mountains. His plans to cross the Shenandoah at Castleman's Ferry were curtailed by high water and further impeded by the Union army crossing the Potomac and pressing southward into Loudoun and the valley. White took his command southward, up the valley to Ashby Gap and the nearby community of Paris. They bivouacked near Paris from July 17 to 20. Here they had some minor skirmishing with the Union advance. White began to take his men further afield, looking for targets of opportunity. On August 7, he learned that a detachment of the 6th Michigan Cavalry was near Waterford. White had 120 men with him. He decided to make a dismounted night attack.

161

Movement and control of troops in a night attack is difficult for men trained in the process. For those accustomed to fighting from horseback by day, attacking on foot in darkness presented special challenges. The Rangers found that they had to cross a field with piles of drying hay scattered across its surface. Blinded by the dark and moving with cocked pistol in his hand, Lige White fell over a pile of hay and inadvertently pulled the trigger on his pistol. The explosion roused the cavalry and confused both sides. Shots were exchanged, cavalrymen jumped to their horses and stampeded off in varying directions. It was not a night of military glory for either side, but men die in such conditions and Captain Richard Grubb and Private John Grubb were killed.

Union Colonel Charles Lowell of the 2nd Massachusetts Cavalry was convinced that White and Mosby operated in conjunction. In an August 12 1863 report he wrote of the two leaders joining. He believed that these two Confederates were dividing up the countryside, White to get the area around Gum Springs and Mosby to have his headquarters near Dranesville. Lowell was rounding up horses from southern farms. He was disturbed that so many sutlers were traveling insecure roads. They made ideal targets for the guerrillas. Lowell was instituting a system of thirty to fifty horsemen running patrols at irregular hours from Centreville to Alexandria. Wagons would not be allowed to travel the roads without escort. They would be required to wait until a convoy could be formed to be escorted. Lowell complained that there were so many sutlers selling whiskey that officers and men were often seen drunk.[35]

Freed from the restraints of army command, Lige White and his men began to use the reports of scouts to exercise independent action.

Colonel Lowell was actively seeking the opportunity to close with White or Mosby, but whenever Lowell moved, the people of Loudoun were reporting his route of march to the Ranger leaders. On Monday, August 17 1863, Lowell had intelligence that White and his men were camped on Goose Creek about 2 miles north of Middleburg. Lowell marched at 2.30 am, hoping his movement would not be seen. Locals informed White, who avoided the contact. Lowell got ten prisoners which he said were White's and Mosby's men. Lowell reported that White had 700 men on his rolls but only about 250 were in the field, the rest being absent at their homes. Lowell reported that Major Ferneyhough was commanding the battalion, while White with an escort of thirty to forty men was scouring the countryside trying to round up deserters and get enlistments.[36]

White had a natural affinity for operating in the area close to the border of Maryland and Virginia where he was well-known to the residents.

ELIJAH V. WHITE AND THE COMANCHES

Toward the end of August 1863, White learned that a detachment of the 11th New York Cavalry known as 'Scott's 900' had established a camp of 125 men at Poole's Farm on the Maryland side of the Potomac River near Edward's Ferry. From this point the New Yorkers sent mounted two-man patrols up and down the towpath of the Chesapeake and Ohio Canal. White decided to attack the camp. On August 27 he led 150 men across the Potomac. Waiting for the opportune time to attack, White sent two men to watch for the patrol. The two men were ordered not to interfere with the passage of the patrol unless they could see that the patrol was hurrying back to camp, obviously bringing Union forces knowledge of the Confederate presence.

One of the men sent on this duty had liquor with him and proceeded to get drunk. When the unsuspecting patrol came down the trail, he attacked them. In order to save the drunken man, his partner had to shoot one of the cavalrymen. The sound of the shot alerted the Union camp. White was forced to launch his attack sooner than planned, but they went in on horseback, leaping their steeds over ditches White reported as being 8ft wide. In all, two Union soldiers were killed, two wounded and sixteen prisoners were taken, along with thirty-five horses and mules.[37] Ranger Robert A. Jones was shot in the spine and rendered a paraplegic for life.

The 6th Ohio Cavalry was sending strong daily patrols through Barbour's Crossroads in Fauquier County. The Union horsemen had fallen into the routine of making this patrol around 3.00 pm. White decided to ambush the Ohio troopers. He took 100 men with him to accomplish the mission. Riding at night, the Confederates reached a place of concealment in a pine forest near the crossroads. White made a reconnaissance and put a few men on outpost down the road to provide early warning of the enemy's approach. At first light on Tuesday, September 1 1863, White stationed Lieutenant Chiswell with seventeen men of Company B in dense roadside brush. Their mission was to fire a volley on the cavalry as they trotted past. White concealed the remainder of the command in the wood, the plan being that when Chiswell fired, the cavalry would be temporarily confused. Then the main body of Rangers would charge.

The men relaxed until the outpost came in and reported that about 100 (actually 50) Union cavalry were coming down the road. Soon White heard the sound of Chiswell's carbines and charged out of the woods. White, Myers and the adjutant Lieutenant Watts were in the lead. They saw the Ohioans responding to Chiswell's fire had left the road. Fences made fields killing grounds for cavalry. As soon they saw White coming, the men of the 6th Ohios under Major Cryer attempted to regain the road. Major Ferneyhough made a wrong turn, leading the main body of the Rangers in the wrong direction. Much to their surprise, White, Myers and Watts learned they were charging the enemy cavalry by themselves. White and Myers had their horses shot from under them. Watts was among the cavalry, fighting for his life. The remainder of the command finally got their bearings and charged into the fight.

In reporting results of battles there is often wide variance between the two sides, but on this occasion they were in close agreement. The 6th Ohio reported 1 man killed, 1 officer and 4 men wounded, 1 officer and 24 men captured and 30 horses captured.[38] White's men claimed 10 of the enemy killed or wounded, 25 prisoners and 30 horses with weapons and equipment.[39] The Rangers lost two horses. One of the unusual aspects of the ambush was that Chiswell's seventeen men fired on the cavalry from a distance of about 12 yards and only killed one soldier. There must have been something about the man that caught the eye, as he had seven bullets in him.

Union commanders had ordered the arrest of two prominent civilians in Loudoun who would not take the oath of allegiance to the United States. The friends and families of these men sought their release. Failing in the attempt, they asked the Confederate government to retaliate. The order was passed to General Stuart to arrest the Quaker Minister William Williams and Asa Bond. Both men were prominent Loudoun County supporters of the United States. Stuart passed the mission on to Lige White to accomplish. If White knew this action would make him a hated man, he did not seem bothered by it. His objection was that the note from Stuart was not signed.[40] The arrests generated anger among many people in northern Loudoun. Bond escaped. A man named Hollingsworth was taken as substitute. Williams and Hollingsworth were sent to Richmond. In time the men were released, but henceforth the Quaker community had a low regard for Elijah White.

Informants told White that the B&O Railroad would be carrying a large shipment of horses passing through Point of Rocks, Maryland on Wednesday, September 16 1863. White decided to go after the horses. While he made a reconnaissance, he would move Lieutenant Crown and Company B to an assembly area where he could quickly bring them forward. This location, at Gray's Farm north of Leesburg, was well within the operating range of Union horsemen.

White made plans regarding Union troops in the area, but his officers either misunderstood or were confused by them. Lieutenant Crown thought Captain Myers was being ordered to take a detachment to attack the Union camp, thus securing Crown's assembly area. Myers thought he was being given the latitude to attack or not. When Myers reached Waterford and the Union camp, he decided they were too strong to attack and pulled off. Crown was caught up in a sense of false security. He did not establish outposts. While Crown was awaiting breakfast at Gray's, Cole's Maryland Union cavalry and the Loudoun Rangers came in from two directions. They scattered the Confederates, capturing Crown and nine men. Lieutenant Dorsey and another of White's men tried to come to the aid of their comrades and were also taken. Once again, the hard lesson was brought home that not posting security is an invitation to disaster.

In 1863, there were a number of Confederate units operating independently as Partisan Rangers from West Virginia through Fairfax County in the east. The Confederate high command was desirous of having these units attack the railroads that were the steel arteries of the massive supply effort of the Union army. The B&O and Orange and Alexandria Railroads were critical to the Northern effort. For the Rangers, attacking railroads often required long treks from home areas, riding by night and staying hidden in woods during the day. It was difficult to carry rations for longer expeditions. Occasionally the tactical situation would change, requiring a longer route to or from the objective. Most locals were friendly, but it only took one informant to ruin the plan. On some missions men exhausted their food supply and went hungry for several days. White took nineteen men on a raid into Fairfax County where he burned a key bridge on the Orange and Alexandria Railroad at Pope's Creek. The men went hungry for three days on that raid, unwilling to risk visiting farmhouses that might betray them. With growling stomachs, they watched heavily-laden sutler wagons pass before their hiding places.

As the junior officers gained experience, White began to divide his command, sending smaller raiding parties over a larger area. There were frequent clashes with Cole's Maryland Cavalry and the Loudoun Rangers who were using the same tactic. Some of the Confederate patrols were guided or led by the guerrilla John Mobberly. There were sudden and unexpected meetings, bursts of gunfire, charge and counter-charge and a rout and pursuit or a mutual breaking of contact. The results of these small unit actions were seldom recorded.

From Vienna, near Washington, Colonel Lowell, his 2nd Massachusetts Cavalry and the Union California Battalion maintained a constant patrol activity in Fairfax, Loudoun and Fauquier Counties. Lowell was a good officer, determined to keep pressure on the enemy. His combat patrols were sizable, often in sufficient number that they could subdivide in their search. Lowell retained his belief that White and Mosby were coordinating their efforts, attacking as a team and dividing up areas of operation. There is scant indication that Mosby, White, Gilmor, McNeill or the many freelance Confederate guerrillas coordinated their actions or that the Confederate government moved to establish a Special Operations Command. When engaged in Partisan Ranger activities, the various leaders of these bands roamed the countryside in the manner of feudal princes.

Around October 1 1863, White took fifty men and a guide named George Tramell to attack a camp of the 16th New York Cavalry and attached infantry at Lewinsville. Tramell did not have sufficient information on the enemy dispositions, so White and Tramell each took along Union uniforms in the hope of getting a closer look. Dressed as Union soldiers, they were able to pass among the cavalry to bring back locations of guards and best routes over which to attack. They found to their gratification that the cavalry outposts had overlooked a little-used forest road that was scarcely more than a path. It was likely one of the narrow roads hewn through the woods that early settlers had used for hauling wood. By using this path, the command could be brought up and formed on a hill that overlooked the 16th New Yorkers. When they swept down on the unsuspecting soldiers the surprise was so complete that the men of the 16th New York Cavalry did not fire a shot. No Union officer was awake, the duty having been passed to Sergeant Shaddock of Company B. When he heard horses coming, he tried to wake the officers. By the time the officers were roused, the camp belonged to Lige White's men: two Union soldiers were killed, three wounded, twenty captured and sixty-three horses and equipment taken. The Union report states that this was all done in five minutes.[41] White's men had no losses.

Meanwhile, other detachments of White's battalion were busy. While moving his company to join White, Frank Myers came upon Vermont infantry on picket duty. Myers captured twenty-five men and a lieutenant. Lieutenant Dowdell with Company C was having a successful fight with Captain Sam Means' Rangers near Harpers Ferry.

Their happy days of independent action were again ended. General Stuart sent orders directing that White's men should report to Brigadier General Thomas L. Rosser, now commanding the famed Laurel Brigade. Stuart did not like 'Grumble' Jones. He relieved the old war horse, replacing him with the young firebrand Rosser.

Rosser was from Louisiana, an April 1861 graduate of West Point, where he was a friend of George Armstrong Custer. The times suited the old mess room toast 'to a bloody war and quick promotion'. On June 20 1862, the youthful Rosser was made colonel of the 5th Virginia Cavalry. Now, just four months later, he was a brigadier general.

Around October 25 1863, Lige White and his men joined Rosser in camp near Flint Hill, Rappahannock County. Rosser's brigade would be part of J.E.B. Stuart's Cavalry Corps in the division commanded by the hard-fighting and enormously wealthy South Carolinian Wade Hampton. The 7th, 11th and 12th Virginia Cavalry regiments were also in the brigade.

Hampton gave White's men an opportunity to settle in to their new existence until mid-November when Hampton's troops were joined by J.E.B. Stuart. This occasioned another of Stuart's flamboyant reviews, an exercise much hated by White's men.

On Thursday, November 16 1863, Union commander General George Meade came across the Rapidan River and began to attack the left flank of Lee's army. Rosser had White's men out in front of his brigade, scouting enemy dispositions. When Lieutenant Conrad did not get back from a mission by the expected time, General Rosser wanted to know why he had to wait for the report. Conrad responded that he had been sent so deep into enemy territory that the only general he could have reported to was General Meade. That satisfied Rosser.[42]

Meade was continuing to push against Confederate positions along Mine Run. At Parker's Store and New Hope Church, Union troops sought to gain the advantage. On Sunday, November 29 1863, at Parker's Store on the plank road, Lige White's men came up against a strong force of Union cavalry. They charged the blue-coated horsemen, put them to flight and took their camp. They in turn were driven from the camp by a counter-attack; they responded and regained the field. Rosser's brigade was in trouble, receiving enfilade fire from a flank. He ordered White to charge. He did, and cleared the flank. Rosser was hit by a larger Union force and his brigade began to falter. Once again, Lige White's horsemen charged, shouting at the top of their lungs. That charge enabled General Rosser to hold his position. Rosser was delighted with the performance of Lige White's men and gave them the nickname 'Comanches'.

As December opened, General Meade decided he could not penetrate the Confederate defense and withdrew to winter quarters. The Confederates also prepared to slow combat action in the face of the impending cold. White's Comanches were placed on picket duty along the Rapidan River; they and their Union counterparts would ride into the middle of the river, trade tobacco for coffee and swap news and experiences. When they came east, General Lee wanted a fast movement with light baggage. As a result, the Comanche tents and other heavy gear had been left behind, stored at Flint Hill. The hard-pressed civilians of that area had raided the baggage and nothing of value was left for the men. White's cold and hungry troops were greatly angered by this, and the Confederate army did not help them. They had enlisted to fight in their home area and did not like service with the army. More than sixty men walked away from the unit and returned to Loudoun County, their homes and families.

On December 16, Rosser's brigade was ordered to move to the Shenandoah Valley to join General Early. The Comanches hoped this would take them home. They were only to see it in passing, however, as they moved westward though Centreville and Upperville, through Ashby's Gap and across the Shenandoah River. It was a winter march, terrible in all its aspects for men ill-equipped for exposure to the elements. Every stream and river was an agony to cross. As the horsemen of the brigade, the Comanches were required to do the scouting and fight the rearguard actions. There was little rest. Myers reported that at one time the command made 90 miles in twenty-four hours. Anxious to get the sixty men who gone home back in ranks, White sent a message asking for their return. The response was that they had heard they would be tried, convicted and shot. Understandably, they would not return on that basis. They would return if Captain Myers came and gave assurances that they would not be so treated. This was done and the men returned.

On January 1, Lieutenant Conrad and six of the men including John Mobberly managed to take on wood and water [get drunk], prepare to attack a Union force, have an argument with Maryland Ranger Harry Gilmor about who would command and launch a successful strike on a Union camp. They captured forty-two Union infantrymen and a large quantity of plunder. Meanwhile, White had been rounding up local cattle for the use of the army.

Jubal Early was retreating up the valley with Rosser's brigade as his rear unit. Lige White's Comanches covered Rosser's movement and skirmishing was frequent. A Union sharpshooter firing at over 1,000 yards missed White but killed his horse. A Ranger named Clendenning from Company C willingly gave White his horse. Courts martial were held for men who had gone absent from the command. Myers reported that Company A had seventy-seven of its eighty-five men being tried and Company C was not much different.[43] The offenders were given double duty for a month.

From February 29 to March 7 the Comanches were sent off in fruitless chase as part of the response to the Kilpatrick-Dahlgren raid on Richmond.

It was an exercise in futility. The unit was not needed, hurried from place to place with frequent orders and just as frequent countermanding of the orders. There was little food for them and their horses and they were overcharged by southern storekeepers when they tried to buy something. Myers was furious at prices such as $3 for a lead pencil and $10 for a pound of butter. On April 27, the winter baggage they had so laboriously gathered was stored at Waynesborough.

On Sunday, May 1 1864, Lige White's command was ordered to join Lee's army along the Rappahannock River. General U.S. Grant was in command of United States forces. The future of the Confederacy did not look bright. Union Colonel Lowell had rounded up a number of the Comanches. White was forced to disband Company D, using its members to fill out the other companies. One of the men of Captain Marcellus French's Company F went absent without leave. When he came back, he told French he would go when he wanted to. French drew his saber and inflicted a deep wound on the skull of the man. There was great anger at French but the captain stood in front of his adversaries and challenged them. They decided it was best to obey Captain French's orders. On Wednesday, May 4 1864, the Comanches bivouacked near Orange Court House. That same day, General U.S. Grant began an assault across the Rapidan River intending to flank Lee and drive on Richmond.

It was clear to the Confederates from the outset that U.S. Grant was a different Union general from those they had faced before. On the night of May 4, a Union prisoner captured by the 11th Virginians was brought to Rosser's camp. The Confederates found the man to be brimming with confidence of Union victory.

'Where is your pontoon train?' asked a Confederate. 'Grant has no pontoon train,' was the response. 'How then, are you going to get back across the river?' asked another Confederate. 'Grant says,' answered the Federal quietly, 'that all of his men who go back over the river can cross on a log.'[44]

On May 5, action was joined between the two armies in the fight that would be known as the 'Battle of the Wilderness'. Rosser's brigade was heavily engaged, often fighting dismounted. The Confederates were so lacking in ammunition that the first action when a prisoner was taken was to relieve him of weapons and ammunition for Confederate use. Having no ammunition, the Comanches were at a disadvantage in this fight. Captain Frank Myers said to White: 'Colonel, how can we fight those fellows with no ammunition? We'd as well have rocks as empty pistols.' White responded:

'What are our sabers for?' These were drawn and the men galloped into the fight, battling using the long knives.[45]

May 5 was a hard day's work. When Lige White's men went into camp at Shady Grove by the Po River that night they counted twenty killed or wounded. An additional twenty men could not be accounted for and had likely been taken prisoner. One of the missing who was never located was John Clendenning, the man who had given Lige White his horse and saved him from capture.

The following day, the Comanches made a charge that took them into battle with George Armstrong Custer's Michigan men. They drove in the Union pickets and hit the 6th Michigan hard, but the 5th and 6th Michigans stayed in line, delivering a high volume of fire from their seven-shot Spencer carbines. Lige White's horse was killed, as was the horse of the adjutant Lieutenant Watts. Both fighter and paper-pusher for the battalion, Watts tried to rescue the saddlebags that carried the Comanche records. The delay caused him to be captured. The Union riders now charged and all of Rosser's brigade was in difficulty. Chew's artillery who had done so much for Turner Ashby now slowed the Union advance.

Myers wrote that Stuart was trying to rally the men, begging them to go back and saying he would shoot them. White ordered French to round up some stragglers and take them back. French declined, saying that his moving toward the rear would appear cowardly. French, who was described as 'cold as ice' under fire, took some persuading before he would make any move that might be looked on as retreating. The Union fire fell on the men like rain; shells were pouring by. As White leaped from his horse to talk to Myers, a shell screamed past their ears. White involuntarily jammed his head into Myer's chest. He quickly raised his head, laughed and said: 'I golly! I believe I'm demoralized myself.' The Union shells were ripping into them, so White had his men dismount and lay prone. A shell tore off the head of Private Broy of Company F, throwing his blood and brains over the men. The horses were being hit. Frantic with fear, the animals were plunging and kicking. Ed Oxley's horse was killed. Oxley was furious to learn that before he could get to it, another Confederate had stolen his saddle and gear. About two o'clock the firing ceased. Lige White's Comanches had been badly shot up.

When soldiers lose a battle it is normal that the first one blamed is the commander who put them in the fight. Many of the Comanches faulted General Rosser. It was not his courage they questioned but his tactical skill. There were fourteen dead, twenty wounded and four captured. Several of the wounded, including Lieutenant Conrad and Color Sergeant Torreyson, would have legs amputated. Myers wrote that Union troops buried the Confederate dead and marked the graves so that the friends of the men could find the bodies. The battlefield was a dreadful sight. The woods were set ablaze by the explosions; fire swept over wounded men, burning to death those who could not escape. There were now fewer than 150 men left of Lige White's Comanches.

On Sunday, May 8 1864, the remnants of the Comanches were back in action. A detachment comprising men skilled with a rifle had been formed as part of Company C. They were commanded by Lieutenant Thomas White who had a premonition of his death. As the sharpshooters moved forward, Lieutenant White called out to Captain Myers: 'Goodbye Frank, I am going and I don't expect to see you any more.' Somewhere on the other side of the line, there was a Union sharpshooter who made the expectations of the gallant Lieutenant White reality.[46]

In the early years of the war, the Union army of the Potomac had taken fearful losses and had withdrawn to regroup. There would be no withdrawal under General Grant. The only way to win the war was to constantly go forward, accept with sorrow the high casualties, but give Robert E. Lee no rest and no room to maneuver.

A battlefield littered with dead has a sickly, rotting smell. In the dark of night, unable to see the ground on which he was spreading his gum ground-cloth, Myers lay down to take a nap. The smell was revolting, but he was exhausted and settled his head on a lump in the cloth. When he woke at first light he found he had been sleeping at an abandoned field hospital with his head on a pile of amputated arms and legs. Nearby was the swollen, putrid body of a Union sergeant.

There were many scenes of horror. When the horsemen rode across the fields, the bodies of the dead so littered the ground that the horses would step on them, stripping rotting flesh from the bones.

Day followed day of sudden clashes and narrow escapes. The under-strength companies were reorganized into two squadrons: one of Companies A and C, the other of Companies B, E and F. They were called squadrons in large part because of the rank of officers, although each squadron scarcely contained the strength to be accurately called a company.

On May 16 1864, Confederate cavalry commander James Ewell Brown Stuart was killed in action at Yellow Tavern, extinguishing another bright light of the Confederate army.

On May 28 Hampton's division, including Lige White's Comanches, marched near Mechanicsville. White's men were to the rear of and supporting Chew's artillery. General Wade Hampton rode by and said to White: 'Good morning Colonel, we've got the Yankees where we want them now.' Myers felt the situation was just the opposite, for it was not long before they were being pounded by fire.[47] Though they were taking casualties they could ill afford, the Comanches were developing a deep affection for Wade Hampton. He was a good general, steady and reliable.

The Confederate government did not supply their men with horses. Men were expected to supply their own animals and received some additional pay for the purpose. In addition to their affection for the animal, it was a financial burden when a soldier lost his horse. Those who did were excused duty to hunt for another mount. Absentees plus casualties put the battalion at less effective strength than Company A had at the beginning of the Wilderness campaign.

The Union cavalry of the army of the Potomac had been consolidated into a single fighting force under General Phil Sheridan. Grant kept Lee occupied. He used the tactic of constantly side-stepping, forcing Lee to strive to keep between Grant and Richmond. Grant planned to slide around Lee's right flank and cross the River James, thus coming against Richmond from the south. As a diversion he ordered Sheridan, with two divisions of cavalry, to head toward Charlottesville, Virginia to operate against the Virginia Central and other railroads. On the return trip the force was to link up with General Hunter who was in the Shenandoah Valley.

Wade Hampton's division was the principal opposing force to Sheridan's movement. The Union cavalry was no longer the whipping boy of the Confederate army. In the early years of the war, they had come from areas where horse-breeding and equestrian pursuits were not as prevalent as in the South. Many Union horsemen had to learn to ride before they could learn to function as a horse soldier. At the start of the war, the heavy and lengthy 'dragoon pistol' was so difficult to use that reliance was placed on the saber. In 1864, well-trained and fully blooded, the Northern horsemen were well equipped with Spencer carbines. They had learned that the revolver was a more effective companion than a saber in a fight and quickly adapted to carrying two or more Colt or Remington sidearms.

In 1864, it was a common tactic for horsemen on both sides to close on each other, fire the loads in their revolvers and then wheel away, clearing the battle area to reload and come back in again.

At Trevillian Station, Sheridan's cavalry hit a Confederate brigade under General Young and smashed all of it, except for one Confederate regiment that kept clear of the fight. While the Union troops were rounding up prisoners, they were charged by Rosser's brigade with White's slender command in the thick of it. Despite a disparity in numbers, the Comanches took a number of prisoners. Custer's troopers flanked Hampton's division, got into their rear area and attacked the Confederate trains, capturing a considerable quantity of vital Confederate supplies. The Comanches and the 11th Virginians then hit Custer's Michigan men. The fight became a swirling action in which men and units were scattered in varying directions. There was no front or rear. White saw an artillery battery getting into position. Fearing that a large force he saw was about to attack the battery, he decided to support the gunners. Lige White had his men tearing down a fence to help them out when General Hampton rode by and asked White what he was doing. White replied that he was going to support the battery. Hampton said: 'Get away from here, Colonel, it's a Yankee battery.'

On the way out of that experience, some Comanches saw a barrel of applejack that had rolled off a wagon. The men were thirsty and stopped to fill their canteens. The Union battery they had tried to protect had no doubt who they were and sent a shell whistling into their midst. One man was killed and two seriously wounded. In all this confusion, Major Ferneyhough was steady as a rock, putting the men into line, counting them off while shot and shell rent the air, riderless horses careened through the formation, and wounded and dying men cried out. A round shot hit to the front of Lige White's horse, which leaped from the ground at the commander and passed over his head. Rosser was hit in the leg and evacuated. Sheridan's 8,000 troopers had the best of it this day. His horsemen now occupied Hampton's previous position. In all that happened during this hectic fight, the puzzling thing to Frank Myers was the unidentified Confederate regiment from Young's brigade. Not bothered by Confederate or Union action, they stayed on a hillside; spectators of a battle that they made no move to join.

On Sunday, June 12 1864, Hampton had his approximately 5,000 troops on good defensive terrain astride Sheridan's route of march. The Confederates were on high ground that sloped away to a creek at their front. Both flanks were protected by thick woods. They had excellent fields of fire; clear ground out to maximum range of their rifles. Artillery was positioned to fire over their heads with a clear view of the field. After a light shower during the night, the day dawned bright and clear.

Around noon, skirmishing began. The Comanches were posted to the front of Hampton's main force. They exchanged fire with Union sharpshooters. In the late afternoon Sheridan made a dismounted attack that was beaten off. Myers was particularly impressed by the courage of new

Confederate regiments having their first experience in battle. Hampton had fought a good fight. Sheridan did not succeed in the details of his mission, but he had the latitude to change his plans. It was not Sheridan's but Grant's move that was the prime effort. Rather than slaughter his men in fruitless attacks on Hampton's superb defense, Sheridan decided not to seek a link-up with Hunter but to return to the army of the Potomac. As darkness fell, Sheridan withdrew his men and began the march back, crossing over the North Anna River. Hampton followed, but could do no serious damage. The countryside was destitute and there was little food for men or horses.

Concerned about Hunter's threat to the valley and hoping to draw off Union forces from his front, Lee sent General Early to try to duplicate Jackson's Valley campaign. On Monday, June 13 1864, Lige White and the Comanches were trailing after the Union cavalry while searching for food and horses. There was little action save for a failed attempt to ambush a courier party and a minor brush with some of the 6th Pennsylvania Cavalry. Patrolling continued till June 26 when they were ordered south of the James River, crossing at Drewry's Bluff. The men viewed going south of the James as a defeat. There was much grumbling that they were being ordered even further from their home soil and families. The analysis of the men in ranks was accurate. Grant now had his vast army across the James River, Sherman was in Georgia, and Union troops were in North Carolina. There was dissension among the Confederate states and a lack of confidence in President Jefferson Davis. Myers had learned from personal experience that war profiteering was rampant and supplies were insufficient to meet the needs of the army. Though there were many desertions, those that stayed could be depended upon. They were men of courage; the unknown soldiers of valor.

From the earliest days of his assumption of command, General Grant understood that his was a war of attrition. Maneuver was a Confederate strength. Grant deprived Lee and his army of that option. He put the Confederates under siege at Petersburg, depriving Lee of the ability to wage a war of maneuver. The destruction of southern railroads was important to the strangulation of the Confederate army and was frequently on the mind of the Union commander. Grant kept the pressure on his subordinates to attack Confederate supply lines.

The brigades of Union Brigadier Generals Kautz and Wilson had been sent west and south of Richmond to cut southern rail lines. Wade Hampton and the Laurel Brigade were sent in pursuit. On Monday, June 27, the Comanches rode through Petersburg. The civilians of the town were becoming combat veterans in their own right, carrying on with their lives despite the heavy shelling that was only a promise of worse to come.

Around 10.00 pm on the 28th, Hampton and his men found a Union raiding party near Sapony Church. Lige White's men were given the mission of circling and striking the left flank of the Union position. This they did with alacrity, but it was accomplished only through heavy fighting. The Union soldiers withdrew, passing over an unguarded bridge. The Confederates followed, going through the weapons, supplies and abandoned plunder that is the garbage and the treasure of the battlefield. They captured bands of terrified slaves who, hoping for freedom, had followed the Union troops. Now they faced a return to that which they had fled.

Throughout the fighting in Virginia, the Confederates had the aid and assistance of local white people. They provided shelter, food and forage and guides that were of great value to Mosby, White, McNeill and Gilmor. The Union soldiers often had assistance from the black slaves. Generations of night movement by slaves slipping away to visit other slaves had taught them the countryside and equipped them to be excellent guides. Being unfamiliar with the military they were prone to exaggeration, but they often provided valuable information.

White planned to ambush a unit of Negro cavalry in Sussex County. Local slaves saw his men and passed on the information. The cavalry patrol came as expected, but behind them was what Myers estimated as 3,000 infantry and 1,000 more cavalry.[48] The hunter became the hunted. It took some quick wit and fast movement to arrive first at the bridges that were their only means of escape.

General Early was having success in the valley and had moved north into Maryland. The thoughts of the Comanches were always turned toward home. They never forgot that they had enlisted to fight at home as Partisan Rangers. They never forgot that J.E.B. Stuart had forced them into the Confederate army. With Early clearing a path through Maryland, most of Company B who were from that state walked away to return to home and family. They reminded people that other men had done this. It was their right to return home when they wished. When pushed to it, the Maryland men could remind people that Maryland had never joined and had no obligation to the Confederate States of America. Among men who left were deserters with a different intent. These included young John Mobberly, an efficient scout and ruthless killer. Captain Frank Myers liked Mobberly, but there were many who did not. Everyone in the Comanches wished they were back in Loudoun County and angry that they were not with Early. On Monday,

August 7 1864, Sheridan took control of operations in the Shenandoah Valley and began to turn the tide of war against Early. Myers wrote that some of the men were so bitter at not being allowed to fight at home that they 'expressed satisfaction' when they heard Early had been driven south of the Potomac.[49]

South of the James, camped where armies had not trodden, the men found good hunting and fishing. They lived better than they had for a long while. They roamed outward on scouts. On one, White cut a telegraph line and had an operator intercepting messages for about two hours. This had been effective early in the war. Now it brought a large detachment of Union infantry in pursuit and White had to withdraw.

Men going into battle are frequently portrayed as praying or at some form of religious service. That does not happen as often as the home folks might like to think. Men have their own ways of getting to grips with the experience of war. If it does include a relationship with their God, it is often via a private channel, not a formal display. Frank Myers noted '... generally, religion in the ranks was unpopular, and many who had been members of church endeavored to hide the fact from their comrades that they ever prayed.'[50]

On Monday, August 8 1864, Major Ferneyhough led a patrol to capture some pickets, but the raid did not succeed. On Friday the 12th, Hampton's troops including the Comanches were ordered to march on a route that took them through Richmond. There the men devoured watermelon and cantaloupes. They moved onward, resting for a night near the South Anna, then terminated the march on the Chickahominy, some 7 miles from Richmond. The troops were happily able to complain that the situation was normal. No one knew what was going on, so the rumor started they were going home. Like most rumors, this one was not true. They were destined for another period of moving and skirmishing and sometimes protecting Chew's artillery.

As part of the effort to strangle Lee's army in Petersburg, General G.K. Warren, hero of Gettysburg and commander of the Union 5th Corps, seized part of the Weldon Railroad, a critical supply route for Lee. With the cannonballs flying back and forth and many coming close, the command party of Generals Butler and Rosser sat on their horses in front of White's men. As a Union shot whizzed by, Butler said: 'They are disposed to be rather familiar this morning.' Rosser replied: 'Yes, politeness is in order this morning, but don't bow too low boys. It isn't becoming.' One of the Comanches, Henry Simpson, observed: 'Yes it is; it's *becoming* a little too damn hot here, if that's what you mean.'[51] Despite hard fighting and many casualties, the Confederates were unable to drive the Union troops from the Weldon Railroad and a critical link was cut.

North and South, the presidential elections were a prime topic of conversation. It was only the presidential election in the North that was being discussed. One of the last hopes of the South was that Abraham Lincoln would be defeated and driven from office. The Confederates knew Lincoln would not settle for anything less than the preservation of the Union and emancipation of the slaves had been added to that. The Southern hopes were moonshine. George McClellan was Lincoln's opposition. They did not care for each other, but both shared the view that the Union should be re-established.

Anxious to know the Northern view of what was happening politically in the North, General Hampton launched a raid behind Union lines to capture newspapers. This most unusual mission included a detachment from the Comanches under the command of Major Ferneyhough. This officer who performed well on many occasions misunderstood a direction of General Hampton's and was severely criticized by that officer. Ferneyhough felt he had no choice but to resign his commission. He resigned and left the command on Tuesday, September 13 1864. Shortly thereafter Captain Frank Myers was promoted back to his earlier position as major of the unit.

The Confederate army was in dire need of meat, so Confederate scouts had located one of the large beef herds kept for Union use near Coggin's Point. On Wednesday, September 14 1864, Hampton took about 3,500 men including Lige White's Comanches to take the cattle. The herd guards were fronted by the 1st District of Columbia (DC) Cavalry and backed up by two companies of horsemen from the 13th Pennsylvanians. Though outnumbered, the Union force declined to surrender. While Confederate cavalry under Fitz Lee and Dearing made diversions to distract Union cavalry, General Rosser was ordered to break the lines at Sycamore Church and get the cattle. The 7th and 12th Virginians cleared a path through initial Union resistance. Rosser told White to 'Come down on them.' In one of their best actions of the war, White's men charged the Union cavalry and put them to flight. About 150 members of the 1st DC Cavalry were captured. The items captured with them were beyond their dreams, including Henry rifles the men called 'sixteen-shooters'. The Union herders stampeded the cattle in an attempt to save them. It took skilled riding to get to the front of the herd and turn it until it ceased running. For the meat-starved Confederates the 2,486 head of longhorn western beef was a sight to make their mouths slaver. Two of the Comanches were killed in the cattle raid. On the way back to Confederate lines the Union forces attempted to catch the raiders at the Jerusalem plank road. Lige White's men were dispatched to delay the Union approach and blocked the way, bluffing his opponents and slowing their movement.[52]

On Tuesday, September 27 1864, the Comanches got the word they so eagerly wanted to hear. Rosser's command, the Laurel Brigade, was going back to the valley to join General Early's army. They marched that very day. Lige White was ill and headed for home and his wife. The Comanches moved under the command of Major Frank Myers. There was sun and rain, dry roads and mud. No matter the weather, the march was a happy one. Men thrilled to the sight of their beloved mountains. However, their good cheer evaporated when they reached the Shenandoah Valley. The once lush land was now wasted. The tramp, foraging, battles and destruction of both armies had changed the life of the valley. The horror of war had come home.

The mills, barns, corn cribs and granaries of the once beautiful Shenandoah Valley were being burned by Sheridan's troopers. Homes of those believed or proven to be supporting Confederate Rangers were sending towering pillars of smoke and flame skyward. A charge against Sheridan's well-equipped men faced weaponry that could deliver a hail of lead. In a give-and-take battle with Custer's troopers, Myers was seriously wounded. On October 9, the Union cavalry flexed its muscle. General Sheridan ordered his cavalry commander General Torbert: 'Start out at daylight and whip the Rebel cavalry or get whipped yourself.' Torbert sent two divisions under his fighting Brigadiers Wesley Merritt and George Custer in a powerful strike on Confederate General Lunsford Lomax and Custer's West Point friend Thomas Rosser. Now commanding a division, Rosser did not do well. The Confederate withdrawal began as a trickle and swelled to a panic, growing to a flood ending in a stampede known as the 'Woodstock Races'. Rosser lost all his artillery. After this day, the famed Laurel Brigade would never recapture the reputation it once had. The running went on for miles. The Comanches were part of the flight. Many of their men were wounded but only one killed. Myers called this experience '...a shameful rout and stampede.'[53]

On September 19, Early made a game try. Attacking Sheridan's position at Cedar Creek, he initially had success. Union camps were taken, along with guns and equipment. Initially Sheridan was not on the battlefield. In a demonstration of the importance of leadership, Sheridan galloped to his command, rallied his troops and changed defeat into victory. The Union

Turner Ashby, the Arthurian knight of the Confederacy, killed in action. At his death, even his opponents mourned him.

Elijah 'Lige' White, founder and leader of the 'Comanches', a Ranger at every opportunity. Animosity with General J.E.B. Stuart cost White and his unit freedom of action.

John Hanson 'Hanse' McNeill, farmer turned Ranger. McNeill and his son Jesse ranged Western Virginia. Hanse McNeill was killed in action.

Henry Harrison Young, Sheridan's eyes and ears. Young was a Rhode Island book-keeper who learned to love the excitement of war. He survived 100 Civil War fights to die in the Rio Grande fighting Mexicans.

Confederate General Rufus Barringer,
North Carolina cavalryman, brother-in-law
of Stonewall Jackson, captured by Henry
Young under embarrassing circumstances.

Sergeant Joseph McCabe,
pictured left. The
Pennsylvanian cavalryman
became the senior non-
commissioned officer of
Henry Young's command.

Harry Gilmor, Maryland's gift to the Confederacy. Both a *bon vivant* and *beau sabreur*, Gilmor was a fighter and a lover or a lover and a fighter. With Harry Gilmor the priority was uncertain. Union Ranger Henry Young captured this gallant.

Major General Phil Sheridan, a rare example of a Civil War general who understood the importance of Rangers and knew how to use them.

John D. Imboden, VMI student, teacher, lawyer, politician and soldier. He formed and led the Virginia Partisan Rangers. On being made a general, he became a line soldier.

Colonel Elijah V. White with some of his officers and ladies of Temple Hall Farm. The women had recently been imprisoned under suspicion of being spies whilst on a mission to smuggle boots and clothes to members of Colonel White's 35th Battalion of the Virginia Cavalry.

Union Generals George
Crook and B.F. Kelley, roused
from sleep in a Union camp
at Cumberland, Maryland.
They became the captives of
Ranger Jesse McNeill.

Archibald Hamilton Rowand, one of Henry Young's Union Rangers. He frequently wore butternut or gray on missions behind Confederate lines.

soldiers turned. They drove Early's army from the Union camps, recaptured the lost guns and equipment and ran the Confederates up the valley. Early lost his guns and his wagon train. He took such a complete whipping that thereafter the Union forces controlled the Shenandoah Valley.

Bad news followed bad news for the Confederate States of America. On Tuesday, November 8 1864, Abraham Lincoln was re-elected as president of the United States. There would be no compromise of his position.

As a fighting unit, the Comanches were badly hurt, low in strength and morale. Frank Myers felt disgusted with the absentees and shirkers, but had a fierce pride in those who stayed to carry the hardship. White recovered from his wounds and was back in command. General Rosser gave up command of the brigade. There was a great hope on the part of the men, many officers and leaders of distinction in Virginia, of having Elijah White appointed as brigade commander but it did not happen. Under White's leadership, the Comanches performed outpost duty. On November 26 they were part of a major raid into West Virginia on facilities of the B&O Railroad.

On December 18, White joined his men with Hanse McNeill's Rangers and the companies of Captains Kirkendall and Woodson. Totaling about 300 men, they went raiding through snow and bitter cold in the Allegheny Mountains, skirmishing with the Union supporters known as the 'Swamp Dragons'.

While cries of outrage filled the South, Grant's policy of destroying the means to fight was taking effect. The Shenandoah Valley could no longer support the Southern army. There was not enough forage to keep horses healthy and strong enough to campaign. The men were hungry and discouraged. The culmination of despair was not the end of the war, but on December 27 1864, companies A, B, C and F left the army and went home. On roll-call on the morning of the 28th the command consisted of forty-three men and three officers. White considered resignation. Friends prevailed upon him to stay. He went to Staunton to get permission to take the command to Loudoun. From there he wired the recovered Myers to lead them home. They found Loudoun hurt but not as badly as the valley. Once home, they were able to regroup and reunite with their departed men. Myers had periodic meetings with the men in a loose form of organization. A few small raids were conducted which yielded little except some store items needed by families.

On Friday, February 17 1865, White and some eighty volunteers tried to organize a raid on a camp of the 6th New York Cavalry Regiment. To the Union men, the war was all but over. Security was lax. White had initial success, but was given bad information on the number of Union troops available to the opposition. He had to hit and run and had one man wounded, while the 6th New Yorkers reported two men killed, five wounded and eight horses taken.

White made strenuous efforts to reunite his command, but the fire of war had turned to embers in the hearts of most of his veterans. Fewer than 100 men rode east with White to Richmond. As well as a small unit could, the remaining Comanches tried to help Lee's army. At the end of March 1865, they were at the disastrous Battle of Five Forks. They fought rearguard and delaying actions in the days that followed. They knew the cities of the South were going down; Atlanta and Savannah had fallen to Sherman's men. On February 17 Columbia, South Carolina was taken. The capture of Wilmington, North Carolina followed. On Monday, April 3 1865, Richmond also fell.

Still those hungry, exhausted men who were the heart and soul of the Comanches fought on. With Lee's army trying to retreat, the bridges over the Appomattox River were of critical importance to the Confederates. The Union army was making every effort to pin down the Confederates by destroying crucial bridges before they could be used. High Bridge was a railroad bridge located some 4 miles from Farmville. Union troops in the area included all or part of the 54th Massachusetts, the 54th Pennsylvania, the 123rd Ohio Infantry regiments and the 4th Massachusetts Cavalry at High Bridge on April 6 1865. The Laurel Brigade under the command of Brigadier General James Dearing found itself surrounded by Union infantry. Dearing discussed the situation with White. They determined to cut their way out. The Comanches took the front, followed by the remainder of the brigade. White and Dearing were to the front of their men. A fierce fight occurred in which General Dearing was mortally wounded. Lige White took command of the Laurel Brigade, his first action leading a brigade. It was so reduced in number as to approximate the size of his original battalion. There was no hesitation in his actions: he kept the men in the attack, pressing it home with vigor. There were not many Confederate units achieving victory on April 6 1865, but Lige White and his Laurel Brigade did, taking 4 regimental colors, some 700 prisoners and their equipment. For one brief moment it seemed like 1862 again.

Dearing would suffer a prolonged death. He would live till April 23, the last Confederate general to die in the war. Myers wrote that while Dearing lay in agony he was visited by Rosser and White. Dearing took White's hand in his. With his other hand Dearing pointed to the brigadier general stars on his collar, then turned his face to Rosser and said softly: 'I want these to be put on his coat.' The promotion would not come to pass. Perhaps Lee did not think White kept a strong enough discipline to warrant his promotion before the battle at High Bridge. At the time White excelled as acting brigade commander, General Robert E. Lee was devoting all his energy to saving what he could of his army. Promotions would not have been high on his agenda.

From saving bridges, the command was assigned the mission of destroying them as Lee's army tried to break out. They could see the long blue lines of Union infantry rolling forward like the ocean wave. Three men were coming from the Union lines. As they walked casually toward the Confederate lines, Myers had them taken under fire. Myers hated the people of the North with a passion. In this case he claimed that he did not see the flag of truce until after the man carrying it fell as the flag was hidden by pines. All three men of the truce party were shot down. It must have been unusual terrain as Myers could not see the flag but could see the man carrying Grant's letter to Lee clearly enough to have him killed. Myers wrote that another 'Yankee' rode forward carrying a white flag but he, Myers, would not allow the courier to bring in Grant's letter until the entire Union advance was halted. Grant's letter to Lee was delivered. Lee sent back word that two of the best-dressed Confederate officers should go back with the truce-bearer. Captain French and Lieutenant James were sent. According to Lieutenant James, they were 'treated handsomely'. Thus men of the Comanches served as couriers in the surrender of the Confederate army.

Myers was shaken by the appearance of the army of Northern Virginia. It was fought out. Many had thrown away their weapons and equipment. They lay exhausted, awaiting capture. Myers wrote a string of hyperbole about how all Lee had to say was where they were to fight and they would rise up and the final success of the Confederate States was assured. It's hard to lose a war. Men who suffer so much in the losing of it need some outlet to still express belief in their cause.

Up till now all the Comanches could see was Union infantry. They questioned where the Union cavalry was. No longer scattered about, the Union horsemen were now a 15,000-man force under General Phil Sheridan. That force now appeared, blocking the path of the Confederate army. White led a charge of the Laurel Brigade, with Myers and the Comanches taking part. They gained the Lynchburg road and readied themselves to attack toward Appomattox. From this point, they could see white flags appearing in the Confederate ranks. The war was over.

Lige White with what was left of the Laurel Brigade and Myers with the Comanches led their men to Lynchburg. The men had seen enough of war and most just wanted to go home. Myers requested his promotion to major be returned to the Confederate War Department 'if that department can be found'. In the bitter sadness of defeat, he added: 'I have no use for any commission now. I wish I had never held one.'[54] The Laurel Brigade was disbanded by White. The men were given the choice of surrender or trying to reach the army of General Joseph Johnston. The latter choice was a forlorn hope that quickly ended.

At the end of the war, Elijah White returned to his farm. Except for one term as sheriff, he avoided politics and controversy, spending his years operating a feed and grain store, a ferry and serving as president of a bank. In time he turned from war and commerce to God and became a Baptist minister. Yet the old war horse could not completely change. Those who dared to sleep during his services were threatened from the pulpit. Elijah White died on January 11 1907. He is buried at Union Cemetery, Leesburg, Virginia.

The young and handsome Frank Myers could not shed himself of his hatred for the United States. He did not take the oath of allegiance until mid-1867 and despised himself for doing it. His heart called for him to be back in the saddle fighting for his cause. Unable to fight, Myers drifted from job to job. He was a deputy sheriff, a storekeeper, a postman, a farmer and in 1870 added a worthwhile chapter to the history of the Civil War by writing *The Comanches*. Frank Myers died in 1906.

Chapter 10

John Hanson 'Hanse' and Jesse McNeill

John Hanson 'Hanse' McNeill was born on June 12 1815 near Moorefield, Virginia. Throughout his youth, Hanse McNeill experienced the argument that grew to hatred over opposing views on slavery. He knew first-hand the divisions within communities and families. McNeill married Jemima Cunningham in 1837 and for twenty-four years lived a successful life as a farmer and stock-breeder. An adventurous man, McNeill on several occasions moved his family to greener pastures, once to Kentucky and later to a 500-acre farm in Missouri where he was at the forefront of the agricultural community. He had knowledge of farm animals and was well-known for his compassionate caring for horses, a caring that would impact on his military career. He placed the Southland before the United States. Neutrality was not an option. As the threat of war grew, McNeill supported the secessionist cause.

McNeill had lived in Missouri for thirteen years when argument boiled over into open conflict. In 1861, at age 46, this farmer of limited education and no military experience organized a company of Confederate cavalry and led them to war. His three oldest sons – William, George and Jesse – rode with him. His first experience in battle was a loss to a larger and better-equipped Union force. McNeill never forgot the lesson. He next fought at Carthage on Friday, July 5 1861, where 4,000 Confederates who were primarily farmers forced the retreat of some 1,000 Union men. He was at the Battle of Wilson's Creek near Springfield, Missouri on Saturday, August 10 1861 when the larger Confederate force won the battle but did not gain the state. The casualties were greater than at the better-known Battle of Bull Run (First Manassas). Each side lost more than 1,200 men and both were in shock from the blood-letting. McNeill gained a distaste for pitched battles. He soon concentrated on hit-and-run tactics. Soon Hanse McNeill's men were capturing wagons, cannon and prisoners. In mid-September 1861, the

Confederates won a significant victory at Lexington, Missouri. In this fight Hanse McNeill was severely wounded and his son George was killed.

While on home leave recruiting, Hanse and his son Jesse were captured. Their captors were men they knew well. Their word that they would not break parole was accepted. McNeill roamed freely, even wearing a new Confederate uniform to social functions with Union officers. Freedom in captivity came to an end when Hanse and Jesse were transferred to the former slave market in St Louis, now a federal prison with miserable conditions. The two McNeills escaped, soon returning to their former home in Hardy County, Virginia. They found that war had already left its mark upon the Virginia landscape. There was opportunity for action and a need for experienced leaders.

On April 28 1862, the Confederate congress passed the Partisan Ranger Act. Colonel John Imboden was raising the First Regiment, Virginia Partisan Rangers. Imboden planned to operate in the area of Western Virginia that Hanse McNeill knew well. McNeill set about raising a company to serve in Imboden's Rangers. To eager recruits, John Hanson McNeill was a successful man and an imposing figure: 6ft tall with blue eyes and a long grey beard, he wore a wide-brimmed black hat, pinned up on one side and sporting a black plume. At his hip was a well-cared-for revolver. At his side, he carried a double-barrel shotgun loaded with buckshot and slugs. The shotgun was his weapon of choice. Legends would grow about him, and one often told after his death was that during a raid McNeill's Rangers found themselves between two columns of Union cavalry. One of the Confederate Rangers cried: 'We're cut off!' Hanse McNeill was said to have responded 'So are they!' and then led a charge that broke through the enemy force.

In October 1862, McNeill's men as part of Imboden's Rangers performed a distraction raid designed to draw attention from J.E.B. Stuart's cavalry while Stuart made his famed ride around McClellan's army. This was followed by winter raids that while small in nature served to train and solidify McNeill's men into a unit. The Union forces most often encountered by McNeill's Rangers were under the command of Union General Benjamin Franklin Kelley. A militia officer whose civilian job was with the B&O Railroad, Kelley was a capable and earnest man. On Monday, June 3 1861, Kelley was wounded in a skirmish at Philippi where the Confederates were routed. The fight was minor, but a great public relations victory for the North. The victory helped to break West Virginia from the mother state. Kelley was promoted to brigadier general of Volunteers and became responsible for the protection of the vital B&O Railroad. His mission was well nigh impossible considering that the vast distance and terrain traversed by the railroad was among the most rugged in the east. Kelley was aided by the Ringgold Cavalry Battalion from Western Pennsylvania. This unit would develop a special adversarial relationship with McNeill's Rangers. Union horsemen were in short supply in Kelley's department when the Ringgolds came down from the Keystone State and reported for duty.

Many units of North and South came to know each other during the war. On a few occasions a mutual respect grew into friendship. Such a respect grew between McNeill's Rangers and this Pennsylvania militia cavalry unit. The Ringgolds started as a cavalry company in the Mexican War, being named for Major Samuel Ringgold who was killed at the Battle of Palo Alto in that war. When President Lincoln asked for 75,000 volunteers after the shelling of Fort Sumpter, the Ringgold Cavalry promptly volunteered their services to Pennsylvania. Only infantry was wanted at the time. The Ringgolds were rural Pennsylvania men who had grown up on horseback, as had their future opponents in McNeill's Rangers. The Ringgolds bypassed the reluctant governor and went to the Secretary of War who let them join the army as horsemen. On June 29 1861, they were mustered into service in Western Virginia for three years and staked their claim to be the first Union volunteer cavalry in the field.[1] The Ringgold Cavalry were joined in November 1861 by the Washington Cavalry, another Western Pennsylvania cavalry company. The two units operated together as a Pennsylvania squadron. In time they would total seven independent companies who, though not organized into a regiment, would work in unison. All would be known in concert as the 'Ringgold Battalion'. This arrangement continued until March 1864 when, against the will of the men, five new companies were added and they were officially named the 22nd Pennsylvania Cavalry. For months the veterans disdained the newcomers calling them 'Militia', they would never give up the name 'Ringgolds'. This unit would fight in fifty-seven engagements during the war and were one of the most experienced and successful organizations in fighting against guerrilla forces. As these companies had bypassed the governor of Pennsylvania to get into the fight, their highly experienced officers were bypassed on promotion in revenge. Several Ringgold officers carried the rank of captain through dozens of battles.

McNeill's Rangers and the Ringgold cavalry were worthy adversaries, oddly bonded in war. Given the opportunity they would quickly kill each other, yet there was a mutual respect that one good fighting man has for another. The two units played a constant game of cat and mouse, alternating roles.

Colonel John Imboden specialized in attacks on isolated United States garrisons. As a result of these raids, Hanse McNeill's daring was the talk of the camp. On one occasion he led his company on a charge into the center of a Union supply train, capturing wagons and supplies. His courage would come to the attention of General Robert E. Lee.

In December 1862, Colonel Imboden was promoted to brigadier general. Requested to change his command from Partisan Rangers to the 'regular' establishment, Imboden allowed those who wished to remain Rangers to do so. Hanse McNeill chose to stay a Ranger and began to reorganize his men into a new unit. His recruits came from all walks of life. John B. Fay, who was one of them, would write:

> Nearly every station, avocation and profession in life furnished its quota to this famous band of partisan Rangers. Aristocrats of the bluest blood and their rough, unpedigreed comrades; lawyers, preachers, doctors, merchants, in fact and embryo; clerks and hardy mountaineers, college graduates, mechanics and sturdy farmer lads; the man of mature age and the inexperienced youth all mingled in harmony, and one would have been hard to please who could not find in this organization an agreeable social circle or congenial mess.[2]

While recruiting was in progress, McNeill continued raiding with his company often attached to the 7th and 81st Virginia Cavalry. A typical comment by an officer was 'Captain McNeill, the old hero, came in with 46 more horses and 25 prisoners.' While reorganizing and recruiting, McNeill scouted, harassed and raided with the twenty men who would form the nucleus of his new command. Hanse's son Jesse Cunningham McNeill, Isaac Welton of Petersburg, Augustus 'Gus' Boggs and Bernard J. Dolan were the lieutenants. Boggs would be captured early in the unit's existence and Dolan would be mortally wounded in a fight with the Union Rangers known as the 'Swamp Dragons'.

During the winter months of 1862/63 McNeill's Rangers continued to make Hardy County their base of operations. They knew the country and had strong support from the populace. The Union cavalry needed hay for their horses and their foraging patrols were frequent. Around the middle of February 1863, a train of twenty-two hay-filled wagons were on the road near Patterson's Creek. Riding on the wagons were seventy-five men of the 116th Ohio Infantry, while to the front were six cavalrymen from the Ringgolds. The wagons took the North-Western Pike and headed toward Romney. The Union soldiers were unaware that they were being observed. Jesse McNeill with twenty-four Rangers was concealed on a hilltop above the road. He saw that the infantry guards had put bayonets on their weapons and used these to stick the rifles down in the hay. The men were lolling in the soft hay, enjoying the ride. When the train halted at a creek to water the horses, McNeill charged. So surprised was the Union captain in command that he did not issue any order for defense.

McNeill captured the infantry and began burning the wagons. The six Ringgolds came riding back and opened fire on the Confederates. Not interested in pitched battles, McNeill and his men withdrew after burning or capturing 19 wagons and capturing 105 horses and mules.[3]

As the Rangers were operating under the provisions of the 1862 Partisan Ranger Act, an auction of captured matériel was held. Each Ranger received $900 as his share of the proceeds. At the time, a private in a regular Confederate unit was being paid $11 a month. When men in the Confederate army learned of this windfall, envy and anger at the favorable rules for the Rangers spread.

By the end of March 1863, Hanse McNeill had recruited fifty-five select men. He placed his headquarters at his home town of Moorefield in Hardy County. Moorefield had a population of about 1,500 people. Hardy County was rural and mountainous, with a beautiful valley whose contour was in large part shaped by the south branch of the Potomac River. Hardy County numbered some 9,864 inhabitants.[4] Approximately 260 men were at one time or another members of McNeill's Rangers. Most raids were performed with sixty men or fewer. Moorefield was a Confederate town where the townspeople would provide early warning and logistical support to the Rangers. McNeill's Confederate Rangers often disappeared into the local population. The Ringgold historian would write: 'The community around Moorefield was so intensely "Confederate" that when our pursuing forces did reach there, no enemy was in evidence, the very men in citizens' clothes to whom you talked were sometimes the very raiders you were seeking.'[5]

An alternate base for McNeill was at Harrisonburg in the Shenandoah Valley where he enjoyed the same privileges.[6] From Moorefield, McNeill could easily strike at the B&O Railroad. McNeill's men rode swift horses, and within a day they could use any of six valleys to get to and attack the railroad. The lack of telegraph communication in the area allowed McNeill to strike and withdraw before the word spread.

McNeill came to the attention of Confederate leaders by attacking Union supply trains. On one occasion he came to the aid of a Southern cavalry force. The gray-clad horsemen had been pursuing Union troopers when they unwittingly rode into an ambush of a large force of Union cavalry who were waiting quietly in the woods with sabers drawn. The Confederates were being cut up when McNeill's Rangers suddenly charged into the action. Their arrival allowed the Confederates to escape. The Union troopers stayed in hot pursuit and burned the Confederate camp. One of McNeill's Rangers was captured, but at this time an exchange policy was in effect and he was back in action in a month. The exchange policy would soon end for any captured Confederate Ranger as the United States army decided to keep them in prison camps for the duration. This was a precursor to a later Union decision to take advantage of larger numbers and to end all exchanges.

The success of McNeill's Rangers opened the highest doors in the Confederacy. On March 10 1863, James Seddon, the Confederate Secretary of War, wrote to Brigadier General W.E. 'Grumble' Jones:

> GENERAL: This will be handed to you by Capt. J.H. McNeill, who has proved himself by past service a gallant and enterprising soldier. He has submitted to me, with the commendation of General Imboden, a plan of a gallant dash, with some 600 or 800 men, to accomplish the destruction of the trestle-work on the Baltimore and Ohio Railroad and the bridge over the Cheat River. These are objects of great importance, and their successful accomplishment has long engaged the attention and special interest of the President. Several efforts heretofore have been, from special causes, frustrated, but the practicability of the enterprise, especially by the sudden dash of a small force, is believed to be by no means doubtful. ...You will be expected to afford a portion, at least, of the force required for the enterprise.[7]

The raid looked so appetizing that senior officers decided more men would be better. The well-planned 'McNeill Raid' became the 'Jones-Imboden raid'. On Tuesday, April 21 1863, 2,500 Confederates moved from the Shenandoah Valley on a raid through North-Western Virginia. General Jones would have one wing of the two-pronged force and General Imboden would command the other. McNeill's Rangers, numbering fewer than 100, were a part of Jones's column. Spring snow and rains hampered movement and early snow melt turned streams and rivers to raging torrents, slowing progress. On April 26, McNeill's Rangers were attached to Colonel Asher Harman's 12th Virginia Cavalry who had the mission of destroying the B&O Railroad bridge at Oakland, Maryland. The small Union detachment at Oakland was taken by surprise and captured, resulting in fifty-seven prisoners. Rejoining the main column, the Rangers learned that General Jones had not been successful in an attempt to destroy the Cheat River bridge. More troops did not make a better raid. Jones's large force had been discovered in time for the Union troops to reinforce the protectors of the bridge. Frustrated, Jones turned his attention to a long bridge over the Monongahela River. The bridge had taken two years to build and cost $500,000. It took a day to burn and destroy it. While the Jones-Imboden raid did not destroy the Cheat River bridge, they dropped more than fifteen other spans and rounded up cattle and horses needed by the Confederacy. Many thought it a good raid. It is likely that if McNeill had been allowed to execute his plan, it would have been a great one.

The raid continued until May 21, while General Lee fought the Battle of Chancellorsville to the east and General U.S. Grant moved on Vicksburg to the west. On return to Hardy County, McNeill's Rangers hurried to refurbish equipment and care for their horses. It would not be long before they were called upon again. General Lee had decided to move north into Pennsylvania. McNeill's Rangers would be part of the left flank of the Confederate army. For the Gettysburg campaign, Hanse McNeill's Rangers would be operating with the 18th Virginia Cavalry, the 62nd Mounted Virginia Infantry and McClanahan's Virginia Battery of Artillery, all under the command of John D. Imboden.[8]

In the first week of June 1863 near Winchester, McNeill and his men struck a small wagon train, capturing horses and prisoners. They then moved on to Romney where they found fifteen more horses Union troops had left behind. McNeill's men lived most of their time in territory controlled by their enemy and thus lived exposed to the elements in the mountains. The comforts of Romney were a welcome distraction.

In late June 1863, Lee's army marched into Pennsylvania. The Ranger mission was to ride through the rich Pennsylvania farmland on a foraging expedition. McNeill's men raided the farms of Franklin and Adams Counties accumulating 740 sheep, 40 horses and 160 cattle. These were taken back to Virginia around June 30, then the Rangers returned north. McNeill's

Rangers did not participate in the great battle of July 1 to 3 that culminated on the third day in the Union defeat of Longstreet's assault.

Near Gettysburg on July 3 1863, John Imboden learned of the disaster that was the attack on Cemetery Ridge. At 11.00 pm, Imboden reported under orders to a mournful Robert E. Lee who told him:

> We must now return to Virginia. As many of our poor wounded as possible must be taken home. I have sent for you because your men and horses are fresh and in good condition to guard and conduct our train back to Virginia. The duty will be arduous, responsible and dangerous, for I am afraid you will be harassed by the enemy's cavalry.[9]

Thus began one of the epic marches of the Civil War, the assembling of what Imboden described as 'thousands' of wagons into a 17-mile-long train of wagons and ambulances carrying the Confederate wounded and supplies back to the South in the midst of a terrible summer storm.

The Potomac River was running high. At Williamsport, Maryland, Imboden was forced to make a desperate defense when attacked by Union cavalry. McNeill's Rangers re-joined Imboden in time to be positioned on line, fighting in the repulse of the blue-coated horsemen.

On July 8 1863, the Pennsylvania Ringgold Cavalry were operating to the west of Hagerstown on the Maryland side of the Potomac River. They were seeking to destroy any boats that could be used to ferry the withdrawing Confederates across the high-running river. McNeill had warned his fellow Confederate officers that the Union cavalry was in the area, but foraging had to be done and a wagon train was sent out under a guard of McNeill's Rangers. Among the guards and probably commanding in his father's absence was Jesse McNeill. Young Jesse took the train out further than intended. Perched on a hilltop at Fairview, Maryland, Captain Andrew J. Greenfield, leader of the Ringgolds, saw the train through field glasses and decided to attack it. He was encouraged by a Union staff officer who said 'Go ahead and I will watch you.' Taking a route concealed from the Confederates and leading his men in single file, Greenfield came down from his hill and attacked the train. McNeill's men attempted to make a stand and let the wagons escape, but were routed. In the fight Jesse McNeill and a Union trooper described as 'a small, active wiry man' fought each other with sabers. The Union trooper knocked the saber from Jesse McNeill's hand and gave him a lifetime scar on his thumb, but Jesse escaped. Others were not so fortunate. The Ringgolds killed several Confederates. Two officers and twenty men of McNeill's Rangers were captured. Sixty horses and mules of the Confederates were taken. The wagon train was burned.

Hanson McNeill tried to lead a relief force, but it did not arrive in time.[10] The elder McNeill was angry at his impetuous young son and gave him a tongue-lashing. The wounded were sent ahead for treatment, and McNeill's Rangers returned to their Hardy County base to rest, refit and plan the next raid. Orders came from General Lee to disrupt the B&O Railroad and on August 2 1863, the Rangers destroyed culverts between Cumberland and New Creek.

In August 1863, United States authorities found Mrs McNeill and an infant son returning from a trip to Ohio. Mrs McNeill was arrested in Maryland and imprisoned at Camp Chase, Ohio. A considerable furore was the result. Hanse McNeill and his sons vowed revenge.

On August 27 near Petersburg, West Virginia, a patrol from McNeill's Rangers met a patrol from Company F of the Ringgold cavalry under Lieutenant Benjamin W. Denny. At the first exchange of fire, Denny's horse was killed and another Ringgold wounded, but the Confederates withdrew, losing two prisoners and nine horses.[11]

Brief, hard fights with the Ringgold cavalry were frequent. On September 4 1863, Ringgold cavalry patrols were operating to the front of General William Averell's expedition through eastern West Virginia counties. Imboden and McNeill were seeking to locate and attack the Union force. Their patrols were searching for Averell's scouts. Jesse McNeill caught one of the Union patrols, capturing five of the Ringgolds. Sergeant Benjamin F. Hassan, the Ringgold patrol leader, escaped and carried back word that the Confederates were at hand. Both sides gained intelligence. When Imboden and McNeill attacked, the battle was a stand-off and Imboden withdrew. The Union command, 600 men under a Major Stevens, occupied Moorefield, West Virginia but were unaware that the Confederates had secreted 70 men in a wood about 4 miles to the north. The Confederates were in perfect position to raid Moorefield. A slave saw the Confederates in their hideout and promptly carried the word to Major Stevens. A strike was planned to hit the Confederates first.

What was unknown to Union forces was that Hanson McNeill and eighty Rangers had joined the hidden Confederates with the intention of raiding Moorefield. Both sides started toward their objectives, McNeill moving first. Using a little-known mountain trail, Hanse McNeill made a night march and brought his men close to Major Stevens' camp. The attack struck home at first light. Stevens and his men were caught sleeping and 147 prisoners, 6 wagons and 40 horses were taken. Ranger Private Mark Westmoreland called upon a Union officer to surrender. The officer deduced that Westmoreland was not commissioned and replied that he would only surrender to another officer. Ranger Westmoreland looked at the man over the barrel of his weapon and replied: 'We are on terms of equality here, sir!' The Union officer surrendered.[12]

Pleased with the result of his attack, McNeill moved off on the South Fork Road. The sound of McNeill's attack had alerted some fifty-five of the Union strike force who had been moving to attack the Confederate camp. These men, a mix of Ringgold and 1st West Virginia Infantry established an ambush position about 2 miles north of Moorefield and opened fire when McNeill appeared. A number of horses were dropped and some prisoners used the confusion to escape. McNeill charged the ambush force and drove them off. He resumed his march, only to run into another ambush set up by other members of the Union strike force. Some of McNeill's men were killed and some captured, more of his horses were lost and more prisoners escaped.

On November 16 1863, Union Captain Clinton Jeffers, commander of Company B, 14th West Virginia Regiment, was escorting a train of wagons bound from New Creek to Petersburg, West Virginia. Jeffers had forty men of his company in advance of the train under the command of Lieutenant George H. Hardman. At the rear of the train were forty men of the 2nd Maryland Infantry (Union) under the command of Lieutenant Edwards. Jeffers and ten men were in the center of the column. The wagon train was more than a mile long, moving along a narrow and crooked mountain road. About 5 miles south of Burlington, they were riding in thick woods when they passed the house of a Confederate named Pierce. Beyond the house, the road made a sharp turn. As the lead Union element completed the turn they were ambushed by McNeill's Rangers. Lieutenant Hardman was killed and the Union advance recoiled. Just at that moment a large number of Confederates came out of the Pierce house to attack the center of the column. Another Confederate force struck the rearguard. The guards fought back, preventing the burning of most of the wagons, but 5 wagons were destroyed and 150 horses taken. McNeill's Rangers quickly broke contact and withdrew with their spoils. In addition to Lieutenant Hardman, one Union enlisted man was killed, twelve wounded and five were missing. One seriously wounded Ranger was left behind.[13]

In January 1864, McNeill's Rangers were part of a large raid that was defeated by cold, ice and snow. On a frozen road, Captain Hanse McNeill had a hot argument with General Thomas Rosser over Rosser's harsh treatment of horses. Rosser was greatly angered that a subordinate would dare to challenge his conduct. In time, General Rosser wrote a letter to General Lee complaining about the Rangers and asking that they be disbanded. That letter would result in greatly reduced Ranger operations.

On January 15 1864, a patrol from McNeill's command was waiting in ambush for Union troops when a Ringgold patrol rode into view. Sergeant Armour Thompson of the Ringgolds saw McNeill's Rangers and gave the alarm. The Ringgolds attempted to withdraw while the Rangers came after them. Seeing his horse was to slow to escape from the Confederate riders, Sergeant Thompson faced about and engaged the closest Ranger. They opened fire on each other with revolvers. Thompson's third shot struck the Ranger in his forehead, killing him.[14] The dead Ranger was Robert R. Rosser. Thompson leaped from his horse, took Rosser's pistol, saber, shotgun and horse, then rode off in a hail of bullets. The Confederates gathered around Rosser's body and did not follow.

By 1864, the Union was growing in strength, tapping its great resource of manpower as expressed in the words of a popular song:

> We are coming, Father Abraham, three hundred thousand more,
> From Mississippi's winding stream and from New England's shore;
> We are coming, we are coming, the Union to restore,
> We are coming, Father Abraham, three hundred thousand more.

On January 11 1864, Brigadier General Thomas Rosser wrote to General Robert E. Lee from his Headquarters Valley District. Rosser pointed out his observation that partisan forces were a nuisance and an evil to the service. Rosser wrote: 'They are a terror to the citizens and an injury to the cause. They never fight, can't be made to fight. Their leaders are generally brave, but few of the men are good soldiers and have engaged in this business for the sake of gain.'

General Rosser felt that the Ranger concept as employed by the Confederacy was bad because it kept men from the battle lines, and it created anger among other troops because the Rangers 'sleep in houses and turn out in the cold only when it is announced by their chief that they are to go on a plundering expedition.' This caused dissatisfaction among other troops, encouraging desertion.

Rosser stressed his difficulties with men of his command who were from the region occupied by Mosby, writing that his troops 'see these men living at their ease and enjoying the comforts of home, allowed to possess all that they capture and their duties mere peacetime pleasures' [compared to that of the line soldier]. The duties of a man in Mosby's, Gilmor's or McNeill's Rangers were hardly peacetime pleasures, but Rosser was determined that all men should be equally put in a conventional battle line.

Rosser paid Mosby a snide compliment by writing that Mosby was of inestimable service to the Yankee army by keeping their men from straggling. He called Mosby a gallant officer and one he respected, but felt the good of the service required the situation to be corrected. He offered two men who also did not like Mosby – Major General Jubal Early and Major General Fitz Lee – as witnesses.

Rosser's letter was endorsed by Major General J.E.B. Stuart, who praised Mosby but condemned the Ranger concept. General Lee forwarded the complaint to the Confederate government, writing that to his knowledge what Rosser wrote was correct, and adding 'I recommend that the law authorizing these partisan corps be abolished. The evils resulting from their organization more than counterbalance the good they accomplish.'

The complaints of Rosser, Early and Fitz Lee were rooted in who they were. They were part of the regular army establishment trained to think along conventional military lines. Their opposition was the same as that offered by British General Gage in the mid 1700s when he sought to have Roger's Rangers disbanded. It was the same argument offered by the opponents of Rangers in the Revolutionary War. It was the eternal cry of the conventional against the unconventional. The word 'Independent' stuck in the craw of many generals. The notion that they might not control everything in their area of operations sits ill with most who wear stars. The generals complained about discipline in the Rangers, yet all of them had discipline problems within their own ranks. They were using the buck and gag, cold water treatment and having men shot as their solutions. There were men in the Rangers who looted when they had the chance and men in the line units who did the same. Confederate generals had deserters who raised havoc with Southern civilians. Looting happens in every major war. These generals were unable to differentiate between those undisciplined units improperly called 'Ranger' which rightly should have been disbanded and those Ranger units who, though few in number, were tying down as many or more Union soldiers than these generals could accomplish. No unit that operates behind enemy lines will survive without discipline. It is true that the provisions of the Partisan Ranger Act which established a profit motive for Confederate Rangers created morale problems in line troops and that justly angered generals.

By General Orders 29 dated March 5 1864, the Confederate House of Representatives abolished the Partisan Rangers. The Act provided for such units to be united with other organizations or be organized as battalions or regiments. They were to be brought under the general conditions of the provisional army with respect to discipline, control and movements and subject to army regulations. The order provided an escape clause for those units deemed serving within the lines of the enemy.

On April 1 1864, General Lee recommended that the Fourth and Fifth North Carolina (59th and 63rd) regiments serving in North Carolina as regular cavalry be so retained. Lee desired that Mosby's battalion be mustered into regular service. If that could not be done, he desired they be retained as Rangers for the present. Captain Kincheloe's company in Prince William County, Captain McNeill's company, Major Gilmor's and Major O'Ferrall's battalion in the Valley Department were recommended for disbandment. Mosby's Ranger unit was the only one Lee recommended for retention.

Kincheloe's unit was disbanded, O'Farrall's battalion would be organized into a regiment, and Gilmor's Ranger battalion became part of the Maryland line as the 2nd Maryland Cavalry with its Virginians transferred to Virginia units. The Secretary of War decided to retain Mosby's and McNeill's command as Partisan Rangers. White's battalion was on service with the army of Northern Virginia and not a part of the decision.

While the life of his unit was in question, Hanse McNeill was fighting for his reputation. He was charged with improper accounting for the sale of supplies he had captured. Profit from war brought envy and anger and he was investigated. McNeill was found innocent, but his legal troubles had not ended. Now General Imboden charged him with accepting a deserter from another organization. Cleared of that charge, with his reputation and his independent Ranger command assured, McNeill returned to battle.

On the night of May 3 1864, McNeill left Moorefield leading sixty Rangers. His objective was the railroad works of the B&O Railroad at Peidmont, West Virginia, a small but vital rail center beneath the Allegheny Mountains on the Maryland line. McNeill's Rangers were joined on the operation by the experienced scout Captain John T. Peerce. May 4 was spent getting close to the objective and resting the men while the leaders laid plans. On the morning of the 5th at Bloomington, McNeill captured a train and placed some of his men aboard. Peerce stayed at Bloomington with a small force to capture any follow-on trains. McNeill sent a few men with a flag of truce on the locomotive, while the rest of the Rangers rode close behind the train. The engineer was forced to take his locomotive and cars and the truce party to the B&O Railroad facilities at Piedmont. The small garrison quickly surrendered. McNeill ordered the telegraph line cut, but the Union operator got off a message to General B.F. Kelley, who had his command only a few miles away on the Maryland side of the Potomac. In less than an hour the Rangers destroyed over $1,000,000 worth of equipment including 9 locomotives, 7 machine shops and more than 100 loaded railroad cars. Other engines were fired up and sent racing down the line, creating havoc. Meanwhile at Bloomington, Captain Peerce had captured three more trains and was disposing of their supplies. More than 100 Union infantryman who were taking trains to report to their units were captured and paroled.

Union General B.F. Kelley sent a column of gallopers to Piedmont including some light artillery. They arrived as the destruction was ending, announcing themselves with a few shells that came whistling over the waters of the Potomac. McNeill and his Rangers moved off rapidly, garnered Captain Peerce and his small force from Bloomington, then withdrew without mishap.[15]

The success of the raid generated a flood of complaint in the northern press. Union General Franz Sigel responded by dispatching a force consisting of 450 men of the Ringgolds and the 15th New York Cavalry to Moorefield and Petersburg, supposedly to cut off McNeill's withdrawal. The Ringgolds were having morale problems. A Union reorganization had made them part of the new 22nd Pennsylvania Volunteer Cavalry. They were ordered to Winchester, Virginia with five new companies that the Ringgold veterans loathed and called 'militia'.[16] Instead of one of the combat officers of the Ringgolds being placed in command, the regiment was put under an inexperienced colonel. The first evidence of the different style of leadership came when the Union cavalry did not get marching orders until thirty hours after McNeill's raid and twelve wagons of supplies accompanied the cavalry on the search. The Ringgolds knew there was little likelihood those responsible would be found.

However, success had spoiled McNeill's Rangers. Many of them were found, resting on a Moorefield hillside, reading the mail they had captured. The good fortune of the Union horsemen was thrown away by the bumbling of the new Union command structure. A delayed attack resulted in no more than three of the Rangers being captured. Confederate General John

Imboden heard of the threat to McNeill's Rangers and sent two regiments of cavalry and a section of artillery to support them. They routed the Union cavalry and took their twelve wagons.

General Benjamin F. Kelley had his headquarters at Cumberland, Maryland. Kelley had long experience of Hanse McNeill and wanted him removed. He sent the following order to Colonel Jacob Higgins, commander of the 22nd Pennsylvania Cavalry:

> Cumberland, May 22 1864, 9 pm.
> Colonel Higgins
> Green Spring:
>
> As soon as practicable, send Captain Hart with 125 or 150 men on a scout up the east side of the river to Moorefield and vicinity, after McNeill. The scout will take three days' rations. It is not necessary for me to give Captain Hart any minute instructions. I will simply say I want McNeill killed, captured or driven out of this valley.
> B.F. Kelley
> Brigadier General.

Captain James P. Hart was one of the best company commanders of the Ringgolds; he was in the saddle the next morning with 100 men behind him. Hanson McNeill got early warning from the local populace and took refuge in wooded mountains where Hart could not find him. On the 31st Hart was sent out again along with Lieutenant James B. Gibson and 100 men. This time McNeill intended to lure the column into an ambush. In one of the oddities of war, another experienced Ringgold leader, Major George T. Work, dreamed that Hart and Gibson were going to be ambushed and killed. The dream was so strong that Work asked Colonel Higgins to be permitted to go in support of Hart's patrol. The request was granted and Work set out with thirty men, ten days' rations and a mountain howitzer.

McNeill had men trailing Captain Hart, and these scouts reported that the Ringgolds were riding on the road for Moorefield. The road led through wooded areas with heavy brush on either side. McNeill knew the area well. He selected an ambush site where the bank on the upper side of the road was high and there was thick brush on the low side. The ambush was established on the higher ground. Forced by terrain into the narrow road, Hart and his men rode cautiously into view. McNeill's Rangers allowed the cavalry to get deep into the ambush and opened fire. Three Ringgolds were killed, another mortally wounded and eight others wounded. More than fifteen cavalry horses were shot and some riders spilled from the saddle. All was gunfire and confusion with wounded animals and men crying out and officers and sergeants shouting commands. Hart's column was split with the Captain, Lieutenant Gibson and about twenty men galloping forward while the rear of the column turned back. Hart's horse had been hit twice and Gibson had his saber shot off. About eighteen Rangers mounted and raced after the lead group. Lieutenant Gibson rallied some of the Ringgolds and launched a counter-charge that killed one Ranger and routed the rest.

Hart and his men were in desperate straits when suddenly howitzer shells began landing in McNeill's position. Major Work had closed upon the scene of the action and from a ridge line could see where McNeill was located. Unaware that another Union force was in the area and uncertain of its size, McNeill and his Rangers withdrew. A dream had saved Captain Hart and his men.

For those who were wounded, the battle was only part of the fight as the medical practice of the time often resulted in swift amputation. One wounded soldier's experience was related in the history of the 22nd PA Cavalry (Ringgolds). George Wogan was shot through the elbow and when he was taken to the hospital, the surgeon wanted to take off his arm but Wogan stoutly refused to submit to an amputation. 'But you will die if it is not done,' said the surgeon. 'Well then I will die with my arm on,' was the determined reply. 'Well,' said the surgeon, 'I will get you a basin of water and a sponge. Keep the bandages well saturated and perhaps the arm can be saved.' The result was that Wogan kept his arm and recovered. Many a poor soldier's arm or leg was taken off when it was unnecessary.[17]

On June 26 1864, at the South Branch River in Hampshire County, near Springfield, West Virginia, a company of the 6th (West) Virginia Cavalry (Union) decided to go for a swim in the South Branch River. Believing themselves secure, they stacked arms and let their horses graze as they frolicked naked in the water. To their surprise and mortification, they found themselves staring at a bank lined with McNeill's Rangers. Brigadier General Benjamin Kelley informed Governor Arthur Boreman in Wheeling that about sixty men plus horses and equipment were captured.[18]

Throughout July 1864, Confederate General Jubal Early had been pressing northward down the Shenandoah Valley. On Tuesday, July 29 1864, a Confederate force under General McCausland crossed the Potomac River. On the following day they moved north into Pennsylvania and arrived at

Chambersburg. McCausland burned the town, destroying more than 500 buildings. Forced to withdraw, McCausland sought to ransom Hancock. Some of his men from Maryland threatened mutiny and his demands were dropped. McNeill's Rangers were not a part of this action but provided a distraction raid at Oldtown, Maryland to help protect McCausland's column.

In early August 1864, Union General William Averell was in pursuit of McCausland. McNeill's Rangers scouted the advancing Union forces. Hanse McNeill knew the terrain, but his advice was ignored by McCausland. More than 400 Confederate soldiers were captured at Moorefield, West Virginia. The loss would have been greater, but the Rangers led many men to safety.

On August 7, General Phil Sheridan assumed command and consolidated Union forces into the Middle Military District. Sheridan's mission was to destroy Early's army and render the Shenandoah Valley incapable of providing a support base for the Confederates. Throughout August and September, the Union forces pressed on up the valley, moving through New Market and pressing on to Harrisonburg. Grant wanted Sheridan to keep moving south, but Sheridan did not have the supplies to do so. He began to withdraw but in the process reported to Grant that 'the whole country from the Blue Ridge to the North Mountain has been made entirely untenable for a Rebel army.'

Sheridan also reported news of an October 3 raid by Hanson McNeill as follows:

> A party of 100 of the 8th Ohio Cavalry which I had stationed at the bridge over the North Shenandoah near Mount Jackson was attacked by McNeill with seventeen men while they were asleep, and the whole party dispersed or captured. I think they will all turn up. I learn that fifty-six of them reached Winchester. McNeill was mortally wounded and fell into our hands. This was fortunate, for he was the most daring and dangerous of all the bushwhackers in this section of the country.[19]

Attacking at dawn, McNeill's Rangers had galloped into the tented Union camp and after a brief fight captured more than forty of their adversaries. The sweet taste of victory turned sour when Hanse McNeill was found laying on the ground beside his horse with a bullet near his spine. Not wishing to delay their escape, he called to them: 'Good-bye boys. Go on and leave me. I've done all I can for my country.'[20] The men would not leave him on the battlefield. Hotly pursued by roused Union cavalry, the

Rangers reluctantly followed McNeill's orders that he be left at the home of the Reverend Addison Weller, a local Methodist minister. McNeill knew he would not survive. Trying to conceal his identity, the family shaved off McNeill's luxurious beard to change his appearance. For several days his hosts were able to fend off Union suspicions that this wounded man was the famed Ranger leader. General Sheridan visited and asked the direct question: 'Are you McNeill?' When McNeill answered in the affirmative, Union doctors examined him and confirmed that the wound was mortal. The doctors did their best to make the Confederate Ranger comfortable. When the Union army left the area, McNeill was allowed to remain. Now the Confederates looked to his care, but again under attack they withdrew, taking McNeill with them. The ride to Harrisonburg in a springless wagon was not conducive to prolonging his life. Hanse McNeill died on November 10 1864 in Harrisonburg, Virginia and was temporarily buried there. In 1865 his remains were reinterred at Olivet Cemetery, Moorefield, West Virginia.

There were then those who doubted young Jesse McNeill's ability to command. Some Rangers left the organization and went with other Ranger leaders. Some of the men favored Lieutenant Isaac S. Welton who was a proven leader and took charge when Jesse McNeill was ill or wounded. General Jubal Early wanted Maryland Major Harry Gilmor to take command and was furious when Jesse McNeill and his supporters balked at Early's order. Jubal Early wrote to Lee wanting the Partisan Ranger command abolished. Early's plans were foiled when Union Ranger Major Henry Young captured Harry Gilmor and Jesse McNeill proved himself of exceptional daring.

While Jesse did not have the maturity of his father, he quickly assumed command as captain of the unit and led it well on far-ranging operations. One venture took some of his Rangers into territory usually reserved for Mosby's operations. Around October 14, McNeill's Rangers found some of Mosby's Rangers preparing to hang the captured Private Francis Marion White of Company A, 22nd PA Cavalry (Ringgold). The hanging would be in retaliation for the September hanging of A.C. Willis, one of Mosby's Rangers, by Union Colonel Powell. Powell claimed that hanging was in retaliation for the execution of a Union soldier. Trooper White had nothing to do with the hanging of Ranger Willis, but retaliation is retaliation. On questioning the prisoner, McNeill's men found that Private Francis Marion White was a member of their respected adversaries, the Ringgold Cavalry Battalion of Pennsylvania. McNeill's men knew the Ringgolds had been worthy foes who had also been kind to Southern families at Moorefield.

They asked that Mosby's officer spare the trooper. When he refused, hands went to guns. Recognizing the insanity of Confederate Rangers killing each other over a Union soldier, Mosby's officer relented and Private White lived to go to the horror of Andersonville prison camp. He would die ten months after his release at the end of the war.[21]

The United States presidential elections would be held on November 8. In one of their less distinguished and futile actions, the command was used to disrupt the election proceedings and to intimidate voters who favored Abraham Lincoln. On November 27, Jesse McNeill's Rangers fought a successful skirmish against a detachment of the 6th West Virginia Cavalry under Lieutenant Colonel Rufus E. Fleming. In early December, Jesse McNeill was injured and he spent much of the month recuperating.

Jesse McNeill was described by his fellow Ranger John B. Fay as 'an officer of great courage and gallantry, though somewhat excitable and indiscreet.'[22] Determined to keep the McNeill Rangers in family hands and disturbed by General Jubal Early's intention of placing Harry Gilmor in charge, Jesse McNeill was looking for an action that would prove his talents. Ranger John B. Fay was from Cumberland, Maryland; a strategic mountain town of some 8,000 inhabitants located at the juncture of the Potomac River and Will's Creek. In 1755, the then Fort Cumberland had been the departure point for British General Braddock's ill-fated attempt to seize the French fort located at the present site of Pittsburgh.

Cumberland was a meeting place of the Chesapeake and Ohio Canal and the B&O Railroad. As it was an important transportation center, Cumberland was occupied by more than 6,000 Union troops and was the headquarters of General George Crook commanding the Department of West Virginia and General Benjamin F. Kelley, commander of the Second Division of that department. In 1863, Kelley had ordered the arrest of Hanse McNeill's wife (and Jesse's mother) and Jesse McNeill was eager to even the score. In February 1865, Jesse made the decision to go after both Generals Crook and Kelley. McNeill was not aware that Union generals Duvall, Hayes and Lightburn were also in the town of Cumberland.[23]

Accompanied by a teenaged Ranger from Missouri named C.R. Heller, Ranger John Fay was sent back to his home town of Cumberland. Fay began to spy out the locations of outposts, the sleeping quarters of the generals and the number of guards and their locations. Meanwhile, Jesse McNeill had selected twenty-five experienced volunteers for what was clearly a hazardous venture. General Phil Sheridan and his army were at Winchester and a large force was at present-day Keyser. Even if McNeill penetrated into the large force in Cumberland, if the alarm was given, the Rangers could be easily cut off and trapped.

Riding cautiously, McNeill moved toward his objective awaiting the critical information from his scouts. With Fay satisfied they had the needed information, the two men left Cumberland and Heller was dispatched to bring McNeill to a forward assembly area. There, on February 21 1865, Fay found that McNeill had added additional Rangers to the party and volunteers from Company F of the 7th and Company D of the 11th Virginia Cavalry.[24] The total raiding force was now some fifty-four men. In the assembly area the men and horses were rested and fed while Fay briefed McNeill and other leaders on his findings.

As daylight ended, the march was resumed. Ranger Fay led the way, describing the route as passing over Middle Ridge and across the valley of Patterson's Creek. They rode through the ridges beyond to the base of Knobly Mountain, then north-east to a narrow gap leading upward to open land on the mountaintop. The chill winds of winter were in the air. The road was icy as they passed through snowdrifts of varying depths. At times the snow forced men to dismount and lead their horses. Reaching a road through a lower gap to the Seymour Farm, they then went down the mountain into the valley and across the Potomac into Maryland.

Jesse McNeill was concerned that the raid was behind schedule and would lose the cover of darkness. He called his subordinate leaders together and led them to a nearby house whose owner was known to be supportive. Here the Ranger leader held a council of war. He told his subordinates that as they were losing the night, it might be better to change the objective and strike at the Union outposts. The subordinate leaders were opposed to this and the decision was made to revamp the route and take a more risky but faster way to the objective. They would go in by the New Creek road. This meant that they must surprise and capture the Union outposts.

It was an hour and a half before dawn before they set out, riding over a thin crust of snow that reflected light, thus aiding visibility. Jesse McNeill, Sergeant Joseph L. Vandiver and Rangers Fay and Joseph Kuykendall formed the point with Lieutenant Welton leading the main body. They followed the New Creek road around the base of Will's Mountain, passing beside the river and the railroad to a point about 2 miles from Cumberland where the river and the railroad tracks came to close proximity in a ravine. It was a likely spot for a Union outpost and they encountered one. A Union soldier standing cold guard by the road called out: 'Halt! Who comes there?'

'Friends from New Creek,' replied McNeill. 'Dismount one. Come forward and give the countersign,' called the guard.

McNeill promptly put spurs to his horse, galloped forward and fired his revolver point-blank in the face of the guard. His speed was such that he missed, but the guard was so terrified that he quickly surrendered. Two other Union soldiers had been off duty. They ran for safety, but were quickly rounded up. The Rangers learned that the prisoners were from Company B of the 3rd Ohio Regiment. Threatened with hanging if he did not talk, one of the men revealed that the password was 'Bull's Gap'.

Fay and others were not pleased that their leader had fired a weapon and felt the sound was likely to give warning of their approach. Fay took the point and the march continued. The next outpost was about a mile further on. Thinking they had an outpost in front of them, the five-man guard from the 1st West Virginians were playing cards. The challenge was late in coming and the Rangers had the password. They were able to quickly capture the outpost. The guards' weapons were broken up or taken. Not wishing to be burdened with prisoners, the Rangers made an unwise move when they paroled their captives, telling the Union soldiers they must remain on the spot until they returned.

At the edge of Cumberland, McNeill halted his men and detailed two ten-man squads under the direction of experienced leaders. Sergeant Joseph W. Kuykendall of Company F of the 7th Virginia Cavalry was a Ranger scout for General Early. He had once been a prisoner of General Kelley and could readily identify him. Ranger Sergeant Joseph I. Vandiver led the squad to capture General Crook. Ranger Fay wrote that included in the Ranger raiders was Jacob Gassman who had been a clerk in the hotel where General Crook was staying and whose uncle owned the hotel. Another Ranger, Sergeant Charles James Daily, had a sister named Mary who would become the wife of General George Crook.

Rangers Fay and Heller led other Rangers to destroy the telegraph lines. The Rangers then rode easily down the pike onto Green Street, around Court House Hill, then over the Chain Bridge across Will's Creek. They then moved up Baltimore Street, the main avenue of Cumberland. As they rode, the men whistled Union songs and exchanged greetings with Union soldiers. Some of the Rangers were wearing captured blue Union overcoats, but the light was still dim and even those wearing Confederate uniform could not be identified. Sergeant Kuykendall led off his party to the Barnum House where General Kelley was staying and Vandiver led his men to the Revere House where General Crook slept. Individual sentries were pacing in front of each building but being accustomed to the coming and going of scouting parties they paid no attention to the raiders.

Maryland Ranger Sprigg Lynn dismounted and captured the guard in front of the Barnum House. Racing upstairs to the second floor, the men captured Captain Thayer Melvin, Kelley's adjutant general, and learned that Kelley was sleeping in the room across the hall. Kelley was understandably nervous and wanted to know to whom he was surrendering. Kuykendall told him 'To Captain McNeill by order of General Rosser.' General Kelley and Captain Melvin were then hurried downstairs and mounted in the saddles of Ranger horses with the owning Ranger springing up behind the captive.

At the Revere House, the guard was taken but the Rangers found the door to the hotel locked. The sound of their arrival caused a porter to open the door. The frightened man quickly admitted that General Crook was in the hotel and told them the room number. While Vandiver and Charles Dailey were getting a lamp, Jacob Gassman used his knowledge of the hotel to get to Room 46 where General Crook was sleeping. In his excitement Grossman did not think of trying the door knob but knocked several times. Wakened from sleep, General Crook called out 'Who's there?' Grossman replied 'A friend' and was told to 'Come in'. Just at that time Sergeant Vandiver and Rangers Daily and Tucker arrived. Having a flair for the dramatic, Vandiver said: 'General Crook, you are my prisoner.' Some generals have an odd way of needing to know the authority for events. Crook responded: 'What authority have you for this?' Vandiver replied: 'The authority of General Rosser of Fitzhugh Lee's Division of Cavalry.' Crook then enquired: 'Is General Rosser here?' 'Yes,' said Vandiver, 'I am General Rosser; I have twenty-five men with me, and we have surprised and captured the town.'[25]

The Rangers took the generals and their flags, then rode casually down Baltimore Street to the Chain bridge. A large stable stood nearby. While Jesse McNeill anxiously fretted, his men took a number of fine horses from their stalls including General Kelley's steed 'Phillippi'. McNeill told Fay to guide them out and Ranger Fay led the column down Canal Street and on to the Canal Bank. They were suddenly faced with about a dozen guards, but reacted quickly and captured them, destroying their weapons and paroling them on the spot. Now moving at a gallop, they raced down the towpath until about a mile below Cumberland they were challenged by another outpost. They raced onward. An alert Union guard shouted: 'Sergeant, shall I fire?' Sergeant Vandiver yelled: 'If you do, I'll place you under arrest. This is General Crook's bodyguard, and we have no time to waste. The rebels are coming and we are going out to meet them.' The explanation satisfied the guard and the Rangers were soon on their way across the Potomac. They had traveled some 4 to 5 miles before a cannon firing in Cumberland told them a pursuit was starting.[26]

The Rangers had 60 miles to go to reach safety. At Patterson's Creek a detachment of Union cavalry closed on them. Two Rangers were taken prisoner. The Union force seemed content to engage and delay. Jesse McNeill decided there must be another Union column closing. Leaving a rearguard to hold off those in the rear, he hurried onward. Sure enough, in time a battalion of McNeill's old adversaries, the Ringgold cavalry of Pennsylvania, appeared in the distance. Jesse McNeill dispatched a small force to lead his opponents on a false trail while he turned the main body and the generals away into concealment. The Ringgolds followed the decoy and McNeill led his men to safety with their prisoners. In total his losses were the two captured Rangers.

General Crook would write: 'Finding ourselves completely at their mercy, there was nothing left for us to do but to go with them. We were mounted on horses provided for the purpose, and were taken to Richmond. After staying there two weeks, a special exchange was made.'[27]

The raid to take Generals Crook and Kelley was one of the most daring Ranger actions of the war. Union reports included the information that the raiders did not spend more than ten minutes at their work, that officers sleeping in the same building, indeed in the next room to General Crook, were not disturbed. When the report came in to General Grant, he fired off a message that read:

> City Point, VA., February 21 1865 – 2 pm.
> Maj. Gen. P.H. Sheridan
> Winchester, Va:
>
> The number of surprises in West Virginia indicate negligence on the part of officers and troops in that department. Hereafter, when these disasters occur, cause an investigation to be made by one of your staff officers of the circumstances, and when there has been neglect, punish it. I have recommended Warren or Humphrey as Crook's successor and Carroll to take the place of Kelley. If you want any change from this telegraph me at once before assignments are made.
>
> U.S. Grant,
> Lieutenant General

Sheridan promptly wired back that he wanted Gibbon, would take Humphrey but his last choice was Warren. Sheridan did not like Warren and before the war was over would relieve and ruin the career of the man whose appreciation of terrain had brought the troops and saved the day on Little Round Top at Gettysburg. Sheridan agreed that the Department of West Virginia was lax, but washed his hands of responsibility by assuring Grant that he was quick to punish those who erred. Grant decided he did not want to give up Humphrey. Sheridan put Brigadier General John D. Stevenson in temporary charge of the Department of West Virginia.[28] Both Generals George Crook and Benjamin F. Kelley were promptly exchanged. Captured on February 21 1865, George Crook was exchanged and reappointed to his former position as commander of the Department of West Virginia on March 20 1865. The resignation of Brigadier General of Volunteers Benjamin F. Kelley was made effective by War Department Special Orders No. 282 dated June 6 1865.

The shot by Jesse McNeill and the paroling of prisoners from the outposts on the way into Cumberland were mistakes, but neither prevented successful accomplishment. This was a classic raid performed with detailed reconnaissance and full knowledge of the objective. From there on it was a matter of the courage and will to succeed. It was no doubt frustrating to Jesse McNeill and his men to know that the captives they had risked so much to get were so quickly exchanged.

On March 30 1865, some forty of McNeill's Rangers captured a party of railroad workers some 3 miles from Patterson's Creek. They ordered the workers to take up some of the rails in order to derail the eastbound train that they were expecting. They had rails taken up that would throw the train into an embankment instead of down an incline. That action would spare as many lives as possible. Their intention soon became reality. At 7.00 am the train appeared. The Rangers rode alongside and fired a few shots to warn the engineer to slow down. The engine and two cars ran off the track, but no one was injured. The Rangers then entered the cars, took the US mail, captured four Union officers and robbed all the male passengers. It was all done in twenty minutes and the raiders disappeared.[29]

The war was ending. On April 9 1865, Lee's army of Northern Virginia surrendered. On Monday, April 24 1865, while the body of the assassinated President Lincoln lay in state, Captain Jesse McNeill and some thirty Rangers came into Union lines under a flag of truce. McNeill met with General Rutherford B. Hayes, asking for an armistice of suspension of hostilities in Hardy County until the Ranger could receive orders from the

Confederate command. No armistice was granted. A force of 200 Union cavalry was operating in Hardy County and Confederate guerrillas were surrendering. McNeill and his men were offered the same surrender terms as those given to General Lee.

On May 8 1865, Union Brevet Major General W.H. Emory commanding at Cumberland, Maryland sent the following message to Governor Arthur I. Boreman of West Virginia:

> SIR: I have the honor to advise you that Captain McNeill has surrendered his command upon the terms given by General Grant to General Lee. The majority have already been paroled, and arrangements have been effected looking to the paroling of the balance of his company as well as those belonging to other commands but operating in the Moorefield Valley and under his direction.

Thirty-six years after the end of the Civil War the members of McNeill's Rangers held a reunion in Moorefield, West Virginia. They invited the men of the Ringgold cavalry of Pennsylvania to join with them. On August 21 1901, thirty Ringgold veterans traveled south and met thirty-four men who had served with McNeill's Rangers. The bond formed in war was solidified in peace. The following year, both groups met again, this time at California, Pennsylvania. The Rangers were given ceremonial cannon salutes and met by Ringgold veterans at the railroad station.

Ranger Captain Jesse McNeill told a newspaper reporter: 'We were enemies once, but, thank God, we are friends now.'[30]

After the war Captain Jesse McNeill married and again moved westward, this time to Illinois. He died on March 4 1912 in Mahomet, Illinois.

Chapter 11

The St Albans Raid

Dawn of Wednesday, October 19 1864 robed the peaceful little town of St Albans, Vermont in the golden hues of a New England fall. Elsewhere, far to the south, many sons of Vermont had gone to fight and on this day some were killing and dying at a place called Cedar Creek in the Shenandoah Valley of Virginia. The war, though often in people's thoughts, was far away from this quiet community located some 60 miles from Montreal and 15 miles south of the Canadian border.

There were no regiments of infantry entrenched, no batteries of artillery in defense or horsemen standing picket to provide early warning to St Albans on October 19 1864. Many of the leading citizens were absent in the larger Vermont cities of Montpelier, where the legislature was in session, or gone to Burlington where cases were being tried before the State Supreme Court.[1]

At the St Albans bank, teller C.N. Bishop and clerk Martin I. Seymour reported for work. Merchants Samuel Breck and Joseph Weeks were at home thinking about the bank. Breck owed $393 on a note that he intended to pay, and Weeks reminded himself to send his clerk, young Morris Roach, down to make a deposit of $210. It was the start of a normal banking day for Marcus W. Beardsley, cashier at the Franklin County Bank, and Albert Sowles who held the same position at the First National Bank.

Elias J. Morrison expected a busy day; he was a contractor constructing a building. Looking forward to a day of peace was Captain George P. Conger of the 1st Vermont Cavalry, home on leave after seeing considerable action in Virginia.

There were strangers in town, but that was not unusual; men came and went on business arriving by train or carriage, spending a brief stopover for a few days and moving on. Most visitors were quiet and minded their own business. There was a fellow at the Tremont hotel who was drawing attention by reading the Bible aloud. Some of the other guests complained. It was not that they were against the good book, but having it dinned into their ears hour after hour was a bit more salvation than warranted.

There was nothing to arouse suspicion: no groups of strangers and no large numbers arriving together. The newcomers came alone, or two or three together. Some townspeople noticed that many of the arrivals seemed to be young, in their early 20s. Some might be draft-dodgers using the Montreal train to pass in and out of Canada. Five of the strangers had been in St Albans since the 10th, and three of those were staying at the Tremont hotel. They had told people they had come south from St Johns in Canada. All the young men seemed friendly; they went about the town meeting people, they looked in the stores and talked about what kind of merchandise was available. Some indicated a desire to go hunting, but said they had no weapons and wondered what kind of guns the townspeople had that they might rent or borrow. St Albans was the residence of Vermont Governor J. Gregory Smith. One of these bright young fellows was anxious to take a tour of the governor's home. He expressed admiration for the house and continued the tour, looking in the stables and admiring the governor's horses.

As the day went on, clouds began to roll in; it looked like rain and most people cleared the streets. Some of the young strangers were looking up, looking at the town clock as it neared the time to strike 3.00 pm. As the clock sounded, teller C.N. Bishop glanced up from sorting and counting notes as five of the strangers came through the doors of the bank. They wore loose coats and had haversacks or traveling bags suspended from their shoulders.

Two of the men pulled Colt Navy revolvers from beneath their coats and pointed them at Bishop. The first instinct of the terrified clerk was flight. Bishop ran through a door to a back room where clerk Martin Seymour was working on the books. The armed men followed after them and both the bank employees found themselves seized by the throat with revolvers at their heads. 'Not a word,' said one of the armed men. 'We are Confederate soldiers, we have come to take your town with a force of one hundred men. We are taking your money and if you resist we will blow your brains out.'

Meanwhile, this scene was being repeated at the other two banks. At the First National Bank, John Nason was reading a newspaper. Though a brigadier general of Volunteers, Nason was nearing 80, a home guard officer who was too deaf to understand what the armed men were saying. 'What gentlemen are these?' enquired the old general of clerk Albert Sowles. 'It seems to me they are rather rude in their behavior.'

The raiders numbered twenty-two and were under the command of First Lieutenant Bennett H. Young. Most were escapees from Union prison camps who had made their way to Canada. The plan, conceived by Bennett

Young and approved by the Confederate government, went far beyond the robbing of banks in a little New England town. This was an assault on one country from the territory of another. The Confederates hoped it would have international repercussions and force the United States into a confrontation with England.

To bring England into the war against the United States was a prime aim of the Confederate government. English factories could supply the arms and matériel so badly needed by the South. The powerful English fleet was the only hope of breaking the strangling blockade established by the United States navy. An English invasion from Canada would have a disastrous effect on the Union cause.

English sympathy for the Confederacy was strong. What England felt, Canada felt, as Canada was but an extension of England's desires. Viscount Monck was then serving as the English governor general of Canada, which would not become a nation until after the American Civil War. Within Canada were numerous descendants of the English loyalists who had fled the United States at the close of the Revolutionary War; the hatred of the United States remained. England was concerned with her own self-interest. An emerging United States was a rival for world power; there were vast lands in western North America that had the potential of being incorporated into the British Empire. To have the United States tearing itself apart was not displeasing to many English politicians. There was also the matter of textiles and jobs. The war had disrupted the flow of the cotton so badly needed by English mills. Thousands of English workers had been made unemployed by the American Civil War. Confederate propagandists were active in blaming the Lincoln government. Their pressure on the English government to intervene was strong. Though their sentiments were with the South, England was hindered in openly supporting the Confederacy by the oft-stated English opposition to slavery. The English objected to slavery, yet were greedy for the cotton raised by American slaves.

In July 1863, R.S. Mallory, Secretary of the Navy for the Confederate States of America, sent twenty-seven commissioned officers and forty petty officers to Canada. The purpose was to organize a large force that would be taken by barge through the Lachine Canal to launch a raid on the Union prison camp at Johnson's Island, Sandusky Bay, Ohio. When the United States government learned of the Confederate plan, Charles Adams, the American ambassador, registered a vigorous complaint before Earl Russell, the British Foreign Minister. That plan foundered, but as many as 20,000 Confederate supporters from across the globe found their way to Canada.

In 1864, Jacob Thompson, a former Secretary of the Interior of the United States, C.C. Clay Jr and George W. Saunders who had been members of the US Congress were in Canada serving as Confederate agents recognized by the British government. They carried $600,000 in gold to influence Canada and therefore Great Britain. The Confederates used anti-United States feeling and money to influence Canadian politicians. A variety of plans to harm the United States were discussed, including one put forth by a Dr Blackburn to introduce clothing infected with smallpox into the Northern states. The assassination of President Lincoln was also discussed.[2]

In May 1864, Confederate agent C.C. Clay Jr met Bennett H. Young at Halifax. Young identified himself as an escaped prisoner of war and proved himself to Clay. The young man was determined to execute a strike on the United States. The initial plan was not approved, but Clay did agree with the idea of raiding New England towns, burning them and robbing the banks to gain money for the Confederacy. Clay viewed this as justifiable retaliation for Union actions in the Shenandoah Valley. The plans were then forwarded to Confederate Secretary of War Seddon and were approved in June 1864. Bennett Young was commissioned a lieutenant and appointed leader of the raid.

The Confederates felt confident that the Canadians would not interfere. Despite US complaint as early as 1862, there was no neutrality law in Canada. There would not be until February 1865 when United States victory was assured. Clay had assurances from Young that the raiders would not plunder or rob individuals, but would burn towns and farmhouses and take money from banks or individuals. Any funds secured by the raiders would be turned over to the Confederate government or its representatives in foreign lands.[3]

To assist in the rapid burning of buildings, Young and his men were to be equipped with a chemical compound they referred to as 'Greek Fire'. The original intent was that Young and his men would make their way south, burning towns and houses along the route. However, the distance to be traveled through a roused enemy territory quickly ended this option. In order to raid an unsuspecting northern town close to the Canadian border, strike and hurry back, the security of another country's soil offered the best chance of success. The Vermont town of St Albans met Confederate requirements.

Reconnaissance showed that for the raid to be successful it would be necessary to confine initial activities to a small area. The three banks of St Albans were all on Main Street and located close to each other. Further off were the railroad depot and machine shops. As there were several hundred men employed by the railroad, it was important to the success of the raid that these workers be unaware of the raid until the fires that would burn the town had a good start. In order not to arouse suspicion, the men arrived in town by train or carriage. They would need horses to escape and planned to get these from Fuller's Livery Stable or the townspeople.

Young had twenty-one men with which to execute his plan. Many of them were escaped prisoners of war. A man named McGrorty was aged 38; the remainder were in their teens or early 20s.

At 3.00 pm on Wednesday, October 19 1864, Lieutenant Young put the plan into action. Eight men were detailed to seal off Main Street near the banks. They stopped anyone who was attempting to leave Main Street and took them at gunpoint to the village green in front of the American Hotel. Thirteen of the raiders were detailed to rob the three banks. Men with pistols forced the staff to stand by while safes and cash drawers were rifled. When Samuel Breck came into the St Albans Bank to pay his note, his $393 were taken from him and young Morris Roach had to hand over the $210 that his employer Joseph Weeks intended to deposit. The raiders were primarily interested in funds that could be easily transported. They found a bag of $1,500 worth of silver but left $1,100 behind as it was too heavy to carry.

At the St Albans Bank, clerk Martin Seymour was doing what he could to save the customers' money. With a pistol held against him, Seymour was questioned about the whereabouts of all funds. Some were in bonds and in uncut sheets and were overlooked by the raiders in their haste. Seymour was concerned with restitution from the Federal government for the bank's clients. He enquired if it would be possible to inventory what the raiders were taking. 'God damn your government, hold up your hands,' was the response. The raiders then required the clerks to hold up their right hands and swear an oath that they would not fire on the raiders or report the loss of the money until two hours after the raiders had left.

At the Franklin County Bank, cashier Marcus Beardsley and woodworker Jackson Clark had been in conversation when the raiders came in. Clark tried twice to escape and was put in the bank safe by the raiders. Beardsley was also pushed into the vault. He protested that the air would soon be exhausted, but the raiders closed and locked the vault door, leaving the two men trapped.

At the First National Bank, a customer named William H. Blaisdell came in, saw the robbery and went into action. Blaisdell saw a raider coming

213

up the bank steps with drawn pistol. He quickly turned around, seized the Confederate and threw him to the ground. 'Shoot him! Shoot him!' yelled some of the Confederates. Two of the raiders came out of the bank and held their pistols against Blaisdell's head. General Nason had followed the raiders and protested that 'two against one was not fair play.' The old warrior then returned to the bank and resumed reading his newspaper. The raiders began to leave the banks carrying their heavily-laden bags. Though the hurried search had left much cash behind, they were making off with over $200,000.

Plans began to go awry when Collins H. Huntington passed into Main Street en route to his children's school. As Huntington walked along, a man touched his shoulder and ordered him to go to the village green. Huntington thought the man was drunk and refused to stop. The man responded that if he did not go to the green, he would be shot. Huntington did not believe him and walked on; as he did the Confederate fired. The bullet struck Huntington in his left side, glanced off a rib and left him with a flesh wound. Now painfully aware of the circumstance, Huntington obeyed instructions to join the group of townspeople on the village green.

It had been Lieutenant Young's intention to read a proclamation to the Main Street residents of St Albans, telling them that the raid was in retaliation for General Sheridan's actions in the Shenandoah Valley. He then planned to use his Greek Fire to set the town ablaze while the raiders made their escape back to Canada.

Meanwhile, the Vermont cavalry officer Captain George Conger was riding into St Albans from the east. Conger saw the crowd of people near the green and was stopped by a man named Basford who was riding out of town spreading the word that the place was being raided. Conger continued on to see for himself what was occurring and met Lieutenant Young and another Confederate. Young questioned Conger, asking if he were soldier or civilian. Conger replied that he was a civilian. Young then directed one of his men to take Conger to the village green. Using the collection of people as a screen, Conger escaped into the American Hotel. He went out a back door and ran down Lake Street, shouting to the railroad workers that a raid was in progress on the town and that they were to bring weapons.

Seeing the men responding, Conger ran back to the front of the American Hotel. Men were coming with weapons and Lieutenant Young was beginning to lose control of the situation. He tried to mount his horse. As he swung into the saddle, a Vermonter named Leonard Bingham ran at him, hoping to drag the Confederate leader from the saddle before he could raise his pistol.

Bingham was too late and raced onward in a fusillade of bullets that slightly wounded him. Confederate firing was frequent now. A saloon-keeper came to his door and asked what the celebration was. Young responded 'I'll let you know', and put a bullet into the doorway, missing the saloon-keeper's head by inches.

Young and his men were spreading the chemical compound on buildings and trying to set them alight, but the compound was not working and resistance was building. Young began to move his men to the north end of town to the livery stable where horses were led out. A townsman handed a rifle to Captain Conger who drew a bead on Young, but the weapon misfired. Young was covering the withdrawal of his men, shouting 'Keep cool, boys! Keep cool!'

Conger had better ammunition now and he and Young exchanged shots. As Young and his men needed not only horses but saddles and bridles as well, they were taking these from a store. The raiders were taking horses that belonged to the townsmen and in some cases the owners were fighting to retain their property. Contractor Elinus Morrison was informed of the raid and brought his workmen to the scene. Lieutenant Young and E.D. Fuller, the owner of the livery stable, were shooting at each other. Morrison found himself exposed to Young's fire and tried to escape into Miss Beattie's millinery store. As he grasped the doorknob, he was shot in the stomach and fell mortally wounded. Morrison was a Southern sympathizer and had been seen talking with the raiders.

The townspeople were civilians who seldom used weapons. Though the men of St Albans attempted to fire at the raiders, there were many misfires. Wilder Gibson was a man who prided himself on his weapon and his marksmanship. As the raiders mounted, Gibson took aim and fired. The body of one of the raiders was seen to suddenly jerk upright.

Townsmen and railroad workers were coming to Main Street carrying arms. Captain Conger had anticipated the need for a pursuit and ordered them to bring horses as well. Under increasing fire and with the chemical compound failing to burn the town, Lieutenant Young ordered his men to ride for Canada. Young had planned to rob the bank at Sheldon, Vermont but Captain Conger and his civilian band were in hot pursuit. Young attempted to fire two bridges to stall pursuit, but the fires were extinguished by the Vermonters before they could take hold.

Conger's band consisted of civilians who were not accustomed to hard riding and were in poor physical condition. Darkness was falling and his men were getting tired. They kept up the pursuit, however, reaching

Enosburg Falls, Vermont. There Conger told his men of his intention to follow the raiders into Canada. Twenty-two men chose to follow him.

They crossed the border and rode to the community of Frelighsburg where Conger put his men in line in front of the hotel. To his disgust Conger learned that on crossing the border, the raiders had dispersed, heading for different locations. Conger withdrew back across the border while he decided what future steps he would take. His thoughts only increased his anger and he determined to go back across the border and hunt the men who had terrorized his neighbors.

Conger learned that another band of men had attempted to cut off the retreat of Young's raiders but had arrived too late to accomplish their mission. As he crossed back into Canada, Conger received a message from local US authorities telling him to pursue the Confederates into Canada if necessary and destroy them. At Montpelier, the Vermont Legislature met in emergency session. There was strong feeling that the St Albans raid was only the beginning of raids and might be followed by a Confederate army striking southward. Governor Smith sent a telegram to Lord Monck, governor general of Canada, making formal notification of the cross-border raid. Monck responded that the law would be impartially administered and that a Montreal judge had been appointed to administer the case.[4]

The Vermont militia was called out and as the months rolled by New England prepared for possible attack. The United States Congress passed legislation building up a naval presence on the Great Lakes. The British representatives north of the border expressed concern and regret that the United States should be raided from Canada, but action against the raiders was slow to take shape. The Americans learned that the raider shot by Wilder Gibson and another man died of wounds taken during the raid and at least two others were wounded. The raiders had planned to have a larger force. An additional fifty men had announced their intention to go south to St Albans but had failed to put in an appearance.

The Americans from St Albans were not content to see their savings disappear into Canada. Many people north of the border were supportive of the raid, but some were not. With assistance from some Canadian authorities, the Americans captured fourteen of the raiders and recovered $86,000 of the money. Livery stable owner E.D. Fuller and another man tracked Lieutenant Bennett Young and arrested him. The unrepentant Young could afford a laugh on his captors as he knew they could not take him out of Canada. Young wrote a letter for newspaper publication setting forth his actions as justified retaliation. He denounced the Americans

216

for coming into Canada to arrest him in defiance of Canadian law and announced his willingness to be tried in Canadian courts. Some Canadian officials acted with impartiality. Others, including officers of the court and lawyers, welcomed the money taken from the Vermont banks. Search warrants were refused.

Judge Charles Coursol, a police judge of Montreal, was given charge of the case and ordered that the money be turned over to Guillaume LaMothe, a police chief of Montreal. The raiders were in prison in Montreal but they were treated as heros. Their cells were furnished as apartments and their lavish meals came with a wine list. Bennett Young amused himself by writing to the editor of the St Albans newspaper.

American representatives were not permitted to address the Canadian court on the basis that they had not been admitted to the Canadian bar. American witnesses were jeered on the streets and in the courtroom. When asked if he intended to return to Canada, one angry American representative responded that if he did, it would be at the head of a regiment.

Judge Coursol had released the prisoners and returned the money to them. There was a considerable smell to his relationship with the raiders and in time he was suspended as a result of his actions. It was widely believed, on both sides of the border, that he had lined his pockets with St Albans money. Chief of Police LaMothe was fired. When the political pressure died down, Coursol was restored to his post.

The Confederate raiders were an articulate group who waged a heartfelt and skillful campaign to raise anger against the United States. They made it clear that they were soldiers engaged in a lawful action on behalf of their country, and that the raid was justifiable retaliation for Northern activities in Virginia. They stressed that they had not broken Canadian law and that pursuit into Canada by the Americans was violation of Canadian sovereignty.

The United States looked upon Great Britain and Canada with cold fury and powerful Americans were for war. President Abraham Lincoln had a wisdom that exceeded that of these jingoistic advisors. The first task was to beat the Confederacy.

Canadian officials openly admitted that they knew raids were being planned from Canada into the United States. Relations on the US/Canadian border deteriorated and a strict passport control was implemented. Canadian regimental bands played for Confederate officers and soldiers bound for missions against the United States. Canadian newspapers vilified the United States and Confederate agents were welcomed. The October 22 1864 edition of the *Montreal Witness* noted that Canada was 'a safe base of operations against the North.'[5] When President Lincoln was assassinated, the Southerners in Montreal were permitted to hold a celebration. Canada remained a refuge for Confederates after the war. General Jubal Early of 'the South will rise again' clique took refuge north of the border for several years. When in later years Early accused Ranger John Singleton Mosby of abandoning the cause, Mosby quickly pointed to Early's swift flight to Canada.

Some $112,000 would remain unaccounted for. Confederate representative Clay blamed the raid's lack of total success on the failure of the chemicals to ignite and the later capture of the raiders in Canada. He did not explain the unaccounted for money.[6] Shortly after the Civil War, a group of several thousand Irish called Fenians sought to invade Canada from Vermont in order to establish an Irish Republic there. They were over the border when they learned they were isolated. United States President Andrew Johnson refused them arms and shut off their supplies. American troops were sent to St Albans and the Fenians were left adrift. Their effort quickly collapsed.

Chapter 12

Bushwhacker, Ranger and Guerrilla Bands

War is organized murder, but even in their darkest hour most men can find some restraint in their hearts. However, that is not true of those psychopathic killers who cloak their depredations in the name of patriotism. Charles Quantrill and William 'Bloody Bill' Anderson were lawless savages who sought to rob and murder while boasting of themselves as Partisan Rangers for the Confederate cause.

The area of operations for Quantrill, Anderson and their gangs was in Missouri and Kansas. Any who seek a true Civil War in the sectional fighting between North and South will find the history of it written in the blood of these two states. Missouri in particular was torn asunder in such hatred that torture, hamstringing, beheading and scalping became accepted practices. Savagery begot savagery, spawning a criminal class that included Jesse and Frank James and the Youngers, all criminals who claimed they were fighting for the Confederacy.

William Clarke Quantrill [his birth name] or Charles W. Quantrell or Charley or Ed Hart as he variously styled himself, was the son of a family who moved west from near Hagerstown, Maryland to Dover, Ohio where the future raider was born on July 31, 1837. At the age of 16, he moved to Kansas to join an older brother. Fighting between abolitionist gunmen called Jayhawkers or Redlegs in Kansas and pro-slavery Missourians had begun in 1854 and was ruthless on both sides. The opportunist Quantrill may have initially been for the Union. A man who never told the truth when a lie would serve, he spread a root falsehood that in 1857 near the Little Cottonwood River in Kansas, Quantrill and his brother were attacked by Jim Lane and a band of Union Redlegs from Lawrence, Kansas. In Quantrill's false tale, his brother was killed, leaving the younger Quantrill to survive his wounds and seek just retribution. As a result of this, Quantrill claimed his most hated enemies were Jim Lane and Colonel (Dr) Charles J. Jennison. In actuality

Quantrill lived in Lawrence, Kansas from 1858 to 1861. He posed as a free state supporter and rode as a Jayhawker. There was profit to be made from slave traffic. Members of the group would entice a slave to escape from slavery in Missouri with the hope of freedom in Kansas. The slave would then be captured, tied and taken back to the owner for reward money.

In Lawrence, Quantrill met James H. 'Jim' Lane who was from Lawrenceburg, Indiana. Lane was 47 years old in 1861 and had been a colonel and fought well at the Battle of Buena Vista in the Mexican War. In Kansas he was the leader of those who opposed slavery and a major general of territorial troops. His raid on Confederate ammunition supplies at Osceola on the Osage River was accompanied by an unnecessary burning of the town, including the destruction of property of those who supported the Union. This became a justification for Confederate raids in Kansas. Lane appointed two subordinates who were as savage as those they fought. There were many who felt that the Union's bands of killers called 'Jayhawkers' and led by Charles R. Jennison and James Montgomery were little different than the 'Border Ruffians' of Quantrill and Anderson. Jennison led the 7th Kansas Volunteer Cavalry, also called 'Redlegs'.

There was no middle ground, no being neutral. The billboard of a Confederate officer raising a company of cavalry trumpeted 'You must FIGHT FOR the South or AGAINST HER. There is no other alternative.' Men were hung for speaking up for the Union or uttering secessionist views. Murder was commonplace and often done for profit. The war offered legitimacy to criminal acts. In no area was the slaughter more indiscriminate, the cruelty routinely carried to the extreme, than in the border fighting of Kansas and Missouri.

When the Confederate States of America was formed in 1861, Quantrill traveled east and secured a commission as a captain from Jefferson Davis. The Confederate president was in need of fighting men and did not investigate Quantrill's background. On return west Quantrill recruited eight men and began raiding in the name of the Confederacy. Among his earliest recruits was Cole (Coleman) Younger. From the outset, Quantrill proved to be a ruthless killer. Those who opposed him might as well go down fighting as his prisoners were shot or hung. Quantrill's command soon grew to fifty men. On November 10 1861, they raided near Independence, Missouri and killed twelve men. In February 1862, they came back and killed seven more. Two Union officers were captured, an elderly captain and a young lieutenant. Quantrill's notion of mercy was to allow prisoners to pray before he shot them. The captain took fifteen minutes; the youthful lieutenant refused the offer, saying 'God knew about as much concerning the disposition it was intended to be made of his soul as he could suggest to him.' Both men were shot.[1]

A series of small but sharp and bloody actions occupied most of Quantrill's time. He searched for small garrisons or outposts that he could attack successfully, kill whoever he found and then scatter his command. He believed that it was much easier for a pursuing force to find a number of men than one. Though scattered, the command was given a rallying point, usually a house they all knew where they would assemble on call or a certain date.

On February 20 1862, acting on information that proved to be false, Quantrill led his band back to the town of Independence. This time they found themselves riding into a fortified town and the attack was beaten off. Quantrill rode toward Kansas City and at a bridge crossing of the Big Blue River killed thirteen Union soldiers and burned the bridge they were guarding. As he moved deeper into Kansas, he and his men were surrounded but managed to shoot their way out. The clothes of a man stripped naked and then shot can be used again. When they killed Union soldiers, Quantrill's command often kept the uniforms of the dead and used these on successful forays into Union lines. When they needed items they could not capture, Quantrill and his men would pose as Union officers or soldiers and go to Union towns where they were unknown to make the purchases. On occasion they used the uniforms to capture and kill Union soldiers in whorehouses where the men would have their weapons set aside and their thoughts on sex. After a fight at Shawneetown, Kansas, Quantrill captured seven men and set about hanging them. The youngest of the captives, a brave youth, begged to be shot rather than hanged and was given a bullet in the face.[2]

Quantrill killed a man named Williams. James Williams, a brother of the murdered man, hunted Quantrill relentlessly and, having no success, tried to infiltrate Quantrill's band. Quantrill was suspicious of Williams and death came promptly on his suspicion. James Williams was hanged.

The hunt for Quantrill was relentless and during the late winter of 1862 he found it necessary to go to Texas to elude pursuit. In the spring of 1863, he returned with thirty men dressed in Union uniforms and operated under the guise of a Union patrol on a special assignment. Union Captain Obediah Smith had been having success against the guerrillas, but he had never met Quantrill. Acting out the part of a Union patrol, Quantrill took his men to Smith's house, took Smith's weapon and killed the captain with his own gun.

Quantrill's operations were usually performed with fewer than fifty men. Frank James had joined Quantrill early on and was later joined by his brother Jesse who was four years younger. Frank James was taller, quiet and sober; Jesse was reckless and laughed frequently. William Anderson from Randolph County, Missouri was one of the band and a ruthless man. As there were many volunteers for a freebooter's life, Cole Younger, Bill Anderson and others began to lead separate attacks. The whole command was available to Quantrill if needed and he began to call himself 'Colonel'. Cole Younger and his group ambushed a Union patrol of thirty-two men and killed all but four. Jesse James was the scout on a raid on a whorehouse where twelve Union soldiers were shot down. The year 1863 began bloody and would be described by one of Quantrill's men as 'the year of the torch and the Black Flag'.[3]

In June 1864, William Anderson crossed the Missouri River and killed eight men of a Union patrol including the captain commanding. One of Anderson's men named Arch Clements scalped the dead captain and one of his squad. At the end of June at Huntsville, Anderson robbed the county treasury of $30,000. Shortly thereafter, Anderson was shot in the shoulder. He quickly recovered and was back in the saddle in July. In another fight, one of Anderson's men named John Maupin cut off a Union officer's head and stuck it on a fence post to dry and shrivel in the sun.

Loot played a major role in the activities of these men. Quantrill had long hated the people of Lawrence, Kansas. He saw the town as the heart of the abolitionist movement in the west and the den of those called Jayhawkers and Redlegs. Quantrill's scout, Fletcher Taylor, was sent on reconnaissance into Lawrence and came back with a report that the town could be taken. After discussion with Anderson and others of his lieutenants, Quantrill decided to raid the town. On August 16 1863, the column set forth from the Blackwater River with the black flag of no quarter as their colors. The march lasted three days and required local guides. Farmers were taken from their land and used to guide the column until they were no longer useful, then they were killed. Some of the men including Cole Younger were dressed in Union uniforms. On the morning of August 21 1863 they reached Lawrence, Kansas. Taylor had estimated that there were 75 Union troops in town and 400 on the other side of the river who could be held off.

With some 600 raiders, Quantrill fell upon the town, ruthlessly killing males regardless of age. Homes and businesses were set ablaze. One raider said that 189 structures were destroyed. People fell on their knees and begged for mercy and were shot down. More than 180 boys and men were killed in a morning of savagery at a cost of one guerrilla dead and two wounded. Quantrill split his men into groups and on departure they fanned outward, raiding homes, killing and burning for a distance of 12 miles until pursuit forces caused them to move rapidly.

A wave of outrage swept through the North. Quantrill gave no mercy and it was vowed he would receive none. Some 6,000 men were involved in the pursuit, but Quantrill disappeared into friendly territory and scattered his men. The Union commander charged with stamping out Quantrill and his men was General Thomas Ewing. Union raids, ambushes and retaliation by burning houses were employed, but nothing stopped the Confederate raiders. Ewing tried another approach. Unable to pinpoint who was supporting Quantrill, Ewing in Order #11 forced the entire population out of Jackson, Cass, Bates and a part of Vernon Counties of Missouri. Some 10,000 people were made to leave their homes. Still the raids did not stop. When he knew of the family of a guerrilla, Ewing captured them. Thus the wives, sisters and mothers of many guerrillas were taken into custody. A number of these were taken to Kansas City and lodged in a ramshackle structure that either burned or collapsed, killing many of the women and injuring others. Among the women were two sisters of William Anderson. One of the sisters was killed, the other badly injured. William Anderson increased his raids and soon gained the nickname of 'Bloody Bill'.

After the Lawrence, Kansas massacre a new atrocity was added. The victims were now scalped. Both sides claimed that the other started the practice. Small but vicious fights were frequent. Men knew that surrender was not an option; it was win or die. At Blue Springs, Quantrill's men killed seventy-five people. They missed the fat and elderly George Rider. When he heard the raiders coming, Rider laid down in a ditch on his back. His belly was so bloated that Quantrill's men thought he had been dead for several days and had swollen up.[4]

The regular Confederate establishment was well aware of what Quantrill was doing; his organization had been given legitimacy by the Partisan Ranger Act of 1862. Confederate General Sterling Price wanted to gain control of Missouri for the Confederacy and saw Quantrill and his men as a vital part of an effort by regular Confederate forces to take the state. In September 1864, Price marched 12,000 Confederates from Arkansas into Missouri. Quantrill and his men were expected to raid rear areas while Price attacked in the front. By October, Price's effort would be a failure and the guerrillas would be left to their own devices, but the fall of 1864 was one bloody episode after another. With some fifty men, William Anderson rode around 50 miles north of Jefferson City and struck at the town of Centralia. He captured a stagecoach and took a train, robbing and killing its passengers including shooting down twenty-four unarmed soldiers on leave. Union Major A.E.V. Johnson led a force of 150 men of the 39th Missourians in pursuit. Some 3 miles out of town, Johnson and his men were ambushed by Anderson and some 260 guerrillas. Frank and Jesse James were among the ambush force. Johnson unwisely drew up his troops in a line. Anderson's men put their reins in their teeth, drew their pistols and charged. They proved a lesson learned time and again in the Civil War: that stationary troops on horseback do not fare well against a charging force. The guerrillas were quickly on the Union troops. Three of Anderson's men were killed outright and another mortally wounded but their revolvers were efficient. Frank James killed Major Johnson and the Union troops broke. Johnson and 123 of his men were killed. The bodies showed that many of the wounded had been executed after surrender.

Anderson formed his own gang but Quantrill's lieutenants such as George Todd, Jim Little, Press Webb, Dick Yager and Dave Poole ranged far and wide, killing as they went. Captured men were made to dig their own graves and were then shot into them. Jim James, Charles Bochman and a man named Perkins died in this way. In October 1864, the Union 2nd Colorado Cavalry killed George Todd. Anderson had been trying to link up with General Sterling Price and had been killing his way toward Kansas City when he learned that Price's effort had failed.

Close to the Missouri River he met a large Union force and could not be dissuaded from an attack. Anderson had recruited heavily and had several hundred men, but they were mostly inexperienced. In the charge, Anderson's horse took the bit and ran away, putting him 75 yards ahead of his men. Three rounds from Union Spencer carbines ripped into Anderson and killed him. A rope was put around his neck and his body was dragged off. The murderous career of Bloody Bill Anderson was over. Now it was his turn to have his head cut off and put on a pole.

With the United States winning the war, the pressure on Quantrill and his men was continuous and many fled to Texas. Jesse James decided to go with this group who, as a going away party, killed twenty-nine men of the 15th Kansas Cavalry. James shot down Captain Emmett Goss, the Union commander. He then rode after Chaplain U.P. Gardner of the Kansas Cavalry who identified himself as a non-combatant minister. James shot Gardner in the face and killed him.

BUSHWHACKER, RANGER AND GUERRILLA BANDS

With the war ending, Quantrill was running out of places to hide. He decided that the pursuit would not expect him to head eastward and planned to ride for Kentucky. Frank James agreed to accompany Quantrill and in June of 1865, the two men left Nelson County with a dozen companions, heading for the Salt River. While they were eating at a wayside house, a column of Union cavalry came up under the command of Captain Edward Terrell. This officer had fought Quantrill before and was not hesitant in attacking. While Quantrill and his men tried to get to their horses, the cavalry were on them. Quantrill's horse ran away and Clark Hockingsmith dismounted and gave the leader his mount. Hockingsmith was killed. Quantrill was shot twice, the killing shot entering close to the collarbone, then traveling down into the spine. Mortally wounded, Quantrill was taken to a military hospital in Louisville. He was a Roman Catholic and it was said that the priest who heard his confession was told everything. The death was a long one, which was fortunate as Quantrill had much to get off his chest and cleanse his soul. He was buried in a Roman Catholic cemetery in Louisville, Kentucky.

Chapter 13

The Raid to Burn New York City

On Friday, November 25 1864, Confederate raiders attempted to burn New York City by setting fires in hotels, theaters and Barnum's Museum. Newspapers reported that three hotels were destroyed and sixteen others damaged with a loss of $442,000. The planning was believed to be the work of Confederate Ranger Colonel Robert Martin who intended to trigger an uprising of the Northern supporters of the Confederacy called the 'Sons of Liberty'.

Robert Maxwell Martin was born on January 10 1840 near Greenville, Muhlenberg County, Kentucky. 'Bob', as he was known, was over 6ft in height and although somewhat slender (about 160lbs), he possessed a well-knit figure. His friend and fellow Ranger Adam Rankin Johnson wrote:

> His hair was brown, his eyes a light blue, the pupils of which would expand thus enabling him to see pretty well in the dark. He had a genial, happy face withal, and a smile like sunshine. There was nothing in his outward appearance that bespoke the wonderful courage and daring that [he] continually displayed during the ensuing years of the war.[1]

Along with Adam Rankin Johnson, Bob Martin had served as lead scout for Nathan Bedford Forrest. When the Confederates suffered their first great defeat of the war at the surrender of Fort Donelson, Forrest refused to surrender. It was Martin and Johnson who made the reconnaissance and found the ice and water path by which Forrest and his men escaped.

When General Van Dorn asked Forrest for reliable scouts, Martin and Johnson went with him. In an engagement with retreating Union forces at the Battle of Farmington, a Union color-bearer stopped and waved his flag in defiance. Martin accepted the challenge and spurred his horse forward. The two men fell into a wrestling match in which the flag tore away, Martin getting the ornate pole, and the color-bearer the cloth. Under heavy fire,

Martin returned safely. Shortly afterward a Confederate staff officer was shot. Van Dorn and his staff watched as a Union soldier rode out to rob the body. Van Dorn was incensed and ordered artillery fire on the Union soldier. Before the guns could fire, Martin went after the man, killed him and went through his effects. Again, under a hail of fire, he made his way to safety and, proudly showing his foe's revolvers, said to Johnson: 'Say, partner, this is a cheaper way to get a dandy pair of navy sixes than to pay seventy-five dollars for them, isn't it?'[2]

Forrest was frequently being asked by other generals for the services of the two scouts. He next loaned Martin and Johnson to General Breckenridge. The two scouts carried ciphered messages through the lines to Kentucky businessmen seeking to recruit behind Union lines.

They began to recruit a Ranger unit without thinking which of them would command. When they saw that men who were recruited needed a chain of command, Martin deferred to Johnson and both swore to support each other. Johnson became captain and Martin his lieutenant. With twenty-seven men Johnson and Martin captured the town of Newburg and its garrison, using stovepipe and wagon wheels to simulate artillery and threatening the town with destruction if there was not immediate surrender. Johnson was henceforth known as 'Stovepipe' Johnson. Recruiting was easy after that. When Johnson formed his command (the 10th Kentucky Partisan Rangers) and became colonel, Martin was lieutenant colonel. These Rangers soon controlled the rural areas of eight Kentucky counties. For six months they operated 250 miles in the rear of U.S. Grant's army.[3]

General Bragg wanted all Partisan Rangers dismounted and put in the infantry, this despite the fact that Forrest with 1,500 and Morgan with 900 Rangers had raised such havoc with Union supplies that they had reduced Don Carlos Buell's army of 50,000 to ten days' rations. Meanwhile, Bragg with 30,000 men, sat in Chattanooga doing nothing.[4] In order to get out from under Bragg, Johnson put his men with John Hunt Morgan. In time Johnson became a brigadier general and commanded one of Morgan's brigades. Martin took command of the 10th Kentucky Partisan Rangers. Just prior to Morgan's departure on the Ohio raid in 1863, Martin was wounded at McMinnville, Tennessee. He was shot in the chest by a Minié ball that lodged in his right lung and remained there. As a result of the wound Martin did not go on the Ohio raid, but his men did and were part of the 1,800 that were captured with Morgan. Adam Rankin Johnson escaped, but Morgan's command was shattered. Despite his wound, Bob Martin continued to lead successful raids. He was again shot, this time a painful wound in the instep.

A cheering note was that Morgan, the brilliant Captain Tom Hines and some of the other Confederate officers escaped from prison and Morgan was attempting to reorganize the remnants of his command. When Morgan went back into action, Bob Martin went also, riding into battle with one foot in the stirrup and the other on a pillow and hooked around the horn of his saddle.[5]

While General Morgan was making plans for his next raid, Colonel Robert Martin was ordered to Richmond in the company of Kentucky politician and Confederate supporter Senator Henry C. Burnett. Martin met with Secretary of War Seddon and President Jefferson Davis and received orders that must have come as a surprise. Martin was ordered to travel to Toronto, Canada and report to Confederate Colonel Jacob Thompson for service along the northern borders of the United States. Martin requested that Lieutenant John W. Headley, a Kentucky officer in whom he had a special trust, be permitted to accompany him. The request was granted.[6]

The Confederate plan to attack the United States from the supposedly neutral English-controlled territory of Canada revealed the increasing desperation of the South. The Confederates were running out of men. Thousands of their soldiers languished in Union prison camps that could be reached by a raid from Canada. Jefferson Davis and his planners clung to the hope that the people in the North were weary of the war and that Northern sentiment on behalf of the South was rising. By sending raids down from Canada, they hoped to stir the pot of discontent with the long and bloody war. This dissatisfaction would create a screen behind which they could free an army of Confederate soldiers from prison camps. These soldiers would be armed by and would support those Northerners who wanted to end the war. Local governments would be deposed and those friendly to the South installed in their place. The key area was in the north-west, in particular Indiana and Illinois, but also in whichever Western states could be induced to leave the Union. The intent was not to have these non-slave-holding states join the Confederate states of America, but to break them away from the United States into a formation of their own. Chicago would be the likely capitol of the North-Western Confederacy of States. In the United States a presidential election was coming up. That seemed a good time to bring all this together and strike south across the Canadian/US border.

Colonel Martin and Lieutenant Headley needed to pass through Union lines to get to Canada and decided to go by way of the west. On horseback and by river boat they traveled from Meridian and Corinth to St Louis to Alton, Illinois and took a train to Chicago. They spent a day seeing the city, then caught a Michigan Central Railroad passenger train to Detroit and from there crossed the border to Windsor and on to Toronto. Within a few days of arrival they had met nearly 100 Confederate refugees and escaped prisoners. They also learned that there were United States detectives constantly seeking to infiltrate this band. One of the key people they met was the youthful-looking Captain Thomas Henry Hines. A true daredevil Kentuckian, Hines was one of Morgan's Rangers. Davis sent him north as Hines had been the brains behind the daring escape that sprang John Hunt Morgan from the Ohio penitentiary. Davis felt that if Hines could achieve that, he could come up with a plan to free Confederate prisoners of war. Hines was involved with an organization of Northern supporters of the Confederacy called the 'Sons Of Liberty'.

In August 1864, planning meetings were held at St Catharine's and at London, Canada. It was decided that sixty of the Confederate soldiers would participate in a raid to free prisoners. Illinois was a prime target. The National Democratic Convention was beginning on August 29 at Chicago and many Confederate supporters or people who just wanted peace were believed to be in their midst. There were 5,000 Confederate prisoners at Camp Douglas and 7,000 at Springfield. Arms were secured in Canada and it was believed that the Sons of Liberty were gathering more weapons in the United States. Confederate hopes were dashed when it became evident that the Sons of Liberty were more vocal than active in their support of the South. The raid to free the prisoners had to be called off.[7]

The next scheme was to seize the fourteen-gun Union gunboat *Michigan* that was anchored near Johnson's Island, a Lake Erie prison camp by Sandusky, New York. This ship was the most powerful naval vessel on the Great Lakes; by capturing it the Confederates would be able to threaten cities in the states of New York, Ohio, Illinois, Michigan and Wisconsin. Captain Charles Cole, one of Nathan Bedford Forrest's Rangers, and a newly-appointed Confederate naval officer, Captain John Yates Beall, were put in charge of this operation. Beall was a Virginian who was badly wounded by a lung shot while fighting as a volunteer with Turner Ashby's Rangers early in the war. While convalescing he developed a plan to strike the Union forces by becoming an inland waterways privateer. He tested the idea on the Potomac River and Chesapeake Bay and though captured, he gained considerable experience. When released he determined to try his luck on the Great Lakes.

Colonel Thompson, in overall charge of Confederate activities in Canada, gave his approval but stipulated 'In all you may do in the premises, you will carefully abstain from violating any laws or regulations of Canada or British authorities in relation to neutrality.'[8]

Captain Cole believed the capture could be made. He asked to be put on secret detached service to accomplish the task. Cole then undertook the reconnaissance in civilian clothes. He made friends of the officers of the Union warship and wined and dined them. He asked for and received tours of the camp where the Confederate prisoners were held and talked with the three Confederate major generals and five brigadier generals that were among the captives. The Confederate officers were kept abreast of the planning. Their task would be to create a prison revolt when they heard a signal gun fired that would mean the *Michigan* was in Confederate hands.

The plan called for Captain Beall and twenty of the Confederate soldiers in Canada to board the *Philo Parsons*, a small passenger-carrying steamboat near Detroit, take control and put the passengers and crew ashore. The innocent-looking craft would then steam to Sandusky until they were close to the *Michigan* when they would turn alongside the Union gunboat, signal 'Away Boarders' and capture her. With this firepower and the revolt from within, the Confederates in prison at Johnson's Island could be freed. As the capstone of the plan, Cole planned to invite the officers of the *Michigan* to dinner on September 19 1864. He planned to drug their wine and be on board the gunboat when Captain Beall arrived. Signal lights would be flashed for the ship and shore to confirm the capture. As a further measure, he bribed the engineer to temporarily disable the ship's engine.

The plan seemed foolproof, but a Union agent had penetrated Colonel Thompson's headquarters in Toronto and learned of the scheme. In Sandusky, the officers of the *Michigan* were informed of the plot. They arrested Captain Cole and put him irons. With that done, the warship got up steam and went to general quarters. They were prepared to go after the *Philo Parsons* if she appeared. They could not have gone far. The engineer had disabled the engine.[9]

Unaware of the capture of Cole, Beall proceeded with his part of the raid. On Sunday, September 18 1864, Beall and his men began boarding the *Philo Parsons* at different points on its route. After leaving the stop at Kelley's Island, Beall and his men drew their pistols and took control of the boat. Around 10 miles from Johnson's Island is Middle Bass Island. Here Beall and his men put the passengers ashore. Another steamboat, the *Island Queen*, was in port and the Confederates also took over this vessel. Heading onward toward Johnson's Island, Beall ordered the *Island Queen* scuttled and she was sunk near Chichanolee Reef. Cole then began to look for the signal lights from Captain Cole, but none appeared. The Confederates under Beall made it clear that they had no intention of going up against a warship that had obviously not been captured. Seventeen of the men refused to go on and signed a note admiring Beall's courage but refusing any further part in his plan. Beall had to turn back. He proceeded to Sandwich, Canada where he dropped off the men and scuttled the *Philo Parsons*. The failed raid drew great publicity. A swarm of US detectives crossed into Canada looking for the raiders. The British authorities in Canada were becoming uneasy about these ventures from their borders.

Undaunted by failure, the Confederate Rangers continued to develop daring plans. The United States presidential election was scheduled for November 8 1864. Colonel Thompson needed to create a circumstance in which Confederate prisoners of war could be released and serve as a rallying point for the Sons of Liberty Southern supporters in the North.

Freeing Confederate prisoners was the mission of Captain Thomas Hines. He was joined by the daring English adventurer Colonel St Leger Grenfell who had ridden with Morgan and other Rangers. The two men would lead a Sons of Liberty-supported raid that would free the Confederate prisoners at Camp Douglas and Rock Island, take over the local government offices of Chicago and launch the North-Western Confederacy.

To disrupt the election it was planned to set election day fires in Boston and Cincinnati. New York was also a prime target. Always contentious, the city of immigrants had erupted in anti-draft riots on July 13 1863. For three days businesses were looted and Negroes were hunted down, shot or hung. It required troops marching from the battlefield at Gettysburg to restore order. To the Confederates, New York looked as though it was ripe for revolution. The Confederates believed the 'Peace' Democrats of the city and state government would not resist New York City being captured. The Confederates were told by supporters that they could count on 20,000 armed men coming to their support. Prisoners of war from the camp at nearby Fort Lafayette could be released and added to this force. It was believed the governor of New York would remain neutral. Thompson, Martin, Hines and the rest of the Confederates believed that once New York was taken, there would be a convention at which New York, New Jersey and the New England states would form their own confederacy and cooperate with the Confederate States of the South and a North-Western Confederacy. The Confederates thought this would be the final dissolution of the United States. The timing of the raid would be the afternoon of the presidential election on November 8. While the takeover of city offices was under way, a distraction was needed. That would be provided by fires set around the city. Colonel Robert Maxwell Martin put forth the plan and accepted the mission to lead the raid to burn New York City.

Colonel Martin and Lieutenant Headley had been held in reserve for some daring enterprise. They kept a low profile, even living apart in Canada. Six other Confederates, who had not been involved in other operations, were chosen for the mission. The eight men came by train from Toronto, traveling most of the route in pairs to arrive in New York City ten days before the election. The path had been smoothed by a New Yorker, Mr James McMasters, who was responsible for in-city arrangements. A Missouri captain named Longmire was also in the city developing the incendiary substance called Greek Fire that would be used to set the flames. New York was a city of primarily wooden buildings with more than half a million people crowded into them. There would be no warning of the attack and the fires were to be started at night. In the euphoria of their planning, there was no consideration of what horror would occur if the unsuspecting masses were trapped in the flames.

Scattered about in different hotels, the raiders made a reconnaissance of their objectives and relaxed in the enjoyment of New York's culture scene. They went to a torchlight rally in support of the Democratic candidate General George B. McClellan. They attended lectures and sermons. What they heard was fodder for their high hopes. The people were tired of war. Meanwhile, the Lincoln administration was not standing idly by. The army was strongly in support of the president and troops were being dispatched to possible trouble spots. General Benjamin F. Butler was ordered to New York City with several thousand troops.

One of the men most hated by the South, Ben Butler was called 'Beast' and 'Spoons' by his Southern adversaries. The former nickname was applied because Butler was no gentleman in Southern eyes. When Butler was in command in New Orleans, women of the city were taunting Union officers, some lifting their skirts and flashing them. From second-floor windows, women were dumping chamber pots on Union officers as they walked the sidewalks. Butler put out an edict that in future any woman that performed these unseemly acts would be treated as a 'woman of the town'. Polite language stripped away, that meant treated as a whore. Butler's action stopped this form of feminine urban warfare. Butler was then accused of stealing silverware, hence he was called 'Spoons' in the South.

The arrival of Butler and the blue-coated troops took the starch out of the Sons of Liberty and Peace Democrats. From brimming optimism, civilian

James McMasters went to quivering fear. Without the support of their Northern friends, the Confederate Rangers were forced to postpone their plans. Though New York City voted heavily against him, Abraham Lincoln was re-elected president. Union action had also forestalled the Confederate raids at Chicago, Cincinnati and Boston. Martin and his Rangers wanted to try again on Thanksgiving Day, but McMasters and his political allies were no longer inclined to risk their necks to a rope. Captain Longmire also deserted the operation.

Colonel Robert Martin and his men felt they had to do something. They decided that uprising or not, they would burn New York City. They consoled themselves with reasoning that Sheridan and Sherman were burning homes in the South and New York in flames would give the hated Yankees a vivid experience in that aspect of war. The plan was to attack the business district on Broadway by setting fires in hotels. Several theaters were later added as objectives, as was P.T. Barnum's famed museum with its animal collection in the basement. Lieutenant Headley picked up the Greek Fire and found it to be twelve dozen 4oz bottles of a substance that looked like water. The valise that he had to carry it in was about 30in long and so heavy that he needed to change hands every ten steps. Headley carried the bag on a crowded horse car on Bowery Street. The smell was so bad that a fellow passenger remarked: 'There must be something dead in that valise.'

Headley finally arrived safely at the meeting-place and distribution of the bottles was made. Each of the eight men had engaged a room at three or four hotels, signing in under fictitious names. Among the false names used were John School Md; Lieutenant Lewis, USA; J.B. Richardson of Camden, New Jersey; S.M. Harner of Philadelphia; George Morse and C.E. Morse of Rochester. Black satchels were purchased for $1 each and each man bought an overcoat. They would put the overcoat and bottles in the bag, go to the three or four hotels each had been assigned and proceed to their rooms. Once inside the rooms, they would take out the bottles and overcoat, collect bedding and furniture and set the fires. They would then put on the overcoats as a form of disguise and leave that hotel for the next one. The fires were to be started at 8.00 pm in the hope that people would still be awake and would escape the flames.

Two of the eight men lost their nerve and failed to appear at the final rendezvous at 6.00 pm on Friday, November 25 1864. Each of the six who remained took ten bottles of Greek Fire and went to their hotels. Colonel Martin was to burn the Hoffman, French's, St Denis and the National Hotels. Lieutenant Headley had as targets the Astor House, City

Hotel, Everett House and the United States Hotel. Altogether the Raiders planned to set fire to nineteen hotels and to attack targets of opportunity. Thirteen hotels were attacked and three other structures: two theaters – the Niblo's Garden Theater and the Winter Garden Theater – and Barnum's Museum. The fires were started, but the men found the so-called Greek Fire to be ineffective. They could have started fires with only a match, but the chemical was intended to create flames that would resist efforts to extinguish them. As each of the men had three or four targets, not all fires could be started at the same time. Fires would be reported at 8.45, 8.55, 9.20, 10.30 and midnight. Five hotel fires occurred after 1.00 am and as late as 2.30 am.[10] All of these buildings were occupied. If the burning went well, many casualties would result.

Fire alarms were ringing about the city and people were crowding into the streets. Headley observed 'the wildest excitement imaginable'. The word spread that rebels were burning the city and crowds were looking for culprits that they could hang from lampposts. New York City fire companies that were often working-class social clubs were racing through the streets. Proud of their strength, many were pulling their equipment by hand. The three Booth brothers, including John Wilkes Booth, were playing in a performance of Shakespeare's *Julius Caesar* at the Winter Garden. The *New York Times* of Sunday, November 27 1864 reported that the theater was crowded and 'the panic was such that for a few moments that it seemed as if all the audience believed the entire building in flames, and just ready to fall upon their devoted heads.' One of the Booth brothers was on stage and cautioned the audience to remain calm. A judge named McCunn joined him in calming the crowd. In the theaters and at Barnum's, strong voices urged calm, and panic was averted. On the day following the attack, P.T. Barnum published a letter in the *New York Times* in which he bragged about the fire safety of his museum and said he had nine different places of egress from his lecture hall. Some questioned if this was for fire safety or to make room for new customers. This genius of hokum played on the ignorance of immigrants and rural folk by taking their money and then having signs about that said 'This way to the egress'! People thought that 'the egress' was another exhibit or strange animal and found themselves in the street. Though the equipment of the fire company was rudimentary, the fires were quickly extinguished and the hunt was on. Attempts were made to burn barge shipping in the harbor, but this also failed.

Arriving at the rallying point, the Confederate Rangers were both delighted and surprised to see that none had been captured. Forced to leave baggage behind, they knew they had to get out of the city as soon as possible. The newspapers were publishing the false names they had used, but the descriptions that accompanied those names were a distinct threat. Two of the least known of the raiders went to the railroad station and purchased tickets for Toronto. There were detectives at the station and Martin told his men they would shoot their way out if necessary and lose the police in the crowd. They boarded a sleeper at 9.00 pm. It left on time, and after an hour of tension waiting for the police to come, they relaxed and slept on the way to Toronto.

On the 26th, General Dix commanding the United States Department of the East issued General Order Number 92 which included 'All such persons engaged in secret acts of hostility here can only be regarded as spies, subject to martial law and to the penalty of death.'[11] There were many refugees from the South living in New York City. All of them were required to report for registration within twenty-four hours or be treated as spies.

It developed that Colonel Thompson, who had overall charge of Canadian-based operations for the Confederates, had a trusted confidante in Godfrey J. Hyams of Little Rock, Arkansas. A double agent, Hyams was selling information to the United States authorities. A month before the operation Hyams had told Northern detectives what would happen. The plot was so outlandish that the Union lawmen refused to believe him. The Confederates who were involved had never been on another operation from Canada, so information on them was minimal. Detectives had followed some of the men around for a few days, but saw nothing suspicious and stopped trailing the men. Hyams had also been responsible for informing on the mission to capture the *Michigan* and the efforts at Chicago, Cincinnati and Boston.

Captain Tom Hines and some of the Chicago raiders were fortunate to escape as their 'Sons of Liberty' friends were arrested. Not so fortunate was the English daredevil George St Leger Grenfell. He was taken captive, tried by court martial, sentenced to death, and then saw the sentence commuted to life imprisonment with hard labor on the Dry Tortugas. On March 7 1868, Grenfell tried to escape from the island in a makeshift craft. Storms arose, and as Grenfell was never seen again, it is believed he drowned. Captain Charles Cole was intended for hanging, but an astute argument was waged by Confederates in Canada. They noted that he was behind enemy lines because he was an escaped prisoner of war and that was why he was in civilian clothes. The Union authorities handling his case allowed him to be treated as any other prisoner of war.

Colonel Martin and his Ranger companions had another raid in mind. Information had been obtained that seven Confederate generals in prison at

Johnson's Island were to be taken by train to Fort Lafayette at New York by train. Martin would lead ten men in an effort to capture the train and release the senior Confederate officers. Whatever money was in the express box on the car would be given to the freed generals to support their escape. On December 14 1864, a ten-man party led by Martin crossed over the border into Buffalo, New York. They moved on to Dunkirk where nine of the men remained. Colonel Martin continued on alone to Erie, Pennsylvania. Martin would attempt to ride back on the train that was carrying the generals. The men waited, checking the trains as they came in looking for Martin. He arrived on the second train, only to tell them that the move of the generals had been postponed. While they waited at the station, what they heard from the local people and read was not conducive to their peace of mind. The patience of the United States regarding raids from Canada was wearing thin.

In the early stages of the war, in November 1861, the warship USS *San Jacinto* had stopped the British mail packet *Trent* in the Bahama Channel and taken off two Confederate diplomats, James Mason and John Slidell, who were on their way to Europe to represent the Confederacy to England and France. Tempers flared in London and there was talk of war. President Lincoln had wisely said 'One war at a time', and the United States backed down and released the Confederates. By December 1864 the end of the Confederacy was in sight. The army and navy of the United States were of an experience and power that England was not eager to challenge in a North American war.

People in Canada had reason to sweat when the following order appeared in the newspapers of Buffalo, New York on December 15 1864:

Headquarters Department of the East
New York City, December 14th 1864
General Orders No. 97.

Information having been received at these headquarters that the rebel marauders who were guilty of murder and robbery at St Albans have been discharged from arrest and that other enterprises are actually in preparation in Canada, the Commanding-General deems it due to the people of the frontier towns to adopt the most prompt and efficient measures for the security of their lives and property.

All military commanders on the frontier are therefore instructed in case further acts of depredation and murder are attempted, whether by marauders, or persons acting under commissions from the rebel authorities at Richmond, to shoot down the depredators if possible while in the commission of their crimes; or if it be necessary with a view to their capture to cross the boundary between the United States and Canada; said commanders are directed to pursue them wherever they may take refuge, and if captured, they are under no circumstances to be surrendered, but are to be sent to these headquarters for trial and punishment by martial law.

Given under the authority of Major General Dix but with the obvious backing of the Lincoln administration, the order was a clear warning to the British in Canada. Sympathy for the Confederate cause was one thing; having Sheridan or Sherman in Toronto was another. The Confederates in Canada were beginning to fear being handed over to the US authorities and the exodus back to the South was beginning.

The raiders spent an uneasy night in Buffalo, checking trains without result. They rented a sleigh and drove outside town to pick the spot where they would stop the train carrying the generals by signaling with a lantern. When the generals were rescued, they would be brought to Buffalo and put on a train to Canada before the alarm was spread. As night fell, Martin directed that a section of rail be laid across the track and covered with snow in case the train did not stop on his signal. The train came sooner than expected, hit the rail and threw it some 50 yards. Further down the track the train stopped and men with lanterns started walking back. It was time to leave. The raiders hurried back to Buffalo and began making their way to Canada. Two of them, including John Yates Beall, were captured.

Confederate operations coming from Canada were conducted on the basis that if it was possible for something to go wrong, it did. Beall was hanged, then Robert C. Kennedy of Louisiana was captured and tried by a military commission. An unusual aspect of his trial was that Kennedy's defense council was Brigadier General Edwin Stoughton, United States Military Academy class of 1859. Stoughton was a general whose military flame burned out when he was rudely awakened from sleep by a slap on the rump from Ranger John Singleton Mosby and taken prisoner on March 8 1863. To his credit, Stoughton worked with diligence to save Kennedy's life but was unable to. In late March 1865, as the army of Northern Virginia was gasping its last breaths, Robert C. Kennedy was hanged.

Leaving Canada, Martin and his men made their way over the border and began to infiltrate their way back to the South. Always looking for some audacious raid, Martin learned that the United States Vice President Andrew Johnson was expected in Louisville, Kentucky. Martin and Headley began to lay plans to kidnap the vice president. Headley scouted the Louisville Hotel, located Johnson's rooms and observed him at a function. Headley also saw Union officers that he knew, resulting in him making a hurried retreat. Martin, Headley and Johnson were from Kentucky and Johnson was from Tennessee. The two Confederates intended to learn when Johnson visited his room, then approach him when he came out. They would act as local people, tell the vice president that they had some important business to discuss, get him alone long enough to draw pistols and give him some hard choices. They intended to get Johnson in a hack downstairs and kidnap him. Told by hotel staff members that Johnson was in his room, they waited around the hall and stairs while three others of their men stayed downstairs with the hack driver. They waited and waited, only to learn that their information was incorrect. Johnson had left on a boat hours earlier.

As they made their way south they encountered or roamed through territory occupied by Confederate guerrillas and bushwhackers, one of these appropriately called 'One-armed Berry'. Another guerrilla was known as both a man and a woman. In his rightful state as a man he was called Jerome Clark but his hair was long and his face and form were feminine so he could pass as the female Sue Munday. The Butcher Quantrill of Missouri had come over to Kentucky and was operating nearby. At length the two Rangers arrived at Abingdon, Virginia. They joined with General Basil Duke and the remnants of John Hunt Morgan's Rangers. In the dissolution of the Confederacy, they roamed about until joining the fleeing president of the Confederate states, Jefferson Davis, in North Carolina. They traveled as part of Davis's escort until May 7 1865, then stopped with the last of the Confederate cavalry while Davis pushed on, trying to reach Mexico. Martin and Headley learned that the Union amnesty did not include any who were in raids out of Canada.

After much wandering, the Confederate Rangers who came over the border from Canada were at length pardoned or ignored by the Federal government. Captain Tom Hines would become the Chief Justice of the State of Kentucky. Lieutenant John Headly became the Secretary of State for Kentucky. Colonel Robert Maxwell Martin was captured at Louisville, Kentucky and put in irons at the request of the New York authorities. He was pardoned and released from prison in 1866. He settled in Evansville, Indiana and operated a tobacco warehouse. In 1874, he came back to New York City, this time to manage tobacco inspections for a Brooklyn firm. The Minié ball he carried in his lung caused frequent hemorrhages and he died on January 9 1901 at 61 years of age. He was buried in Greenwood Cemetery in the city he had once tried to burn.[12]

PART TWO

YANK RANGERS

Chapter 14

Ranger Abraham Lincoln

Abraham Lincoln is the only president of the United States to be part of a battle and under enemy fire while in office. Though he is the most famous of the Ranger brotherhood, Lincoln is enshrined in the US Army Ranger Hall of Fame under the principle of 'Once a Ranger, always a Ranger.'

Lincoln learned much of the art of leadership in his short military experience in the Black Hawk War. The brief conflict had its roots in a land purchase by the United States government in 1804 when Winnebago Indians gave up land in North-West Illinois. The Indians did so on the understanding that they could hunt and plant corn there until the land was settled by the newcomers. Both sides violated the agreement. Squatters moved on the land and prevented the Indians from hunting, and the Indian chief Black Hawk unilaterally rejected the agreement and sought to use force to drive all settlers from the land.

Numerous militia units were organized by the settlers. Much to his surprise, Lincoln was elected captain of a militia company. His opponent in the election for the captaincy was an influential man named Kirkpatrick, a former employer of Lincoln who had treated the future president badly. Lincoln would later write that no success in life gave him so much satisfaction.[1]

The young Abe Lincoln was a large and powerful man. He could lift a full barrel of whiskey head-high and had the good sense to put it down full. Lincoln did not know military drill, but common sense is critical to military leadership and Lincoln had it in abundance. On one occasion when marching his company across a field in a twenty-man front, Captain Lincoln encountered a fence and a narrow gate. Lincoln did not know a military command equal to the situation, so he shouted: 'This company is dismissed for two minutes, when it will fall in again on the other side of the gate.'[2] When an old Indian was captured, Lincoln's comrades, who were full of frontier hate, wanted to put the Indian to death. Lincoln would not allow it. He invited the others to try to take the captive from him. The men protested that Lincoln was too physically strong for them. Lincoln then invited them to 'choose your weapons'. It was decided to let the captive live.

When the militia army was mustered out, Captain Abraham Lincoln enlisted as a private in Captain Elijah Iles company of Independent Rangers, a unit whose commander described it as being made up of 'generals, colonels, captains and distinguished men from the disbanded army'.

The Ranger company was kept on special duty, performing reconnaissance missions and courier duty.[3] Black Hawk and his followers were quickly defeated. Thereafter, Ranger Abraham Lincoln made light of his military service of approximately one month's duration. The closest Lincoln came to combat was when his company arrived on the scene shortly after Indians had killed and scalped five Rangers. He was a witness to the burial. Lincoln said:

> It is quite certain that I did not break my sword, for I had none to break, but I did bend my musket pretty badly on one occasion... I had a good many bloody struggles with mosquitoes; and although I never fainted from loss of blood, I can truly say I was often very hungry.[4]

Abraham Lincoln believed that the United States could not remain half-slave and half-free. However, he did not run for president on an anti-slavery platform and was not elected to eliminate slavery in the United States. He despised the practice of slavery, comparing it to a skunk whose stink would result in its own demise.[5] Lincoln knew the Constitution of the United States permitted slavery. He believed that the extension of slavery to new states was not automatic. It was Lincoln's view that the national government had the power to prevent the extension of slavery to new states. Many Southerners knew that if slavery was not extended, it would cause the demise of the base on which much of the prosperity of the South rested. Lincoln's primary goal was the preservation of the Union. U.S. Grant noted in his memoirs:

> The fact is the constitution did not apply to any such contingency as the one existing from 1861 to 1865. Its framers never dreamed of such contingency occurring. If they had foreseen it, the probabilities are they would have sanctioned the right of a State or States to withdraw rather than that there should be war between brothers.[6]

No such sanction existed. Lincoln was firm in his conviction that the success of the United States rested on those states continuing united.

Lincoln was a towering, gangly figure, often referred to as 'the ape' by his opponents. An English correspondent saw him as a crane walking among bulrushes. He was also described as a marriage between a derrick and a windmill. It was said that Lincoln could sit cross-legged and have both feet flat on the floor. The president stood 6ft 4in tall and was frequently given to measuring his height against other men. Once, when visiting a hospital, Lincoln met a Pennsylvania soldier who stood 6ft 7in tall. Lincoln gazed up at the man in silence, then said: 'Hello comrade, do you know when your feet get cold?'[7] Not knowing Lincoln, many Southerners thought they had the better leader in West Point-educated Jefferson Davis. In the South there was a children's rhyme that showed their disdain for the new president of the United States:

> Jeff Davis rides a milk-white horse,
> And Lincoln rides a mule –
> Jeff Davis is a gentleman,
> And Lincoln is a fool![8]

President Abraham Lincoln loved his soldiers. Whenever he saw a column of troops marching through Washington, Lincoln would call to them to find out which unit they were and where they were from, applauding and praising them. Once, when seeing a body of troops marching, he opened the door to his carriage, leaned out and yelled in excitement: 'What is it?' A nearby wiseacre youth who did not recognize the president replied: 'It's a regiment, you damned old fool!'

Until he got Grant and Sherman, Lincoln had a better grasp of the essentials of war than his generals. He was frustrated by George McClellan's lack of aggression. Lincoln said McClellan had 'the slows'. General McClellan often spoke of 'saving' his army and at one point his chief of staff said the army might be forced to capitulate. Furious, Lincoln called the officer before him and said: 'General, I understand you have used the word capitulate – that is not a word to be used in conjunction with our army.' When Lincoln demanded reports, the petulant McClellan sent him a telegram saying: 'Have captured two cows. What disposition should I make of them?' Lincoln replied: 'Milk 'em, George.' When the National Army had 400,000 men in the field, Lincoln told a reporter that the Confederates had 1,200,000 men fighting in rebellion. Aghast, the reporter asked how he knew that. Lincoln replied that every time his generals got whipped, they claimed that the enemy had three times more men. With a disarming grin, Lincoln observed that three times four makes twelve.[9] When General Hooker said the nation needed 'a dictator', Lincoln set him straight with a letter reminding him that 'Only those generals who gain successes can set up dictators.' Hooker kept bragging that he would take Richmond. Lincoln reminded Hooker that it was the destruction of Lee's army that was important. On June 14 1863, the observant Lincoln wrote Hooker: 'If the head of Lee's army is at Martinsburg and the tail of it on the flank road between Fredericksburg and Chancellorsville, the animal must be very slim somewhere; could you not break him?'

Lincoln was greatly disappointed when General Meade did not attack after the defeat of Longstreet's assault on the third day of the Battle of Gettysburg. He cautioned Meade not to hold a council of war but Meade, who wanted to attack, listened to tired subordinates and missed the chance to crush Lee's badly wounded army. When Meade talked of 'driving the enemy from our soil', in one of the most penetrating observations of the war, an anguished Lincoln asked: 'When will they understand that it is all our soil?'

After he had his fighters in Grant and Sherman, Lincoln had the good and rare presidential sense to support them and let them win. Ranger President Abraham Lincoln did not shrink from visiting the battlefront and putting his life at risk. Carl Sandburg, Lincoln's famed biographer, told of Lincoln putting himself at risk while pointing out weaknesses in enemy positions. When Jubal Early attacked Fort Stevens in the defense of Washington on July 11 1864, Abraham Lincoln, over the objections of Union officers, stood on the parapet to observe the conduct of the battle. A Union officer was hit within 5ft of the president. In Washington, Lincoln was constantly in danger of assassination and twice had his hat shot off.

Lincoln understood the Ranger philosophy of offensive action. On August 1 1864, General Grant sent a message to General Halleck telling him that the youthful Phil Sheridan was being put in command in the Shenandoah Valley and used the following words: 'I want Sheridan put in command of all the troops in the field, with instructions to put himself south of the enemy and follow him to the death. Wherever the enemy goes, let our troops go also.' Lincoln saw this message. For years Abraham Lincoln had known only commanders who vacillated, who withdrew or tried grand maneuvers, then collapsed. Lincoln knew that what he needed were generals who would fight and never stop fighting until they won. He wired Grant his support, but cautioned him 'it will never be done or attempted unless you watch it every day and hour and force it.'[10]

Few men have ever carried a burden as heavy as that borne by Abraham Lincoln. From inauguration to death he was plagued by war, but his burden was not limited to the saving of his country. His brother-in-law Confederate General Benjamin Hardin Helm died of wounds received at Chickamauga. Lincoln's wife, Mary Todd Lincoln, was a mentally unstable person who ridiculed her husband, upbraiding him before others. She was a spendthrift and began to believe she could communicate with the dead. Her violent jealousy caused other wives to avoid her company. On the night of Lincoln's death, the Grants did not go to the play with the Lincolns as Julia Grant had had enough of Mary Lincoln's violent temper. Lincoln bore it all with the patience of a saint, but the sadness in his eyes revealed the tragedy he faced daily. Lincoln and his wife were attacked because Mary Todd Lincoln had relatives fighting for the Confederacy. Mrs Lincoln's half-brother A.H. Todd was a Confederate Ranger killed in fighting near Baton Rouge, Louisiana.

As the war dragged on and the casualty lists mounted, a minister wrote the president and asked if he were a Christian. Lincoln replied:

> When I left Springfield, I asked the people to pray for me; I was not a Christian. When I buried my son, the severest trial of my life, I was not a Christian. But when I went to Gettysburg and saw the graves of thousands of our soldiers, I then and there consecrated myself to Christ. I *do* love Jesus.[11]

Abraham Lincoln stood for the preservation of the United States and held that view above all others. Two of his generals, John C. Fremont and David Hunter, freed slaves in their jurisdictions before Lincoln did. It cost Fremont, who was a political rival, his career. Lincoln did not relieve Hunter for the action, but disallowed it. Lincoln was opposed to slavery, but felt the question could be resolved without the nation being torn apart. In this he was likely wrong. Abraham Lincoln did not bear malice toward the South or toward its president Jefferson Davis, who he hoped would escape to some other land. Lincoln touched men hardened by war. General William T. Sherman said: 'Of all the men I ever met, he seemed to possess more of the elements of greatness, combined with goodness, than any other.'[12] The bullet that John Wilkes Booth fired into Abraham Lincoln's skull at Ford's Theater on April 14 1865 killed not only a great president and a great American, it also brought years of additional suffering to the South that Lincoln would have prevented.

Chapter 15

Loudoun Rangers

In the summer of 1862, President Lincoln called for 300,000 volunteers for military service. Famed songwriter Stephen Foster wrote a ditty entitled *We Are Coming, Father Abraham, 300,000 More*. The volunteer spirit was high in 1862, and almost 600,000 men answered the call. Among this number was a small group of men who lived in Loudoun County, Virginia. These men fought for the United States, despite their homes being within the operational area of such skilled Confederate Rangers as Elijah White and John Singleton Mosby.

Within Loudoun County were descendants of Germans who had never held slaves. Most of their sires had fought in the Revolutionary War to establish the United States. Those for the Union believed that while a state had rights, those rights must be subordinate to the will of elected national authority. These men were willing to fight to uphold the United States. In Loudoun there were also Quakers opposed to slavery, secession and war.

The secession of Virginia from the Union was critical to the formation of the Confederacy. Initially Virginia was in no mood to leave the Union it had done so much to form. In April 1861, a state convention was called. The delegates voted nearly two to one against secession. Southern states that had seceded exercised maximum pressure to draw Virginia to their cause, including sending 50,000 troops into the state to assist the Confederate cause. Citizens who supported the Union were threatened or roughed up. Many fled to Maryland. Another vote was called for. At a time when Virginia had a population of more than 1.5 million people, approximately 146,000 voted, all but 20,000 voting for secession. Those for the Union felt the election was rigged with the decision backed by bayonets. Some communities, including Hoysville, Lovettsville, Neersville and Waterford voted to remain in the Union. Their inhabitants would live surrounded by opponents.

In April 1861, Confederate cavalry visited the German and Quaker settlements of Loudoun County to take horses and wagons. When their supplies and livestock were confiscated and their leaders taken hostage, some peaceloving Quakers became US Rangers. One who was aiming his musket at a Confederate was heard to say: 'Friend, it is unfortunate, but thee stands exactly where I am going to shoot.'

Foraging and arresting opponents was the norm, but hatred followed in their wake. To avoid arrest, many men left their families to manage property as best they could and went north to enlist. Rebecca Williams, a young woman of Waterford, kept a diary. She recorded an event as follows:

> The election passed off quietly. A large majority in the precinct for the Union but in other parts whole bodies of troops have been taken to the polls to vote for disunion and Union men have been intimidated & many have left the states. How long will such tyranny & anarchy prevail? Until their father shall be pleas'd to say it is enough?[1]

One of the men who left was a prosperous miller and businessman named Samuel C. Means of Waterford. Though strongly for the Union, Means did not wish to fight against the South as he had a brother supporting the Confederate cause. When the Confederates seized his property, Means slipped away to Maryland.

Though at this point Means was not involved in military activities, the Confederates incorrectly believed he was guiding raids by Union forces. He was denounced as a renegade and a price of $5,000 put on his head. This brought him to the attention of Federal authorities who offered him a captain's commission and asked him to recruit a company of Union Rangers.

On June 20 1862, at Lovettsville, Virginia, the Loudoun Rangers, a new independent unit with Captain Sam Means in command, was mustered into service. The unit was created on the direct authority of Secretary of War Edwin M. Stanton.

While recruiting went forward, Means led a detachment of some thirty men to guide Union forces moving into Loudoun County. A small party of the Rangers trapped a Confederate captain named Simpson and killed him, securing important documents from the body. The killing was done by Ranger Charles A. Webster, the Ranger drill master. Charles Webster was a mysterious figure, cool in battle and quick to kill. Webster was not a local man; something of a stranger in their midst. He was the only well-trained fighting man in the unit. Webster knew arms and their use and he spent hours training the others. Webster and the other Rangers had called upon Simpson to surrender, but he was a brave man and tried to break free. Wounded, Simpson raised his pistol to shoot. Webster wrestled the weapon from Simpson and used it to kill him.

By August 27, the company had grown to fifty men. Welcomed in their home communities, they found that only a short ride saw them the object of scorn and derision. As the Confederate army advanced, Union forces withdrew. The small band of Rangers was the only Federal unit left in the area and they were about to pay the price.

At 3.00 am on the 27th, the Loudoun Rangers were hit in a dawn attack by Elijah White's Confederate Rangers. Union Colonel D.S. Miles reported to Major General Halleck:

> Captain White, by crossing the fields avoided the pickets, and attacked about 23 of Captain Means' men in a church at daybreak this morning, who fought as long as ammunition lasted. One private killed; 1 second lieutenant and 6 privates wounded. Fifteen surrendered (on parole); two, engaged in killing Mr. John, carried away; also 30 horses and all the arms of the Company except those belonging to the men on the picket. The enemy lost 6 killed and 9 wounded. Retreated toward Snicker's Ferry.[2]

Captain Means was not present. He had been at his home and, having no opportunity to join his men, rode for safety. Trapped in a church, the US Rangers had fought bravely until their ammunition and water were exhausted. Senior officer Lieutenant Slater had five wounds and another bullet through his hat. Colonel Miles' statistics were incorrect. Two Union Rangers would die, nine were wounded and captured along with another ten men. The Confederate Rangers lost two killed, one known to have been shot by Charles Webster who fought well. Though Webster was an enlisted man, he negotiated the surrender on favorable terms. All those captured in the church were immediately paroled and released.

With a strength of some thirty-five men, the Loudoun Rangers kept critical fords under observation and conducted limited raids. On patrol, they captured two of White's men who had been at the church fight, then joined with a 125-man Union cavalry force. Near the strongly secessionist town of Leesburg, the US troops were hit by a large Confederate force and driven through the distinctly unfriendly town. As they formed on the other side of town, they were suddenly struck from the rear by the 2nd Virginia

Cavalry. Union Ranger Frank Mormon was killed, six men were wounded and taken, together with another four men. In a tragic case of mistaken identity, Rangers Baker, Miles, Shoemaker and Welch were thought by the Confederates to be men who had violated their parole. They were taken to the infamous prison at Castle Thunder in Richmond. There Baker, Miles and Shoemaker starved to death. In 1865, Ranger Welch was found close to death, confined in a Richmond dungeon.

The Loudoun Rangers now numbered fewer than twenty men. Having been mauled in two engagements they found that men were unwilling to enlist in a unit that performed such exposed and precarious duty, living without support in enemy-controlled territory.

Confederate commander General Robert E. Lee moved north, seeking to recruit Maryland to the Southern cause. Lee divided his army, sending General Thomas J. 'Stonewall' Jackson with three divisions to seize Harpers Ferry. McClellan muffed the chance to attack the separate elements of his foe while a disaster was shaping up at Harpers Ferry. Units of the Union, the 1st and 8th Corps, were stationed at this mountainous juncture of the Potomac and Shenandoah Rivers. Command of the Harpers Ferry garrison fell to Colonel Dixon Miles, a regular army officer. As the enemy drew closer, Miles began to drink heavily and refused advice. His actions, including abandoning the high ground overlooking the garrison and ordering that considerable Union artillery on these heights be spiked, was a gift the Confederates would not ignore.

Seeing the potential for catastrophe, Captain Means buried all company records and anything not required for rapid movement. He sent riders to General McClellan's headquarters informing him of the situation and telling him that the garrison only had sufficient food for four days.

When it soon became evident that Colonel Miles would have to surrender the garrison, Captain Means determined to break out with his Rangers. When Means and Ranger Charles Webster developed a plan, they informed cavalry officers who concurred. During the night of September 14 1862, the Rangers led some 2,000 Union horsemen under the command of Colonel Voss of the 12th Illinois Cavalry across the Potomac River on a pontoon bridge and made their escape. En route they heard the sound of a wagon train and, knowing it to be enemy, the Rangers and cavalry men charged. It was Confederate General Longstreet's ammunition train escorted by several hundred Confederate cavalry. The Union horsemen rode down the Confederates and captured 80 wagons and more than 200 prisoners. It was a significant prize, but pale compared to the disastrous surrender of the

Harpers Ferry garrison on Monday, September 15 1862. Union commander Dixon Miles was mortally wounded and 12,000 Union soldiers with arms and equipment were captured, largely because of inept leadership. Means believed he could have led the entire garrison out of the trap.

Means' Rangers next action followed quickly. Lee moved his army into Maryland. What Lee got was not Maryland, but the bloody Battle of Antietam, fought on September 17. Robert E. Lee was outnumbered, but outfought the glacial effort of Union Commander General William McClellan. 'Little Mac', as he was affectionately called, knew how to equip and train an army. However, he did not know how to use one effectively in battle, even when presented with a copy of the enemy's plans. McClellan kept his army so stationary that when a man told Lincoln he was going to visit the army, Lincoln assured him he would have no difficulty in finding it. 'It's there,' said the president, 'that's the difficulty.' Committing units piecemeal and leaving large numbers not engaged, George McClellan botched an excellent chance to destroy Lee's army.

Withdrawing after bloody Antietam, some exhausted men of the Confederate army found themselves separated from the main body. Approximately eighty of these stragglers were taken prisoner by the Rangers. Separated from the remainder of the company during the break-out, four Rangers rode out through Maryland into York, Pennsylvania where they cheerfully displayed three Confederates they had captured en route.

As the Union forces moved south, the Rangers served as guides and scouts. When the army went into winter quarters along the Rappahannock, the Loudoun Rangers rejoined the 8th Corps at Point of Rocks. They ran patrols and had frequent skirmishes with Elijah White's Confederate Rangers. While Captain Means was absent, Charles A. Webster decided to hold an unauthorized election for first lieutenant. Means was a patriot, but a grinder of grain, not a soldier. Webster was a well-schooled fighting leader who was unanimously elected. When Captain Means returned, he cancelled the election. The anger between the two men would result in Webster leaving the company.

The 'Dear John' letter from the girl of one's dreams happened then as now. One United States Ranger was told that a loving relationship must end as the Confederates might win and he would not be allowed to come home. He became obsessed with offensive action, demanding to go raiding. He survived the war and married the girl. Dances in homes of family and friends were a frequent form of entertainment and a good time to raid. Some ended in laughter. Lieutenant Marlow and a number of White's Rangers raided a dance and captured a Union Ranger. The captive's pretty sister begged that he be released. Marlow agreed, provided she would dance a set with him. The Union Ranger played *The Girl I Left Behind Me* on his violin while his sister and the Confederate Ranger danced. Then White's Confederate Rangers paroled their prisoner and left.

At another dance, Sergeant Anderson of the United States Rangers got his saber caught in a chair when a mixed group of Mosby and White's Confederate Rangers attacked. Thus encumbered, Anderson was shot repeatedly and died in his mother's arms. The men of both sides were careful, but at one dance fight a female dancer was wounded.

Operating with a variety of regular cavalry units, the US Rangers passed the spring of 1863 by participating in raids on Confederate positions. Battles with White's men continued to be frequent. When the Confederates slipped away with some of the Loudoun Rangers' horses, the Rangers pursued and recovered their horses plus some of the Confederates'. White's Rangers responded with a raid that captured thirteen US Rangers. Throughout Lee's move north and the Battle of Gettysburg, Union Rangers were employed on foraging operations. They followed this in August with a raid on White's men, capturing sixteen enlisted men and two officers.

On August 8 1863, Captain Means sent a message to Union General Heintzelman. As they were local to the area, the Rangers had much better intelligence than the regular Union forces. Means felt that the Union forces were not making sufficient use of Ranger knowledge. His message read in part as follows:

> I know that there is a large force in Loudoun waiting an opportunity to make a raid into Maryland. Send me the force and I will clean them out. Strangers cannot find them. Send on the Maryland side. Keeping far enough from the Potomac not to let the news go over. Let me know when you send, and sooner the better.[3]

In October 1863, the Rangers reported a large Confederate force under General John Imboden was attacking Charleston. The Charleston garrison commander Colonel Simpson decided to fight, but Imboden's artillery created a panic in the Union garrison and Simpson's men were forced to surrender. The Rangers decided to cut their way out. Fighting their way through the 18th Virginia Cavalry and the 62nd Virginia Mounted Infantry, the Rangers lost seventeen of thirty men. The Rangers who broke out led a relief force under Colonel George D. Wells back to the scene of the action that hastened the withdrawing Confederates but could not rescue the surrendered garrison.

Death did not always come from bullet or shell. While the Loudoun Rangers were in camp conditions, smallpox killed several Rangers and scarred others. Tempers were short. There were fist-fights over coffee or saddle-blankets or oats for the horses. They amused themselves by trapping bees and putting them in another Ranger's blankets. Though they were expert horsemen, the men found themselves baffled by a mule that no one could ride. Camp life, often in enemy territory, was not boring.

In the spring of 1864, Union General Franz Sigel was assigned to command the department of West Virginia. Captain Means was ordered to consolidate the Rangers with the 3rd West Virginia Cavalry. Means refused to obey the orders, stating that his independent authority came from the Secretary of War. He was sustained, but the bitterness of the dispute ended with his resignation from the service. Lieutenant Daniel Keyes was promoted to captain and set forth with thirty men to attack part of Mosby's command. The attack was a success, with three prisoners taken. Pressing the advantage resulted in four additional members of Mosby's command being taken.

Celebrating their success, the US Rangers rode to the friendly town of Waterford for breakfast. This mistake cost them heavily as some 150 of Mosby's men trapped their outposts. The Confederate Rangers killed two Union Rangers, wounded another man in four places and captured five of his comrades. Mosby's Rangers then began a foraging expedition in the area, rounding up horses and wagons which they loaded with hay and grain. As it began to rain, the US Rangers donned blankets over their uniforms and began to track the Confederate foragers. Hiding their weapons under the blankets that concealed their blue uniforms, the US Rangers captured nineteen wagons, fifteen prisoners and twenty horses. A day later they ambushed another of Mosby's foraging parties, killing one Confederate and capturing two others. In a thirty-eight-man raid they hit a small force of White's Rangers, wounding and capturing three, one of whom died.

The Confederates were having success foraging in Maryland and Pennsylvania. Howls of outrage sounded in Washington. Despite the displeasure of Secretary Stanton who did not like him, General Phil Sheridan was selected by General Grant as the solution. What Grant wanted, Grant got. The people of the North recognized U.S. Grant as the general who would not back off. The feeling was expressed in a slogan of the time, 'God-Grant-Victory'.

Sheridan was a US Military Academy graduate. Though he possessed a monumental ego and was given to swagger, Sheridan was a fighter. His bad grammar upset some senior officers; Sheridan spoke of licking the enemy or hammering them. Lincoln was not put off by this; he observed that the worst whipping he ever got was from a boy who did not know the alphabet. At the Battle of Cedar Creek, Sheridan would prove his mettle and turn retreat into victory.

In October, the US Rangers found Mosby's command on a raid and attacked the larger force. A nearby Union force did not join in the attack and Mosby led two companies to the relief of his men. One Union Ranger was killed, two wounded and four taken prisoner. This was followed by a skirmish in which M.H. Best of the Loudoun Rangers killed Captain Mountjoy of Mosby's command, and Colonel Coleman of the 5th Virginia Cavalry and Captain Smith of General Early's staff were taken prisoner. On November 10, the Rangers located and reported the position of a Confederate infantry division under General Hill.[4]

On November 30, Corporal Tritapoe of the Rangers captured the marauder French Bill, a Union deserter who joined White's Confederates. White's Rangers were too legitimate for French Bill who again deserted, this time to join the outlaw band of John Mobberly. Among the many crimes of Mobberly and his men was the robbery and murder of the surgeon of the 6th Pennsylvania Cavalry. On December 1 1864, General Sheridan was informed of French Bill's capture. Sheridan sent a wire ordering the culprit hanged as soon as positively identified. His captors knew French Bill. Within twenty-four hours, Sheridan received a return message that the execution was accomplished.

Rangers Best and Tritapoe slipped away to visit some girls and found themselves in hand-to-hand combat with two Confederates. Shooting and flailing with revolvers, the four men fought back and forth until Best killed one Confederate and the other fled. Best had his thumb ripped open under the hammer of his opponent's weapon, while Tritapoe had two bullet holes in his clothes. Other Rangers captured five of Mosby's men, four of whom were taken while filling their canteens with whiskey from a still.

The last significant action of the Loudoun Rangers involved John W. Mobberly who at age 18 joined Elijah White's Rangers. Mobberly was from Harpers Ferry and knew the area well. He was valuable as a scout and courageous, but he was a vicious man. In 1864, Mobberly deserted from White's command and formed a band of robbers who claimed to be Rangers. As the war progressed, his activities centered on theft and brutality.

256

The story persisted that he had beaten a 15-year-old girl with his pistol so badly as to leave permanent injury. On one occasion Mobberly and his band ambushed a small party of United States Rangers, one of whom was Charlie Stewart. With Stewart on the ground wounded, Mobberly rode his horse back and forth over the injured man (another version says stood over him) and fired two shots into Stewart's face. Thinking Stewart was dead, Mobberly then left. Ranger Charlie Stewart did not die.

The termination of Mobberly was much desired by the United States, as the following letter through channels from General Stevenson at Harpers Ferry to Sheridan's headquarters demonstrates:

Harpers Ferry, April 1, 1865
Brigadier-General MORGAN
Chief of Staff

There is a gang of murderers infesting Loudoun, who have done incalculable service for the rebels for the last four years. The leader of the band is named Mobberly, and is one of Mosby's right-hand men.

Some citizens of Loudoun have proposed to me that if I will arm them and give them the means of living away from home for a while they will kill or capture the band. The band consists of Mobberly, Riley, S. Mocks and Tribbet. All of them have murdered our soldiers time and again. The band originally consisted of about fifteen men. During the last summer we have killed most of the band, leaving these four men who are the head devils of the concern. I think promising these men a reward of $1,000 for Mobberly and $500 for each of the others dead or alive will clean out the concern. The Government could readily afford to pay $50,000 for them and save the amount in the prevention of the destruction of public property in six months' operations of the band.

Respectfully,
John D. Stevenson.[5]

Stevenson was wrong about Mobberly being connected with Mosby, but right about the need for special action. Sheridan agreed that Mobberly must be dispatched, but did not want to publicly offer a reward as he believed offering rewards could backfire and bring support to the target.

Stevenson was instructed to keep a low profile on the rewards, but take what steps were necessary to kill Mobberly.

Understandably, Ranger Charlie Stewart wanted to put the finishing touch to John Mobberly's career. When angry citizens of Harpers Ferry provided information on Mobberly's location, Ranger Sergeant Stewart accompanied by Rangers Joseph Waters and M.H. Best set his trap. Stewart spread the rumor that a valuable horse was stabled at a certain barn. It was on April 5 1865 that Mobberly rode to the barn to steal the horse. He found himself looking into the barrels of US Ranger pistols. Mobberly cried out 'Oh Lord, I am gone', and he was. The Rangers took his body back to Harpers Ferry. Mobberly had his supporters. The wording on his tombstone reads like the eulogy for a knight instead of a nightmare.

Worthy of remembrance as a United States Ranger is a man carried on the roster of Company A, Loudoun Rangers as Charles A. Webster, also known as Alfonso C. Webster. His true name was Charles W. Brown, but he renounced the name of his father. Comrades in the Loudoun Rangers believed Webster changed his name because his father was a Confederate sympathizer. Webster came from Weld, Maine. He was bright, aggressive, and happier as a leader than a follower. He had military training, most likely at the Cavalry School of Practice at Carlisle Barracks, PA.

Webster was a young man with a sense of destiny, a true fighting man who, early after the formation of the unit, served as drill master for Company A of the Loudoun Rangers and proved himself in battle. Webster's record would indicate he deserved promotion, but he was denied it because his personality clashed with that of Captain Sam Means. In November of 1862, their enmity came to a head and Charles Webster left the command. His friends believed he then set out on a desperate mission to ambush and kill Elijah White, believing that success would bring the leadership role he sought. Webster failed and was taken prisoner by White's Confederate Rangers. White knew of Webster's ability and is reputed to have had the prisoner 'bucked and gagged' to ensure he would not escape. It was torture and White's officers raised such a fuss that Elijah White relented. Webster was transported to Castle Thunder, the Confederate prison in Richmond where he began organizing plans for an escape. However, a fellow prisoner betrayed him and Webster was handcuffed and chained to a post.

Webster befriended a member of Andrews' Raiders who made a bone key and unlocked his irons. Webster escaped, but was soon recaptured. He was handcuffed, irons were riveted on his ankles and he was imprisoned on the third floor. Somehow he succeeded in shedding his irons, his only option then being to jump from a third-floor window into the darkness. The fall broke both his legs. Webster crawled under a woodpile and eluded search for most of a day before being recaptured. This time he was brought to trial accused of murdering Captain Simpson of the 8th Virginia Cavalry, the man Webster had beaten and killed in hand-to-hand combat. Also charged with breaking parole, Webster was sentenced to be hung.

In Richmond on April 10 1863, Ranger Charles Webster was brought before 2,000 fellow prisoners who were assembled so that the death of Webster would be a deterrent to escape attempts. With both legs broken, Webster could not stand and was strapped in a chair. Permitted to say his last words, Ranger Webster used his drill master's voice to damn the Confederacy and pledge his allegiance to the United States. He tossed his hat to the crowd as a signal for the trapdoor to open beneath him.

Chapter 16

The Snake-Hunters

Early in the war, the Union adopted retaliatory bushwhacking tactics by employing mountain men to hunt mountain men. In Western Virginia were a select group of Union woodsmen who were skilled in the bushwhacking trade. As they were hunting the Confederate Moccasin Rangers, the men decided that the name of their unit would be the 'Snake-Hunters'. The formal title of the unit was Company A of the 11th Virginia Infantry (Union). Their leader was the youthful Captain John Baggs. Powerful and standing about 6ft 2in tall, Baggs lived to fight. He ruled his command with his fists. John Baggs had no understanding of military drill. As misunderstanding his orders might cause a man to be beaten bloody, the troops paid close attention to his words.

An exuberant Northern writer characterized them as follows:

> The Snake-Hunters are stalwart, rugged, foresters, mountaineers and 'original backwoodsmen' – shrewd, wary, and daring as they are athletic and active – fleet of foot, nimble climbers and perfect in the use of knife and gun. They were enlisted at Wheeling and mustered into service there, under that most half-horse, half-alligator and the rest snapping turtle-est of human beings since the demise of the lamented Colonel David Crockett. Captain Baggs, who beat every county in Western Virginia for the right breed, and sent them to Wheeling as fast as he found them to be licked into the shape required to constitute a Snake-Hunter in good standing. They were recruited for mountain service, and they were usually kept on the trail of guerrillas and for other independent enterprises; but when attached to an army, their business was to 'trot' in the extreme front in the capacity of guides, scouts and spies. For a while they were with Rosecrans' army of the Kanawha and Gauley and came often in contact there with their rebel rivals, the Moccasin Rangers.

As to their arms, the only peculiar feature, I believe, was their variety, each separate Snake-Hunter being at liberty to indulge his fancy and consult his early habits, the training of his hand and eye, in the choice of his weapons. But in their 'toggery' everything was peculiar. A magnificent contempt for uniform distinguished them, and motley was their only wear. No two were got up alike, and rarely did the accomplished Snake-Hunter permit himself to be seen two days in succession on parade (if their extraordinary system of tactics included such a dandyism), in the same eccentric combination of 'duds'.

But most peculiar of all was their drill. Every movement was accomplished on the double-quick or in a run. They acknowledged no 'common time', and if reduced to a dead march, they would surely have mutinied.

This, for instance, was Captain Bagg's very original style of dismissing his company:

'Put down them thar blasted old guns, and be d–d to you!'
(Which, being interpreted, is 'Stack Arms!')
'Now to your holes, you ugly rats, and don't let me see you again till I want you!'
(Which, being reduced to the Hardee vernacular, means 'Break ranks – march!')
(*Exeunt*) Snake-Hunters on the run, with grand divertisement of whoops, yells and squeals, interspersed with lifelike imitations of birds and beasts.[1]

Two gentlemen from Philadelphia witnessed Captain Baggs dismiss his men in this unusual fashion. Later at a bar room they asked Bagg how he reassembled his men. Baggs went to the door and fired three shots from his pistol. His men came running and gathered around him in the bar. They certainly were 'active – fleet of foot' and also very thirsty. The two Philadelphians paid for a round of rum.

Captain Baggs' style of punishment, like his drill, was peculiarly his own. He knocked down the refractory Snake-Hunter with his fist, and mauled him to his heart's content. He was once tried for cruelty to one of his own men while the man was under arrest, but Baggs was acquitted.[2]

THE SNAKE-HUNTERS

Disguised as a Quaker, Baggs put a small Confederate flag in his hat brim and went into the camp of former Secretary of War and now Confederate commander in Western Virginia John B. Floyd. Baggs convinced Floyd that he was a loyal Confederate and obtained a signed pass that allowed him to go to and fro through Confederate lines. He told Floyd that a force of Union guerrillas was gathering and needed to be dealt with before they organized. Floyd sent three companies and arrested the men Baggs had named as Unionists. Floyd found they were men gathering together to fight for the Confederacy.

The Snake-Hunters were effective. They killed or captured many of their Confederate foes, including Dan Dusky who it was said kept a private graveyard for Union soldiers and supporters he had killed. Despite the killing, there were friends and relatives on both sides and in some cases ties were still close. In 1863, John Baggs was dismissed from the service for willfully letting a prisoner escape.

Chapter 17

The Swamp Dragons

For the Union, another equivalent of the Confederate Moccasin Rangers in Western Virginia were several companies of men known as the 'Swamp Dragons'. The Dragons inhabited mountainous areas in what is today the panhandle of West Virginia. While primarily based in Pendleton County, they operated in other eastern counties of West Virginia including Grant, Hardy, Pocahontas and Greenbrier under the command of Captain Bond. They employed ambush tactics and were considered bushwhackers by their opponents in the Pendleton Rifles and Dixie Boys who tried hard to eliminate them. The most serious threat to their existence was McNeill's Rangers who were within striking range from their headquarters at Moorefield in Western Virginia. On December 31 1862, the Ringgold Cavalry of Pennsylvania went to the assistance of the Swamp Dragons and recorded the event as follows:

> On the morning of December 31st, every man of both companies was ordered to saddle up bright and early. We marched out the New Creek Road and over the mountain, striking New Creek above the station; then turned up the Creek and marched all night, reaching Greenland Gap [near Scherr], where there were two companies of loyal Virginians who had organized to defend their homes. The Rebels hated these companies, whom they called 'Swamp Dragons', and had attacked them at this Gap, where they fortified themselves in some log buildings, and we had been sent to their relief. On our approach, the Rebels withdrew. The 'Dragons' were still holding the fort, and we had some difficulty in convincing them that we were Union soldiers as they feared it was a trick of the enemy. They were greatly rejoiced when they found that we were their friends.[1]

In April 1864, McNeill's men struck the base camp of the Swamp Dragons and were in turn ambushed by Union men as they withdrew. No significant casualties were suffered by either side.

Chapter 18

Grant's Ranger

C. Lorain Ruggles was born in Copley, Summit County, Ohio on June 17 1823. His father, a blacksmith named Alfred Ruggles, was married twice, in total fathering twelve sons and seven daughters. Lorain Ruggles was the youngest of these children. Alfred Ruggles whipped his offspring for any infraction, real or imagined. To avoid these beatings Lorain Ruggles learned to be an accomplished liar when necessary. Later in life he would consider deception as the key to his survival.[1]

When Alfred Ruggles died, Lorain was 10 years old. The older brothers and sisters quarreled over the estate and incurred legal fees that exhausted their inheritance. Ruggles became a cabin boy on a packet-boat on the Ohio Canal, then at age 14 began to drive the mule or horse shore teams that pulled the boat. As he grew, he became a woodchopper. While still a teenager, Ruggles lived as a hunter and trapper in the mountains of Arkansas. He roamed west to Colorado and to Salt Lake, was for a time a plantation overseer and in 1861 was the foreman of a team of woodsmen cutting shingles. His early life had combined to make Lorain Ruggles a man inured to hardship, accustomed to finding his way about and an expert marksman. His many years in the south-west gave him a knowledge of speech and mannerisms that would serve him well in war.

Though his older brother Daniel would become a Confederate general, Lorain Ruggles deeply believed in the preservation of the Union and was willing to fight for that cause. Despite a hazardous journey, he worked his way north and in 1862 joined the 20th Ohio Infantry. Ruggles had no familiarity with army equipment. When seeing a pack extending from a soldier's back he called it a 'Bunker Hill'. He was given the nickname 'Bunker' and in time a joking promotion to 'General Bunker'.

Ruggles was not good at drill, thinking it a waste of time. He knew he did not need to drill to kill a bear. He believed that what would kill a bear would kill a Confederate. Accustomed to freedom and demonstrating courage if not wisdom, he was not hesitant about speaking his mind to colonels. His first experience of war would be on February 15 1862 at Fort

Donelson, then at the battle soldiers called 'Bloody Shiloh', he became a hardened soldier. It was after this battle that he volunteered for and became a Ranger, scouting ahead of the Union army.

Ruggles was a natural for his missions. He frequently operated from the Union camp at Bolivar, Tennessee, some 40 miles east of Memphis. Before leaving Union lines, he ascertained sufficient knowledge of the Confederate forces in opposition that he could pose as a Southerner rejoining his unit. While roving behind Confederate lines dressed as a civilian or as a Confederate soldier, his ability to deceive was invaluable. Encountering Confederates, he would say he was searching for his unit and believed it to be at a certain location. The Confederates would quickly correct him and tell him where the unit was located. In casual conversations he learned strength, disposition, supply status and intentions of Confederate units. He frequently stopped at farms and learned the names of their owners. This enabled him to act as though familiar with the country. When stopped by a Confederate patrol, part of the conversation with a Confederate lieutenant ran as follows:

> 'Soldier, what road did you come in on this morning?'
> 'I came down on the Somerville road, across the Hickory flats, by the old man Pruett's and then over on to the Salem and Grand Junction Road.'
> 'You came a very good route indeed.'
> 'I am aware of that, I know this here country all through in here. Lieutenant, where did you boys stay last night?'
> 'At Davis' Mills.'
> 'Haven't we got a cavalry force there?'
> 'No, there was only fourteen of us there last night.'
> 'That old man Pruett told me yesterday that there was, that we had three brigades of cavalry at the White Church on Wolf River.'
> 'The old man is mistaken. There is none of our forces nearer then Tupelo except the three regiments that you saw to-day, and a few of the same company that I belong to, that are scattered about the country on the same business that we are on.'[2]

By such seemingly innocent conversations, Ruggles gathered information. On occasion he would meet men that he knew in Arkansas or in the west. They did not know he had returned north and assumed he was a Confederate.

Sometimes these men vouched for him. When all else failed, he could truthfully claim that he was the brother of Confederate General Ruggles.

Ruggles knew his life would quickly end if he were discovered ranging the Confederate rear area in Confederate uniform. He killed without hesitation anyone he could not convince with words. Many Confederate sympathizers took the oath of allegiance to the United States and were permitted to travel about. While Ruggles was making a report to a Union general, he was seen by the overseer of a plantation who was having his pass renewed. Ruggles followed the overseer, who tried to shoot him. That night Ruggles took two sergeants and went to the overseer's house. In the yard they found a Negro slave chained around his neck and waist. He had been sent to work on Confederate fortifications, run away and been captured. Ruggles was furious. The overseer feigned illness, but was hauled from his bed and forced to stand on a box with the chains of the slave around his neck and over a beam. The slave was given the opportunity to hang his tormentor. The black man said 'I reckon he won't do dat box no good standin' there', and kicked the box out from under the overseer. The overseer's wife complained that her husband had been hanged, but no officer knew that Ruggles and the two men had left camp. They did not believe it was Union troops who were responsible.[3]

Ruggles had known Confederate General Joe Wheeler in Memphis before the war. Posing as a member of the 2nd Arkansas Cavalry, he went into Wheeler's camp. He found Wheeler with General Van Dorn. Ruggles asked for a pass to go through Confederate lines to scout Yankee positions. Van Dorn intended to attack and took the opportunity to ask if Ruggles could check out a particular road he intended to use. Ruggles said he would do his best. He got the pass and used it to get through Confederate outposts. Ruggles knew that the Union force on the road Van Dorn planned to use would be crushed by the Confederate army. He was able to reach them in time to allow them to rejoin larger Union forces. Van Dorn never knew that he had missed the opportunity.

Occasionally Ruggles would reveal his true status when behind enemy lines, but the only people with whom he did this were Confederates he promptly killed or with black slaves. He was known to the slaves as 'Bunker' and they frequently told him the location of Confederate units or paths by which he could travel unseen. On one mission, a slave told him of Confederate cavalry hiding in woods keeping watch on the Union army. Ruggles scouted the position and found that the Confederates had an observation point that allowed them to view whatever the Union camp was doing. His report, based on the information of a slave, ended the Confederate advantage.

His experience made Ruggles adept at spotting Confederates who came into Union lines on scouting missions. Ruggles was leading a nine-man foraging party after some Confederate butter he knew about when he came upon a man dressed in civilian clothes. The man saw the Union soldiers and immediately sat down under a tree and began to read a Bible. When questioned, he told Ruggles that he was a preacher of the gospel, that he had taken the oath of loyalty to the United States and that he had a pass through Union lines. Skilled at deception, Ruggles sensed it in this man and had him searched. They found he was concealing a map 18in x 22in that was an accurate drawing of Union lines and the position of Union troops. They hanged the pseudo preacher on the spot.[4]

Dressed as a civilian behind Confederate lines, Lorain Ruggles was taken prisoner by a conscription patrol scouring the countryside looking for men to draft into the Confederate army. On reaching the Confederate camp, Ruggles was seen by men he had known well in Arkansas; they ensured he was taken into their cavalry regiment. Ruggles saw he was in a good position to gain information. He did not have a horse, so he requested he be permitted to penetrate Union lines and get one. Few expected that he could succeed. Ruggles passed through Union lines, told his commanders what he had learned and was given a superb horse to ride back to the Confederate camp. There he told of stealing the horse from a Union colonel. He was then the camp hero. Ruggles stayed with the unit through a raid to burn cotton and prevent it from falling into Union hands. He then turned up 'missing' and returned to Union lines.

Ruggles frequently voluntarily rode with or was recruited by Confederate cavalry. When encountering a large Confederate force he moved his horse at a slower pace, pretending he was a local citizen returning home. On one occasion, riding a mule, he dropped behind the Confederate column and thought he was clear. The Confederates were suspicious and he had to gallop away with a cavalry patrol in hot pursuit. He evaded the patrol, but suspected that all bridges would be covered. Moving at night, he found his escape route by road guarded. Ruggles had no choice but to make a crossing of a cypress swamp inhabited by swarms of mosquitoes and water moccasin snakes. When he made it through the swamp he found himself trapped by three robbers who took his money and his mule.

Though Lorain Ruggles took extraordinary risks while gathering information in Confederate lines, he was careful to ensure that his cover was not penetrated. On occasion Confederates he knew from Arkansas or previous raids were captured and saw him talking with Union officers. Ruggles made certain they were sent to prison camps in the North. Any of them who were released or who escaped could have unmasked him.[5]

His travels behind Confederate lines brought him in occasional contact with guerrilla bands who used the war as an excuse to murder, steal and torture. On one mission, Ruggles hid in a wood watching such men burning things that screamed while the men would shout 'Bring on another'. Ruggles saw some thirty men using long poles to push their victim into flames. Ruggles could not see those screaming things being burned, but he felt strongly that they were human beings. He was convinced it was Union soldiers taken captive that were being burned.[6]

There were many times when Ruggles led from six to thirty-six men on ranging expeditions. In this war of retaliation Ruggles and men he sometimes took with him were merciless with any guerrilla they caught. While he was questioning one captive, his men took a Confederate guerrilla, tied a short rope around his neck and attached the rope to a tree. Another rope was tied around his feet and attached to the harness of a mule. The animal was lashed and pulled away, stretching the man until his head separated from his body.

The success enjoyed by Ruggles brought him to the attention of General U.S. Grant. His reputation was such that though he worked for several subordinate generals, he could communicate directly with Grant. During the siege of Vicksburg, Grant gave Ruggles a Henry rifle. Ruggles used this advanced weapon in a sharpshooter role. His long years as a hunter had given him considerable skill. Firing with great accuracy, he picked off Confederate artillerymen and engaged Confederate sharpshooters. Though they shot within inches of his head, he escaped injury, killing or wounding several of his opponents from 900 yards.

When Grant went east, Ruggles was deeply saddened. He sought to leave the mission of solitary patrols and form a unit that would operate behind Confederate lines. Generals Logan, Leggett and Oliver O. Howard approved, but when the request was forwarded to General Sherman, now in overall command in the west, Sherman disapproved. He wrote: 'There is no general law for such organization.'[7] The North did not have a Partisan Ranger Act as did the South, and what likely would have been a successful Ranger organization was not formed.

Ruggles sought aid from Grant, who wrote:

Head-quarters Armies of the United States
City Point, Va., October 13 1864.
I know Private Ruggles well, and the services he rendered in Mississippi as a scout. With an independent company of such men as himself, he would be more worth in the Shenandoah

Valley, and over the district of country over which Mosby roams, than a regiment of Cavalry.

I would recommend that he be authorized to raise a battalion of men and be put in the Department of West Virginia.

U.S. Grant, Lieutenant General[8]

The troops would be raised in Ruggles' home state. The request went to the Secretary of War where a clerk put the wrong year on the endorsement recommending approval to the governor of Ohio. As it was dated 1863 instead of 1864, the paper-pushers would not recognize the validity of it and the effort died in the rat-holes of administration. Thus ended what might have been a very interesting duel of wits and skill between Ruggles, Mosby and McNeill in Virginia.

As the war continued, Ruggles was a part of Sherman's march to the sea, then was sent to Florida and to Mobile, Alabama. Steadily working west, he ended up scouting for General Grierson. The war ended, but Ruggles had roamed between commands so much that he could not find one to give him a discharge. It was February 1866 before he could get out of the service.

Ruggles wrote of his experiences and closed with a review of things that men who operate behind enemy lines should remember:

> It is true that war is hardening to the finer sensibilities, but, nevertheless, if a man is unconscious of the danger of his undertaking, he is not apt to exercise the necessary precautionary measures to ensure his safety, and consequently fails in his mission.... I had to learn as I went along. At first I only ventured a short distance out... I increased gradually... in making trips of several hundred miles in length.

Ruggles summed up his experience in words that men of any generation who have gone behind enemy lines know to be true. He wrote of the importance of 'presence of mind, when suddenly and unexpectedly confronted' and that 'A man should never lose confidence in his own case, nor despair of escape if captured.' Ruggles guarded his tongue. He once told a loose-lipped scout: 'General Grant pays me for *seeing*, and not for *talking*.' He took calculated risks, but not unnecessary risks. He wrote of the importance of studying the terrain as one passes and knowing its features. Ruggles also wrote of the importance of reporting failure as accurately as success.[9]

Chapter 19

Scouts

The army of the United States had men and units who specialized in infiltration of enemy lines for intelligence-gathering or raids. These tactics developed when commanders identified junior leaders who had a flair for Ranger activities. An example was Theodore A. Boice of the 5th New York Cavalry who was promoted from first sergeant to first lieutenant on December 29 1862. On December 20 1863, Boice became captain of Company B of the 5th New Yorkers.

Boice was a skilled soldier who specialized in behind-enemy-lines reconnaissance for Brigadier General James Wilson's 3rd Cavalry Division. On September 3 1864, Wilson, who was located at Millwood in the valley, reported to the cavalry commander Brigadier General Alfred Torbert that Boice had just returned from a scout on the road to Newtown. Boice had led a detachment of horsemen into Confederate pickets near the Front Royal pike and determined that the Confederate regiment was the 9th Virginians. Leaving his men in a concealed area, Boice made his way through the Confederate outposts to their reserve positions near Stephensburg. Taking advantage of darkness, he moved close to a camp fire where officers warmed themselves and listened to their conversations, gaining information on the movements and strength of the Confederates.[1]

Wilson liked the courage of Boice and, by Special Order Number 85 on September 5 1864, put him on special duty to head Wilson's scouts. Each brigade commander was required to 'send in the names of five of the most daring and enterprising men in each regiment of their commands to be put under charge of Captain Boice for Special Duty.' General Wilson required that 'these men will be selected with care and only such will be recommended as are sure to be a credit to their regiment and the division in every particular.'[2]

General William T. Sherman had an audacious Ranger in Corporal James Pike who came out of the 4th Ohio Cavalry. Pike was from Leesburg, Ohio and was a printer by trade. His love of adventure took him to Kansas in 1858/59 when the border wars between slavers and abolitionists were raging. In Kansas, Pike fell in with a man from Texas who encouraged him to join the Texas Rangers. Pike became a Ranger and fought Comanche and Apache in Texas until the outbreak of the Civil War. Pike believed in the Union and many in Texas who did were being hanged or shot down. A skilled fighter and willing to try any mission, Pike moved into Arkansas where he posed as the nephew of Confederate General Albert Pike while gathering information for Union commanders. By the summer of 1861, Pike was in Portsmouth, Ohio where he enlisted in the 4th Ohio Cavalry. His regiment moved to Louisville and to Bowling Green, Kentucky as part of General Ormsby Mitchel's division. Pike's daring came to the attention of Mitchel who began to use him for reconnaissance missions. He was soon leading raiding parties against Confederate bushwhackers. Pike seemed to court death with schemes that went beyond reason. He rode into the Confederate town of Fayetteville, Lincoln County, Tennessee in full Union uniform, stabled his horse, rented a hotel room and sat down to breakfast as a curious crowd gathered.

The rumor spread that he was one of John Hunt Morgan's Confederates dressed in Yankee garb. Pike informed his onlookers that he was a Union soldier who had come to demand the surrender of the town. The citizens thought he was joking and Pike rode on. A short distance out of town he came upon several Confederate supply wagons. At gunpoint Pike forced the teamsters to bring the wagons together, then burned them. He put the teamsters on the mules and ordered them to go to Fayetteville and tell the townspeople what had happened.[3]

In his memoirs, Sherman described him as follows: 'This Pike proved to be a singular character; his manner attracted my notice at once...he said he wanted to do something *bold*, something that would make him a hero.' While Sherman was at Chattanooga preparing to move on Atlanta, Pike set off ranging behind Confederate lines disguised as an East Tennessee refugee. Pike's orders were to move through the mountains of western North Carolina with instructions to float down the Savannah River to destroy a bridge at Augusta, Georgia. Pike was unable to destroy the bridge or get back and the two men would not meet again until February 1865 when Sherman was at Columbia, South Carolina. An individual looking much the worse for his experience called from the ranks of prisoners taken by Sherman's men. It was Pike, who had been captured by the Confederates, put on trial for his life, escaped and made it to Union lines only to be captured by Sherman's men who thought he was a rebel. Sherman freed his Ranger and put him to work carrying messages through Confederate lines to the Union commander at Wilmington. After the war, Sherman gave Pike a regular army commission, but the adventurous Pike was bored with chasing Indians; he wrote Sherman that he wanted to be on the other side and planned to become a Cheyenne. Sherman was obviously much taken by this man. He wrote back that Pike must behave himself and be a gentleman and an officer and do his duty. James Pike never adjusted to life as an officer or became a Cheyenne Indian; he was killed in the accidental discharge of a pistol.[4]

Chapter 20

Rangers and Indians

As President Buchanan's term of office came to an end, the dissolution of the Union was being actively sought by many spokesmen in the South. Because of the location of the lands of the Indian Territory, many of the United States Indian agents were Southerners. These were quick to embrace the cause of the Confederacy and to use their influence on the Indians to also renounce the United States. The Choctaws and Chickasaws were willing to do so, the Cherokee were not. Increasingly, the Indians found themselves caught in the middle of a great struggle that was not theirs. The Creek Indians under Chief Hopoeithleyohola were firm in their support of the United States and the Confederates were determined to crush these Indians. In November and December 1861, at the Battles of Chusto Talasah and Chustenahlah, the Creeks who fought for the United States were defeated by a Confederate force primarily consisting of Indians who supported the Confederacy. The defeated Creeks were forced into the Kansas plains in winter. In the spring and summer of 1862, Union troops recaptured all the Indian country north of the Arkansaw River. In July, Tahlequah, the capital of the Cherokee nation, and Fort Gibson, a critical post in the Indian territory, were retaken by Union soldiers. Three 1,000-man regiments of Indians loyal to the United States were formed. The senior command positions were occupied by Union officers. The company level officers and non-commissioned officers were Indians.

On the Confederate side, Texas Ranger Ben McCullough and Indian Commissioner Albert Pike used their considerable influence to encourage Indians to side with the South. Stand Watie, a Cherokee man of mixed white and Indian ancestry, was appointed colonel of a force of Indians to fight Kansas 'Jayhawkers'. John Ross, the primary chief of the Cherokee, was opposed to an alliance with the South, but after the Southern victory at the Battle of Wilson's Creek, the voice of Stand Watie prevailed. It was Watie who formed a Confederate Cherokee regiment and led them against the Creeks on December 9 1861 at Chusto-Taloash in the Indian territory

277

near present-day Tulsa, Oklahoma, where Confederate Indian fought Union Indian. Stand Watie led a regiment and Pike's Confederate command of some 1,000 men were over 90 per cent Indians.

The Confederates raised three regiments from the Choctaw, Chickasaw, Cherokee, Creek and Seminole nations. These fought with Stand Watie at the Battle of Pea Ridge on March 7–8 1862. On April 1 1863, Watie was authorized to raise a brigade that was primarily made up of Cherokee Confederates. They were employed in raiding. In 1864, Watie's command captured the steamboat *Williams* with 150 barrels of flour and 16,000lbs of bacon. The command nearly disintegrated when troops left with the loot. In mid-1864, Watie was promoted to brigadier general. By the war's end he would command a cavalry brigade that consisted of the First Cherokee Regiment, a Cherokee battalion, First and Second Creek Regiments, a squadron of Creeks, the First Osage Battalion and the First Seminole Battalion.

In September 1864, shortly after the death of John Hunt Morgan and the acceptance of George McClellan of the Democratic nomination for president, Watie's force joined with a Texas brigade under Brigadier General Richard Gano for a raid into south-eastern Kansas. Typical of the ruthless war of no quarter in the Kansas/Missouri theater, the raid turned into a slaughter of prisoners. The Confederate Indians butchered members of the black 1st Kansas (Colored) Cavalry who surrendered and did the same to Union Indians on September 19 at Cabin Creek. Stand Watie remained true to the Confederacy. He died in August 1877.[1]

Battles between white and Indian continued during the Civil War. In Texas, the Comanche took advantage of the absence of white men who had gone east to fight, and terrorized the frontier. In Minnesota, in September 1862, one of the bloodiest Indian attacks in American history occurred. The ever-growing white settlements had pressed upon Indian land. Treaties were made with the Indians agreeing to exchange land for money, but the Indians felt that the money was slow in coming. This was true. The great war that was raging made Indian matters of small concern. A hunting and warlike people, the Sioux could not easily adjust to being farmers. They had been conquerors before the arrival of the more powerful whites and now resented their loss of control. On August 6 1862, Indians briefly seized an agency warehouse. Some of the tribal chiefs cautioned against war, but five chiefs headed by Little Crow responded to the urging of a group of renegades and the bloody work began. It is likely that communication between tribes occurred as attacks began from Pike's Peak and Salt Lake eastward, with the worst violence being in Minnesota. Only a few hundred United States troops were available to guard this vast area.

There had been indications that the Indians were angered and home guard units had been formed in preparation for conflict. On August 17 1862, one of these under a Captain Strout was surprised by Indians and defeated. The same occurred to Captain Marsh's command the following day as they were caught crossing a river and cut down. Raids began on isolated farms and spread among the small settlements. Herds of cattle were taken by the Indians, homes looted and put to the torch. Few of the white families were able to mount a defense. In the initial days of the attacks estimates of the number of whites killed ranged from 300 to 1,000. It is probable that some 800 white people were killed, including children and women. Some of the captive girls and women were raped. More than 30,000 people were made homeless and whites were killed within 30 miles of Minneapolis.

Emboldened by their success, the renegade Indians cut a path of destruction as they headed toward the German community of New Ulm. Fort Ridgely was held under seige until August 28. On September 2, Indians surrounded a force of white soldiers at Birch Coulee until the troops were relieved the next day. On September 6, General John Pope was assigned to command the newly activated Department of the North-West which included Iowa, Minnesota, Wisconsin and the Dakota and Nebraska territories. Pope had been defeated by Robert E. Lee at the Second Battle of Manassas in late August and Lincoln was still searching for a general who could win. Furious at his relief, Pope went off to Minnesota, blaming Lincoln and all senior army officers and saying 'I feel shame and mortification that we should live under such a system of things as prevails in Washington.' The Indian attacks continued, and on September 23 skirmishing with Indians in the Dakota territory occurred. The same day, at Wood Lake near Yellow Medicine, Minnesota governor and General Henry H. Sibley defeated the Indians in battle. On October 10, Sioux fought miners on the upper Missouri River south of Fort Berthold in the Dakota territory. The Sioux took several hundred prisoners and Sioux chief Little Crow told Sibley that Indians were angered over the manner in which their government annuities were being handled. Sibley replied he would not talk to Little Crow until the prisoners were returned. In the meantime, he sent messengers to the peaceful tribes of Sioux seeking to isolate Little Crow and the five chiefs who were his allies.

Early on it was recognized by the whites that infantry could not maintain the rapid pace at which the Indians could move. The infantry were primarily confined to stockades in a defensive posture. An organization was needed that could patrol the long lines of the frontier. Under the authorization of the War Department, the First Regiment of Mounted Rangers was organized in the fall of 1862, with most men being mustered into service in the months of September and October at Fort Snelling, Minnesota. It was not difficult to recruit the command. Many of the men involved in the fighting of August and September had lost family members to the Indian attacks. They were men who thirsted for revenge. The Ranger regiment consisted of twelve companies well-armed and mounted. Commanded by Lieutenant Colonel Samuel McPhail, they were quickly sent forward to patrol the frontier.

As the more numerous whites began to gain the ascendancy, Sibley reported in mid-October that he was holding some 2,000 Indians prisoner and the Indian attacks were dwindling. Many of the Indians captured had not participated in the attacks. They came in willingly as they knew the sword of revenge was being lifted. Pope convened a military tribunal. He reported the names of 303 captive Indians to Washington who were accused of being involved in the murders and proposed to hang them. Minnesota's politicians endorsed the executions, then pressed Lincoln to order it done. Pope warned that all these Indians were guilty to a greater or lesser degree of murder or violating young girls and warned of mob violence if the executions did not take place.

Lincoln looked at the crimes compared to the government policy he felt was in part responsible for the Indian unrest. To the outrage of the whites in Minnesota, Lincoln stalled the order for executions while he reviewed the list carefully and selected those he felt most warranted the death penalty. As captive Indians were led through New Ulm they were stoned by an angry crowd. After reviewing the charges, President Lincoln directed that 39 of the 303 prisoners should hang. On Friday, December 26 1862, thirty-eight Indians and mixed bloods were executed by hanging on a single gallows in Mankato, Minnesota. An Indian named 'Round Wind' was spared when it was learned that he had helped whites during the attack. A crowd of some 4,000 people cheered as the Indians sang their death song and called out to each other in support. William J. Duly who had lost half his family in the Indian attacks was granted the privilege of springing the trap. The rope suspending an Indian named 'Rattling Runner' broke. It appeared that his neck was broken, but he was strung up again to be certain.

The hatred engendered by the bloody attacks of August and September now fell upon the entire Indian community. Many of those who had been guilty and those who were not headed toward the west. Indian attacks were continuing in the Dakota territory. In the spring of 1863, General Sibley decided on a punitive expedition westward. The task force included the 6th and 10th Minnesota Infantry and the First Regiment of Mounted Rangers. They marched in July over land that was not settled, contained no railroads and very little forage. The drought of 1863–64 had left the plains with little grass. The alkaline dust that rose from the horses' hooves choked men and animals. Dogs died of thirst. The primary fuel was buffalo dung. Wells had to be dug to a depth of 10 to 12ft at the edge of marshes. The heat was so intense that the column started its march at 2.00 am and ended at noon.

On July 24, the Rangers encountered large numbers of Indians at and to the east of a place called 'Big Mound'. The chaplain of the Rangers, Dr Weiser, said he could identify some of the Indians. He went to them and returned saying they wanted peace. When Weiser went back to discuss terms, the Indians killed him. Furious at this action, the whites attacked. As the fight began, a violent storm arose. One Ranger was killed by lightning and two others had their horses knocked down. The battle became a running fight with the Rangers in pursuit of the Indians while the storm raged about them. Scalps of Minnesota victims were found and the Rangers showed no mercy. The pursuit continued for 10 miles, then the Rangers were ordered back to camp. Many felt this was a mistake. There was nothing to eat in camp except what was taken from the Indians and the advantage of the attack was lost.

The exhausted horses of the Rangers had to be rested and the Indians were quick to take advantage of the break in fighting. They moved their families ahead of them, gaining a three-day start. The warriors remained behind to provide cover for the Indian families and to rally for an attack. On July 26 1863, at Dead Buffalo Lake, the Indians, under a distinguished war chief named Grey Eagle, made an attack on Sibley's command. The Rangers leaped to their horses and met the attack head-on. The dust raised by the swirling horsemen made observation difficult. Grey Eagle wore a magnificent feathered headdress and was covered in war paint. Being this distinguishable made him a prime target and Grey Eagle was killed in the action.

The Teton Sioux from across the Missouri River came from the west to reinforce their kin and a force of Indian warriors estimated at 2,500 gathered. At Stony Lake on July 28 this band of expert horsemen attacked Sibley's men. Brightly painted and naked but for shot pouches and knife belts, many

Indians were armed with both guns and bows. The Rangers considered the bow and arrow more dangerous at close quarters than muskets or rifles as the Indians could shoot numerous arrows in the time it took to load one rifled musket. The arrows were iron-tipped and would penetrate to a depth that would show the barb on the opposite side of the wound entrance. The battle was a draw. Sibley's men could not destroy the Indian force as they had hoped, but they cleared the Sioux warriors from Minnesota and ended any threat of future massacres.[2]

Chapter 21

The Blazer Scouts

Of all the Confederate Rangers the United States forces had to contend with in the Shenandoah Valley, John Singleton Mosby's force was the greatest threat (see *Ghost, Thunderbolt, and Wizard*, Stackpole Books, by the author). To General U.S. Grant and his blue-clad troopers, Mosby was a bandit; a criminal operating outside the rules of war.

On August 16 1864, Grant sent a message to General Phil Sheridan: 'Where any of Mosby's men are caught, hang them without trial.' The following day Sheridan responded: 'Mosby has annoyed me and captured a few wagons...we hung one and shot 6 of his men.' Sheridan was well aware that Mosby was more of a problem than he expressed to Grant. Whoever he hung and shot, they were not Mosby's Rangers.

In Sheridan's command was General George Crook. A pre-Civil War Indian fighter in the north-west, Crook had enlarged his guerrilla warfare experience fighting bushwhackers in West Virginia. While there, Crook had made good use of a band of volunteer scouts under the command of Lieutenant Richard R. Blazer of the 91st Ohio Volunteer Infantry. Crook proposed putting together 100 well-armed volunteer marksmen who would dispose of Mosby and his band. Sheridan agreed and recruiting commenced.

Sheridan sent a message to General Christopher Augur, head of the Department of Washington, on August 20: 'I have one hundred picked men who will take the contract to clean out Mosby's gang. I want 100 Spencer Rifles for them. Send them to me if they can be found in Washington.'

The Spencer repeating carbine was one of the most significant weapons of the war. The Spencer used a completely self-contained .52 caliber cartridge. Loaded through a seven-shot tubular magazine in the carbine butt, the weapon provided firepower that Confederate muzzle-loading weapons could not match.

Selected to lead the new force was newly-promoted Captain Richard Blazer. An undistinguished civilian with scant military experience until he became a Ranger, in Western Virginia he had shown an appreciation of the art of intelligence-gathering. There he led his men in a series of successful operations. By the time Sheridan wanted a force of his own to meet Mosby's Rangers, Blazer was experienced in independent behind-the-lines operations and could recruit men who were equally adept.

By late August of 1864, the required 100 men were raised and equipped with Spencer rifles. They were well mounted, many on fleet horses taken from the enemy.

The fights that followed between Mosby's Confederate and Blazer's United States Rangers were frequent. Often, clashes were between small numbers of men and sometimes affairs in which each was wearing the other's uniforms. Despite Mosby's denials, considerable evidence including statements by his own men prove that Union blue was often worn to allow the Confederate Rangers more flexibility in operating behind Union lines. Conversely the same was true of United States Rangers. Both Richard Blazer and Henry Young often dressed their men in Confederate butternut or gray. Casualties were frequent but hard to prove, as both sides tended to underestimate their own and overestimate harm to the enemy.

On Tuesday, November 16, Captain Montjoy of Mosby's Rangers led Company D through Ashby's Gap and crossed the Shenandoah at Island Ford within a mile of Berry's Ferry. They rode taking advantage of concealed routes. Close to Winchester they hid, resting for the remainder of the night in a wood with security posted. At first light the men were mounted, while Montjoy scouted activity on the Winchester-New Town road. Blissfully unaware of Mosby's men, a detachment of Union cavalry was on the road riding without point men in advance or flankers. A hill located beside the road offered concealment for Captain Montjoy and Company D. The Confederate Rangers waited until the unsuspecting Union cavalry rode by, then charged into their flank, coming at them from only a few yards distance with revolvers blazing. Those of the cavalry who could, fled. A number were killed or wounded and seventeen prisoners with horses were taken.

His action completed, Montjoy led his men through Berryville and began dispersing the men to their homes or hideouts. Those who lived in Loudoun crossed the Shenandoah at Castleman's Ferry. Montjoy, with some thirty men and the prisoners, rode south-west toward Berry's Ferry intending to cross into Fauquier County. Some 2 miles short of the ferry, near a house owned by Mr Frank Whiting, Montjoy and his men were ambushed by Richard Blazer and his independent scouts. Ranger Edward Bredell was killed by one of Blazer's Spencer rifles. Montjoy's men tried to make it to the river. Captain Montjoy and Lieutenant Grogan attempted to rally the men near 'Vineyard', the home of John Cooke, but Blazer pushed his advantage, freeing the prisoners and taking back the captured horses. Accounts of killed and wounded differ, but the Union Rangers clearly won the fight. The Confederate Rangers broke contact as quickly as possible.

Though the Union army occupied the country, it could only control that portion where its troops were present in large numbers. While there were exceptions, the population generally supported the Confederacy. Captain Blazer's scouts were a small band of Union Rangers operating independently in a hostile environment. Their movements were frequently under the eyes of Confederate sympathizers. Small parties of five to ten US Rangers were frequently detached on patrol or ambush duty. While performing this duty, Lieutenant Ewing and five men were attacked and only Ewing got away. Sergeant Fuller and ten men were located and attacked by guerrillas. In this fight only three Union Rangers escaped. Dispatching small parties to cover his large area of operations and then losing them without replacement was whittling away at Blazer's numbers. He was left with a functional strength of about fifty men.

Mosby ordered Dolly Richards to take Companies A and B in pursuit of Blazer. Ranger Williamson wrote that 110 men made the November 17 roll-call at Bloomfield; other sources state that all Mosby's command rode out and place the number at 300 or more. Scouts picked up Blazer's trail at Snickersville, but Blazer was gone when the Rangers got there. The Rangers knew that Blazer made his headquarters at Kabletown on the west side of the Shenandoah. Continuing the search, Richards and his men crossed the river below Castleman's Ferry and bivouacked in Castleman's Woods. This then put him in position to attack Kabletown the next day.

A heavy fog lay on the land when, early on the 18th, Mosby's Rangers Puryear and McDonough were sent forward to scout. Puryear was a young man; McDonough was an able soldier but a ruthless killer and robber who was hardly a credit to the Rangers. Unable to see clearly, the two scouts stumbled on to one of Blazer's outposts. McDonough got away, but young Puryear was taken prisoner and hustled to Blazer's camp. According to Confederates, Puryear was roughly interrogated by Lieutenant Tom Cole, Blazer's second-in-command. When Puryear refused to give information, Cole had a rope put around Puryear's neck and twice hoisted him off the ground. Puryear was left hanging to the point of unconsciousness. Unable to secure information, Cole let Puryear down and put him with four other Confederate prisoners.

The capture of Puryear gave Blazer early warning. As a result, Blazer broke camp. As the fog lifted, the opposing Ranger commands began to search for each other. Richards located Blazer's camp. He led the Confederate Rangers forward, charging in with revolvers drawn, but it was to no avail; the camp was empty. Blazer had gone toward the Shenandoah searching for Richards.

Near Myerstown, the opponents came in sight of each other. Richards was in the open, but Blazer had a woodline to offer some concealment. It was to the Union advantage to fight the battle at long range, pitting seven-shot Spencer rifles against the six-shooter hand guns of the Rangers. Richards recognized this disadvantage. Leaving Company B to form a line, Richards withdrew Company A, simulating a withdrawal of his command. Blazer's caution failed him. Seeing what he believed to be a Confederate Ranger withdrawal, he ordered his men to attack.

Company A had disappeared from the view of the Union soldiers. Now, as Blazer's men clashed with Company B, Richards led Company A in a slashing assault on Blazer's flank. Fighting at close range, the Union Rangers threw down their cumbersome Spencers, drew revolvers and a furious but brief fight ensued. Richards was a skilled leader who knew how to use his advantages. He clearly had superiority of numbers and brought his command into a favorable tactical position where their firepower could be employed.

Despite Blazer's efforts, his men began to waver, then break. Puryear was freed and grasped a riderless horse. Riders on both sides were well mounted, so the flight and pursuit lasted for several miles. Though he had emptied his pistols, Ranger Sydnor Ferguson of Company B had a fast horse. He managed to ride abreast of Captain Blazer and strike the Union officer with the empty weapon, knocking him from his saddle and then capturing him.

Confederate Ranger McDonough saw with Blazer's scouts a man named Harrell who he recognized as a deserter from a Confederate regiment in which they had both served. The two men exchanged shots and McDonough was wounded. Harrell's horse was hit and fell, pinning its rider under it. McDonough had emptied his revolver and borrowed one from another Ranger. Standing over Harrell, he pulled the trigger three times only to have the weapon misfire. On the fourth pull of the trigger, the bullet shattered the skull of the helpless man.[1]

Ranger Alexander had pursued and captured a wounded Union officer who had holstered his revolvers. As he began to take the officer's weapons,

Ranger Puryear rode up in a state of agitation. Puryear had taken a hand gun from a Union soldier and was now after this officer. It was Puryear's former captor, Lieutenant Cole. Alexander said: 'Don't shoot this man; he has surrendered.' Puryear cursed and said: 'The rascal tried to hang me this morning.' Alexander asked Lieutenant Cole if that was true. Cole hesitated and made no response. Then Puryear shot and killed him. Lieutenant Cole fell between his and Alexander's horses, giving Alexander a dying look that seared itself on the Confederate Ranger's brain. With mixed emotion, Alexander dismounted and unbuckled Cole's holsters. Both revolvers had all chambers fired. Cole had fought as long as he could. Blazer's scouts were finished. Twenty-two of Blazer's men were killed, the same number of prisoners taken and a large number of these wounded. Fifty horses were captured. Dolly Richards had one man killed and five wounded.

Mosby's men had varying views of Captain Richard Blazer. Ranger Williamson wrote that 'Captain Blazer was not only a brave man and a hard fighter, but by his humane and kindly treatment...he had so disarmed our citizens that instead of fleeing on his approach and notifying all soldiers, thus giving them a chance to escape, but little notice was taken of him.'[2] Ranger Crawford thought the Union officer's name was Brasher. Crawford did not have a high regard for the fighting ability of the Union scouts, but praised their conduct.[3] Mosby's Doctor Monteiro named the Union officer 'Blaizor' and promoted him to major. Monteiro, who gained his impressions of Blazer through Mosby's younger brother and adjutant William Mosby, called the officer a 'desperado' and had the impression that Blaizor 'must be one of the most uncouth bipeds that ever aspired to military honors.'[4] Mosby said his men named their adversary 'Old Blaze' and were eager for a fight with him. Contradicting himself, Mosby described Blazer as 'a bold, but cautious commander.'[5]

The survivors of Blazer's scouts who came back to Union lines were ordered relieved of special duty and returned to their original units on January 2 1865. Captain Richard Blazer was held at Libby Prison in Richmond. After exchange, Blazer returned to the 91st Ohio Regiment. Post-war he lived in Gallipolis, Ohio. He died on October 29 1878.

Chapter 22

The Jessie Scouts

In early 1861, Missouri was in turmoil. Men were hung for merely saying they were for the Union. A strong commander was needed. On May 14 1861, President Lincoln appointed John C. Fremont a major general and assigned him to command the Western Department with headquarters in St Louis. Fremont was not a surprising choice. Born in South Carolina on January 21 1813, he grew up in a time of 'Manifest Destiny'. Fremont's nickname was 'Pathfinder', and many a western city today stands where he opened the path.

Fremont was given the command because he was a proven leader of men, a famed explorer with a national following. It was John Fremont who led the way in finding paths through the Rocky Mountains and grew rich in the California gold rush. He then played a major role in efforts to take California from Mexico. These successes led him to politics. Fremont was the first presidential candidate of the fledgling Republican Party. Though in the same political party, he was a potential political thorn in the side of Abraham Lincoln.

Lincoln was uneasy about Fremont, but was under pressure from the Republican Party to treat his in-house rival well. Fremont had no qualms about leading men in combat. He was a confident, determined man with a mate to match. Fremont had eloped with and married Jessie Benton, the 16-year-old daughter of Missouri Senator Thomas Hart Benton. Jessie Benton Fremont was a bright, strong-willed woman who did not hitch her wagon to any man's star; she was up front, in the traces with her man. As the daughter of a senator, Jessie Fremont had many social contacts. She was at ease in Washington society and the White House. Jessie Fremont captivated most people she met. Albert D. Richardson, a risk-taking war correspondent for the *New York Tribune*, met Jessie in St Louis and wrote of her: 'In a lifetime one meets not more than four or five great conversationalists. Jessie Benton Fremont is among the felicitous few, if not the queen of them all.'

John Fremont threw himself into his work, putting in fifteen-hour days of decisive action. What mistakes he made, he made with a will. He had a penchant for recruiting foreign officers into his military household. Critics said the inability to speak English was a requirement to serving on his staff. He sent out scouts to keep him informed and set about fortifying St Louis at the expense of the rest of his command. He declared martial law on August 30 1861, issuing a proclamation confiscating the property of all Missourians in rebellion against the United States and freeing all their slaves. President Lincoln's private thoughts of Fremont remained private. Lincoln publicly said he thought Fremont was a good man surrounded by men who were not. Lincoln was trying to preserve the Union and keep Missouri in the fold. He was not ready to take rebel property and free slaves. Fremont's actions and his unwillingness to back down got him in trouble.[1]

Jessie Fremont stood by her man. She wanted explanations for what the Fremonts deemed a lack of presidential support. Her letters to Lincoln were in the tone of demands. When Jessie sought an audience with him, Lincoln was so incensed that he left her standing. The president shocked Jessie Fremont when he said sneeringly: 'You are quite a female politician.'[2] Fremont was finished in Lincoln's eyes and was relieved of his command. Abolitionists were strongly supportive of Fremont's efforts to free slaves. Fremont's national popularity was such that Lincoln was soon pressured to give him the command of the Mountain Department of West Virginia. Lincoln was skilled in political in-fighting. Getting command did not mean that Fremont would get the necessary resources. The Mountain Department included West Virginia, parts of Kentucky, Tennessee and Virginia. Wheeling, West Virginia was Fremont's headquarters. He was soon the darling of the *Wheeling Intelligencer*, a newspaper that saw Fremont as a man of action.

In the South Branch Valley of West Virginia, Confederate guerrillas were creating problems. Jessie Fremont suggested scouts who had worked for Fremont in Missouri be brought east. Jessie proposed a Ranger organization be formed that would provide her husband with information. On April 30 1862, Captain Charles Carpenter and some twenty-five men arrived in Wheeling. They were described by a *Wheeling Intelligencer* reporter as wearing uniforms 'velvet faced with brass buttons, red sashes and mystic shoulder straps.'[3]

The men were called 'Jessie Scouts' in Mrs Fremont's honor. When they went out on a mission they went in civilian clothes or in the butternut or gray of the Confederates. They had some successes, but lacking discipline they left much to be desired. Without strong leadership this type of unit frequently delivers false reports or becomes criminal. With Carpenter in command, the Jessie Scouts seem to have been guilty of both faults.

Their publicity value was significant, however, and the Confederates were concerned. A commander who knows enemy scouts are going about his rear area is likely to be looking over his shoulder. Those who don't roam around behind enemy lines tend to think such duty is romantic, so the Jessie Scouts were much talked about on both sides of the lines.

Fremont won the premature praise of the *Wheeling Intelligencer*, which on May 1 1862 praised him for having driven the main body of the enemy from West Virginia and going to work on the guerrilla bands that infested the country. Unfortunately for Fremont, his next opponent was Thomas 'Stonewall' Jackson. This ferocious pray-and-kill puritan would thrash several Union commanders during his 1862 Valley campaign and Fremont was one. Suitably disgraced, Fremont was then reassigned under John Pope who it was well known he despised. In a fit of pique, Fremont resigned his commission. He resurfaced briefly in the 1864 presidential election as a third-party candidate for president, but the effort fizzled out and he and Jessie, always a team, went from pomp and circumstance to a dreary future and even poverty.

While he was recuperating from a gunshot wound, Captain Carpenter of the Jessie Scouts met a correspondent and regaled him with epic tales of encounters. He informed the newsman that he had been a charter member of the John Brown raid at Harpers Ferry and escaped by crawling through a covered drain that led from the famed engine-house to the river. Carpenter modestly admitted that no army that he had ever scouted for had ever suffered from a raid in its rear or been 'surprised'. When asked if he had ever been in Confederate General Sterling Price's headquarters, Carpenter responded: 'Several times.' He mentioned dressing as a woman and passing into Confederate lines. On the way back out he had the personal escort of a Confederate officer. Carpenter continued his brag by telling the correspondent that he had suspected that the telegraph operators between Hannibal, Missouri and St Joseph were disloyal. A woman revealed that one of these telegraph operators had asked her to go to the theater. Carpenter learned of this and paid $50 to the woman to plead illness at the last moment but to introduce him to the operator as a Confederate agent. As the telegrapher's female companion was not available, the two men went drinking and the true Confederate told all. Taking two of his men, Carpenter followed the telegrapher to a hut in the brush which was the enemy signal station. They found the telegrapher and another man there, but determined these Confederates could not be taken prisoner and must be killed. Carpenter shot one of the men. Another scout named Hale only wounded his target, so when they rushed in Carpenter had to shoot that man also. They made a complete haul of the telegraph equipment, got two horses and $65. Carpenter also said he captured two daguerreotypes but did not mention who or what they were pictures of.

Carpenter related that Henry Hale was one of his best scouts. Hale was carrying dispatches when he saw an old rebel with a horse. Hale put his pistol to the man's head, took the man's shotgun and horse and rode off. The old Confederate must have had Olympic qualities as he somehow got another gun, then sprinted ahead of the horseback Hale about a mile on. In turn he captured Hale, took back his horse, all weapons and Hale's pants. Hale thought his shirt would be next, but the old man told him to 'Skedaddle'. Hale had nothing on but a shirt; still he was content as that was where his dispatches were.

Carpenter said he was the man who burned Randolph, Missouri which was a Confederate supply center. With 22 men he attacked and routed 250 Confederates. He did that by attacking from all points of the compass with all of his men pretending to be officers and calling out commands to imaginary units. The Jessies took seventeen prisoners and destroyed the Confederate supplies. Carpenter and a deserter from the First United States Dragoons fought with sabers. Captain Carpenter was wounded over the eye but killed his man.

Coming east to Kentucky, Carpenter and a Jessie Scout named Robb were captured. They had thirteen guards, but the guards got drunk and Carpenter and Robb took their revolvers and killed them. He then went to Platte City dressed as a Confederate and made a speech in favor of Jeff Davis. Someone recognized Carpenter and he was imprisoned. He escaped and took a horse, but on the way back to Union lines the horse fell. Now on foot, he met two Confederate videttes and told them that he was on a recruiting mission. One of them walked a way with him and Carpenter stabbed and killed him with a knife that came from somewhere. He then went back and killed the other man. The correspondent probably had not been aware that it was Carpenter who went into Confederate-held Fort Henry and brought out the information that enabled Grant to capture it. He did the same thing at Fort Donelson. On the way out he saved the fine battle flag of a Union cavalry regiment. Writing furiously, the correspondent must have been fascinated to be in the company of such an accomplished warrior and a wounded one at that.[4]

No one could be certain how much, if any, of Carpenter's stirring tale was the truth. It was known that Captain Charles Carpenter's wound did not come from Confederates. He was wounded in Cumberland, Maryland when a woman put a pistol ball into his hip under circumstances that were less than heroic for the officer. The totality of Carpenter's mendacity and questionable activities closed his scouting career. With the departure of John and Jessie Fremont and Captain Carpenter, the organization called the Jessie Scouts was ended.

Some men of the Jessie Scouts may have remained to serve in the same role under General Robert Milroy, then followed with service under General William Averell. Irascible General George Crook did not have a high opinion of any of them and would later write 'Gen. Averell had a lot of bummers who he called scouts and spies, who were thoroughly unreliable and worthless.'[5] Crook was opposed to the men, not the tactic. In his memoirs he left no doubt that it was George Crook, not Phil Sheridan, who founded the Blazer Scouts.

Despite being disbanded, the name 'Jessie Scouts' hung on throughout the war. Any Union soldier engaged in behind-the-lines operations might be considered a 'Jessie' by the Confederates. In May 1864, Samuel T. Haviland of Company H, 15th New York Cavalry was serving as a Ranger scout. Haviland and another man were riding over Mount Jackson to Orkney Springs on a reconnaissance patrol. The two men were dressed in Confederate uniform. While returning from the patrol, they encountered a Confederate mail carrier. They rode with him for a while, encouraging the Confederate to take them to General Imboden's headquarters. The three men stopped at a house to ask for dinner, and the two Union Rangers felt secure in their disguise.

Unfortunately a Union cavalry patrol also stopped at the house. Some of the cavalry knew Haviland's partner, so the two Union men and the Confederate were not arrested. When the cavalry left, the Rangers knew that with their true identity revealed, they could not continue their search for Imboden. They told the Confederate mail carrier he was a prisoner. The two Union Rangers continued eating their meal. The prisoner, who was facing the door, suddenly jumped to his feet and yelled, 'Take them; they are Yanks.' The two Rangers drew their pistols and raced outside to their horses, only to find that they were surrounded by a group of Confederate guerrillas.

The mailman and the guerrillas wanted them promptly hung as Jessie Scouts. A rope was secured, but a line unit Confederate lieutenant on recuperative leave stopped the proceedings to question the two men. He first told them that as 'Jessie Scouts' they had to hang. Haviland and his partner denied being Jessies. The lieutenant observed that it was all right. He had found them in Confederate uniform and would hang them on that basis. The United States War Department had published an order that any Confederate captured in Union uniform was to be hanged. The Confederate lieutenant felt that a *quid pro quo* was in order.

The Rangers continued to claim they were Confederates. At length the lieutenant decided to let his senior hang them. He put the two captives on their horses and the party rode off. A pretty young woman came out of a house and asked what was going on. When told they were Union Rangers, she asked the lieutenant for his revolver so that she could shoot the two men. However, the Confederate lieutenant was a stickler for the rules of war, so they rode on.

They were brought before Captain William Miller who commanded at the Columbia Iron Works and his brother, who was the local sheriff. Surrounded by guards, the two Rangers sat on their horses during the brief trial. The sheriff wanted them hung promptly, while the captain and his womenfolk felt they deserved more time to prove they were not Jessie Scouts. For several days the two men were held tied. Another prisoner of their unit was brought before them and wisely claimed they were just regular Union troops. They were sent on the prisoner-of-war trail to Libby Prison at Richmond, then on to Andersonville in Georgia. At Richmond, Haviland's companion was recognized by a Confederate as a 'Jessie Scout' and was hung. At Libby, Haviland made the mistake of standing at a window. A guard shot at him and barely missed. At the infamous Confederate prison of Andersonville, Haviland got his first sight of its commandant, Captain Wirz. The captain, who would be executed at the close of the war, was counting the prisoners while carrying a revolver in his hand. Haviland was tired and sat on the ground. Wirz said: 'Stand up, God damn you, or I will blow your head off.' That welcome was minor compared to the hell Haviland was about to endure. Yet he was a tough man and survived Andersonville. Haviland was one of the few Union Rangers to be captured and come back alive.[6] After the war, Haviland often thought about the pretty Southern girl who had wanted to shoot him. He wished he had gotten revenge by going back and marrying her.

Ironically the name 'Jessie Scouts' fired the imagination on both sides of the line. Civilians, Confederates, even some of the Union scouts used the term 'Jessie', but with the departure of the Fremonts 'Jessie Scouts' became a misnomer. Those men who remained were now military and the scouts of other commanders. Few of those Rangers who would in future go behind Confederate lines ever had contact with the Fremonts. These men were Averell's scouts, Milroy's scouts, Kilpatrick's scouts, Meade's scouts and Grant's scouts. A man with the ego of Phil Sheridan would not have used or suffered to be used the name 'Jessie Scouts'. It was the 'Sheridan Scouts' that became the most famed of all these Union Ranger organizations and their work was done under the brilliant leadership of Major Henry Young.

Chapter 23

Henry Harrison Young and Sheridan's Scouts

Phil Sheridan did not like the information-gathering organization he found on taking command in the Shenandoah Valley. The existing system relied too much on Confederate deserters and local citizens. Sheridan decided that his principal reliance would be on an all-volunteer force of picked men to serve as his Rangers. Sheridan began by soliciting the best scouts from his subordinate commanders. As numbers grew, he decided his Rangers would need a structured organization. Sheridan decided on Major Henry Harrison Young of the 2nd Rhode Island Infantry to head those who would go behind Confederate lines. When Sheridan told Young's commander Colonel Oliver Edwards that he wanted Henry Young on his staff, Edwards replied: 'I would rather you take my right arm than take him from me.'[1] Sheridan had the wit to see he could not gain much intelligence from Edwards' right arm, so he insisted on Henry Young. Being a general dealing with a colonel, Sheridan got his way.

On October 12 1864, Henry Young was promoted to major and assigned to Sheridan's staff as Chief of Scouts. Sheridan told Young his men must be carefully selected. They would operate wearing Confederate uniforms behind Confederate lines. With the exception of Major Young, the men would be paid from the Secret Service fund. The better the information they brought in, the better they would be paid.[2]

Henry Harrison Young is little known to Civil War history, yet he was the d'Artagnan of the North. Born on February 9 1841 in Mendon, Massachusetts, he grew to be handsome but slight of build. In the opinion of friends, he was too frail to be a soldier. From his childhood, Henry Young had an interest in military affairs and Ranger activities. He studied the life and campaigns of Revolutionary War Ranger General Dan Morgan. When he failed to be accepted at West Point, Young attended a commercial college and became a Jack-of-all-trades cashier and bookkeeper at Lippitt and

Martin, a large firm in Providence, Rhode Island. This financial training taught him to pay attention to detail; a useful practice for one involved in reconnaissance. In the office and the field, his reports would prove to be clear, complete and concise.

When South Carolinians fired on Fort Sumpter, President Lincoln called for 75,000 volunteers to put down the rebellion. Henry Young was among the first of his community to volunteer. He wanted a commission and that meant recruiting. He spoke to friends of how Dan Morgan had recruited his Rangers in the Revolutionary War and announced his intention to form a command. With his 10-year-old sister driving the rig, the 20-year-old Henry roamed street after street encouraging men to join. He recruited sixty-three men and was so persistent that Colonel John S. Slocum, who was commanding the 2nd Rhode Island Regiment, got him a commission as a second lieutenant. Mustered into service on June 8 1861, Young joined Company B of the 2nd Rhode Island Infantry. From the beginning, Henry Young proved himself an officer who looked after his men. He led from the front and did not ask men to do what he would not do himself.[3]

Young's first challenge came when the new soldiers were assigned to barracks that had no beds or bedding. The troops were furious and in a state of near mutiny. Henry went to the barracks and told the men it was time to turn in. He laid down on the floor to go to sleep. 'Lie right down,' he called out to the men. Soon they joined him on the floor, wrapping their blankets around them. From then on the men followed him anywhere.[4]

Henry was a dutiful son who had frequent correspondence with home. When his mother wrote about the suffering of the times, he wrote in reply:

> You say you think it would discourage any one from going to the war. The fact is that no one knows what fighting is until they have seen it; and they that have, after it is over and they think about it, would like to see it over again. There is an excitement about it, there is a longing for it again that no one knows who has not experienced it.[5]

On November 13 1861, Young was promoted to captain and was commanding Company B. His company was the first to cross the Rappahannock River at Fredericksburg on December 11 1862. There he led his men across the pontoon bridges established by the 15th and 50th New York Engineers into the fire of Barksdale's Mississippi marksmen. After the battle, one of the more seriously wounded men of Company B was sent home to Rhode Island.

Young's mother visited the soldier and in the course of the conversation she asked: 'Do you like your captain?' 'Like him, ma'am,' responded the soldier, 'we think God A'mighty of him! There never was any one like him; the men would lay down their lives for him any day.'

Though opportunity presented itself, Henry Young would not take a furlough from the battlefront. He preferred to stay with the men. He fought at Bull Run, the Siege of Yorktown, Williamsburg, Seven Pines, Malvern Hill, Fredericksburg, Marye's Heights, Salem Heights, Gettysburg, Rappahannock Station, Mine Run, Wilderness, Spottsylvania and Cold Harbor before he joined Sheridan. When he became a staff officer, Young could not stay away from the sound of the guns. His brigade commander wrote of him:

> When you wished an order carried to any part of the field he did not look about for the safest route, but took the most direct one, no matter how the bullets whistled. He was always ready to dash through the hottest place to cheer on a wavering regiment or rally a disorganized one.[6]

At Fredericksburg where the Northern Lights wept over Northern dead, Young was commended for leaping from his horse and dragging a wounded man to cover in a hail of gunfire.

Henry Young lived happily on the knife-edge of danger. Staff life did not offer sufficient challenge, so even before Sheridan's call, he began to go ranging. He wrote to his mother: 'A scout's life is a dangerous one to a certain extent, but I don't know after all that it is more so than a great many other positions.'

When his command was moved to the Shenandoah Valley, Henry Young was made Inspector Adjutant General, Fourth Brigade, Second Division, Sixth Corps. On June 5 1864, his friend Colonel Oliver Edwards was placed in command of Winchester and Young worked under his direction. Much of Young's work was as a freelance Ranger. He had maximum latitude to go where he felt he could do the most good. Part of this experience was the opportunity to go out on missions with Captain Richard Blazer and Blazer's scouts. Young learned much from Blazer's successes and from his defeat at the hands of Mosby's Adolphus 'Dolly' Richards. Young developed battlefield techniques that were more akin to the scalpel than the hammer.

Henry Young genuinely enjoyed working alone, roaming behind Confederate lines. There were many close calls. Once when he was hotly pursued in a violent storm, he hid among leaves in a forest. The senior Confederate had ridden close to Young's hiding place. It appeared that the Union Ranger's life would be ended. A bolt of lightning struck near the Confederate leader, causing his horse to shy and strike the man against a low bough, injuring him. The search was called off and Young narrowly escaped.

Now Henry Young had the mission he loved. Phil Sheridan fully supported his Rangers. He was a commander who understood the need for having intelligence of the enemy's strength, dispositions and intent. While at Winchester in the fall of 1864, Sheridan was anxious for information concerning Confederate movement on his flank. Young volunteered and took three additional volunteers with him on the mission. The four dressed in Confederate uniform, then passed into enemy lines. Young soon returned with the information Sheridan needed.

A battalion-sized organization was too unwieldy for Young's methods. Sheridan authorized Young to choose 100 men. Though it may have reached those numbers in the latter stages of the war, Young was very selective and his command usually consisted of between thirty to sixty men. The roll book of Sergeant Joseph McCabe, the senior NCO, carried the names of fifty-eight men.

Volunteers were carefully screened. Each man would be mounted and armed with two revolvers and the Spencer carbine that some Southern units had acquired by the fall of 1864. Some men also carried sabers. They were issued Confederate gray uniforms[7] but were free to use any other garb that suited their purpose. It was unlikely there was any of this foolish business of consistently using one means of identifying each other while in enemy territory, such as wearing a white neckerchief. The unit was small enough for the men to know each other. No one working behind enemy lines wants to draw attention to themselves and have people start asking questions.

A few of the first men to be selected began to infiltrate the Confederate positions and had immediate success. Sheridan wrote: 'They had learned that just outside of my lines near Millwood, there was living an old colored man, who had a permit to go into Winchester and return three times a week, for the purpose of selling vegetables to the inhabitants.'[8] The scouts had questioned the old man, Thomas Laws, and found him to be the ideal courier. He was intelligent, loyal and willing. Now someone was needed with access to information inside Confederate lines. General Crook had many friends inside Winchester and suggested Miss Rebecca Wright, a young Quaker schoolteacher loyal to the United States. Sheridan personally interviewed the old man who said he knew Miss Wright well.

Sheridan's message requesting specific information was written on tissue paper and put in a small capsule that would be carried inside the courier's mouth. In the unlikely event he was searched, the messenger had only to swallow the capsule. The message was a complete surprise to Rebecca Wright, but thinking it over, she liked the idea of helping to win the war. There are many men who cannot keep their mouths shut when in the presence of a woman. The night before the message came, a wounded Confederate officer had been telling Rebecca Wright's mother of planned dispositions of Jubal Early's Confederate army. Rebecca Wright's first message gave Sheridan the vital information he needed to initiate the Battle of Opequon (Winchester). Miss Wright went to her new-found calling with a will and produced a flow of useful information.

Meanwhile Henry Young and his Rangers were prowling Confederate territory. Lieutenant George B. Peck Jr of the 2nd Rhode Island Infantry wrote of the time he first saw Henry Young:

> ...we met a man in butternut suit, beardless, with very red, blooming cheeks and yet darkly tanned, long-haired with broad-brimmed hat, and dilapidated horse equipments. I was amazed to see the cordial greetings he received, and the many hearty hand-shakes from many of our officers and men as we still kept marching on. It was none other than our Major (Henry H. Young, chief of scouts on General Sheridan's staff), who had just returned from a tour through enemy lines, and imparted information upon which the conduct of the impending battle would be based.[9]

Confederate Rangers such as Gilmor, McNeill, Mosby and White were a constant threat to Sheridan's command, and another problem was Confederate deserters. Often men who had considerable combat experience, these deserters had gone home on pass or recuperation leave and stayed there. They knew the countryside and had friends who would shelter them. They lived by ruthless robbery, were a plague to both armies and to any Southern civilians they did not know. Henry Young was assigned the mission of bringing these men in, and a shot from Young's pistol or short shrift and a stout rope was the end of many of them. With two men, Young went after one such individual. Though his two men were wounded, Young pursued the deserter and beat him in a hand-to-hand fight, though the man was much taller and heavier.

With each success, Young's confidence grew. When a Union attack was being held up by the accurate fire of a Confederate artillery battery, Young made his way through the lines on horseback. Approaching the battery from the rear, he assumed the role of a senior Confederate staff officer and ordered the battery commander to withdraw his guns to a new position. When the order was complied with the Union attack continued.[10]

In this war in which opponents spoke the same language, Henry Young had the great advantage of being believable. He would dress in Confederate uniform, enter Confederate camps and charm his enemies into revealing information. Dressed in civilian clothes, Young entered a Confederate recruiting station and joined the Southern army. On learning when and where the recruits were being assembled, Young led Union troops back and all the would-be Confederate soldiers received their first taste of army life as prisoners.

The Sheridan scouts would penetrate Confederate lines and visit towns and units, often posing as Southern soldiers on leave. After getting useful information they would ride away under the guise of rejoining their commands. One man would be detached to take the message back to Union lines. These Union Rangers practiced thinking, acting and speaking like Southerners. The slightest miscue could cost them their lives. One man said 'I guess' instead of the expression 'I reckon' and that mistake almost cost the lives of men. The Confederates quickly became aware of these Union Rangers who were behind their lines, but there were many Confederate cavalry patrols, soldiers going to or from the battle area or straggling. It was difficult to distrust every man who wore the same uniform. For Major Young and his men life was difficult and dangerous. Those who were caught were shot or hung.

The Sheridan scouts served under hard masters. It was possible the men were more afraid of Sheridan and Young than the Confederates. Sheridan's questions were penetrating and came at a subject from directions that would detect an exaggeration or a lie. John Landegon, who served as a scout for Kilpatrick and Grant, served briefly in that capacity under Sheridan before Henry Young came on the scene and related:

> My first report to General Sheridan. I'd been out for three days – somewhere in the enemy's lines...and when I came in to report to the General I thought it would be my last report.

'Well,' he says, 'what did you find?' 'Nothin',' I answered – just that. 'By Gee!' he yelled, and he jumped up from his chair. 'That's the best report I ever heard a scout make!' I thought he was mad and just making fun of me, and I stood still and didn't say anything. He walked up close to me. 'Do you know why I think so much of that "nothin'" of yours? It's because you didn't think you had to make up a lot of lies for fear I'd think you hadn't been working. If you saw "nothin'" in three days, that means there was nothing to see, and that's the one thing I wanted to know.[11]

None of the scouts tried to fool Henry Young. He was either on the mission with them or following them about. 'It's no use trying to stump up his eye,' a Ranger would say.[12]

Henry Young used flexibility of organization as a tool of war. He tailored his unit to the mission. On some occasions they worked as teams of fifteen to twenty men when going raiding, but many of their missions were lonely operations performed by one, two or three men.

Of the first two months of operations Sheridan wrote in his memoirs (after Young's end-of-war promotion): 'I now realized more than I had done hitherto how efficient my scouts had become since under the control of Colonel Young, for not only did they bring me almost every day intelligence from within Early's lines, but they also operated efficiently against the guerrillas infesting West Virginia.'[13]

A Ranger named George Valentine was behind Confederate lines when he saw two soldiers in butternut who were obviously stragglers from their command. Assuming the manner of a provost guard, Valentine approached the two men and demanded to know why they were not with their unit. The men responded that because they had been so tired, they could not continue and did not know where their unit had gone. Valentine demanded to know what unit they belonged to. When the men responded, Valentine assured them that he knew the location of their unit and would guide them. He took them through the lines and into Union captivity.[14]

Rangers Dunn, Tone and Goubleman were on the trail of some Confederates when they found three others following them. The Union Rangers were soon attacked by these men. Goubleman was shot in the arm and Dunn's horse took a bullet. Galloping in the escape, they turned left quickly, masking their movement with a small hill, then rode to its top and charged down on the Confederates. Goubleman killed a Confederate with his saber. Rangers Dunn and Tone trapped another gray-coated horseman between them. The Southerner was a skilled rider who would not surrender. The three men galloped along, riding stirrup to stirrup, cutting at each other with their sabers. Finally, a horizontal slash of a blade took the Confederate in the mouth. The force of the blow drove his body from the saddle and he turned a full somersault before hitting the ground.[15]

Sergeant Joseph E. McCabe was born on January 6 1841 at Bridgewater, Pennsylvania and grew up learning the trade of a carriage-painter. He enlisted in the army on September 6 1862 as a member of Company A of the 17th Penna Volunteer Cavalry Regiment. McCabe soon began to catch the eye of his seniors and was promoted to sergeant on November 1 of that year. Joe McCabe fought at Chancellorsville, Gettysburg, Boonesborough, Brandy Station, Rappahannock, Kilpatrick's raid to Richmond, and Cold Harbor. On Sunday, September 18 1864, just prior to the Battle of Winchester (Opequon Creek), McCabe was ordered to find a place where the regiment could cross the creek. McCabe knew of a ford, which he expected would be guarded. He crossed at another place and circled around. At the ford he found a Confederate lieutenant and sixteen men on guard. Coming from their rear, McCabe took the men prisoner and freed the ford for movement.

On September 19 1864, the 17th Pennsylvania Cavalry was ordered to provost duty at Winchester. The provost was Henry Young's mentor and friend, Colonel Oliver Edwards. On September 21, McCabe was ordered to take ten men and carry dispatches to Harpers Ferry. On the way, McCabe was attacked by some thirty of Mosby's Rangers. He managed to elude the Rangers and brought in his men and his dispatches without injury or loss.

On return from this mission, Colonel Edwards interviewed McCabe, liked what he saw and heard and sent for Harry H. Young. The new head of Sheridan's Rangers was looking for a good sergeant to play a major role in a prisoner raid on Jubal Early's army. Edwards recommended McCabe and Young agreed. McCabe was allowed to select twenty volunteers and good horses. Major Young decided to also take twenty infantry volunteers. They marched toward Winchester throughout the day on the 21st and stopped near a brick house on the road to Romney. Security was posted, and the Rangers lay quietly throughout the night. The next morning they continued movement and soon captured a Confederate straggler. McCabe saw a place where fence rails had been let down and there were tracks in the earth. He followed these tracks to a cabin where six horses were tied outside. After a brief firefight, two of the six Confederates in the house were wounded and all were captured. McCabe returned to Major Young with his prisoners. As McCabe was leading out again, they encountered a Confederate patrol. The Southerners fled, but McCabe captured one prisoner when the Confederate was thrown from his startled horse. The captured man was Charles Sibert, a wanted guerrilla. The march continued till midnight when the infantry being exhausted, the Rangers halted. They stopped at a friendly house and posted security. While Young and McCabe were eating buckwheat cakes, eggs and drinking applejack, firing broke out. Young and McCabe had kept their horses saddled and quickly led their men into line and drove off the Confederates. On the way back to base camp McCabe captured several more guerrillas. The Union Rangers came back from the patrol with seventeen prisoners.

This exploit led to McCabe being detached from line duty on November 27 1864 and working with Major Young as his senior non-commissioned officer. The two men would scout the countryside by themselves, gather information and bring in prisoners.[16]

The ability to attack in the worst possible weather and over the most difficult terrain is a hallmark of the American Ranger. In January 1865, when the bitter cold had men huddled close to camp fires, Young took his scouts raiding on Confederate pickets. One such post was at Edinburg Bridge and another at Columbia Furnace. These were ideal targets; small detachments located in advance of the main body of their army. John Singleton Mosby had built a reputation picking off such plums. Young had twenty scouts and a detachment of fifty cavalry and spent the night rounding up Confederates. As the dawn cracked over Massanutten Mountain, Young turned his command and the prisoners toward the Union lines at Kernstown. He and his men were hungry and stopped for breakfast at Woodstock. Arch Rowand finished eating and went out in the street. A butcher named Kuhn passed close to Rowand and whispered: 'Three hundred on the "Back Road", coming!' Rowand hurried back to where Young was eating and told him of the Confederate reaction force. Young had kissed success too often and threw caution to the wind. 'I'll not budge till I finish my breakfast,' he replied.

This bravado did not go down well with Young's men. James Campbell and Arch Rowand urged that they mount and ride, but Young continued eating. By the time he finished and gave the order to ride, the Confederate cavalry was at the upper end of the long street. Firing erupted and the Union cavalry fled. The prisoners saw their opportunity to escape and scattered. Young sent Rowand to order the Union horsemen back, but they were panicked and clearly had no intention of returning. It was up to the Rangers to fight a delaying action that would let them break free. Major Young took position at the tail end of the Union column.

Rowand was riding to obey Young's orders when James Campbell yelled: 'Rowand, come back, Young is down!' Rowand turned. As he did so, he saw that Young's horse was down and the major was fighting on foot. Rowand put spurs to his horse and galloped toward Young. Before he could get there, Rangers Campbell and Harry K. 'Sonny' Chrisman[17] had charged toward the assistance of their commander. Campbell rode past Young, swung his horse sideways, dismounted, then stood, firing two pistols from behind the horse. Chrisman leaned out of the saddle and grabbed Young's arm, then swung the major into the saddle behind him.

They galloped away and after a time the Confederates gave up the pursuit.[18] On October 30 1897, Ranger James A. Campbell was awarded the Medal of Honor for his part in the rescue of Major Henry Young and for the capture of two Confederate battle flags at Amelia Courthouse in 1865. Campbell remained in the post-Civil War army and served in the Indian campaigns. He died on May 6 1904 and is buried in Section 3 of Arlington National Cemetery. His grave marker lists the award of his medal and identifies him as 'Capt. Co A 2nd NY Cav'.

Born on March 6 1845, Archibald 'Arch' Rowand was from Pittsburgh, Pennsylvania. Looking for action, he joined Company K of the 1st West Virginia Cavalry on July 17 1862. Rowand served under General Milroy who from the assumption of his command found himself dealing with a mountaineer enemy that fought Indian-style from ambush. Fighting bushwhackers took up much of Milroy's time and he developed good scouts. Rowand had been a railroad clerk. He was boyish-looking, giving the appearance of someone's kid brother. As wars are primarily fought by boys hurled into manhood, Rowand quickly adapted to his new profession. In the fall of 1862, Rowand and his buddy Ike Harris had volunteered for hazardous duty. Rowand said that when they were issued with Confederate uniforms, 'We wished we had not come.'[19]

Union and Confederate Rangers played a battlefield chess game with each other and checkmate was done with a pistol ball or a rope. Rowand told of a man coming into Union lines at Salem who claimed to be one of General Averell's scouts. He was recognized as a Confederate Ranger and without further conversation, was shot where he stood. The hazards were not only from the enemy. One of the most difficult times for a Ranger is coming back into friendly lines from a mission. In that circumstance, trigger-happy friendly troops have killed a number of men. The difficulty increased in the Civil War when these scouts wore the enemy uniform. Once safely returned, the Rangers lived a good life for a soldier. There was no guard or picket duty, no camp details or routine formations, none of the drudgery or eye-wash aspects of military life. The Rangers lived well and relatively free of military discipline. Each man was allowed four horses, each animal carefully selected for speed and stamina. When they were behind Confederate lines posing as 'our boys in gray', Rowand said the unsuspecting Confederate families 'fed them like wedding guests.'[20] There are indications that Rangers on both sides who wore the uniform of their opponents romanced unsuspecting females in enemy territory when the opportunity arose.

Arch Rowand had many adventures with his friend Ike Harris. Once, when acting as couriers, they were seen by the commander of a Confederate artillery battery. Guessing what duty they were performing and having no other immediate target of priority, this servant of the King of Battles turned his four guns on the two riders and added terror to their mission. Shortly after Sheridan took command and fought the Battle of Winchester, Ike Harris was killed and Rowand became a scout for Custer, then for Averell with whom he went raiding.

A Southern civilian named Creigh had killed a Union soldier with an axe and thrown his body into a well. Creigh was tried by drumhead court martial and sentenced to be hanged. Captain Jack Crawford of Averell's staff was ordered to hang the prisoner, but did not want the duty. Crawford ordered young Rowand to perform the execution. Rowand refused the onerous task, but Crawford made him believe the order came from the general so Rowand hanged the man. It was his first hanging and he did not know that the hangman should tie the hands and feet of the man being executed.[21]

While behind the lines eating dinner in a Confederate household, Rowand and Ranger Townsend were taken into custody by a Confederate patrol headed by a very suspicious captain. The two men had their cover stories well rehearsed, but were throughly questioned. The Confederates separated them for questioning, but made the mistake of not taking them far enough apart. Both Rowand and Townsend could hear the other man's answers. After long and difficult questioning, the 18-year-old Rowand managed to convince the captain that he was a Confederate courier en route to take a message to Confederate General Breckenridge. Once the officer was convinced, he related that he had a letter for the general. With instructions to hurry, the two scouts were sent on their way. Rowand delivered the letter to a general... Union General William Averell.

Rowand gained great experience as a scout under William Averell, but his training had its rough spots. Early on, a report he had delivered to a subordinate of Averell's went astray and a furious Averell sent Rowand back to the 1st West Virginia Cavalry. When he learned the truth of the matter, Averell brought Rowand on his staff and insisted that from that time on the reports of the Rangers would be given directly to him. This technique proved vital for those commanders using Rangers to gather intelligence.

Rowand was in the dismal retreat when Jubal Early marched north and ordered McCausland to burn Chambersburg. Laying in concealment, Rowand watched the flames devour the town. Eternal vigilance is key to survival behind enemy lines. On a reconnaissance with several other Rangers, Rowand saw a snake trying to eat a bull frog and the men stopped to watch the contest. The bull frog was resisting being swallowed so the men began to place bets, giving the money to Ranger Mike Smith to hold. While they avidly watched the struggle, some nearby Confederates came to the conclusion that they were Union Rangers and opened fire. Smith's horse was killed and the Rangers had to ride for their lives with Rowand dragging Smith up on his horse with him. On a peaceful day in the middle of a sun-kissed pasture, Rowand was riding into Confederate lines when he encountered a Confederate Ranger riding into Union lines. Both men recognized each other for what they were and drew their pistols. The quiet was shattered by the roar of gunfire and in this peaceful setting the Southern youth fell dead from his horse.

In the towns that frequently changed hands, there were girls who knew Arch Rowand was a Union soldier but did not know he was a Ranger. When the Confederates had retaken Martinsburg, Rowand was in the town on a mission, dressed in Confederate uniform and walking among Confederate soldiers. Miss Sue Grimm saw him and cried out: 'Why Archie Rowand, what are you doing with----?' 'Shut up your mouth!' screamed the terrified Rowand, who saw suspension from a rope as his immediate future. Sue Grimm was furious at such impolite treatment. Arch Rowand must have had a fondness for Sue Grimm, as over the next three months he tried hard to get back in her good graces.[22]

When General Phil Sheridan came to the valley in 1864, the 19-year-old Rowand was the longest-serving scout in the area. Sheridan had not yet found the officer he wanted to lead his scouts and was recruiting proven enlisted volunteers for the service. Rowand brought Jack Riley, Dominic Fannin, Jim White, Alvin Stearns and John Dunn. James A. Campbell and Harry K. 'Sonny' Chrisman were from New York cavalry regiments,

Campbell from the 2nd and Chrisman from the 8th.[23] These Rangers were soldiers, but Sheridan also hired civilian scouts. One who enlisted while Sheridan was at Winchester was William H. Woodall who was likely a deserter from the Confederate ranks of Harry Gilmor.

Sheridan listened to his scouts and did not lightly dismiss their words. That was not always true of other commanders. In October 1864, when Sheridan was absent in Washington to make a report, General Crook was in command. Crook sent out a reconnaissance patrol that did not go deep enough to reach the Confederate main line. As they did not make contact, the patrol reported that the Confederates were in retreat. Rangers Dominic Fannin and Alvin Stearns had penetrated the Southern lines, learning that they were planning an imminent attack. When the men reported this to Crook they made the suggestion of a confirming reconnaissance and strengthening a part of the line. General Crook became angered at their presumption and asked: 'How long have you been in command of this department?' The two Rangers were dismissed. The next morning, October 19 1864, the Confederates attacked and the Battle of Cedar Creek began. The Union army was routed and a disaster was in the making. Arch Rowand credited the timely return of Sheridan to the battlefield with a Union counter-attack that saved the day.[24] Confederate General Thomas Rosser said of Cedar Creek: 'The sun never rose on a more glorious victory and never set on a more inglorious defeat.'[25]

On the night of January 21 1865, twenty Sheridan scouts captured the Confederate picket reserve at Woodstock, Virginia. As they were returning to Union lines, they were attacked by 200 Confederate cavalry. Fifty Union cavalry were sent in support, but they were new troops who panicked and fled. The Rangers fought a delaying action in the course of which four of them were captured. Ranger Tom Cassidy was taken prisoner while wearing the Confederate uniform. Knowing the Confederates would hang Cassidy, Sheridan sent Major Baird of his staff under a flag of truce to attempt an exchange of prisoners. Dressed in Union blue, Arch Rowand was a part of the Union escort. A major of the 17th Virginia Cavalry informed Baird that Cassidy would be hanged. Baird replied that if so, a Confederate officer would be hanged in retaliation. While the officers argued, civilians gathered. A girl recognized Rowand, identified him as a Ranger and called him a spy. The life of Rowand and the safety of the Union truce party was at risk. Dressed in Union uniform, Rowand had participated in a charge against the major's men at Fisher's Hill when the Confederates were routed and he reminded them of the incident. The Confederate officer angrily closed the interview and the two parties separated. Tom Cassidy could not be rescued and was hanged.[26]

Sergeant George D. Mullihan of Webb City, Missouri was a strong-jawed, rugged individual who had first enlisted at age 13 in the 12th Pennsylvania Cavalry. He fought in five major battles including Antietam before that first enlistment ran out. Mullihan then enlisted in Company D of the 17th Pennsylvania Cavalry and proved his worth as a trusted courier for general officers. With two other volunteers, Mullihan carried a critical message 100 miles in twenty-four hours through guerrilla-infested territory.[27] Mullihan became one of Sheridan's scouts.

In January 1865, Mullihan and fifteen of the Rangers accompanied by forty men of the 5th New York Cavalry made a raid on Woodstock to save a farmer who supported the Union cause. The Confederates had detected the man and were going to hang him, but Mullihan and his party brought him to safety.

Moorefield was a strongly pro-Confederate village some 90 miles south-west of Winchester. It was the headquarters of the Confederate McNeill's Rangers. Henry Young's men were roaming the area in Confederate uniforms. The scouts included the senior NCO Joseph McNabe, James Campbell, Archibald Rowand, George Mullihan and Nick Carlisle. Two of these men learned that Major Harry Gilmor and another Confederate guerrilla, George W. Stump, were in the area and that under General Jubal Early's orders, Gilmor was seeking to consolidate with and control McNeill's Rangers and other Western Virginia guerrilla organizations. The talented Confederate Partisan Ranger Hanse McNeill had been killed; his manner of death caused some to think that one of Sheridan's scouts, George Valentine, had managed to infiltrate the ranks of McNeill's command. Valentine was a Sheridan scout, but it is unknown if he joined the organization before or after the death of Hanse McNeill.

Jesse McNeill and his friends did not want to be under a stranger's leadership, but Gilmor had orders to take command. He planned to rally all the Confederate Rangers in the area under the guise of a camp meeting and to add to his force a party of recruits from his home state of Maryland. When he had the Confederate Rangers organized the way he wanted them, the B&O Railroad would be Gilmor's objective.

Major Young's Rangers learned that Gilmor was in the area of Moorefield. Sheridan sent Sergeant Joseph E. McCabe and Arch Rowand on a three-day scout to gather information. The two men learned that Gilmor and key subordinates were staying at two spacious and comfortable houses belonging to the Williams and Randolph families. The houses were outside of town on the South Fork River road some 2 miles from Moorefield. These houses could be approached with a good chance of success.

Major Young reported this information to General Sheridan. With the death of Hanse McNeill, Harry Gilmor was becoming more of a problem in West Virginia. Sheridan wanted Gilmor dead or in captivity. He described the Confederate Ranger as 'Harry Gilmor, who appeared to be the last link between Maryland and the Confederacy, and whose person I desired in order that this link might be severed.'[28]

Sheridan issued orders to Young to conduct the operation. The plan would include a back-up force of 300 men of the 3rd Cavalry Division under Lieutenant Colonel Edward W. Whitaker of the 1st Connecticut Cavalry. Strict secrecy was maintained. No one in the cavalry knew the mission except Colonel Whitaker.

It was 58 miles to Moorefield. The command would leave on Saturday morning, travel through Saturday night and make the raid early on Sunday morning. Fifteen Rangers dressed in Confederate uniforms would lead the way. They would pass themselves off as Maryland volunteers for Gilmor, saying they were being pursued by Union cavalry. When accepted as Confederates, the Rangers would make the captures. The cavalry would come on fast at the sound of firing, overpower any resistance, then protect the withdrawal. Rowand wrote that on arrival, he and his men were ordered by Young to secure the Williams house. They did, and captured one of Confederate General Tom Rosser's men. Meanwhile, Young and a small group of Rangers were heading for the Randolph house.

Ranger Mullihan's account of the operation against Harry Gilmor was told in the history of the 17th Pennsylvania Cavalry. According to Mullihan, the movement cross-country went well. Major Young and his men passed easily through the Confederate lines and were welcomed as volunteers to the Confederate cause. The Rangers timed their entrance into Moorefield just prior to sunrise. Mullihan was one of five scouts detailed to follow Major Young to the house where Gilmor was staying. While the others stood guard, Young and Mullihan went into the bedroom. The famed guerrilla was sharing a bed with his cousin (Hoffman Gilmor). Both were sound asleep, but Gilmor had his pistols laying close to hand on a chair beside the bed.

Rudely shaken from their sleep, the two Confederates were captured and Mullihan ran to the stables to saddle the captives' horses. Gunfire had broken out between the Rangers and Gilmor's guard and Whitaker's cavalry came in at a gallop. Mullihan was concerned when he saw the splendid horse owned by Gilmor. It was a sturdy black charger that Gilmor had taken on the Chambersburg, Pennsylvania raid. Mullihan suggested to Young that the Confederate be required to ride a nag. Young was busy with Gilmor's guards and ignored him. Gilmor mounted and promptly tried to escape, but Mullihan seized his bridle. The Confederate Ranger was then put aboard a nag that could not outrun pursuit.

After-action reports of participants usually give differing versions of events. Lieutenant Colonel Whitaker stated he had under his command detachments from the 2nd Ohio, 8th New York, 1st New Hampshire, 22nd New York and 1st Connecticut Cavalry regiments. Whitaker found it necessary to pause briefly on the march to organize this task force. En route, two men of Southern birth deserted from the column of the 8th New Yorkers, but these men did not know the mission. Whitaker felt that Young's men did not know the house that Gilmor was in and that it was the large number of horses in the stable at Randolph's that caused Major Young to have sternly enquired of a colored woman 'what soldiers were in the house'. The woman replied: 'Major Gilmor is upstairs.' The capture was made by Young. In his writings, Harry Gilmor said that when he was first mounted on his horse, his men fired on the Union column and he shouted words of encouragement. Whitaker confirmed that occurred. After an operation that Whitaker described as riding nearly 140 miles in a little over forty-eight hours through mountains and ice-filled streams in enemy territory, they came back to Winchester, mission accomplished without losing a man.

Whitaker complimented Young while reserving his senior rank. He wrote: 'I cannot commend too highly the zeal and hearty co-operation evinced by Major Young commanding General Sheridan's scouts, who accompanied me. To his personal gallantry is due the successful "bearding of the lion in his den".' Whitaker signed his report as 'Lieutenant Colonel First Connecticut Cavalry, Comdg [Commanding] Expedition.'[29]

Harry Gilmor's account of his capture is that he was in bed with his cousin when the door suddenly opened and five men entered with drawn pistols; Gilmor could not get to his weapons which were on a chair under his uniform. A man said 'Are you Colonel Gilmor?' When there was no reply Gilmor felt the muzzle of the pistol against his skull and the man repeated the question. 'Yes,' said Gilmor, 'and who in the devil's name are you?' 'Major Young, of General Sheridan's staff,' was the response. 'All right. I suppose you want me to go with you,' said Gilmor. Young's answer probably came with a tight smile: 'I shall be happy to have your company to Winchester, as General Sheridan wishes to consult you about some important military affairs.'[30]

Gilmor wrote that he did shout to his men and as a result had a pistol shoved in his face, accompanied by the words: 'Hush up, or I'll blow your brains out.' Young took away his fast horse and mounted him on a slow runner. Gilmor was under constant guard by four Rangers with drawn and cocked pistols. The cavalry were moving too slowly to suit Major Young. When they got to the Big Capon River, Young wanted to take Gilmor and his scouts and ride hard for Winchester. Whitaker was senior officer and refused to let Young have the captive. Greatly angered, Young took his Rangers and rode off. Whitaker sent to his column for some guards and dismounted. Gilmor now saw an opportunity to escape. Whitaker was a well-built and intelligent man, but while they were dismounted he had carelessly allowed Gilmor to get behind him. Gilmor took cautious steps forward and was immediately behind the unsuspecting officer when suddenly Arch Rowand and three other Rangers came up. The sound of their horses had been muffled by the snow. Major Young's anger had cooled and with it came recognition that Gilmor might get away. His returning of the Ranger guards came just in time to prevent Gilmor from attempting to break free. One of Harry Gilmor's guards was a deserter from his command. Gilmor wrote: 'He was a consummate scoundrel, and told me that he was anxious for a chance to shoot me.'[31] That scout was likely William Woodall.

Sheridan was delighted with the success. In his memoirs he would write about the effectiveness of Henry Young and his men in working against Confederate Rangers:

> Harry Gilmor of Maryland was the most noted of these since the death of McNeill, and as the scouts had reported him in Harrisonburg the latter part of January, I directed two of the most trustworthy to be sent to watch his movements and ascertain his purposes. In a few days these spies returned with the intelligence that Gilmor was on his way to Moorefield, the center of a very disloyal section in West Virginia, about ninety miles south-west of Winchester, where under the guise of a camp-meeting a gathering was to take place, at which he expected to enlist a number of men, be joined by a party of recruits coming from Maryland, and then begin depredations along the Baltimore and Ohio railroad. Believing that Gilmor might be captured, I directed Young to undertake the task...

I directed Young to take twenty of his best men and leave that night for Moorefield, dressed in Confederate uniforms, telling him that I would have about three hundred cavalry follow in his wake when he got about 15 miles start, and instructing him to pass his party off as a body of recruits for Gilmor coming from Maryland and pursued by Yankee Cavalry... Young met with a hearty welcome wherever he halted along the way, and as he passed through the town of Moorefield learned with satisfaction that Gilmor still made his headquarters at the house where the report of the two scouts had located him a few days before. Reaching the designated place about 12 o'clock on the night of the 5th of February, Young under the representation that he had come directly from Maryland and was being pursued by Union Cavalry, gained immediate access to Gilmor's room. He found the bold guerrilla snugly tucked in bed with two pistols lying on a chair nearby. He was sleeping so soundly that to arouse him Young had to give him a violent shake. As he awoke and asked who was disturbing his slumbers, Young, pointing at him a cocked six-shooter, ordered him to dress without delay and in answer to his inquiry informed him that he was a prisoner to one of Sheridan's staff.[32]

Harry Gilmor had a considerable following in Maryland. His removal had both military and political implications. Gilmor was brought to Winchester, then sent on to prison at Fort Warren in Boston Harbor with Henry Young guarding him all the way.[33] Sheridan would take no chances with Harry Gilmor. The general wrote: 'He is an energetic, shrewd, and unscrupulous scoundrel and a dangerous man. He must be closely watched or he will escape.'[34]

The raid to capture Harry Gilmor had yielded other prisoners. One was John Casler who was from Dayton, Virginia and a long-time member of the Stonewall Brigade. Casler had spent the night with Confederate Captain George W. Stump at Stump's sister's place. There the two men planned to meet a third Confederate named Lovett and ride to the home of Stump's father near Romney. The next morning their horses were saddled and ready to ride, but Lovett had not yet arrived. Casler went on ahead, soon reaching a place where the road forked with one road leading to Moorefield and the other going to Lost River, the direction of Casler's travel. Near the forks, Casler saw some horsemen in the woods. He decided to take no chances and tried to gallop away. In the escape process, he rode into a group of men dressed in Confederate uniform who seized the bridle of his horse and held their pistols on him. The men told him they were Confederates. Casler said he was also, but the men accused him of being a dammed Yankee spy. They wanted to know what other Confederates were around and then performed the usual process of 'going through' a prisoner. Almost everything he owned was taken, from his hat being snatched from his head to throwing him on the ground and stripping off his good boots. Rags of clothing and boots too small were given in exchange. Most of these men rode on, but one guard stayed with him; this guard continued to say that he was a Confederate. After a time, Casler saw blue-coated cavalry coming through the trees and knew he was not with a fellow Southerner. Lacking knowledge of order of battle, Casler believed the men to be what he called 'Jessie Scouts', part of Captain Blazer's band. The cavalry came up and Casler saw Harry Gilmor and his cousin, thirteen prisoners in all. The captured rode in single file with two guards to each side of a man. Lovett was soon brought in as a prisoner and accused Casler of causing his captivity. Casler was wondering what happened to Captain Stump.[35]

George W. Stump had been one of Imboden's Partisan Rangers and became company commander of Company B, 18th Virginia Cavalry. Stump went about with a carbine and three or more pistols; he was so heavily armed that his troops referred to him as 'Stump's Battery'.[36] He was hated by Union soldiers. Working with McNeill on raids on Union pickets posts, George Stump had gained a reputation for leaving the occupants dead with throats cut or hung. As a result he was wanted dead or alive, preferably dead. There are a variety of stories about the encounter with George Stump. Many of the accounts have the action taking place on the way to seize Gilmor, but this seems unlikely. The mission from Sheridan was to get Gilmor and it is unlikely that mission would be put at risk. It is probable that Stump was a bonus objective or a target of opportunity. Casler's writings are that what happened with Stump was part of the return trip.

Ranger Mullihan's account of the encounter with Stump is that he guarded Gilmor till about 30 miles from Winchester when he was relieved. As a scout, Mullihan was dressed in Confederate uniform and rode to a house nearby to get some breakfast and information. A female slave told him the house belonged to Captain Stump. At the time the Union Rangers came up with him, Stump had been wounded and was recovering. Still pretending to be a Confederate, Mullihan told the slave that he had important dispatches for Stump. He was then informed that Stump had gone to church about half a mile down the road. Rounding up several of his comrades, Mullihan rode for the church where he said he had dispatches for Stump and was told that the officer had left for the house of his brother. Leaving two men to guard those at the church, Mullihan took two others and rode to the brother's house nearby. Stump suspected he was being sought and was in the act of mounting his horse when the Union Rangers rode in. Gunfire was exchanged. Stump called out that he was wounded in the thigh and would surrender. He did not admit to being George Stump, claiming he was a brother of the guerrilla. On the way back to rejoin Young, Stump tried to escape, but the Union Rangers had him under their pistols and foiled the attempt. When brought before Major Young, he admitted his identity. Young informed Stump that they intended to kill him, but would give his horse a ten-rod start. On Young's command Captain Stump spurred his horse, but the Rangers were all marksmen and they quickly killed him.[37]

According to Arch Rowand, Stump was taken prisoner from a house while Young and his men were on a routine patrol. The day was bitter cold and the roads slippery with snow. The Rangers were tired after a hard ride and had Stump riding in the middle of their group to prevent him trying to escape. Suddenly one of the men yelled that Stump had tried to take his pistol. Major Young warned Stump that if he tried it again, he would be killed. Some time later, Rowand saw Stump trying to get at Major Young's pistol. 'He's trying to get *your* gun,' yelled Rowand. Young pulled his horse aside and said: 'I told you! Ride aside, boys – plug him Rowand!' At least six Rangers fired and Stump fell from the horse. They left his body lying in the snow.[38] Another version of what transpired is that when Stump said he was sick, Major Young replied: 'Make him sicker.' Casler wrote that Young's men gave him differing versions of what happened.[39] All accounts end with the termination of George B. Stump.

Those losing ask that war be civilized and seek scapegoats. When Sherman cut a 50-mile-wide path of destruction through Georgia, people along the way asked: 'Why don't you go to South Carolina and do this to them; they started this war.' Sherman and his 60,000 men did move north. If Georgia 'howled', South Carolina screamed as Sherman went through its plantations, towns and cities. Kilpatrick's cavalry and foraging bummers were free with the torch and the town of Barnwell was renamed Burnwell. It would not be long before Sherman could strike Lee from the South, but Grant was wary. There was the chance that the wily Lee would slip away and join forces with Joe Johnston's army or prolong the war by drawing Grant's army from its base of supply.[40]

HENRY HARRISON YOUNG AND SHERIDAN'S SCOUTS

With Early routed from the Shenandoah Valley, Grant wanted Sheridan to move his army south-east and join Sherman, en route ripping through Lee's rapidly shrinking lines of supply. The combined forces of Sherman and Lee would then come north. Lee would be caught between a gigantic Union hammer and anvil. Sheridan argued against being required to join Sherman. His motives were likely a mix of tactical imperative and personal desire. Sheridan believed that going south-east to join Sherman only to march north again would not end the war as quickly as using his 10,000 horsemen to come east and slash into Lee's flank. It was also obvious that if he joined Sherman he might well be a subordinate to Grant's subordinate and lose the independence he had enjoyed in the valley. Commanders like freedom of action to take advantage of opportunity as they see it. If that means more fame for those who are successful, it's earned. Grant gave Sheridan the opportunity to use his own discretion.

With Early no longer a threat in the valley, Sheridan decided to take his three cavalry divisions commanded by Custer, Devin and Crook to join Grant's army. The mountains were covered with fast-melting snow and heavy spring rains turned the roads to mire as Sheridan began his march from Winchester in the Shenandoah Valley to join Grant's army in front of Petersburg. Starting on the morning of February 27 1865, the blue-coated troops crossed Cedar Creek and marched the 30 miles to Woodstock on the first day. The second day took them near Staunton which they entered the following morning, moving through driving rain. Sheridan was intent on destroying Early's army. At Waynesborough, George Armstrong Custer found the entrenched enemy and routed them. Custer flanked the beaten Confederates and the fight was soon over, with the South losing 1,600 officers and men, 11 guns and 17 battle flags. Sheridan then moved to Charlottesville where the rain caused a delay of two days while the teamsters tried to bring their wagons of supplies through the mire. At that point Sheridan had not yet made up his mind about going to Lynchburg. The rain and the scouts assisted him in the decision to come east. Sheridan wrote: 'This necessary delay [trains delayed by rain] forced me to abandon the idea of capturing Lynchburg, but trusty scouts had been sent there to find out the state of affairs in the vicinity.'[41]

Sheridan had control of the area north of the James River. Based on the reports of his Rangers that the Confederates were mustering at Lynchburg, he decided to let them wither on a military vine as he set about destroying the Virginia Central and Fredericksburg Railroads and James River Canal. By destroying these transportation systems he was cutting a critical supply line of Richmond. He now made the final decision to bring his army east to

315

join Grant. Rangers Arch Rowand and James Campbell were sent through Confederate lines to deliver the message of Sheridan's intent to Grant.

The story of their adventure was written in a letter from Arch Rowand to his mother. The letter was sent from City Point, Virginia and dated March 13 1865:

> MY DEAR MOTHER – I suppose you will be surprised to receive a letter from me from this place. I arrived here yesterday afternoon from Gen. Sheridan's raiding forces with dispatches for Gen. Grant. There were two of us. We left Gen. Sheridan at Columbia on the James River Canal, one hundred miles West of Richmond. At the time we left he had destroyed the Virginia Central Railroad between Charlottesville and Staunton; blew up both bridges of the Rivanna River near Charlottesville. It will be impossible for the rebels to rebuild their bridges during the war. We were forced to stay in Charlottesville two days on account of the heavy rain. Leaving there, we struck out for Lynchburg, destroying the Railroad as we went, burned the large bridge over the Tye River, eighteen miles from Lynchburg. By this time the Rebels had collected a large force of Infantry and Cavalry at Lynchburg. When Gen. Sheridan got all of the Rebels at Lynchburg, he turned around and came north, destroying the Canal beyond repair during the war. He burned and blew up every lock, culvert, and aqueduct to Columbia – a distance of forty miles.
>
> We left at one o'clock Saturday morning and came into our pickets near Harrison's Landing on Sunday morning at eleven o'clock. Came from there here in a special boat under charge of Gen. Sharp of Gen. Grant's staff. On arrival at headquarters after delivering our dispatches, the Acting Adjutant-General took us around and introduced us to Mrs. Gen. Grant and several other ladies whose names I have forgotten. They had expressed a wish to see the two men who came through the Rebel lines in open day. Gen. Grant was well pleased with our success in getting through. The staff was surprised at our getting through at all. They quite lionized us last night. Several of them invited us to drink with them. Then the Sanitary Commission took charge of us. We had a nice bath, good underclothes given us, and a bed that felt better than all, considering we had no

sleep for forty-eight hours. We rode one hundred and forty-five miles in thirty-six hours, and walked ten miles and came north of Richmond. Of course we came a roundabout way or rather a zigzag way. Several times we were within ten miles of Richmond and talked to some fifty Rebels; gained valuable information. We had quite a confab with four of Gen. Lee's scouts; passed ourselves off for Gen. Rosser's scouts. Being dressed in Gray, they never suspected us. They, in fact, never expected to see two Yankees right in the midst of their lines in broad daylight. We were never suspected until we were within two miles of the Long Bridges, where suspicion was raised and we were forced to leave our horses at the Bridges and paddle across in a small boat to the south side. When we came to the river there was a small boat floating down the river. I swam with my horse to the boat, got off my horse into the boat and went back for my partner. We left our horses and made quick time across the swamps. We got into the woods before the Rebels got to the river, they, of course, got our horses – the two best in the Sixth Cavalry. The fleetness of our horses alone saved us, as we had time to get across the river before the Rebels got to the bank. Although we could see them coming down the road, they did not follow us any further than the bank of the river, as there is no boat, and they could not swim their horses across. Then we got from there to our picket, most of the time being in the woods; the compass father gave me has done me great service as I have a military map of Virginia. With both, it is not difficult to get to the nearest way to any point. When I swam my horse I got my clothes wet and boots full of water. When I got to our pickets I was perfectly dry, but was so crippled in my feet I could scarcely walk. I am all right to-day.

We are today quartered with Gen. Grant's scouts. They think it is the biggest and boldest scout trip of the war.

We will start back in a couple of days. We are to be sent to the White House (landing) on the York River Gunboat, and with good fast horses start for our command again.

Love to all. Hoping these few lines will find you in good health, I remain,

Your Affectionate Son
Archie H. Rowand[42]

Sheridan moved on, reaching Frederick's Hall. He was uncertain of the situation ahead of him, but his questions were soon answered. He wrote:

> Major Young's scouts from Richmond notified me of preparations being made there to prevent me from getting to the James River, and that Pickett's division of Infantry was coming back from Lynchburg, via the South Side Railroad, as was also the cavalry, but that no advance from Richmond had yet taken place.[43]

This was the critical information that Sheridan needed. He now saw a clear road to join Grant. He crossed the James River on Sunday, March 26 1865. Writing of this epic march (27 February–26 March), Sheridan penned: 'There perhaps never was a march where nature offered such impediments and shrouded herself in gloom such as this; incessant raid, deep and almost impassable streams, swamps and mud were overcome with a constant cheerfulness on the part of the troops that was truly admirable.'[44]

Sheridan recognized the value of the reconnaissance work done by his Rangers. He wrote: 'To Maj. H.H. Young, of my staff, chief of scouts, and the thirty or forty men of his command, who took their lives in their hands, cheerfully going wherever ordered, to obtain that great essential of success, information, I tender my gratitude. Ten of these men were lost.'[45]

The endless rain did not deter Sheridan, who was eager to attack. He told Grant's staff that if he had an infantry corps added to his command he would drive in Lee's flank. 'I tell you I'm ready to strike tomorrow and go to smashing things,' he told Grant's delighted staff. The officers thought Sheridan 'chafed like a hound on a leash'.[46] Grant believed Sheridan could handle the rain and the enemy and had Warren's Fifth Corps added to his command.[47]

Sheridan now controlled a wing of the army of the Potomac as on Wednesday, March 29 1865, Grant began the final campaign. General Porter wrote it was raining so hard that 'it looked like the saving of that army would require the services not of a Grant, but of a Noah' and that soldiers were shouting to their officers, 'I say, when are the gun-boats coming up?'[48] Sheridan had his scouts operating around the clock constantly probing Confederate lines. The hard-charging Phil Sheridan was beginning his attack at Five Forks and was riding his famed black charger. The horse had once been named 'Rienzi' but was now called 'Winchester' after Sheridan's famous ride to battle from there. There was a popular poem about that battle,

Sheridan and his horse, and the horse seemed to get most of the credit, the horse saying to Sheridan:

> I have brought you Sheridan all the way
> from Winchester, down to save the day.

Sheridan said he thought that the poem was popular because of the horse.

Now Little Phil and his charger were back in action. Sheridan was like a berserker, seizing his battle flag and waving it as he led from the front. A soldier was shot through the throat, cried 'I'm killed' and dropped to the ground. Sheridan yelled: 'You're not hurt a bit, pick up your gun man and move right on to the front.' The man staggered to his feet, took his weapon and moved forward a dozen more paces before he fell dead.[49]

When Grant heard the news of Sheridan's advance he ordered an attack all across the front. The next day, April 2 1865, at 4.15 am, the crash of hundreds of guns rolled like thunder across the land. The infantry went in and all across the front what was left of Lee's army was disintegrating. His trenches would no longer serve and he must come out of them and seek to preserve what was left. At Sailor's Creek, Sheridan's cavalry rode over what was left of Ewell's corps, capturing the Confederate general and his staff.

On April 3 1865, the Ranger scouts were operating within Confederate lines checking movement on each of the roads. Around noon, Henry Young, Joseph McCabe and some fifteen of the scouts dressed in gray uniforms were riding as part of one of Lee's columns. As they rode among a Confederate cavalry brigade, they came alongside the commanding general, two of his staff officers and two orderlies and began casual conversations. Young said: 'Good afternoon General.' Not knowing the officer who addressed him, Brigadier General Rufus Barringer responded: 'You have the advantage of me, Sir!' Young laughed and replied: 'You're right, I have, General!' Young and his Rangers then drew their revolvers and took the Confederates prisoner, easing them out of the column as though the general were making a wayside stop to review his troops. North Carolina Brigadier General Rufus Barringer of Fitzhugh Lee's Cavalry Corps was Stonewall Jackson's brother-in law and commanded the 1st, 2nd, 3rd and 5th North Carolina Cavalry regiments. In the Civil War the capture of an enemy flag was sufficient in most cases for the Medal of Honor to be awarded. The chief of the civilian scouts William Woodall captured the flag of Barringer's brigade and was awarded the Medal of Honor on April 25 1865.[50]

In these last days of the war, the static lines of the siege of Petersburg were broken and the action was fluid with men and units scattered about. This was an ideal situation for Young and his men. On the day following the capture of Barringer, Young, dressed as a Confederate colonel, was back tracing the movement of Barringer's former brigade. Young had the good fortune to meet the Confederate colonel who, accompanied by an orderly, was en route to take Barringer's place. When the officer said of Barringer 'I am to command; I take his place', Young responded: 'You do not take his place; you go to the place where he is!' Young then drew his pistol, capturing the unsuspecting officer.[51]

Sheridan was bowling over Confederate defenses and sent Ranger James A. Campbell to carry a report to Grant. The lieutenant general commanding was riding his black pony 'Jeff Davis' with his headquarters staff about midway between Burkeville and Nottoway. The light was fading and on the north side of the road where the Confederates were, dense woods blocked observation. Suddenly a rider in full Confederate uniform trotted out in the road in front of them. Grant's escort and staff went berserk trying to protect their general. Some of the escort charged the rider. Brigadier General Porter recognized that it was Campbell as he had previously brought messages to Grant. Porter freed the man and Grant, who knew Campbell, came up. The Ranger took a wad of tobacco from his mouth, broke it open and pulled out a ball of tin foil. Wrapped in the foil was a message in which Sheridan described the situation at Jetersville and told Grant: 'I wish you were here yourself.'[52]

Lee's demoralized remnants were making their way across country as best they could, often traveling in small groups. Young sent his disguised men among them to act as guides. The weary Confederates found themselves guided to an improvised prison camp in the woods where they were disarmed and their war ended for them.[53]

General Gordon wrote that at Petersburg, when the Southern army was being broken into fragments, a young Southern soldier was running for his life and when asked why by his commander, he responded: 'Golly Captain, I'm running 'cause I can't fly!'[54]

These were desperate hours for the Confederates. When they could, the men held impromptu prayer gatherings. At one being held in a log cabin, General Heth stepped to the door and asked another general who was riding by to join him in prayer. The other officer did not properly hear the last word of the request and replied: 'No, thank you, General; no more at present, I've just had some.'[55]

General Gordon was riding about his lines on the night of April 6 1865 when he was approached by a Confederate scout named George and some guards who had two men in Confederate uniform as prisoners. The men claimed they were from Fitzhugh Lee's cavalry, but the Southern scout believed they were Union soldiers. Gordon wrote of the incident in his memoirs:

I questioned the men closely and could find no sufficient ground for George's suspicions. They seemed entirely self-possessed and at ease under my rigid examination. They gave me the names of Fitzhugh Lee's regimental and company commanders, said they belonged to a certain mess, and gave the names of the members, and without a moment's hesitation gave prompt answers to every question I asked. I said to George that they seemed to me all right, but he protested, saying: 'No, general, they are not all right. I saw them by starlight counting your files.' One of them at once said: 'Yes, we were trying to get some idea of your force. We have been at home on sick leave for a long time, and wanted to know if we had any army left.' This struck me as a little suspicious and I pounded them again with questions:

'You say that you have been home on sick leave?'

'Yes, sir; we have been at home several weeks, and fell in with your command to-night, hoping that you could tell us how to get to General Fitzhugh Lee's cavalry.'

'If you have been at home sick, you ought to have your furloughs with you.'

'We have, sir. We have our furlough papers here in our pockets, signed by our own officers, and approved by General R.E. Lee. If we had a light you could examine them and see that they are all right.'

George, who was listening to this conversation which occurred while we were riding, again insisted that it did not matter what these men said or what they had; they were Yankees. I directed that they be brought under guard until I could examine their papers.

We soon came to a burning log heap on the roadside, which had been kindled by some of the troops who had passed at an earlier hour of the night. The moment the full light fell upon their faces, George exclaimed: 'General, these are the two men who captured me nearly two months ago behind General Grant's headquarters.'

They ridiculed the suggestion and at once drew from their pockets the furloughs. These papers seemed to be correct, and the signatures of the officers, including that of General Lee, seemed to be genuine. This evidence did not satisfy George nor shake his convictions.

The Southern scout asked permission to search the two men and went through every article of clothing seam by seam. Under the lining of a boot he found a message from General Grant to General Ord ordering him to make certain moves to cut off Lee's retreat. With the evidence in hand, Gordon told the scouts that he would have them shot in the morning. The older of the two could not have been more than 19 or 20, but they gave no sign of nervousness. One of them pointed out that the war was in its final days and it would not help matters to shoot them. Gordon had already considered that and decided not to shoot the Union Rangers, but he let them sweat. He sent them to General Sheridan on the morning of Lee's surrender.[56] Like John Casler and many Confederates, General Gordon erroneously thought of the captured men as 'Jessie Scouts'.

The 1st US Cavalry Regiment captured a Confederate Ranger carrying telegrams in his boot from the commissary general of Lee's army. One message was 'The army is at Amelia Court House, short of provisions; send three hundred thousand rations quickly to Burkesville Junction.'

Sheridan was moving fast, as he would later recall:

> My command was pinched for provisions, and these dispatches indicated an opportunity to obtain a supply; so calling for Lieutenant-Colonel Young, commanding my scouts, four men in the most approved gray, were selected – good, brave, smart fellows, knowing every regiment in the Confederate Army, so far as bearing and language were concerned. They were directed to go to Burkesville Junction and there separate.'[57]

On April 8 1865, Sergeant Joseph McCabe led out his three companions to track the trains that would bring the supplies. At Burkesville Station they separated into two-man teams with McCabe and Ranger Jim White going along the Lynchburg branch of the railroad. As they rode, McCabe held conversations with groups of Confederates and learned that four trains of rations and supplies for Lee had arrived at Appomattox Station. Locating the trains, the two Rangers returned to find Sheridan's command on the move with Custer's division in front followed by Devin's and Crook's. McCabe stayed with the cavalry to guide them and dispatched Ranger Jim White to Sheridan with the information. Sheridan immediately ordered his divisions to move with speed. Guided by Ranger McCabe, Custer and Devin captured the trains before Lee could move them.

At Appomattox when General Lee met General Grant to surrender, the subject of rations and food was discussed. Lee said to Grant:

> I have, indeed, nothing for my own men. They have been living for the last few days principally upon parched corn, and we are badly in need of both rations and forage. I telegraphed to Lynchburg, directing several train-loads of rations to be sent on by rail from there, and when they arrive I should be glad to have the present wants of my men supplied from them.

General Horace Porter was present when General Lee spoke the foregoing words. Porter wrote: 'At this remark all eyes turned to Sheridan, for he had captured these trains with his cavalry the night before, near Appomattox Station.'[58] Sheridan's cavalry had captured the trains and Sheridan, Custer's cavalry and Jim White who was the messenger got the credit. Sergeant Joe McCabe who had located the trains was forgotten. Good soldier that he was, McCabe had finished off his adventure by capturing a lieutenant and ten pickets for questioning by Sheridan's staff.

The capture of the supply trains deprived the Confederate army of Northern Virginia of their food and put an end to any hope of continuing the fight. Sheridan wrote that he met Confederate General Cadmus M. Wilcox who he had known at West Point. Wilcox gave Sheridan his saddlebags and said: 'Here, Sheridan, take these saddlebags; they have one soiled shirt and a pair of drawers. You have burned everything else I had in the world, and I think you are entitled to these also.'[59]

Sheridan expected that Jefferson Davis and his officials would attempt to escape south on the Danville Railroad. With the help of a black guide, Young's men reached a critical trestle where they could stop the train. They were cutting the telegraph line to isolate communications when Davis's train and the Confederate Treasury roared by. General Lee surrendered on April 9 1865.

On April 19, at Petersburg, Sheridan wrote:

> I desire to make special mention of the valuable services of
> Maj. H.H. Young, Second Rhode Island Infantry, chief of my
> scouts, during the cavalry expedition from Winchester, Va., to
> the James River. His personal gallantry and numerous conflicts
> with the enemy won the admiration of the whole command.
> In the late campaign from Petersburg to Appomattox Court
> House he kept me constantly informed of the movements of
> the enemy and brought in prisoners, from brigadier-generals
> down. The information obtained through him was invaluable.
> I earnestly request that he be made lieutenant-colonel by
> brevet.[60]

To his regret, Sheridan did not march at the head of his troops in the final
grand review of the army at Washington. Sheridan was GTT (Gone to
Texas). While his surface mission was to track down Kirby Smith, Jubal
Early and other Confederates who had not surrendered, it was understood in
both America and in Europe that his arrival would be a 'hands off Mexico'
message to the French and the Austrians. Sheridan took Wesley Merritt and
George Custer and started two columns of cavalry going from Shreveport
and Alexandria heading for San Antonio and Houston.

The rapidly-shrinking US army had no place for a citizen soldier. Brevet
Lieutenant Colonel Young was mustered out of service on August 1 1865.
He was free to go home to Rhode Island, his mother and younger sister.
However, Young had nothing else to go home to. He had learned to live and
love a life of danger. It was impossible for him to return to being a cashier
and bookkeeper. Sheridan asked Young to go with him to the west. With four
men who had served with him as Rangers, Rowand and White included,
Henry Young accompanied Sheridan. On July 17 1865, an individual who
signed his name L. Barry sent a letter to Henry Young's mother. The letter
began 'Mrs. Young, your son has gone to Texas...'[61]

While they did not directly intervene in the American Civil War, it
was in the long-term interest of European powers that the United States
dissolve. As a result, covert support had been given to the Confederacy.
Western lands in present-day Canada and some of the American west were
not developed and offered possible opportunities for England. The French
ruler Napoleon III had fostered the installation of his puppet Hapsburg
Archduke Maximilian to the crown of Mexico. Desperately seeking help

from Europe, the Confederacy had not opposed this territorial grab. Now that the Civil War was ended, the United States could turn its attention to keeping the ambitions of the Europeans in check.

Sheridan established his headquarters at Brownsville at the mouth of the Rio Grande. He had immediate use for the Rangers. He wrote of Young and the scouts: 'From Brownsville I dispatched all these men to important points in northern Mexico, to glean information regarding the movements of Imperial forces, and also to gather intelligence about the ex-Confederates who had crossed the Rio Grande.'[62]

Seward, the United States Secretary of State, was seeking to get the Europeans out of Mexico by negotiation; the army was on the scene and sought more direct methods. Sheridan reviewed troops as though readying them for a campaign and visibly opened communication with the Mexican nationalist leader President Benito Juarez. Every indication was given to the Emperor Maximilian that the United States was preparing to march against him. Sheridan provided funds, guns and supplies to Benito Juarez and other liberal leaders. US troops were given free rein. The United States had developed a hard-bitten, combat-proven army. Maximilian's officers were insulted and some of his troops were shot down by Americans.[63] As a result, the French and Austrian soldiers withdrew from most of Northern Mexico and it became a safe haven for the Mexican nationalists. Sheridan's actions did not go unnoticed in the State Department and he was ordered to remain neutral. Maximilian was seeking the aid of former Confederates, even to the point of establishing land grant communities that would be headed by former Confederate Generals Price, Magruder and Maury. Henry Young and his men kept Sheridan informed of these plans. As a result, no one could sail from southern ports to Mexico without a pass from Sheridan. This frustrated the plans of the ex-Confederates.

Jealousy and bickering erupted between Mexican leaders Cortinas, Canales and the US-backed Carvajal. Sheridan used Young as a go-between with Carvajal, but while Sheridan was on a trip to New Orleans, Carvajal paid Young $7,000 to raise and equip a bodyguard and told Young the idea had Sheridan's concurrence. When Sheridan returned from his trip he learned of the plan. Sheridan wrote in his memoirs: 'I at once condemned the whole business.... He told me he had entered upon the adventure in the firm belief that I would countenance it; that the men and their equipment were on his hands; that he must make good his word at all hazards.' Sheridan felt he could not refuse the man who had served him so well and agreed to let Young proceed. He wrote: 'I have never ceased to regret my consent, for misfortune fell upon the enterprise almost from its inception.'[64]

After spending the money to raise and equip fifty volunteers, Young found that in the hot mix of Mexican politics, Carvajal was no longer a leader. He had been deposed by Canales who was not interested in Young and his men as bodyguards. Now without funds and the leader of fifty mercenaries, Young attempted to cross the Rio Grande to reach the camp of Mexican General Escobedo to seek employment. Mexico was in turmoil with Maximilian's troops, revolutionaries, former Confederate soldiers turned renegade and Mexican bandits all seeking opportunities to kill for money. It is possible that rumors spread that Young and his men were escorting a quantity of gold.

In the winter of 1866/67 Young and his men were attacked while crossing the Rio Grande. From that point on Henry Young was never heard from again. Sheridan could not believe that a man who had survived so much could have perished. He clung to the hope that Young was alive and sought to give that comfort to Young's mother and sister. For years, Henry Young's mother and sister prayed for his return. His sister Eleanor wrote:

> It was a sad time indeed when the letters ceased coming, and when all efforts to find him proved unavailing.... Although I know that no tidings of him have cheered us in thirteen years, still I cannot conscientiously say that I believe him dead. I have no foundation on which to build hope, indeed, unless it be the private conviction of General Sheridan.[65]

In his memoirs Sheridan sought to penetrate the fog of Young's disappearance and, putting together rumor, came to the conclusion that Young and his men were attacked by ex-Confederates and Mexican bandits while crossing on the American side of the river:

> Being on American soil, Young forbade his men to return the fire and bent all his efforts to getting them over the river; but in this attempt they were broken up and became completely demoralized. A number of the men were drowned while swimming the river. Young himself was shot and killed, a few were captured and those who escaped – about twenty in all – finally joined Escobedo.[66]

Not returning fire does not sound like Henry Young. He may have been killed in the battle or wounded and taken prisoner and died in a Mexican jail. All that is certain is that he disappeared. For the rest of her life his mother mourned him, while hoping in vain for his return.[67] On July 12 1911, the state of Rhode Island erected a monument to the memory of Lieutenant Colonel Henry Harrison Young at the capitol city of Providence. Ranger Sergeant Joseph McCabe was among those in attendance at the dedication.

Deserted by the French and Austrians, the Emperor Maximilian fell from power. He was taken prisoner and scheduled to be executed by the Mexican revolutionaries. Secretary Seward sent a plea for mercy from the United States government to Sheridan who entrusted delivery of the message to Ranger Sergeant Jim White. This errand of mercy has been frequently confused with the famed 'Message to Garcia' that took place in Cuba. Jim White's mission was at least as dangerous. He carried the document from Tampico to General Escobedo's headquarters at Querétaro and arrived in time. However, the hatred and desire for retaliation were too strong and Maximilian was executed by firing squad.

Sergeant Joseph E. McCabe was mustered out of service on June 16 1865. He spent a year in St Louis, then moved to Allegheny City (part of Pittsburgh), Pennsylvania, where he was foreman in the painting department of a carriage manufacturer until 1871. He remained in his home state but moved to Bridgewater and was in the construction business. From 1873 to 1882 he was a grocer. Politics became an interest and he was elected to the general assembly to represent his county. He took a strong interest in the veterans' affairs and served in the highest Pennsylvania offices of the Union Veterans Association, the GAR. Joe McCabe and his wife Tillie had three daughters but there are no known descendants of them. McCabe died in 1922 aged 81 and the inscription on his faded headstone in the Beaver Cemetery reads 'Sheridan Scout'.[68]

Ranger Arch Rowand did not remain in the west. He returned to Pittsburgh, worked for the railroad, married into a family of means and entered local politics. In 1885 he became a lawyer. Archibald Rowand died in 1913.

Epilogue

Founded in the 1600s, the Rangers came into being as citizen soldiers who in defense of home and family became the cutting edge of ground combat. From their beginnings in colonial times through the Civil War, the great American Rangers were not trained at the United States Military Academy at West Point or other military institutions. Nathan Bedford Forrest, Henry Young, John Singleton Mosby, Harry Gilmor, John Hunt Morgan, Hanse and Jesse McNeill, and Elijah White all came from civilian pursuits to prove themselves on the battlefield. None of these men commanded large armies; those are reserved for the so-called 'professional' officer.

Uninhibited by standard military doctrine, the Rangers of the Civil War used methods inherited from their colonial and revolutionary war ancestors, then suited these techniques to their challenges. They operated on raids into enemy territory or lived for years surrounded by opposing forces. They survived and prospered by audacity, doing the unexpected, often at the least likely time. No individual or area could be considered safe from their attack, therefore enormous resources had to be diverted in the hope of protecting against them.

The Rangers of the Civil War built upon the accomplishments of their predecessors and left a legacy of high military standard that continues. Both the large armies and those units who specialize in ambush, reconnaissance, raid and spearhead operations are needed in any war of significant size. Today the all-volunteer, highly-trained Rangers are part of the Special Operations forces of the United States.

In wars that followed the Civil War – the Indian Wars, the Second World War, Korea, Vietnam, Grenada, Panama, the First Gulf War, Somalia, Afghanistan and Iraq – the Ranger has remained faithful to the trust of the American people.

When the Civil War ended, many men who fought in it asked themselves: 'What the hell was that all about?' Then they thought about the war and came to the conclusion that whatever it was, it was likely the biggest event in their lives. War looks better when you are out of it. They formed veterans groups, resumed their friendships forged in battle and experienced the in-fighting that is the curse of all such associations. Time began to take them, but not their feelings of brotherhood and their legacy of courage.

Many works written by men who fought from 1861 to 1865 were consulted in the writing of *Yank and Rebel Rangers*. The last book read was *Minty and the Cavalry*, the story of a Union horseman and his men. The author, a former captain of the 7th Pennsylvania Cavalry, signed the introduction 'JOSEPH G. VALE, Carlisle, PA., May 4, 1886'. Vale wrote: 'We are old now, and to the young generation of to-day, the spectacle of a lot of gray-haired old daddies and grand-daddies coming together and "getting crazy over the old war memories" is almost absurd – they "don't know", boys; they "don't know", do they?'

Through this author's writings, it is hoped that the American people and the leadership of the American army will know more about the Rangers. For 400 years the Rangers have fought and bled for the people of these shores. When used in its military sense, 'Ranger' is American. We are not 'Commandos'; they are British. We are not Special Forces (SF). The SF are superb soldiers (many Ranger-trained), with a different mission. At the time of writing, the Ranger course at Fort Benning, Georgia is the finest patrolling school in the world. Its well-tested graduates proudly wear the 'Individual' black and gold Ranger tab, as they infuse Ranger techniques throughout the services. The cutting edge of our fighting force is the Ranger Regiment, consisting of three highly trained battalions of volunteers who wear the red, white and black Ranger scroll as a 'Unit' insignia. At the call of our elected leaders, the Rangers stand ready to carry on the proud tradition built over the centuries of American experience; a service defined by the motto 'Rangers lead the Way!'

Endnotes

Preface
1. Amann, William Frayne, (ed.), *Personnel of the Civil War*, 2 vols (NY, Thomas Yoseloff).
2. Annual Report of the Adjutant General State of New York for 1899, p.743.
3. Twain, Mark, *The Private History of a Campaign that Failed, from The Family Mark Twain* (NY, Harper, 1896), pp.1281-94.
4. Sherman Memoirs, American Library edition, Chapter XIII, pp.360-63.

Opening Moves
1. Lang, Theodore F., *Loyal West Virginia* (Baltimore, Deutsch Publishing Co., 1895), pp.17-21.
2. *Picket Line and Camp Fire Stories*, p.45.
3. Brooks, *Butler and His Cavalry*, p.138.
4. *Picket Line and Camp Fire Stories,* p.104.
5. Casler, John O., *Four Years in the Stonewall Brigade*, pp.19-20 (henceforth Casler).
6. Moore, Frank, *Anecdotes, Poetry and Incidents of the War North and South 1860–1865* (NY, The Arundel Print, 1882), pp.144-45 (henceforth Moore).
7. *Wheeling Intelligencer*, November 11 1861.
8. Long, E.B., *The Civil War Day By Day* (NY, Doubleday, 1971), p.713.
9. US War Dept. (comp). *The War of the Rebellion: A Compilation of the Official Records of the Union and Confederate Armies (Washington, 1880–1901)*, Ser. I, II, 211 (henceforth referenced as O.R.).
10. *Cincinnati Times* report noted in *Bushwhackers' War, Insurgency and Counter-Insurgency in West Virginia* (eds Curry, Richard O. and Ham, F. Gerald).

Coming of Age
1. Crook, General George, *His Autobiography*, pp.86-87.
2. Lonn, Ella, *Desertion During the Civil War*, p.231.
3. Statement from Alfred Pike to Thomas Settle, contained in Thomas Settle to Governor Zebulon Vance October 4 1864, Thomas Settle Letters 1863–1864, North Carolina State Archives from 1988 doctoral dissertation by William Thomas Auman.

4. Linger, James Carter, *Confederate Military Units of West Virginia* (1989), p.17.
5. O.R Series I, Vol. XXXIII, 1891, p.526.
6. Ibid., p.531.
7. Scott, *Partisan Life With Mosby*, Preface.
8. Mosby Memoirs, p.371.
9. Crawford, *Mosby and His Men*, pp.156-57.
10. Sheppard, Captain William Eric, *Bedford Forrest* (NY, The Dial Press, 1930), p.320.
11. Crawford, *Mosby's Men*, p.155.
12. Miller, *Photographic History of The Civil War*, p.50.
13. Tsouras, *Dictionary of Military Quotations*, p.517.

Chapter 1: The Moccasin Rangers

1. Armstrong, *19th and 20th Virginia Cavalry*, p.3.
2. Ibid., pp.130 & 16.
3. Moore, p.65.
4. *Wheeling Intelligencer*, April 15 1862.
5. Ibid., April 12 1862.
6. Ibid., April 21 1861.
7. *The West Virginia Heritage Encyclopedia*, Vol. 7, p.1405.
8. Matheny, *Wood County WVA in Civil War Times*, pp.232-40. Also article and photo in the *West Virginia Hillbilly*, November 20 1986, Lang, 'Loyal West Virginia', p.269.
9. Osbourne and Weaver, *The Virginia State Rangers and State Line*, p.179.

Chapter 2: The Hatfields and the McCoys

1. Weaver, *45th Battalion Virginia Infantry*, pp.103-104.

Chapter 3: The Thurmond Brothers

1. Witschey, *The Thurmonds of Virginia* (Gatewood Co., Richmond), p.287.
2. Sandburg, *Abraham Lincoln, The War Years*, Vol. 1, p.416.
3. Weaver, *Thurmond's Partisan Rangers*, p.29.
4. Weaver, *Thurmond's Partisan Rangers*, pp.33-34 from an article by C. Shirley Donnelly in the *Fayette Tribune*, 1935.
5. O.R. Vol. XXIX, Part 1, pp.946-49.

Chapter 4: The Iron Scouts

1. Brooks, U.R. *Butler and his Cavalry* (Coumbia, S.C., The State Company, 1909), p.140.
2. Ibid., p.140.
3. Ibid., p.234.
4. Ibid., p.99.

5. Ibid., pp.287-88.
6. Ibid., pp.463-64.
7. Ibid., p.48.
8. Ibid., pp.395-96.

Chapter 5: The Border Rangers
1. Dr Roy Bird Cook, Collection 27, Box 9, Civil War (University of West Virginia Library).

Chapter 6: John D. Imboden
1. Evans, *Confederate Military History*, p.609.
2. 'Haviland Harris Abbot', *West Virginia Quarterly Magazine* January 1960, Vol. XXI, Number 2, p.24 and from Imboden's undated advertisment in the West Virginia University Library.

Chapter 7: Turner Ashby
1. Ashby, *Life of Turner Ashby*, pp.17-27.
2. Avirett, *Memoirs of General Turner Ashby* (henceforth Avirett), pp.15-20.
3. Avirett, p.31.
4. Avirett, p.62.
5. Ashby, *A Life of Turner Ashby*, p.55.
6. Moore, p.171.
7. Sandburg, *Lincoln: The War Years*, Vol. 1, p.530.
8. Southern Historical Society Papers (henceforth SHSP), p.525.
9. McDonald, *Laurel Brigade*.
10. Avirett, p.70.
11. O.R. Series 1, Vol. 2, p.772.
12. Ibid., pp.775-76.
13. Ibid., p.787.
14. Ibid., p.805.
15. Ibid., p.825.
16. Ibid., pp.871-72.
17. Ibid., p.896.
18. Ashby, *Life of Turner Ashby*, p.65.
19. O.R. Series 2, Vol. 1, p.904.
20. Ibid., p.908.
21. O.R. Series 2, Vol. 1, pp.952-53.
22. Armstrong, *7th Virginia Cavalry*, pp.88-91.
23. Avirett, p.101.
24. McDonald, *Laurel Brigade*, p.30.
25. Jones, *Gray Ghosts and Rebel Raiders*, p.75.
26. Freeman, *Lee's Lieutenants*, p.309.

27. O.R. Series 1, Vol. 2, p.963.
28. O.R. Series 1, Vol. 2, p.986.
29. Ashby, *Life of Turner Ashby*, pp.101-104.
30. Light, mobile artillery contributed greatly to the success of Gustavus II 1594–1632, the Swedish warrior king known as the Lion of the North.
31. Avirett, p.131.
32. SHSP, Vol. III, pp.2-3.
33. Avirett, p.138.
34. Beach, *The First New York Cavalry*, pp.201-202.
35. Douglas, Henry Kyd, *I Rode With Stonewall*, p.150.
36. Strother, *A Virginia Yankee in the Civil War*, pp.28-29.
37. Davis, William C. (ed.), *Diary of a Confederate Soldier (John S. Jackman)* (University of South Carolina Press, 1990), p.174.
38. Avirett, p.146.
39. Ashby, *Life of Turner Ashby*, p.129.
40. Gordon, General John B., *Reminiscences of the Civil War*, p.7.
41. Taylor, *Destruction and Reconstruction*, p.50.
42. Ibid., p.66.
43. Esposito, *West Point Atlas of American Wars*, Vol. 1, Map 39 text.
44. *Battles and Leaders*, Vol. II, p.300.
45. Ashby, *Life of Turner Ashby*, p.135.
46. Taylor, *Destruction and Reconstruction*, pp.79-80.
47. Ashby, *Life of Turner Ashby*, pp.150-55.
48. SHSP, p.528.
49. Ashby, *Life of Turner Ashby*, pp.181-82.
50. Avirett, pp.196-97.
51. Freeman, 'Lee's Lieutenants', pp.433-34 from Avirett, J.B., *The Memoirs of General Turner Ashby and His Compeers*, p.206.
52. O.R. Series 1, Vol. 51, p.639.
53. Ashby, *Life of Turner Ashby*, p.227.
54. Ibid., p.197.
55. Ibid., p.198.
56. Ibid., p.199.
57. Ibid., p.264.
58. Ibid., p.228.
59. Ibid., pp.235-36.
60. Pyne, *The History of the First New Jersey Cavalry*, p.24.
61. Ibid., pp.24-25.
62. Ibid., pp.55-56.
63. Rauch, *History of the Bucktails*, pp.154-55.
64. Swayne died of his wounds. Blanchard and Gifford both survived but their wounds forced them out of the service and their remaining years of life were spent in pain.

65. Rauch, *History of the Bucktails*, p.156.
66. O.R. Series 1, Vol. 12, p.732.
67. Rauch, *History of the Bucktails*, p.160.
68. Avirett, p.223.
69. Ibid., p.232.
70. SHSP, p.525.
71. Ashby, *Life of Turner Ashby*, p.211.
72. Ibid., p.233.
73. Evans, *Confederate Military History: Virginia*, pp.577-79.

Chapter 8: Harry Gilmor
1. *Dictionary of American Biography*, Vol. IV, p.309.
2. Gilmor, *Four Years in the Saddle*, p.13 (henceforth Gilmor).
3. Ibid., p.18.
4. Ibid., p.23.
5. Ibid., p.26.
6. Ibid., p.28.
7. Ibid., pp.32-33.
8. Ibid., pp.32-34.
9. Ibid., p.38.
10. Ibid., pp.41-42.
11. Ibid., p.52.
12. Ibid., p.61.
13. Ibid., pp.65-66.
14. Ibid., p.66.
15. Ibid., p.69.
16. Ibid., p.74.
17. *Southern Bivouac*, Vol. 4, 1877, pp.1-7.
18. Gilmor, pp.77-78.
19. Gordon, pp.41-42.
20. Ibid., p.38.
21. Gilmor, pp.87-88.
22. Ibid., p.96.
23. B&L, Vol. III, p.424.
24. Ibid., p.428.
25. O.R. Series 1, Vol. 51, part 2, p.770.
26. O.R. Series 1, Vol. 29, p.210.
27. Gilmor, pp.111-12.
28. Ibid., p.112.
29. Gray, John A. and Green, *Rebellion Record, NY*, (1864), pp.565-67 and Beach, *The First New York*, pp.283-84.
30. O.R. Series 1, Vol. 29, pp.490-91.
31. Gilmor, p.116.

32. Ibid., pp.127-28.
33. O.R. Series 1, Vol. 51, part 2, p.795.
34. Ibid., p.796.
35. Beach, *The First New York*, p.300.
36. Gilmor, pp.137-38.
37. Beach, *The First New York*, pp.305-307.
38. Gilmor, p.141.
39. *Wheeling Intelligencer*, February 16 1864.
40. O.R. Vol. 33, p.222.
41. Gilmor, p.147.
42. Gordon, p.417.
43. Gilmor, p.160.
44. Norton, *History of the 15th New York Volunteer Cavalry, pp.33-34.*
45. Beach, *The First New York*, pp.355-58.
46. O.R. Series 1, Vol. XXXVII, Part 1, p.152.
47. Gilmor, p.174.
48. Ibid., p.177.
49. Ibid., p.178.
50. Douglas, pp.290-91.
51. Wallace was a well-rounded man. He was the future author of the classic novel *Ben-Hur* and governor of the territory of New Mexico.
52. *New York Herald*, July 13 1863.
53. Gilmor, p.202.
54. O.R. Series 1, Vol. XXXVII, Part 1, p.349.
55. Gilmor, p.208.
56. B&L, Vol. IV, p.495.
57. O.R. Series 1, Vol. XXXVII, Part 1, p.333.
58. Gilmor, p.210.
59. Farrar, p.307.
60. Gilmor, p.211.
61. O.R. Series 1, Vol. XXXVII, Part 1, p.335.
62. Gilmor, p.214.
63. Ibid., p.215.
64. Ibid., p.221.
65. O.R. Series 1, Vol. XLIII, Part 1, p.726.
66. Gilmor, p.241.
67. Ibid., p.245.
68. Ibid., p.247.
69. Ibid., p.254.
70. Ibid., p.260.
71. Gordon, p.415.
72. Gilmor, p.264.

73. Ibid., p.271.
74. Ibid., pp.272-73.
75. Ibid., pp.273-74.
76. Ibid., p.274.
77. Ibid., p.276.
78. Brooks, p.481.
79. Gilmor, p.276.
80. O.R. Series 1, Vol. 51, Part 2, p.1061.
81. O.R. Vol. XLVI, Part 2, p.44.
82. Gilmor, p.291.
83. *Dictionary of American Biography*, Vol. IV, p.309.

Chapter 9: Elijah V. White and the Comanches

1. Myers, *The Comanches*, p.8 (henceforth Myers).
2. Armstrong, *7th Virginia Cavalry*, p.91.
3. Myers, p.9.
4. Ibid., pp.13-16.
5. Ibid., pp.17-18.
6. O.R. Series 1, Vol. 29, p.69.
7. Taylor, *Destruction and Reconstruction*, p.39.
8. Myers, p.38.
9. Taylor, *Destruction and Reconstruction*, p.37.
10. SHSP, Vol. 7, pp.526-27.
11. Myers, pp.86-87.
12. Ibid., pp.94-95.
13. Ibid., p.98.
14. Goodhart, *The Loudoun Rangers*, p.33.
15. Myers, p.101; Goodhart, p.35.
16. Gillespie, Richard, *Leesburg in the Civil War* (Loudoun Museum, Leesburg VA, 1998).
17. Myers, p.106.
18. Douglas, Henry Kyd, *I Rode With Stonewall*, p.145.
19. Myers, p.112.
20. O.R. Series 1, Vol. 21, p.12.
21. Ibid., p.20.
22. Ibid., pp.691-92.
23. Myers, pp.158-59.
24. Ibid., p.172.
25. Ibid., p.175.
26. Ibid., p.181.
27. Ibid., p.183.
28. McDonald, *History of the Laurel Brigade*, pp.138-39.

29. SHSP, Vol. X, pp.294-95. On receiving orders to join Lee at Gettysburg, General Ewell marched his corps through the mountain gap at Paper Town (Mount Holly Springs) and left the buildings of the old post standing.
30. Myers, pp.192-93.
31. SHSP, Vol. X, pp.294-95.
32. Ibid., p.295.
33. Myers, p.204.
34. JCCW, 1868, part 2, p.10; Pleasonton, Alfred, *The Campaign of Gettysburg'*, *Annals of the War, Written by Leading Participants, North and South* (Philadelphia, 1879), p.455.
35. O.R. Series 1, Vol. 29, p.69.
36. Ibid., p.75.
37. Ibid., p.92.
38. Ibid., p.91.
39. Myers, p.216.
40. O.R. Series 1, Vol. 29, pp.92-93.
41. Ibid., p.202.
42. Myers, pp.236-37.
43. Ibid., p.250.
44. McDonald, *History of the Laurel Brigade*, p.225.
45. Ibid., p.228.
46. Myers, p.280.
47. Ibid., p.290.
48. Ibid., p.314.
49. Ibid., pp.316-17.
50. Ibid., p.319.
51. Ibid., pp.325-26.
52. McDonald, *History of the Laurel Brigade*, p.295.
53. Myers, p.339.
54. Divine, *35th Battalion Virginia Cavalry*, p.71.

Chapter 10: John Hanson 'Hanse' and Jesse McNeill

1. The 1st New Yorkers also make that claim, but their date is August 7 1861.
2. Fay, *The Capture of Generals Crook and Kelley*, p.2 (henceforth Fay).
3. Elwood, *Old Ringgold Cavalry*, pp.135-36 (henceforth Elwood).
4. Bright, *The McNeill Rangers: A Study in Confederate Guerrilla Warfare*, p.1 (henceforth Bright).
5. Farrar, *Twenty-Second Pennsylvania Cavalry and Ringgold Battalion*, p.197 (henceforth Farrar).
6. Ibid., p.2.
7. O.R. Series 1, Vol. XXV, Part 2, pp.660-61.
8. O.R. Series 1, Vol. XXVII, Part 2, p.291.

9. B&L, p.422.
10. Farrar, pp.120-22.
11. Lieutenant Charles Johnson of McNeill's Rangers was wounded and taken prisoner. He became part of what Southern historians would call the Immortal 600 (600 officers) sent to a 2-acre stockade in front of Fort Wagner and used as human shields for forty-six days in retaliation for 600 Union officers held at Charleston.
12. Delauter, *McNeill's Rangers*, p.53.
13. O.R. Vol. XXIX, Part 1, pp.650-51.
14. Farrar, p.153.
15. O.R. Series 1, Vol. XXXVII, Part 1, pp. 382-83; Delauter, p.66; Bright, pp.9-11.
16. Farrar, p.183.
17. Ibid., p.344.
18. O.R. Series 1, Vol. XXXVII, Part 1, p.687.
19. Farrar, pp.399-400.
20. Lyman, *Civil War Quotations*, p.185.
21. Farrar, p.477.
22. Fay, *The Capture of Generals Crook and Kelley*, p.1.
23. Ibid., p.3.
24. Ibid, p.5.
25. Ibid., p.8.
26. Ibid., p.10.
27. *General George Crook*, p.136.
28. O.R. Vol. XLVI, Part 2, pp.619-28.
29. Farrar, p.458.
30. Elwood, p.269.

Chapter 11: The St Albans Raid

1. Royce, Edmund H., *St. Albans Raid* (St Albans North Country Press).
2. Sowles, Edward A., 'Vermont Historical Society Annual Address', Tuesday, October 17 1876, pp.7-10.
3. O.R. Vol. 43, Chapter LV, pp.914-15.
4. Ibid., p.20.
5. Ibid., p.41.
6. O.R. 43, pp.915-16.

Chapter 12: Bushwhacker, Ranger and Guerrilla Bands

1. Burch, John P., *Charles W. Quantrell* (Vega, Texas, 1923), p.266 (henceforth Burch).
2. Ibid., pp.92-93.
3. Ibid., p.128.
4. Ibid., pp.163-64.

Chapter 13: The Raid to Burn New York City
1. Johnson, *Partisan Rangers*, p.40 (henceforth Johnson); Headley, John W., *Confederate Operations in Canada and New York* (New York, Neale Publishing Company, 1906), p.480 (henceforth Headley).
2. Johnson, pp.80-81.
3. Headley, p.480.
4. Ibid., p.102.
5. Ibid., p.199.
6. Ibid., p.210.
7. Ibid., pp.223-30.
8. Ibid., p.233.
9. Ibid., pp.231-38.
10. The *New York Times*, November 27 1864.
11. Ibid., November 27 1864.
12. Headley, *Confederate Operations in Canada and New York*, pp.239-461.

Chapter 14: Ranger Abraham Lincoln
1. Tarbell, Ida M., *The Life of Abraham Lincoln* (New York, McClure, Phillips & Co.), p.76 (henceforth Tarbell); McClure, J.B., *Anecdotes of Abraham Lincoln* (Chicago, Rhodes & McClure, 1884), pp.38-39 (henceforth McClure).
2. Tarbell, pp.76-77.
3. Ibid., p.80.
4. McClure, J.B. (ed.), p.40.
5. Rice, Allen Thorndike, *Reminiscences of Abraham Lincoln* (New York, North American Publishing Company, 1886), p.447 (henceforth Rice).
6. *Personal Memoirs of U.S. Grant*, Chapter XVI, pp.146-47.
7. McClure, p.109.
8. Moore, p.251.
9. *Camp Fire and Picket Line*, p.42.
10. Farrar, pp.322-33.
11. Oldroyd, *Words of Lincoln*, p.154.
12. *Sherman Memoirs*, Library of America Edition, Chapter XXIV, p.813.

Chapter 15: Loudoun Rangers
1. Divine and Souders (eds), *To Talk is Treason*, p.24.
2. O.R. Series 1, Vol. XII, Part 3, p.705.
3. O.R Vol. XXIX, Part 1, p.67.
4. O.R. Series 1, Vol. XIX, Part 2, p.568.
5. O.R. Series 1, Vol. XLVI, Part 3, pp.444-45.

Chapter 16: The Snake-Hunters
1. *The Picket Line and Camp Fire Stories*, pp.7-10.
2. Ibid.

ENDNOTES

Chapter 17: The Swamp Dragons

1. Farrar, *Twenty-Second Pennsylvania Cavalry and Ringgold Battalion*, p.33.

Chapter 18: Grant's Ranger

1. Downs, Edward C., *Four Years a Scout and Spy*, p.3.
2. Downs, *The Great American Scout and Spy*, pp.42-43.
3. Ibid., pp.55-56.
4. Ibid., pp.88-90.
5. Ibid., pp.128-38.
6. Ibid., p.151.
7. Ibid., p.353.
8. Simon, John Y., *The Papers of Ulysses S. Grant*, Vol. 12, p.457; Downs, *Four Years a Scout and Spy*, p.364.
9. Ruggles, pp.399-402.

Chapter 19: Scouts

1. O.R. Vol. 43, Part 2, p.20.
2. Ibid., p.33.
3. Hazelton, *Scouts, Spies and Heroes of the Great Civil War* (Jersey City, Star Publishing Co., 1892), pp.34-66.
4. *Sherman Memoirs*, American Library Edition, Chapter XIV, pp.383-85 and Chapter XXIII, p.775.

Chapter 20: Rangers and Indians

1. Evans, *Louisiana and Arkansas: Confederate Military History*, pp.417-19.
2. The First Regiment of Mounted Rangers was mustered out of service on December 30 1863. Material contained in this chapter is taken from *Minnesota in the Civil and Indian Wars 1861–1865* by the Board of Commissioners, Saint Paul, Minnesota (Pioneer Press Company, 1891) and newspaper reports of the period.

Chapter 21: The Blazer Scouts

1. In time McDonough would be trapped in a wood by Union cavalry. Knowing he faced a rope, he committed suicide.
2. Williamson, *Mosby's Rangers*, p.301.
3. Crawford, *Mosby and His Men*, pp.285-86.
4. Monteiro, *Reminiscences*, pp.59-60.
5. *Mosby Memoirs*, p.320.

Chapter 22: The Jessie Scouts

1. Johnson and Malone, *Dictionary of American Biography*, Vol. IV, p.23.
2. Herr, Pamela and Lee Spence, Mary, *The Letters of Jessie Benton Fremont* (Chicago, University of Illinois Press), p.266.

3. *Wheeling Intelligencer*, April 30 1862, and Comstock, *The West Virginia Heritage Encyclopedia*, Vol. 12, p.2528.
4. Moore, Frank, *Anecdotes, Poetry and Incidents of the War, North and South* (New York, Arundel Print, 1882), pp.45-46.
5. *General George Crook*, p.120.
6. Norton, *History of the Fifteenth New York Cavalry*, pp.113-25.

Chapter 23: Henry Harrison Young and Sheridan's Scouts
1. Beymer, William Gilmor, *On Hazardous Service* (New York, Harper Bros, 1912), p.112.
2. *Sheridan Memoirs*, p.1.
3. Rider, Sidney S., *The Campaign Life of Lieutenant Colonel Henry Harrison Young* (Providence, 1882), pp.6-22.
4. Beymer, p.102.
5. Ibid., pp.102-103.
6. Ibid., p.105.
7. Moyer, p.222; Beymer, p.113.
8. *Sheridan Memoirs*, pp.2-3.
9. *Personal Narratives of Events in the War of the Rebellion, Rhode Island Soldiers and Sailors* (Providence, N. Bangs Williams & Co., 1880–81, reprinted by Broadfoot Publishing Co., Wimington, N.C., 1993).
10. Rider, Sidney S., *The Campaign Life of Lieutenant Colonel Henry Harrison Young* (Providence, 1882), pp.39-40.
11. Beymer, pp.220-21.
12. Rider, p.27.
13. Beymer, pp.115-16; *Personal Memoirs of Philip Henry Sheridan*, p.105.
14. Beach, *The First New York*, p.498.
15. Ibid., p.498.
16. Moyer, *History of the 17th Penna Cavalry*, pp.219-21.
17. The 1894 records of the adjutant general of the State of New York for the 8th New York Cavalry show the name as Christman, but he was also shown as Crisman.
18. Beymer, pp.119-21.
19. Ibid., p.3.
20. Ibid., p.5.
21. Ibid., p.7.
22. Ibid., pp.8-13.
23. Ibid., p.15.
24. Ibid., pp.17-22.
25. Gordon, p.361.
26. Beymer, pp.25-28.
27. Moyer, pp.224-25.

ENDNOTES

28. O.R. Vol. 43, Part 1, p.56.
29. O.R. Series 1, Vol. XLVI, Part 1, p.457.
30. Gilmor, pp.277-78.
31. Ibid., pp.280-81.
32. *Personal Memoirs of Philip Henry Sheridan*, pp.105-107.
33. Ibid., p.107.
34. O.R. Vol. 46, Part 2, p.442.
35. Casler, John O., *Four Years in the Stonewall Brigade* (original publication Guthrie, OK., 1893; second edition 1906. Reprinted by Morningside Bookshop, Dayton, Ohio, 1982).
36. Ibid., p.265.
37. Moyer, *History of the 17th Penna Cavalry*, pp.223-28.
38. Beymer, p.23.
39. Casler, p.265.
40. Porter, Brevet B.G., *Battles and Leaders*, Vol. IV, p.708.
41. O.R. Series 1, Vol. XLVI, Part 1, p.477.
42. Beymer, pp.31-33.
43. Ibid., p.479.
44. Ibid., p.480.
45. Ibid., p.481.
46. Ibid., p.710.
47. Sheridan wanted the 6th Corps as he was familiar with them in the Shenandoah. Grant could not give him the 6th Corps as it was near the other end of the line and could not be pulled out in time. According to General Porter, Grant told Sheridan he could relieve Warren if he wanted to and Sheridan soon did. Warren, a hero of Gettysburg, would spend some fourteen years trying to clear his name.
48. Beymer, p.709.
49. Ibid., p.713.
50. Beymer, *Hazardous Service*, pp.126-27; Moyer, *History of the 17th Penna Cavalry*, p.360. The 1901 book *Deeds of Valor* by Walter F. Beyer and Oscar F. Keydel credits McCabe with the capture of General Barringer. Confirmation of the award has not been found.
51. Beymer, pp.126-27.
52. Porter, Brevet B.G., *Battles and Leaders*, Vol. 4, p.719.
53. Rider, Sidney S., *The Campaign Life of Lieutenant Colonel Henry Harrison Young* (Providence, 1882), pp.58-59.
54. Gordon, p.424.
55. Ibid., p.416.
56. Ibid., pp.425-28.
57. Sheridan, *Last Days of the Rebellion: Military Essays and Recollections*, Military Order of the Loyal Legion Vol. 1 (Chicago, A.C. McClurg & Co., 1891; republished by the Broadfoot Publishing Co., Wilmington, NC, 1992), p.428.

58. Porter, B&L, Vol. IV, p.741.
59. Sheridan, *Last Days of the Rebellion: Military Essays and Recollections*, Military Order of the Loyal Legion, Vol. 1 (Chicago, A.C. McClurg & Co., 1891; republished by the Broadfoot Publishing Co., Wilmington, NC, 1992), pp.436-37.
60. O.R. Series 1, Vol. XLVI, Part 1, p.1113.
61. US Army Military History Institute Misc. collection, the letters of Henry Young.
62. *Sheridan Memoirs*, Vol. II, p.215.
63. Haislip, Joan, *The Crown of Mexico* (New York, Holt, Rinehart & Winston, 1971), p.365.
64. Beymer, p.130; *Sheridan Memoirs*, pp.221-22.
65. Beymer, p.132.
66. Beymer, p.132; *Sheridan Memoirs*.
67. Rider, Sidney S., *The Campaign Life of Lieutenant Colonel Henry Harrison Young* (Providence, 1882), pp.62-63.
68. In October 2002 the author told his Korean War foxhole buddy Nick Tisak of the 8th Airborne Rangers about Ranger Joe McCabe. Nick visited McCabe's grave at the Beaver Cemetery and Mausoleum, Beaver, PA. He found the McCabe family plot in disrepair and Joseph McCabe's headstone scarcely legible. Both Ranger Nick Tisak and Ranger Lew Villa of the 1st Airborne Ranger Company live in the area and they engineered a program to restore the grave site of this brave Ranger and to bring his deeds to the remembrance of his home community.

Bibliography

Alexander, Edward P., *Military Memoirs of a Confederate* (New York, Charles Scribner's Sons, 1907)

Ashby, Thomas A., *Life of Turner Ashby* (New York, Neale Publishing Co., 1914; reprinted by Morningside House Inc., Dayton, Ohio, 1991)Avirett, Reverend James B., *The Memoirs of General Turner Ashby and His Compeers* (Baltimore, Selby & Dulany, 1867)

Beymer, William Gilmor, *On Hazardous Service* (New York, Harper & Brothers, 1912)

Brandt, Nat, *The man who tried to BURN NEW YORK* (Syracuse University Press, 1986)

Breihan, Carl W., *Quantrill and his Civil War Guerrillas* (New York, Promontory Press, 1959)

Brooks, U.R., *Butler and His Cavalry* (Columbia, South Carolina, The State Company)

Burch, John P., *Charles W. Quantrill* (Vega, Texas, 1923)

Bushong, Millard K., *General Turner Ashby and Stonewall's Valley Campaign* (Varona, VA, McClure Printing Co. Inc., 1980)

Collins, Darrell L., *General William Averell's Salem Raid* (Shippensburg, Pennsylvania, 1999)

Comanches (A History of White's Battalion, Virginia Cavalry) (Baltimore, Kelly, Piet & Co., 1871. Reprinted by Butternut Press, Gaithersburg, Maryland, 1987)

Connelley, William Elsey, *Quantrill and the Border Wars* (Cedar Rapids, Iowa, The Torch Press, 1910)

Crouch, Richard E., *Rough-Riding Scout* (Arlington, Virginia, Elden Editions, 1994)

Delauter, Roger U. Jr, *The Virginia Regimental History* series, *McNeill's Rangers* (Lynchburg,Virginia, H.E. Howard Inc., 1986)

Divine, John E., Souders, Bronwen C. and Souders, John M., *To Talk is Treason* (Waterford, Virginia, Waterford Foundation Inc., 1996)

Downs, Edward C., *Four Years a Scout and Spy, 'General Bunker'. One of Lieut. General Grant's Most Daring and Successful Scouts* (Zanesville, Ohio, Dunne, 1866, republished as *The Great American Scout and Spy, 'General Bunker'*, New York, Olmstead, 1870; attributed to C. Lorain Ruggles)

Dupuy, R. Ernest and Trevor, N., *Brave Men and Great Captains* (McLean, Virginia, Nova Publications, 1993)

Dyer, Frederick H., *A Compendium of the War of the Rebellion*, 2 Vols (F.H. Dyer, Des Moines, Iowa, 1908)

Eckart, Edward K. and Amato, Nicholas J. (eds), *Ten Years in the Saddle: Memoir of William Woods Averell* (Presido Press, San Rafael, 1978)

Edwards, John N., *Noted Guerrillas or the Warfare of the Border* (St Louis, Missouri, Bryan, Brand & Co., 1877)

Fay, John B., *Capture of Generals Crook and Kelley by the McNeill Rangers* (Cumberland, Maryland, Laney Souvenir Co., 1865)

Freeman, Douglas Southall, *Lee's Lieutenants (A study in command)* 2 Vols (New York, Charles Scribner's Sons, 1943)

Frost, Lawrence A., *Custer Legends* (Bowling Green, Bowling Green University, Popular Press, 1981)Gilmor, Colonel Harry, *Four Years in the Saddle* (New York, Harper & Brothers, 1866)

Goodhart, Briscoe, *History of the Independent Loudoun Virginia Rangers* (Washington, D.C., Press of Mcgill & Wallace, 1896)

Gordon, John B., *General Reminiscences of the Civil War* (New York, Charles Scribner's Sons, 1904)

Grant, U.S., *Personal Memoirs of U.S. Grant* 2 Vols (New York, The Century Co., 1895)

Haislip, Joan, *The Crown of Mexico* (New York, Holt, Rinehart and Winston, 1971)

Hakenson, Donald C., *This Forgotten Land* (2002)

Headley, John W., *Confederate Operations in Canada and New York* (New York, The Neale Publishing Company, 1906)

Herr, Pamela and Spence, Mary Lee, *The Letters of Jessie Benton Fremont* (Chicago, University of Illinois Press, 1993)

Hurst & Company, *The Picket Line and Camp Fire Stories: a collection of war anecdotes, both grave and gay, illustrative of the trials and triumphs of soldier life; with a thousand-and-one humorous stories told by Abraham Lincoln, together with a full collection of Northern and Southern war songs. By a member of the G.A.R. (18---)* (Library of Congress Rare Book Room, Call Number E655)

Johnson, Adam Rankin, *The Partisan Rangers (of the Confederate States Army)* (Louisville, Georgia, G. Fetter & Co., 1904)

Johnston, Milus E., *The Sword of Bushwhacker Johnson* (Memoirs published in Guntersville, AL Democrat, April-December 1902. Edited and annotated by Charles S. Rice and published Huntsville, Alabama, Flint River Press, 1992)

Jones, Reverend William J., *Southern Historical Society Papers*, Vol. VII (Morningside Bookshop, Broadfoot Publishing Co., 1990)

King and Derby, *Campfire Sketches and Battlefield Echoes* (Springfield, Massachusetts, 1887)

Lang, Theodore F., *Loyal West Virginia from 1861 to 1865* (Baltimore, The Deutsch Publishing Co., 1895)

BIBLIOGRAPHY

Long, E.B. with Long, Barbara, *The Civil War Day By Day: An Almanac 1861–1865* (Garden City, New York, Doubleday & Co., 1971)

McDonald, William N., *History of the Laurel Brigade* (Gaithersburg, Maryland, Old Soldier Books, 1987. Originally printed 1907)

McPherson, James M., *Battle Cry of Freedom* (New York, Oxford University Press, 1988)

Miller, Francis Trevelyan, *The Photographic History of the Civil War*, Vol. 4 (Cavalry) of 10 (New York, The Review of Reviews Co., 1911)

Monaghan, Jay, *Custer* (Lincoln, University of Nebraska Press, 1959) Moore, Frank, Anecdotes, Poetry and Incidents of the War, North and South 1860–1865 (New York, The Arundel Print, 1882)

Morton, Joseph W. (ed.), *Sparks from the Camp Fire* (Keystone Publishing Co., Philadelphia, 1891)

Mosby, Colonel John S., *Mosby's Memoirs* (New York, Little, Brown and Co., 1917. Republished by J.S. Sanders & Co., Nashville, 1995)

Ness, George T. Jr, *The Regular Army on the Eve of The Civil War* (Baltimore, Toomey Press, 1990)

Osborne, Randall and Weaver, Jeffrey C., *The Virginia State Rangers and State Line* (Lynchburg, Virginia, H.E. Howard, 1994)

Pollard, E.A., *The Lost Cause. A facsimile of the original 1886 edition* (New York, Gramercy Books, 1994)

Pond, George E., *The Shenandoah Valley* (New York, Charles Scribner's Sons)

Porter, General Horace, *Campaigning With Grant* (New York, The Century Co., 1897)

Ramsdell, Charles W., *Behind the Lines in the Southern Confederacy* (Baton Rouge, Lousiana State University Press, 1944)

Rice, Otis K., *The Hatfields and the McCoys* (University Press of Kentucky, 1982)

Richardson, Albert D., *Secret Service* (Hartford, American Publishing Co., 1865)

Sandburg, Carl, *Abraham Lincoln*, 3 Vols (New York, Dell, 1959)

Schmitt, Martin F. (ed.), *General George Crook: His Autobiography* (Norman, Oklahoma, University of Oklahoma Press, 1946 & 1960)

Sheridan, Brigadier General Michael V., *Personal Memoirs of Philip Henry Sheridan*, 2 Vols (New York, D. Appleton & Co., 1904)

Sherman, William Tecumseh, *Memoirs of General W.T. Sherman*, 2 Vols (New York, Charles L. Webster & Co., 1892)

Siepel, Kevin H., *Rebel (The life and times of John Singleton Mosby)* (New York, St Martin's Press, 1983)

Sifakis, Stewart, *Who Was Who In the Civil War* (New York, Facts on File Publications, 1988)

Simpson, Colonel Harold B. (co-ordinator), *Soldiers of Texas* (Waco, Texas, 1973)

Strother, David Hunter (Eby, Cecil D. Jr, ed.), *A Virginia Yankee in the Civil War* (Chapel Hill University of North Carolina Press, 1961)

Surby, R.W., *Grierson's Raid: (part of) Two Great Raids* (Washington D.C., The National Tribune, McElroy, Shoppell & Andrews, 1897)

Taylor, Richard, *Destruction and Reconstruction* (New York, D. Appleton & Co., 1883)

Vale, Joseph G., *Minty and the Cavalry: A History of the Cavalry Campaigns in the Western Armies* (Harrisburg, Pennsylvania, Edwin K. Meyers, 1886)

Vasvary, Edmund, *Lincoln's Hungarian Heros* (Washington D.C., The Hungarian Reformed Federation of America, 1939)

Veil, Charles Henry (ed. Viola, Herman J.), *The Memoirs of Charles Henry Veil* (New York, Orion Books, 1993)

Waller, Altina L., *Feud (Hatfields, McCoys and Social Change in Appalachia 1860–1890)* (Chapel Hill, University of North Carolina Press, 1988)

Waring, Colonel George, *Whip and Spur* (New York, Doubleday & McClure, 1897)

Warner, Ezra J., *Generals in Blue* (Baton Rouge, Lousiana State University Press, 1964)

Wert, Jeffry D., *Custer (The Controversial Life of George Armstrong Custer)* (New York, Simon & Schuster, 1966)

Woodward, Harold R. Jr, *Defender of the Valley (Brigadier General John Daniel Imboden C.S.A.)* (Berryville, Virginia, Rockbridge Publishing Co., 1966)

Regimental Histories

3rd PA Cavalry Association, *History of the Third Pennsylvania Cavalry* (Philadelphia, Franklin Printing Co., 1905)

Armstrong, Richard L., *7th Virginia Cavalry* (Lynchburg, Virginia, H.E. Howard Inc., 1992)

Armstrong, Richard L., *19th and 20th Virginia Cavalry* (Lynchburg, Virginia, H.E. Howard Inc., 1994)

Beach, William H., *The First New York Lincoln Cavalry* (New York, The Lincoln Cavalry Association, 1902. Reprinted by Bacon Rice Books, 3717 Pleasant Ridge Rd., Annandale VA 22003)

Benedict, George Grenville, *Vermont in the Civil War*, 2 Vols (Burlington, Vermont, The Free Press Association, 1881. Includes history of the First Vermont Cavalry)

Boudrye, Reverend Louis N., *Historic Records of the Fifth New York Cavalry, First Ira Harris Guard* (Albany, New York, J. Munsell, 1868)

Delauter, Roger U., *18th Virginia Cavalry* (Lynchburg, Virginia, H.E. Howard, 1985)

Divine, John E., *The Virginia Regimental History Series: 35th Battalion Virginia Cavalry*
(Lynchburg, Virginia, H.E. Howard, 1985)

Elwood, John W., *Sgt. Elwood's Stories of the OLD RINGGOLD CAVALRY* (Coal Center, Pennsylvania, self-published, 1914)

Farrar, Samuel Clark, *The Twenty-Second Pennsylvania Cavalry and the Ringgold Battalion 1861–1865* (Their association, 1911)

BIBLIOGRAPHY

Hard, Abner, *History of the Eighth Cavalry Regiment, Illinois Volunteers* (Aurora, 1868)

Lee, William O., *Seventh Regiment, Michigan Volunteer Cavalry 1862–1865* (7th Michigan Cavalry Association)

Loyal Legion of the United States War Papers and Personal Reminiscences 1861–1865, 60 Vols (St Louis, Becktold & Co., 1892. Republished by Broadfoot Publishing Company, Wilmington, North Carolina, 1992) Moyer, H.P., *History of the Seventeenth Regiment, Pennsylvania Volunteer Cavalry* (Lebanon, Pennsylvania, Sowers Printing Co., 1911)

Newcomer, C., *Armour Cole's Cavalry, or Three Years in the Saddle* (Baltimore, Cushing & Co., 1895)

Norton, Chauncey S., *History of the Fifteenth New York Volunteer Cavalry* (Ithaca, New York, Journal, Book and Job Printing House, 1891)

Parker, John L., *History of the Twenty-Second Massachusetts Infantry* (Boston, Rand Avery Co., 1887)

Price, George F., *Across the Continent with the Fifth Cavalry* (New York, Noble Offset Printers Inc., 1883)

Rauch, William H., *History of the Bucktails* (Philadelphia, Electric Printing Co., 1906)

Regimental Association, *History of the Eighteenth Regiment of Cavalry, Pennsylvania Volunteers* (New York, Wynkoop-Hallenbeck Crawford Co., 1909)

Ripley, William Y.W., *Vermont Riflemen in the War for the Union* (Rutland, Tuttle & Co. Printers, 1883)

Rodenbough, Theo F., *Everglade to Cannon with the Second Dragoons, Second U.S. Cavalry* (New York, D. Van Nostrand. 1875)

Todd, Glenda McWhirter, *First Alabama Cavalry U.S.A.* (Bowie, Maryland, Heritage Books Inc., 1999)

Weaver, Jeffrey C., *45th Battalion Virginia Infantry, Smith and Count's Battalions of Partisan Rangers* (Lynchburg, Virginia, H.E. Howard, 1994)

Weaver, Jeffrey C., *Thurmond's Partisan Rangers and Swann's Battalion of Virginia Cavalry* (Lynchburg, Virginia, 1993)

Young, J.P., *The Seventh Tennessee Cavalry (Confederate)* (Nashville, M.E. Church, 1890)

Newspapers

Charleston Mercury (SC)
Harper's Illustrated
Leslie's Illustrated Weekly
New York Herald
Richmond Examiner (VA)
Wheeling Intelligencer

Index

INDEX

357

INDEX

INDEX

INDEX

INDEX